Praise for *Gangland Chicago*

"Richard C. Lindberg is the reigning authority on Chicago bad guys. It didn't start with Capone, and Lindberg's got the goods on them all, from Roger Plant to the El Rukns." **—Sam Reaves**, coauthor of *Mob Cop: My Life of Crime in the Chicago Police Department*

"Everyone loves Chicago history, especially Chicago history involving crime and gangsters. This wonderful book will be snapped up by enthusiasts and recruit others. Enjoy!" **—Leigh Bienen**, senior lecturer, Northwestern University School of Law; author *Florence Kelley, Factory Inspector in 1890s Chicago, and The Children*

GANGLAND CHICAGO

GANGLAND CHICAGO

Criminality and Lawlessness in the Windy City, 1837–1990

Richard C. Lindberg

ROWMAN & LITTLEFIELD
Lanham • Boulder • New York • London

Published by Rowman & Littlefield
A wholly owned subsidiary of
The Rowman & Littlefield Publishing Group, Inc.
4501 Forbes Boulevard, Suite 200, Lanham, Maryland 20706
www.rowman.com

Unit A, Whitacre Mews, 26-34 Stannary Street, London SE11 4AB

British Library Cataloguing in Publication Information Available

Library of Congress Cataloging-in-Publication Data

Lindberg, Richard, 1953–
Gangland Chicago : criminality and lawlessness in the Windy City, 1837–1990 / Richard Lindberg.
pages cm
Includes bibliographical references and index.
ISBN 978-1-4422-3195-5 (cloth : alk. paper) — ISBN 978-1-4422-3196-2 (electronic) 1. Crime—Illinois—Chicago—History. 2. Organized crime—Illinois—Chicago—History. 3. Criminals—Illinois—Chicago—History. 4. Chicago (Ill.)—History. I. Title.
HV6795.C4L56 2016
364.106'609773110904—dc23

2015019909

∞™ The paper used in this publication meets the minimum requirements of American National Standard for Information Sciences—Permanence of Paper for Printed Library Materials, ANSI/NISO Z39.48-1992.

Printed in the United States of America

This one is for Helen

CONTENTS

PREFACE AND ACKNOWLEDGMENTS

Chicago is a city under siege, awash in street-gang violence, criminality, and increasing hopelessness. How did it start and what can be done when the old remedies no longer work?

The gangs of Chicago have a long and disreputable criminal history. The problem the police, the courts, and society confront today is nearly as old as the city itself and has only worsened with the passage of time. Between 1870 and 1920, when the early gangs of Chicago coalesced in the streets of misery where the weak, the disenfranchised, and the downtrodden lived, the city crime rate grew steadily as Chicago's population soared from 298,977 to 2,701,705.

High population density and a policy of "warehousing" the poor into crowded residential districts segregated by geography, ethnicity, and economic status, mapped out by the Chicago Relief & Aid Society in the years accompanying the Chicago Fire of October 8 and 9, 1871, established firm boundary lines separating the slums from the business district and the city's affluent "better element." Consequently as the socially isolated poor got poorer, the criminal gangs grew bolder and stronger.

The flow of the Chicago River from the foot of Lake Michigan, extending west and then splitting into its southern and northern forks, provided a natural hermetically sealed barrier limiting access to the commercial business district to the bridges spanning the waterway that formed the hub of the city's early commerce. Only from the south could Chicago's downtown be easily accessed without having to cross a bridge. Zoning ordinances and man-made obstructions, including railroad viaducts and, in later years, expressways, effectively divided the city's diverse ethnic and racial composition.

The Relief & Aid Society was responsible for building the squalid wooden tenements intended to serve as "temporary" lodging for the hoi polloi that became the permanent "barracks of poverty" and a point of entry for generations of immigrants to come. The splintered, unsanitary buildings with outdoor privies lasted well into the twentieth century. The Relief & Aid Society, in its patrician "missionary" zeal to rescue and segregate the "savages" of foreign lands, cemented the foundation of a crisis of poverty, despair, lawlessness, and gangs that resonates into the twenty-first century.

Conditions in the slums were exacerbated by the manipulation of crooked, meddling politicians offering material rewards, protection, and superficial influence for election-eve thuggery and voter intimidation by the gangs. Seedy subcultures of prostitution and vice controlled by "organized" criminal gangs in connivance with corrupt, bribe-taking ward bosses and police court magistrates applied the downward push to the city's reputation as Chicago prepared to host its first World's Fair in 1893.

This Chicago crime survey tracks the history and evolution of three primary gangland classifications dating back to the nineteenth century: (1) gangs organized for the self-serving needs of local political bosses, (2) disruptive youth gangs defending "turf" by seeking social acceptance and respect among peers through the commission of both petty and serious criminal offenses, and (3) gangs of professional criminals organizing a structured enterprise with strength in numbers and financial resources to suborn police and lawmakers.

The Prohibition war of the 1920s hatched Chicago's "traditional" and monolithic organized crime group—the "Outfit." The saga of the bootlegging gangs of that chaotic epoch of our history parallel the rapid rise of the "new organized crime" in the 1960s. Chicago's modern-day gang crisis is a by-product of a lethal blend of alienation, societal neglect, murder, drug trafficking, and decades of institutional racism prevalent within troubled African American and Hispanic neighborhoods on the South and West Sides.

In Chicago and elsewhere around the country, gangs have become more violent, better organized, and more widespread than ever before. The Drug Enforcement Agency (DEA) concluded that gangs are responsible for more serious violent crime in our major cities than any other criminal enterprise. The Justice Department's National Youth Gang Center reported that the number of youth gangs in 2002 was pegged at 21,500 with 731,500 members. According to published FBI data the number of violent street gangs, prison gangs, and motorcycle gangs has dramatically risen to thirty-three thousand with about 1.4 million criminally active members.

In Chicago various estimates drawn from Chicago Police Department and Chicago Crime Commission research identifies seventy to one hundred active gangs and seventy thousand to a hundred thousand hard-core members, "pee-wees" (children), and associates.

In a larger sense the street gang is a highly organized criminal enterprise, the "new organized crime" if you will, with a hierarchical structure of command, constitutions, and defined responsibilities. Although Illinois lawmakers have treated it as such in recent years and responded by arming law enforcement with new prosecutory measures, including the Illinois Street Gang and Racketeer Influenced and Corrupt Organizations (RICO) Act, to charge those involved with street gangs with serious felonies, the effective *containment* of violence may be the only hope left to us in our troubled times.

The spillover of "gangster nations" into nearly every suburb, every school district, public park, and out into the cornfields of Illinois exposes every community and social class to the lurking danger of losing a son or daughter to the streets. The crisis is not exclusive or unique to Chicago. It extends into nearly every corner of America.

The homicide rate, our most accurate barometer of crime conditions in large urban areas, reminds us that despite fluctuations and sporadic reductions in violence, Chicago is losing the battle to save the most vulnerable and exposed segment of the population, our inner-city youth. Up to 80 percent of all city homicides and shootings are gang related.

Crack cocaine consumption in the 1980s and early 1990s contributed to a meteoric rise in the murder rate. In 1992 Chicago recorded 943 homicides. The figure includes ninety-six young people age sixteen and under.

Homicides in Chicago have dropped proportionately with the end to the crack consumption epidemic, evolving police tactics, and the incarceration of important gang leaders. However, in recent years, New York City, with a population nearly twice the size of Chicago, has stood at the vanguard of a nationwide crime reduction during the recession years of 2009 to 2012, while conditions in Chicago have remained static. The city lags behind both New York and Los Angeles, both of which have higher populations but less gun violence. The proliferation of assault weapons and the easy availability of handguns as a means of conflict resolution between inner-city gangs, differentiated the problems police and social workers faced in the 1950s from the killing fields of the 1990s and beyond.

Chicago Homicides 1985–2014

Year	*Chicago Homicides 1985–2014*
1985	666
1986	744
1987	691
1988	660
1989	742
1990	851
1991	928
1992	943
1993	855
1994	931
1995	828
1996	796
1997	761
1998	704
1999	641
2000	633
2001	667
2002	656
2003	599
2004	453
2005	451
2006	471
2007	448
2008	513
2009	459
2010	436
2011	435
2012	516
2013	441
2014	432

In 2012 Chicago announced a plan to hire forty "interrupters" from the Chicago-based CeaseFire, the local branch of a national initiative called Cure Violence, from the award of a $1 million grant. Its purpose, not unlike the forty-nine member Chicago Intervention Network launched by the late Mayor Harold Washington in 1985, was to deploy ex-gang members into city neighborhoods to mediate sporadic conflicts contributing to the escalation of violence in nineteen city neighborhoods, including Woodlawn and Lawndale, two of the worst gang hotspots in Chicago. After just one year, however, the program in the two troubled communities had to be cancelled after it was revealed that six of the interrupters returned to gang life.

CeaseFire claims credit for reductions in gun violence, but state funding for this program is continuously imperiled by potential rollbacks of the grant money and massive budget deficits that have plagued Illinois in the second decade of the New Millennium.

With no end in sight to the killings, Attorney General Eric Holder announced that he would dispatch fifty-two agents from the Bureau of Alcohol, Tobacco and Firearms (ATF) following a bloody Fourth of July weekend in 2014.

The City of Chicago, under the direction of Commander Lee Schmitz of the Chicago Police Department Gang Enforcement Unit, centralized four hundred police officers from twenty-five districts to form the largest dedicated unit in the nation to address a pattern of violence that threatens to overwhelm our schools and communities and tear apart the fabric of society.

"The only consistent action taken to stop violence and homicide in this city has been of the law enforcement variety," wrote *Chicago Tribune* columnist Rex Huppke in an opinion piece on February 26, 2015. "Little is done to address the factors that lead to violent behavior. Little has been done to improve the communities where violent behavior has become the norm."

In point of fact, divergent remedies *have been put into practice* by earlier generations of civic leaders, philanthropists, and community-service agencies to curb the contributing factors to juvenile delinquency with varying degrees of success. Social workers, criminologists, and community leaders tend to agree on four core strategies for curbing gangs: (1) Encourage gang members to evolve into neighborhood clubs as a means to better their lives, stem the violence through greater tolerance, and improve neighborhood quality of life. During the "Great Society" years of the 1960s, influential political leaders, the clergy, Dr. Martin Luther King Jr., and even officials within the Johnson and Nixon White House believed that they had "transformed" the feared Blackstone Rangers into a force for social good; but after squandering substantial amounts of federal grant money that ended up in gang coffers, the plan of rehabilitation failed; (2) Campaigns to steer youth away from joining gangs. This too yielded only temporary results and marginal success. With barriers to employment and higher education for Chicago's youth, who are trapped in slums of vacated storefronts, derelict buildings, social isolation and incidents of physical abuse, there are few viable alternatives to counter the pressure of the strong-arm tactics employed by older gang members to recruit the younger, vulnerable children left to fend for themselves in the street; (3) Mediation and intervention to quell violence among warring gangs, a strategy that has yielded positive, albeit short-term, gain; (4) Greater emphasis placed on instituting restorative justice programs to replace zero-tolerance policies in the schools in order to encourage conflict resolution, dialogue between perpetrators and victims, with less reliance on the presence of metal detectors and uniformed guards, and immediate suspension for students committing minor infractions. The restorative justice movement, with less threatening school environments, has scored victories and yielded positive results in large urban areas. Educators and social workers have long insisted that keeping troublesome kids in the classroom instead of sending suspended students into the streets is one way of discouraging negative perceptions of learning among young people that feeds active gang recruitment. Could such a program work in Chicago neighborhoods where "safe passage" to and from schools has become the overriding issue in recent years? Restorative justice strategies were never part of the game plan in Chicago's juvenile correctional facilities dating back to the first reform schools and work farms of the late nineteenth century.

Our contemporary crisis of gangs and criminality exists in the vacuum of our collective historical amnesia—all too common in this age of technology that ignores history and the teachings of the past. Modern criminal justice theorists have either discounted or forgotten the earlier work of socially conscious penologists, progressive reformers, settlement-house workers, educators, faith-based ecumenical leaders, and grass-roots youth organizations including the YMCA and the Boys & Girls Clubs that have at one time or another employed each of the strategies. In the ebb and flow of city history dating back to the post–Civil War period, they have all grappled with the crisis of youth crime in areas of the city the acclaimed 1920s sociologist Frederic Milton Thrasher identified as having the highest vulnerabilities: the "West Side Wilderness," the "North Side Jungles," and the "South Side Badlands."

Over time, the central debate pitting the advocates of harsh and unrelenting punishment against compassionate, liberal-minded proponents of community-based outreach programs—educational and job opportunity over long incarceration—has had no clear-cut winner, although the effectiveness of harsh punitive reform-school measures against youthful offenders has long been discounted. The focus has shifted away from seeing the problem solely as a criminal justice issue. Writing in the June 2015 journal of the National Disabilities Network, Executive Director Curtis L. Decker correctly notes that,

> "We have been searching for a humane way to treat children with bad behavior and still we have not found our way," adding, "We have locked them up in orphanages, so called schools for the retarded, mental hospitals, training and reform schools. We have dispatched them across the nation on orphan trains, farmed them out, drugged them, shocked, lobotomized and beaten them. We have exorcised and broken their spirits. We have scared them straight, made them climb mountains, in wilderness camps, and dig holes in boot camps hoping they would learn to behave through starvation and sheer exhaustion."

While generations of juvenile offenders, many suffering developmental disabilities, were rescued from the streets and went on to live productive lives free of criminal associations, many more have not. If it were as simple as street-level intervention, we would have no gangs today. Other groups, including the Boys Clubs of Chicago, pioneered CeaseFire's intervention approach in Chicago during the 1950s and early 1960s. The early results were promising but proved unsustainable.

Infrequent gangland "summits" and conferences convened for the purpose of establishing a framework of peaceful coexistence mimicked earlier attempts made by the bootlegging gangs of the 1920s with the same dismal results. In 1966 Chicago police superintendent O. W. Wilson believed he had succeeded in quelling gang violence on the South Side. It was a gamble that failed. Gang leaders from Chicago, Boston, Minneapolis, and Los Angeles agreed to seek a nationwide truce following an epidemic of eight hundred gang-related killings in Los Angeles County in 1992. Organizers signed-off on a six-point action plan and a 1993 summit in Kansas City to agree upon a permanent solution to end the killing. "We appreciate these efforts," Chicago police spokesman Billy Davis told the *Chicago Sun-Times*, "but a truce is not something the police can look at in a short span of time. With a gang truce, all we see is a displacement of crime in different areas than before." Davis was right.

The historic current, weighed against the short-term successes of early reform movements, community intervention, and truce agreements, suggests that the gang problem in Chicago is unsolvable and the hopes for a peaceful outcome and the permanent eradication of these gangs seem increasingly remote.

The gangland problem looms large in Chicago. It is the latest chapter in the city's frightful struggle to shake off its unwanted reputation for crime and unchecked lawlessness, which dates back to the time when vice and prostitution rings menaced the late Gilded Age and continues up through the era of street gangs calling themselves nations. Unlike the anarchic gangs of Los Angeles with their more diffuse and ad hoc leadership styles, Chicago gangs of the 1990s and into the New Millennium tended to be more entrenched, militaristic, and hierarchical, and aware of their origins and roots. Contemporary gang leaders imitated the management structure of the Capone Gang, and drew inspiration from Mafia hierarchical command leadership and methods of internal discipline enforcement by a centralized ruling cadre.

In this sense Chicago gangbangers of the present day operate on a parallel track and, in so many ways, are irretrievably linked to historic patterns of earlier criminality and lawlessness that has adversely defined the character of the city down through the years.

What can we deduce about Chicago? Perhaps it is summed up best in the words of the great muckraking journalist Lincoln Steffens, who said, "First in violence, deepest in dirt, lawless, unlovely, ill-smelling, irreverent, new; an overgrown gawk of a village, the 'tough' among cities, a spectacle for the nation."

It is that today.

I would be remiss if I failed to cite the scholarship of colleagues, criminologists, sociologists, historians, social workers, and fellow authors, all of whose scholarly work helped provide me with the necessary framework to shape my latest inquiry into Chicago's criminal past. John Hagedorn, professor of criminal justice at the University of Illinois at Chicago, has drawn Chicago's massive gang problem into sharper focus through research, published volumes, and symposia.

The Chicago Crime Commission has generously supported my research down through the years. Special thanks to the distinguished Crime Commission leadership team I was privileged to work with during my tenure editing the *Illinois Police & Sheriff's News* in the 1990s: Wayne Johnson, John Jemilo, Robert R. Fuesel, and Arthur Bilek, who retired as executive vice president in 2015 after decades of meritorious service to the profession of law enforcement.

The Illinois Academy of Criminology (IAC), founded in 1950, has dedicated its resources these many years to providing balanced academic inquiry into the issues and problems confronting the criminal justice system at the local, state, and federal levels. Pattie Banas, Sy Adler, Edward Mogul, the late Ken Dooley, Robert "Mickey" Lombardo, and many other expert practitioners and academicians have effectively driven IAC's important mission down through the years. I thank each of them.

William J. Helmer, Richard "Dick" Bales, Rose Keefe, Rick Kogan, R. Craig Sautter and June Skinner Sawyers are notable authors I much admire, who have covered the gamut of Chicago history and crime-related subject matter. Thanks to James Bigham for his input on juvenile reform and to Daniel Kelley for his study of the portrayal of crime in cinema. My deepest gratitude and thanks to Helen Kossler, a novelist who has championed my work, made many timely and helpful suggestions, and completed manuscript edits for me as I finalized the initial first draft. And finally, I extend appreciation and thanks to Brooke Goode for her superior editing skills, to Elaine McGarraugh for handling the production, and to Kathryn Knigge, associate editor at Rowman & Littlefield, who first approached me in 2013 about a book idea for a history of Chicago gangs, and without whose commitment to the project this book could not have been possible.

Richard C. Lindberg
Chicago, Illinois
June 2015

1

OUTLAWRY AND THE RISE OF A CRIMINAL CLASS IN THE EMERGING CITY

In its earliest, embryonic years, the future City of Chicago was viewed by outsiders with a mixture of dismay and pessimism. The sparsely populated settlement, with its cluster of shanties adjoining a military fort, stood on the marsh populated by roughs and men of low character in this rather insignificant trading post on the edge of civilization. In an expedition to the Upper Mississippi and Red River Valleys, geographer and adventurer William R. Keating recorded his dismal impressions of the frontier village encircling Fort Dearborn on the Lake Michigan shoreline upon arrival June 5, 1823. "We were much disappointed at the appearance of Chicago and its vicinity. The village presents no cheering prospects as it consists of but a few huts, inhabited by a miserable race of men. . . . As a place of business it offers no inducement to the settler."[1]

This tract of brown, wind-beaten grass and scrub oaks comprising the modern city of Chicago had been ceded to the U.S. government by the native Miami tribe through the terms of the Treaty of Greenville, Ohio, formalized on August 7, 1795, with General "Mad" Anthony Wayne. The name given to this marshy swamp by the Potawatomie was Che-ca-gou, meaning "wild onion"—for the indigenous plant of a distinctive odor that grew here. Near the south bank of the river, bisecting the north and south divisions, stood Fort Dearborn, housing the military garrison in a half dozen barracks and officer's quarters. The garrison was wiped out and the fort burned to the ground during the War of 1812 but was rebuilt four years later. Chicago's slow ascent to become the preeminent city of the mid-continent began four years later when the fort was rebuilt and the easterners with ambition matriculated west to stake their fortune in the "land of the onion."

Barely a hundred souls clustered around Wolf Point. Its three tavern hotels and John Kinzie's store occupied the town proper in 1830, but all that was soon to change. In 1823 workmen completed the first survey of the proposed Illinois & Michigan Canal. This important waterway (which required twenty-five years to finish) established Chicago as a gateway to the west for a young country on the move, and sparked a mad land rush for opportunists, both rich and poor.

The availability of "canal lands" and vacant property offered for sale at just $1.25 an acre by storefront agents on Lake Street gradually shifted the main business district from Wolf Point. It beckoned migratory adventurers, immigrants from all over Europe (notably Ireland) as well as "Hardy pioneers; sharpers of every degree; peddlers, grog-sellers, horse dealers, horse stealers . . . rogues of every description, white black, brown and red . . . half breeds, quarter breeds and men of no breed of all," wrote English traveler Charles Joseph Latrobe.[2] As one of its first orders of business, on December 8, 1829, the Court of County Commissioners of Peoria County awarded the first tavern license to twenty-three-year-old Archibald Clybourn who had ridden into the settlement on horseback from Fort Wayne two years earlier. The double-log-house tavern advertised its business with a painted wolf on the shingle over the door, but operated without a formal name.

Packs of indigenous wolves were a constant threat to the public safety, and the wolf packs gave Wolf Point its name. Another tavern license for a fee of seven dollars a year was awarded to Elijah "Old Geese" Wentworth to operate Wolf Tavern at the Forks and to run a hotel on the premises. James and Robert Kinzie built stores nearby for the convenience of the soldiers garrisoned at Fort Dearborn who were known to hoist a tankard of beer or two inside Wolf Tavern. A cantankerous sort when provoked, Wentworth threatened any potential adversary by "geesing [sic] him." In 1830 Wolf Point was Chicago's town center.[3]

Scottish pioneer James Kinzie opened the Green Tree Tavern, a two-story frame building at the corner of Canal and Lake Street, in 1833, the same year that the native people—Ottawa, Sauk, Fox, Potawatomie, and Chippewa were removed to the lands west of the Mississippi River by terms of their treaty with the white man's government. This location became a destination point at the south fork of the river. In subsequent years it was called the Chicago Hotel and later the Lake Street House. In 1880 the entire structure was uprooted and moved northwest to a location out on Milwaukee Avenue so it could be preserved as a historic landmark of Chicago's earlier times.

With the threat of native uprising removed, settlers confidently poured into Chicago. The years of the speculative "western fever" were at hand. Immigrants poured into the city. "Hardly a vessel arrives that is not crowded with immigrants and the stage that now runs twice a week from the East is thronged with travelers," reported the *Chicago Democrat* on June 11, 1834. "Loaded teams and covered wagons, laden with families and goods are daily arriving and settling upon the country back." In 1835, 255 sailing boats put into Chicago, depositing bewildered newcomers. Sleeping accommodations were poor and provisions scarce. In the muddy shallows that passed for streets, livestock roamed freely. Outside the new Tremont Hotel, cattle and pigs were slaughtered in plain sight of travelers.

By July 1837, the year the townsmen drafted Chicago's charter, the population of the frontier town had swelled to 4,066. Among the 4,066 residents crowded into just 398 residential dwellings, there were 1,800 white men and only 845 white women, according to the research of author Edith Abbott. The city was a bachelor community. Cheaply constructed wooden boarding houses and taverns catered to transient men, canal laborers from Ireland, and the goings on inside these places at all hours could not be successfully policed or regulated.

The first duly appointed constable, Orsemus Morrison, former street commissioner, coroner, town collector, and later an alderman, was tasked with "the maintenance of public health, the reporting of fires and the preservation of property thereof."[4]

Morrison did not wear a uniform but he carried with him at all times "a staff of office," painted white so that his authority, or lack of it, could be acknowledged. Fragmentary public records of the day reveal that the constable made his first arrest in 1833 after farmer Luther Hatch accused a dangerous cutthroat of assaulting and robbing him of thirty-four dollars inside "Old Geese's" saloon. The offender was stripped of his clothes before the money was recovered from a rucksack. The legal proceeding that followed marked Chicago's first recorded criminal trial.

Chicago did not as yet have a jail to hold a criminal offender. Therefore Morrison sat up all night in his carpenter shop guarding the prisoner. The following afternoon, Hatch was put on trial inside "Old Geese's" saloon. He was found guilty. He put up a "straw bail" (a worthless, insufficient bail) and fled the Chicago settlement, never to be seen again.

Morrison could not enforce the first Sunday closing laws passed into law in 1834, the first statutes outlawing gambling a year later, or the ordinance criminalizing the use of firearms in a hotel or tavern. If Morrison deemed a man or woman a lawbreaker or public nuisance, the offender paid a small fine, typically three dollars, half of which was paid to the constable and half to the informant for his cooperation.

The Green Tree, another frontier bucket of blood, named for a nearby oak tree, was a swaggering, raffish kind of place for the pleasure of the newcomers. There was a taproom within, the center of considerable merriment for the 1830s "rounders," who were typically attired in skintight pantaloons, socks in black or red, and puffy shirts with swallow-winged collars. They were gamblers, dandies, and dudes of the green-cloth trade who plied their business in the three taverns with the old settlers who came to imbibe with the traveling men.

They would listen to the fiddle music of Mark Beaubien playing "Money Musk" and "Fisher's Hornpipe" inside the Sauganash, Chicago's first real "hotel," opened in 1831 by Beaubien and his wife, Monique, and named for the famous Indian chief who suggested the idea to him. Beaubien, flamboyant, colorful, and often amusing, established the first ferry service to convey drinkers and revelers to the taverns across the forks of the Chicago River before the first bridge was constructed.

"Lights burned all hours of the night," recalled a historian of the period. "Here boisterous public meetings and dances were held."[5] The first theatrical performance witnessed in Chicago was staged at the Sauganash on October 17, 1837. The rowdy, unkempt audience of three hundred drank, hooted, and whistled as the theatrical troop struggled to be heard. A young Irishman attached to the company contributed to the mayhem and had to be thrown out on his ear by the innkeeper-turned-theater-operator. Fearing for his life, the actor likely asked, "Where can I go with Lake Michigan roaring on one side and bloody prairie wolves on the other?"

Beaubien had arrived from Detroit in 1826 to strike his fortune in the hospitality industry. He sired twenty-three children who delivered him fifty-three grandchildren. "I keep tavern vigorously," he boasted in a mix of French and broken English. Addicted to gambling, he was a familiar figure in the "turf" world, appearing trackside in his swallowtail coat, brass buttons, and summer nankeen trousers. Over time, his name became synonymous with the patronage and sponsorship of early horse racing.

Despite the rowdy charm and geniality of the proprietor, Charles Latrobe found nothing about the Sauganash to recommend to his friends back in London, calling the tavern a "vile two-storied barrack." By the mid-1830s the Sauganash, the first frame house built in Chicago, was rated the main center of entertainment and amusement in town. It was a rollicking haven for gamblers, eastern thugs, sports, and criminal profiteers, some of whom were just passing through and others planning to lay down roots. Saloon life in the early frontier days established Chicago's dubious reputation for recklessness and criminality—a carnival city of vice, gangs, and violence that it has not been able to outlive.[6]

The growing menace of the "social evil" of prostitution and criminal pandering so alarmed the town council in 1835 that they imposed a twenty-five-dollar fine against the keepers of houses of ill repute. For the New England Yankees coming west to speculate, invest in the future, and establish schools, churches, and the rewards of civilized society, it was an early indoctrination into the malignancy of crime that would form the locus of 150 years of failed reform movements, temperance advocacy, demonization of the poor, the introduction of jails, state prisons, reformatories, and juvenile courts to punish youthful offenders.

For the common laborers and other down-and-outers coming to Chicago beginning in 1836 to build the Illinois & Michigan Canal and to work in the planing mills, machine shops, grain depots, and animal stockyards of the West and South Sides, the city was either an irresistible lure—or a desperate last chance. For the waves of potato-famine

Irish and others trying to escape the grind of poverty, the pogroms, and political repression of the old world, destitution and shabby wooden tenement housing segregating one ethic tribe from the other, awaited.

Young toughs formed neighborhood "associations"—street gangs—hell-bent on violence, intimidation, and imposing a cruel feudal reign (in the name of self-protection) upon small geographical territories within squalid slums often lying in close proximity to the railroad yards and the river. Sociologist Frederic Milton Thrasher identified the existence of organized criminal gangs plaguing the Illinois frontier in 1810, "when a gang of murderous thieves operating throughout the State victimized travelers. They had taverns and inns as their hangout and were recognized murderers."[7]

The Chicago River, praised by author Theodore Dreiser as "the smallest and busiest river in the world," drew immense maritime traffic to the emerging city.[8] Two- and three-masted 125-foot wooden schooners laden with North Woods lumber, iron ore, grain, and other commodities choked the river and established Chicago as a port city and the reigning "Queen of the Lakes," beginning in the 1840s.

In the long winter months, itinerant sailors, stevedores, and other rough and ready men laid low by the lack of maritime work and with time on their hands, fed the vice trade, or formed criminal gangs of their own.

"Bum boats," permanently anchored to the river wharves, functioned as surrogate brothels and gambling dens for the schooner sailors. Shipping companies had to keep a watchful eye out for the presence of cutthroats, river pirates, footpads and marauding gangs laying siege and stealing the cargo and contents of legitimate commercial vessels moored in the ice-choked Chicago River until spring. So dangerous were the wharves and piers that Chicago police routinely avoided the risk and peril associated with nighttime patrol.

Quoting an original 1883 news report filed in the *Chicago Times*, Professor Theodore J. Karamanski of Loyola University described the treacherous river docks extending from the North Branch down to Twenty-Second Street as "a narrow rotten footway, ill-lighted and unpoliced, the abode of vermin, biped and quadruped. Occasionally a drunken sailor or wharf rat is passed and at rare intervals the solitude is broken by the brawling of some inebriated dock-walloper who is making night hideous in one of the many low doggeries that abound."[9]

By 1855 it was estimated that 60 percent of the city population was foreign born, and by 1900, with the schooner traffic in eclipse, Chicago had evolved into the railroad capital of the United States and the convergence point for trains traveling east, west, north, and south, carrying with them refugees from old-world famine, disease, and war.

Other cities tended to outgrow the spasms of outlawry that characterized their early development. The Five Points neighborhood in Lower Manhattan, controlled by tightly organized gangs of cutthroats, thieves, and murderers, existed as a crime district for seventy-five years before its evolutionary transformation to a solid, earnest residential community adjoining the city government district of New York. Storyville, New Orleans, once a cesspool of gaudy dives expired before the end of World War I. Similarly, San Francisco's Barbary Coast is a page out of a book from another time.

In Chicago, however, matters did not follow the same evolutionary progression. In its earliest years, saloons and boarding houses for transient bachelors, drummers, grain merchants, railroad men, and soldiers and sailors with time on their hands outnumbered churches and schools. Chicago could never shake loose its lusty reputation, and the resources of law enforcement failed to keep pace with the rapid population growth.

Chicagoans went to the polls on May 2, 1837, to vote in the city's first charter election. They elected John Shrigley, an Englishman, to continue on as "high constable" on the Democratic ticket in the William B. Ogden mayoral administration. At the same time, he established the first municipal court. The number of under-constables the city allowed Shrigley to appoint were fixed at just one in each of Chicago's six wards. Since colonial times, Americans harbored deep suspicions and hostility of standing armies, uniformed soldiers, and others engaged by the civil authorities to enforce local statutes. Shopkeepers, private businessmen, and average citizens engaged professional "thief takers" (or private detection agencies charging a fee for their services), to recover stolen property or provide security and personal protection. In the public mind, police agencies were abhorrent and most often equated with repression, unwarranted search and seizure, and standing militias. It was not until civil disorder and a series of urban riots occurred in the big cities in the years leading up to the Civil War that public attitudes slowly changed.

The actions on the part of voters in 1837 did little to deter rising criminality or assuage the concerns of the citizenry, and the *Chicago Democrat* noted on July 12, 1839, that "it is a great evil that the number of police is so contemptibly small."

Constable Shrigley owned the Eagle Hotel. He operated the Dutchman's Point Tavern and was a friend and colleague of other grogshop owners and tippling houses. He had no formal law enforcement training or fundamental understanding of criminal law, such as it existed at the time, and mostly relied on his intimidating physical presence and fisticuffs to drag a miscreant through the unpaved, mud-filled streets to the city's first bridewell (an early jail), a crude frontier log cabin measuring a hundred feet long and twenty-four feet wide, and concealed behind a high plank palisade.[10] Located on the northwest corner of Polk Street and Wells Street, the jail accommodated up to two hundred inmates assigned to a work detail piling up stacks of lumber used for paving the streets. After the city discontinued street planking, prisoners toiled in a stone yard adjacent to the jail.

Shrigley selected two men, Samuel J. Lowe, an 1834 arrival from England, and George M. Huntoon, formerly of Massachusetts, as his under-constables. These three upholders of the peace were all that stood between the reign of lawlessness and the city population of four thousand. It wasn't long, however, before the *Democrat* drew public attention to the inadequacy of the constabulary, decrying "brawls in whiskey shops, street fights, and the fact that small pigs and fowls are running at large in the sixth ward."

It was reliably reported that Shrigley's men engaged in frequent altercations with the remaining soldiers still deployed to duty in the Fort Dearborn garrison instead of taking on their rightful role of thief taker. One of their assigned duties was to hunt down and shoot "worthless dogs," prompting the editor of the Jackson, Michigan, newspaper to remark in 1839: "The population of Chicago is said to be principally composed of dogs and loafers."

Constable Samuel Lowe succeeded Shrigley in 1839, but his official title was changed to "chief of the city watch" until he was succeeded by Orson Smith as city marshal in 1842. Smith deputized just three assistants: Henry Rhines, a grocer and cabinetmaker accused by abolitionists of being a slave catcher; Hugh Henry; and William Wesencrest.

Meanwhile, the night watchmen operated independently of the daytime constabulary with little interaction and the sharing of information among them. Citizens of the growing metropolis went about their lives, often in great peril to their person and property. Only the constabulary was empowered to arrest criminal malefactors. Under Lowe's watch, Chicago carried out its first execution, a public affair occurring on the afternoon of May 1, 1840, when the citizens of the town streamed to the south lakefront, to what is now Fortieth Street, to witness the hanging of one John Stone, a woodchopper convicted of murdering Mrs. Lucretia Thompson. Sixty militia men kept order, assisted by two hundred armed citizens perched on horses.

In 1847 the ranks of the city watch swelled to nine members (one for each district of the city), but their principal accomplishment was to combat the city's frequent cholera epidemics. With sunset, their day's labors ended and the unarmed watchmen took over. It was during these precarious times that incidents of burglary, armed robbery, garroting, and assault increased. In 1849 Chicago claimed the dubious distinction of having more gambling hells than either Philadelphia or Boston. With one hundred houses of ill fame in operation by 1859, the city earned dubious notoriety as the "wickedest city in America."

After describing a burglary in the Hubbard Building, the *Chicago Tribune* declared on May 3, 1850: "The city watch knew nothing of it of course. They were probably regaling themselves in pleasure quarters at the time."

The daytime force, each man elected to his post by the Committee on Police earned a meager eight dollars a week, was no better equipped to confront and deal with a rising tide of crime than the night watch. In March 1853, the committee authorized and detailed just nine officers to the day police.

Inefficient, outnumbered, and untrained, the inadequacies of the constabulary and night watch were fully revealed on April 21, 1855, when a mob action that history records as the "Lager Beer Riot" threatened to engulf the entire city. Mayor Levi D. Boone, grandnephew of frontiersman Daniel Boone and a proponent of the Know Nothing political movement that traced lawlessness and the ills of society to the immigrant Irish and Germans and their fondness for the gin spirits, attempted to impose temperance measures on an unwilling populace.

"The reputation that Chicago then had as a hard town may be freely confessed now to have been warranted by the actual conditions," wrote an "Old Citizen" to the *Tribune* on January 29, 1882. "A free and easy tone pervaded society and politics and the privilege of selling whiskey ranked with the privilege of selling dry goods. A large part of the people who regarded their residence as temporary, were predisposed to lawlessness."

The righteously prim but fiercely bigoted Boone, a Kentuckian and physician by trade, delivered a series of lectures advancing the proslavery agenda by attempting to prove the scriptural warrant for human bondage. "Notwithstanding his views concerning slavery, he was a kindly mannered man, gentle and courteous to all, of perfect integrity, hospitable as became his Southern origin and much beloved by all who knew him," praised A. N. Waterman in a 1908 civic booster screed titled "Historical Review of Chicago & Cook County."

Meddling in both politics and medicine, Dr. Boone contrived to close the saloons on Sunday and raise the yearly licensing fee from $52 per year to an onerous annual assessment of $300, placing the keepers of Irish whiskey saloons and German *brau houses* in peril of having to relinquish their businesses.

The passage of the 1851 "Maine Law" prohibiting the sale of intoxicants except for medicinal purposes established a growing national trend among ecumenical leaders and reformers for imposing abstinence by legislative fiat. By 1855 twelve states had already voted themselves dry—but not in Illinois where the yen for liquor could not be stopped. The coordinated attack against saloons, dram shops, and other pillars of immigrant culture was precisely what Boone and his supporters—the Unitarians, Methodists, Baptists, and Universalists who prayed for the salvation of the wretched foreigners from churches clustered along Washington Street between Dearborn and Clark—had in mind.

East of Dearborn, a north-south street, Washington Street reigned as the most desirable and pastoral community of verdant green gardens, cabbage patches, and pleasing little cottages in the years leading up to the Civil War. Peace and tranquility prevailed. Mayor Boone's residence at State and Madison was far removed from the streets of ill repute south of the river and west of the public square. The imposing Randolph Street courthouse afforded him safe refuge from the mob. From its early frontier days, the City of Chicago was resolutely segregated by class, social position, and ethnicity.

Saturday, April 21, 1855, dawned bright and clear in Chicago. On Judge Henry L. Rucker's docket that day was a list of saloon owners arrested for not paying their licensing fee. The police court was then held in the basement of the courthouse. Eighth Ward alderman L. D. LaRue, whose North Side constituents were mostly German, Irish, and Swedish immigrants who demanded that no legal disruptions be placed on spending their "continental Sundays" in a beer garden, encouraged them to voice their dissent and solicit Rucker to discharge their friends from the jail. They stormed into Rucker's chambers and were forcibly dragged from the court and jailed.

Outside, a large gathering of men and women numbering a thousand, from the poorer areas of the city hugging the river, massed. A trombone player and a drummer beat out a somber tune under the warm April sun. Their mood was sullen, and their tone of voice threatening. A small detachment of constables under the command of Captain Luther Nichols, himself a Know Nothing sympathizer, were posted in front of the courthouse doors. Nichols armed himself with a cane. Violence followed after Nichols shoved the wooden staff into the chest of a man from the North Division. Angry shouts arose.

An assembly of rough and violent men who turned out to voice opposition initially pushed forward, swinging at the officers, tossing debris about, and causing a melee. Eighteen rioters were seized and locked up. After a half hour's time, the mob retreated to Clark and Wells to regroup. Their anger, fueled by liquor, did not subside. Reinforcements from Milwaukee Avenue and Wright's Grove in the North Division, armed with fowling pieces, meat cleavers, spokes from carts, and other crude weaponry, joined the Wells Street throng and marched back to the Courthouse Square in a second attempt to free their compatriots from jail. They marched in solemn military order to the beat of the fife player and drummer, ready to engage in combat. The balconies and windows of the original Sherman House Hotel were packed with spectators, there to witness the insurrection. Boone ordered the city to be on lockdown. Martial law was declared.

The mob opened up on the constables and an armed militia, the Montgomery Guard, had been deployed to the public square to lend support. Hundreds of ordinary citizens had been sworn in as special policemen.

Rioters fired upon the police, but were unable to reload and discharge a second round. Officer G. W. Hunt lost an arm in the affray, but many of the rioters were arrested. The following day, Mayor Boone had his proclamation read aloud in the churches. All good and law-abiding citizens were thus ordered to remain inside their homes upon return from their worship. However, by now, emotions were spent and the threat of cannon fire from the Montgomery Guard discouraged the rioters from a further assault on the courthouse. To ensure the peace, the objectionable licensing increase was cancelled.

Boone, a one-term mayor, accomplished one noteworthy and remarkable reform during his two-year term. He added a midday squad of patrolmen, reducing the hours of the beleaguered and overworked nighttime force. In 1858 Chicago police officers were ordered to wear uniforms consisting of a short blue frock coat with a plain brass star affixed, a navy blue cap with a gold band, and with that these changes the modern Chicago Police Department was born.

No longer could the city solely rely on a part-time police force with divergent responsibilities, not with the threat of mob violence hanging in the air, the viral spread of saloons, gambling "hells," and houses of prostitution run by organized criminals and gangs pressing down upon quiet Washington Street, suburban in appearance and character, with its white picket fences and residential cottages.

Over the next ten years, 1855 to 1865, the towering steeples of the churches and most of the single dwelling homes in the heart of Chicago's business and commercial center disappeared. The prairie lands to the south and west were to be driven farther and farther back from the city center with each passing year. Frontier village life and the peaceful agrarian existence of the city of Kinzie, Beaubien, and Wentworth in the 1830s, was soon to be torn asunder by the forces of urbanization, industrialization, the railroads and waterways, and the explosion of immigrants and easterners into its realm.

Pleasure quarters abounded in this wickedest of cities west of the Alleghenies. Mark Beaubien had opened another public house, a large frame hotel he called the Illinois Exchange, at the corner of Lake Street and Wells. The hostelry did a thriving business on Wells Street (named for Captain William Wells, the martyred hero of the Fort Dearborn Massacre), which evolved from a narrow, unpaved, and ill-appearing street that ran only as far south as Polk Street and the wooden calaboose housing petty criminals, vagrants, gamblers, and scalawags.

To the south, songbirds twittered in the swampy marsh. Chicago had yet to fully spread its wings, but as the ominous shadow of the Civil War spread over the land, the optimistic hope of Beaubien and other original settlers that Chicago might escape the social evil of New York and the older cities of the East, faded as dens of vice sprouted on Wells Street, arguably the city's first "controlled" business district given over entirely to the pursuit of vice and crime.

Wells Street, an unpaved road of muck and mire lined by cheap one-story hovels on both sides, was a carnival of crime from the 1850s through the Great Chicago Fire. The wooden plank sidewalks were an exhausting series of up-and-down steps separating one unpretentious dump from another. If a pedestrian missed his footing on a cloudless dark night, it was a treacherous six-foot fall into the muddy, brackish pools of water that swarmed with cholera bacteria. Cholera was a constant summertime threat to Chicagoans. To improve sanitary conditions, the city laid the first wood-block paving in 1859 on Clark Street and began the task of elevating the street grade—an unparalleled feat of engineering at the time. Meanwhile homeless and destitute children often huddled in the space beneath the elevated sidewalks that provided shelter.

The most notable criminal of the period to control this dissolute spot was Englishman Roger Plant, a veritable bulldog of a man, born and bred on the Liverpool waterfront. Around 1850 or so he opened a notorious house of ill fame at the southeast corner of Monroe and Wells.

Plant started life as a poor man. He had a wife and together they had twenty children (including several sets of twins) to support, but his double-frame resort with its narrow gable windows and upstairs assignation parlors not only provided a livelihood and fed his hungry brood but in short order made him a wealthy man. In front of the resort stood three willow trees that provided a poetic appellation for the dangerous bucket of blood operated by Plant and his gang of henchmen, which included the house manager Gus Anderson, assigned to directing the unsuspecting into a barracks of vice that was raided from time to time with little effect. The inmates of the resort paid the usual fines and drifted back into the slums coalescing in the developing Irish enclaves of Bridgeport, where the canal immigrants settled, and Conley's Patch in the southwest corner of the business district near the "Willows."

Roger Plant enjoyed friendly relations with the bribe-taking magistrates and Assistant Police Superintendent Jack Nelson, who commanded the Armory Police Station, an imposing prison replacing the original jail stockade. Nelson permitted Plant to sell liquor without a license at a saloon Plant operated at 531 Clark Street. He supplied recognizance for his clients thrown in the stir, and collected their bond payment one way or another. With solicitude mixed with occasional brute force, Plant managed his girls, who were making do in their shabby hovels that would have astonished city missionaries if had they ever dared navigate their way into the rabbit warren of depravity that sprouted up and down Wells Street.

Marie Filkius and Lib Woods were two of the "Willows" harlots who subscribed to Plant's own personal business credo of "Why Not?" In the parlance of the time, fallen women and their consorts—often shady political types, or tin-horn gamblers traversing the Mississippi and Ohio Rivers in the years of the river boat trade—were referred to by police as "bummers."

Swarms of gamblers congealed in second-floor rooms on Randolph Street between Dearborn and State Street, located in 65, 68, 72, and 79 McCormick's Building, where day after day faro and keno dens operated full tilt. At the foot of the stairways the "blackleg" (gambler) accosted passersby, urging them to partake in rigged games of chance. Itinerant gamblers had come to Chicago in the 1840s to carve out Randolph Street fiefdoms. Colonel "Wat" Cameron, George "One Lung" Smith, John Sears, George Rhodes, Cole Martin, and other men whose names are lost to history ran their bunko gangs and crooked games in the early “gambling hells” of the city. In the early years of the C numbers multiplied as gamblers fled their usual haunts avoid impressments into the Confederate Army. Samue and George Trussell, owner of the famed racing steed “Dexter (who lent his name to the racing grounds Dexter Park), lined up consortiums of gamblers into their respective camps and battled for customers, patronage, and cash proceeds—often with a resulting exchange of gunfire and men falling dead in the muck.

In Chicago, a city of easy virtue, a tolerance for liquor, vice, and the green-cloth trade, they found their safe haven. By 1867 McCormick’s Building and the adjacent Randolph Street dens came to be known as Hairtrigger Block, because of the many drunken quarrels and shooting affrays that resulted inside the concert saloons and bagnios. The men with “hair-trigger tempers” loaded pistols and, angry defiance in their eyes, made this district a mecca of vice in the years leading up to the Great Fire, and immediately thereafter.

Many of the Randolph Street dives, some showy and others common, were fronts for prostitution. Pimps stood on the sidewalk advertising their business. Idle men uttered profane wisecracks and lewd comments to the women shoppers scurrying past. “The existence of these dens is not only a fearful danger to those who become their victims but an outrage and a damage to those whose businesses are under and adjoining them. The brazen gamblers are not content to angle for their legitimate bait but they hang in knots about the sidewalk blowing their smoke into the faces of respectable passers-by, spitting over their dresses and giving vent to the rottenness of their own hearts and imaginations by coarse and insulting comments on every lady who ventures to pass under the stare of their licentious eyes,” the *Tribune* commented on May 23, 1867.

The police officers, ill-trained and undermanned, were often seen drinking inside the establishments, collecting payoffs and free beer in return for their patronage and protection.

“Chicago was a bad town,” author Dorsha B. Hayes wrote in 1944. “That was the name it had now, no blinking it. All over America it was known as wild, lawless, full of wickedness and the stories of its shootings spread. And that reputation served to attract yet more lawbreakers who sought to live by violence and stealth. To these also, the big, rich city was a magnet.”[11] Unemployed men roamed the streets.

Farmers driving their livestock and produce to market down former Indian trails fashioned into wooden plank toll roads (Milwaukee Avenue, Clybourn, Elston Avenues in the modern era) from the distant hinterland were robbed by highwaymen, or waylaid into vice dens controlled by Plant and his minions, and relieved of their cash. Gangs of pickpockets called the fleecing of the country grangers in Chicago the "Saturday night rolls."

Ruffian and desperado Cornelius "Con" Brown, with his brothers, Jim and Bill, operated a small farm in Lemont, Illinois, a distant south suburb of Chicago. They were recognized as the leaders of gangs of highwaymen, burglars, and cow thieves preying upon tradesmen, farmers, and merchants making their way to the Chicago markets to sell their wares. Policing of the hinterland was sporadic, and few officers even dared to take Con on. Law enforcement managed to pick off Jim and Bill, sending them to an early grave. For a time Con stewed over this misfortune, working as a boatman on the Illinois & Michigan Canal, but a thief's life was more to his liking. He knew the woods and prairies beyond Chicago and managed to escape into the backwash. Inside a Lemont saloon the night of February 29, 1868, Brown drew a Bowie knife on a man named Peter Boyle. Through the element of surprise, a brandished knife usually beats a gun in a saloon fight, but Boyle was a little faster and drilled Con Brown through the heart, ending his reign of terror.

"He lived a miserable, worthless vagabond and died an ignominious death," the *Chicago Times* commented on March 1, 1868. "No mourner will follow his body to the grave, no tear of sorrow or regret will be shed but the death of Con Brown will rather be celebrated as an event which has the rid the world of a bold, Bad dangerous man—a man who is better under the ground than over it."

The heyday of Roger Plant and his bummers faded after 1869. With riches accrued from the poor unfortunates in his employ, Plant, like other criminals interested in ascending into the "upper world," aspired to become a respectable uptown "swell." With a fancy suit of clothes, and a diamond stick pin protruding from his cravat, he dangled a gold watch and chain and invited the unsuspecting into his vile den. The *Tribune* reported on July 23, 1871, that old Roger resembled a "bird of gorgeous plumage just arisen from the ashes." In the same article, it was reported that Roger had abandoned his old haunts and had turned to the church for salvation after more than a decade in business, but upon running into Lib Woods, the colorful harlot in his former employ, he greeted her as one would embrace a long lost daughter.

"I'm living from hand to mouth, sometimes in the bridewell and whiles out of it [sic]. Ah Mr. Plant, times have changed, ain't they since we were on Wells Street? Them were gay old days!" Lib Woods, one of the city's most colorful and best-known courtesans of the Civil War period, fell on hard times.[12] Following her passing from the ravages of smallpox on September 16, 1870, even the pious, devoutly Republican *Tribune* couldn't help but express remorse over the death of a once beautiful woman who had been driven by despair to the lower depths.

> Lib Woods was a poor outcast. Her death will relieve the policemen from a good deal of personal trouble picking poor Lib up from time to time; in carrying her from the gutters to the Armory to the Bridewell and from the Bridewell back to her old haunts on Jackson Street. Ten years ago Lib Woods was one of the gayest, prettiest and most fascinating creatures that could be found among her class in the city. Many fine gentlemen who are not quite gray may remember the day when they were flattered with the preference of the gay courtesan. In her palmy days she was the mistress of Billy Meadows, a notorious prize fighter and dog fancier. Lib Woods was the 'Nancy' to this 'Billy Sykes.' This Billy Meadows was more than suspected to be a murderer. After the death of her paramour, Lib became dissipated. She found her way in later years to that shadowy haunt of sin known as Under the Willow and while there she was seized with the small pox. That disease disfigured her once comely features. She drank whiskey and sunk gradually, but surely, to the gutter of Wells Street before it was raised to the grade.[13]

The Great Fire of 1871 spared Roger Plant any financial anguish. Soon after, he escaped to St. Louis where he opened a brothel on Green Street—the scene of a murder in 1874—and then it was on to California and his final oblivion.

Pawn brokers and secondhand clothing stores with large awnings covering the front of the abode operated adjacent to Wells Street vice dens. Plant and the first criminal "gangs" to emerge in Chicago during the pre-Civil War period were the early purveyors of gambling and the flourishing vice trade. There were others, of course. Steve Stamp, a burly African American man with a frame likened to Hercules, kept a saloon-dive and gambling den facing Plant's operation at Wells and Monroe. Stamp, a name otherwise lost to the vapors of history, turned his resort over to Ed White and George Crutchon, who turned the place into a seedy restaurant where, over servings of greasy food, assignations were arranged. The street had a tough reputation. The Wells Street saloons operated by the brutish George Dupont and "Captain" Rounds did a land office business. Roxanna Brooks was a fearsome barkeep, a woman of no mean reputation, who put to flight numerous Chicago constables ordered to bring her in. "Con" Weeger, a well-known local thug, ruled a Wells Street gang, but later moved to Cheyenne, Wyoming, where he was hanged by a vigilante mob.

"Long John" Wentworth, editor of the *Chicago Democrat* newspaper and mayor of Chicago in two rollicking terms of office, 1857–1858 and again in 1860–1861, is principally remembered today for discharging the entire city police force at the stroke of midnight, March 27, 1861, after the Republicans wrested control of the department by appointing a partisan metropolitan board. Wentworth, an imposing force of nature obsessed with eradicating vice and criminal gangs, traced the moral decay of Wells Street to "inefficient city officers [who] allowed gamblers to settle and with them came the disciples of Potiphar's wife and that crowd of moral and social outcasts which gamblers instinctively draw around themselves wherever they go."

During his first term of office Wentworth closed the book on one of the darker chapters in the history of the young city—the forced removal of the criminals, impoverished social outcasts, and the befuddled prostitutes whose behavior was tempered with laudanum that congregated in a row of hastily erected squatter shanties lying on the edge of Lake Michigan north of the Chicago River. The district gained national prominence as "the Sands," a detached neighborhood of dingy tenements set upon a triangular-shaped formation of white, clear sand given over to sin and the flaunting of public decency. "From 1844 for 12 years, these desert Arabs of Chicago lived on an area of yellow sand that drifted about into their shanties, was piteously bleak in Mackinaw breezes and shone blindingly in the summer suns," the *Tribune* observed in a retrospective look back on October 20, 1872. The police never "visited" there of course. "It was a neighborhood sure to attract the stray sailor, the country greenhorn seeing life, the innocent gull from the interior, the low and the vile, and the idly curious," the reporter made note.

With the opening of the first Dearborn Street bridge spanning the Chicago River in the 1840s, the district opened up to a wider clientele of thrill seekers and habitués previously cut off from the North Side. The "Sands" became a focus of newspaper attention. Dead bodies were found floating in the lake or upon the city streets. Missing men straying into the "Sand Houses" from the safety of the Lake House a few hundred feet away (then the city's finest hotel) stayed missing.

Constable James Quinn of the Ninth Ward, the first Chicago police officer to fall in the line of duty, ventured into the "Sands" to arrest a sneak thief named Paul Parmilee for pilfering items of clothing. As he struggled with Parmilee, a waterfront thug answering to the name William Rees pounced on Quinn and flailed away at him, breaking a rib and injuring his jaw. In the ensuing melee, Parmilee escaped. Quinn returned to the dismal shanties the next night to recapture Parmilee, but Rees was waiting for him inside a dive owned by criminal Stephen Crosby and Wilson Perry, an anti-Irish Know Nothing, and meted out a second terrible beating. Quinn, a potato famine immigrant from Ireland, died in the hospital three days later on December 5, 1853. Rees was captured by Marshal James Howe two months later and convicted on a charge of manslaughter. His sentence was light—just five years—and he was paroled by Illinois governor Joel Matteson after serving just two years.

Up to that point, there had not been a single murder conviction in the City of Chicago in over ten years. Facing destitution as a result of loss of income, the widow, Margaret Quinn, petitioned the city for compensation. They awarded her and her children the paltry sum of fifty dollars.[14]

As editor of the *Democrat* in his nearby office on Water Street, Wentworth observed firsthand this daily spectacle of vice, murder, and misery, and ragged, unwanted children running loose outside the houses of ill fame and gambling dens, and decided that he would do something about the matter. Up to that time, writs of eviction and civil litigation to force their removal mostly failed. William B. Ogden, Chicago's first mayor and its wealthiest citizen, had purchased the rights of some of the claimants' lots. He ordered the trespassers off the lakefront but the squatters defied him. Ogden persisted in his demands, and after months of stubborn refusal he prevailed upon Wentworth to take sterner measures.

On a bright, sunlit April afternoon in 1857, while the ring leaders of the criminal enterprise were lured off somewhere on the pretext of betting on a horse race and a dogfight, Wentworth and a posse of police descended on the district. After completing their first assault, the mayor's men returned to burn down six remaining brothels. With grappling chains, the flimsy wooden dives were pulled down while screaming women hurled profane epithets at the mayor, who personally directed the assault. "Where shall we go?" they demanded, but there was no ready answer from police or the mayor. The work went on all day long. The remaining men responsible for the conditions that had not gone off to the horse races were savagely beaten. The battle of the "Sands" was only a temporary victory in the crusade to rid the city of its crime problem.

The Chicago Fire accomplished for the city what "Long John" could not—the destruction and rebirth of Wells Street, later called Fifth Avenue, into a bright and gleaming commercial thoroughfare lined by fashionable stores, hotels, apothecaries, public houses, and dry goods stores to mimic the famed New York City thoroughfare. The conflagration swept away the last of the ramshackle dives and the disreputable element was driven out. Self-conscious city folk sensing an imminent change for the better immediately petitioned the city council to rename Wells Street "Fifth Avenue." By the mid-1870s, Fifth Avenue (née Wells Street), beckoned only the best people to its newly built retail emporiums of brick and stone. The criminal throngs and the vice mongers vacated but quickly coalesced in other shambling districts of the city.

Wells Street did not harvest all of the wretchedness, poverty, and desperation spreading like a cancer through Chicago. Misery abounded in all quarters of the city. "At the head of the list of the squatter villages of Chicago stands Kilgubbin, the largest shanty settlement within its limits," observed a *Chicago Times* reporter on November 3, 1866. "It has a varied history, having been the terror of constables, sheriffs and policemen in days that are past. The advance of time and civilization has removed this classic locality several times. Its first side was on Kinzie Street westward along the river *ad infinitum* [North Branch of the Chicago River]. It numbered many thousands of inhabitants of all ages and habits, besides large droves of geese, goslings, pigs and rats. It was a safe retreat for criminals; policemen not venturing to invade its precincts or even cross the border without having a strong reserve force."

Kilgubbin's collection of lean-to shanties, divided into three apartments, all sitting on a swamp, represented squalor. Between ten and twelve children often slept in a single room, lying on the floor upon squalid rags and accumulated filth. Chicago's earliest juvenile gangs formed in these districts, often under the direction of adult criminal profiteers and thieves not unlike the character of the fiendish Fagin in Charles Dickens's 1837 novel *Oliver Twist*.

Children and adolescents were pressed into the criminal life, often selling stolen property procured for pawnbrokers, dealers in old copper, iron, and appliances. In May 1859 Chicago's pioneering stockman John B. Sherman[15] reported the loss of cattle and hogs from his Cottage Grove Avenue pens by a thieving gang that had slipped dexterously past the wooden fences and the watchman to procure stolen livestock for certain unscrupulous city butchers. Three gang boys under the age of seventeen were eventually nabbed by the watchmen and dragged before the magistrate. "All are of the hardest class of the rising generation of who are in training for felon cells," the *Chicago Times* reported. "They are not of course subjects for the penitentiary, but lack only years to meet its fullest requirements."

"Is it a fact that little children steal?" a *Tribune* writer asked rhetorically on May 9, 1853, as the city council pondered the ways and means of dealing with youthful crime in the immigrant communities. "Is it a fact that there are monsters of iniquity who openly and secretly make it a business to buy off children, no questions asked?"

An epidemic of juvenile crime and residential burglary erupted after the Civil War, as the boundaries of Kilgubbin shifted to Conley's Patch, bounded by Wells, Polk, and Madison on the city's Near West Side on the south branch of the Chicago River. It was the fastest-growing area of the city, adjoining manufacturing plants, lumberyards, the first Chicago stockyards, factories, and planing mills, and it drew the greatest number of working poor, mostly Irish in the early years, but later they came from every corner of Europe. It is possible that Phillip Conley, the U.S. Collector of Customs, alderman, and a leader in Irish-American fraternalism, gave his name to this corner of deprivation—but the name is immaterial to the legacy of the district. It was home to the city's first gas works, and a collection of shanties, rookeries, grogshops, and cheap bordellos. A large African American woman named the "Bengal Tigress" operated a profitable house of ill repute during the Civil War but became a holy terror when she went on a drinking and fighting spree.

Denizens of the poor neighborhoods preyed upon the Terrace Row swells as they socialized in their dwellings. The press reported on the infamous deeds of the "Break O'Day Boys," Chicago's first home-invasion gang. Covering their faces with boot-blacking, this vicious gang of toughs spent considerable time conducting surveillance of their intended targets' homes before entering the premises under the cover of darkness. They often carried out these crimes during social gatherings and private house parties where rich friends sipped sherry and dined on breast of squab before being brutally accosted by the invading gang. Poverty and desperation bred this kind of crime.

The population of the West Side quadrupled from 57,000 to 214,000 in a ten-year period, from 1862 to 1872. Slum areas sprouted quickly. Double lots of frame houses in the front and back of the property lacked plumbing, ventilation, and paved streets. With nowhere to go, and school attendance lax and mostly unenforceable, children congregated in alleys and were often recruited into a life of crime.

"The little Arabs of the streets of whom the public have much cause to be afraid are here becoming an actual nuisance because of their continued depredations in the larcenous line," the *Tribune* reported on October 1, 1868. "Lacking the practical caution of the adult and hardened burglar or thief, yet having the essential qualities of thieving—surprising knowledge of the modus operandi, they succeeded well in their risk taking. Their practice appears to be to closely watch certain houses, await the departure of occupants, and then enter and carry off what they can conveniently lay their hands on."

The Chicago police superintendent's report to the city council for 1869 revealed that 125 children under the age of ten had been arrested and charged with felony crime in the previous twelve months. The police reported 2,404 arrests of children and adolescents ages ten to twenty for property crime and other offenses. Ten of the convicted children were sent to one of two functioning reform schools operating in the city at that time. Fifty more were turned over to the Roman Catholic Asylum.

Desperate, poverty-stricken parents, unable to provide for or discipline their children, often surrendered them to the police magistrates who dealt with them in the usual and customary ways. The *Tribune* reported on August 29, 1871, that "Thomas Mort, a willful youth who his mother cannot manage was sent to the Catholic Asylum."

For the other unfortunates, if they were not discharged back into the street, the Bridewell was the last stop. Drawing attention to the appalling conditions of the criminal justice system that spawned hard-core criminals from the population of "Street Arabs" a member of the Board of Charities noted on May 7, 1869, that he had "remembered visiting the jail last summer during the hottest weather and found five boys between the ages of nine and seventeen confined in one cell in a perfect state of nudity, so that they might not be eaten up with vermin. But one need not go back to last summer to find such scenes as they are daily occurrences in both bridewell and jail, where they associate with the most hardened criminals. What we are most in want of is a compulsory educational system; but as we cannot have school palaces, ten or 15,000 children must roam the street in idleness."

The homeless "Street Arabs" were often the children of distant lands—orphans, runaways, the throwaway children of a society ill equipped to provide rudimentary schooling and the slightest chance of opportunity but receiving tutoring in the practice of burglary, pickpocketing, and armed robbery from adult Fagins safely hidden away in the recesses of the ghettos and otherwise immune to arrest and prosecution.

As the railroads extended their tentacle-like reach across the continent, runaway children rode the boxcars to Chicago from eastern cities. In New York City rescuing children from the shackles of crime became the personal mission of Charles Loring Brace, who founded the Children's Aid Society in 1853 and spent the majority of his remaining years attempting to place street children in the homes of secure parental households in the West. But the big cities west of the Hudson River offered little relief from slum life and the organized gangs of New York. Chicago waifs were frequently forced to take refuge beneath the city sidewalks, or under the wharves, bridges, and inside empty hogsheads. A large population of street urchins suffering cold and hunger went to work as bootblacks and newsboys, subsisting on pennies a day and the charity of strangers.

An estimated five hundred newsboys dispensed papers from city street corners in 1868. Another 120 boys worked as bootblacks. Three-quarters of them were homeless and motherless. Beaten and whipped by drunken fathers, boys ran off and took these lowly jobs, acquiring a street sense and underworld connections.

Relief agencies administered to poor families, but places of safety and nurturing for children were lacking. In 1868 Chicago established a "Newsboys' Home" in Wright's Block at the corner of Kinzie and State Streets for the express purpose of "domesticating the wild little vagabonds," boys from eight to fourteen years of age attired in cast-off boots, ill-fitting hand-me-down trousers, and shabby, discarded coats that once belonged to adults. The first Newsboys' Home accommodated forty or so boot-blacking urchins in a room measuring twenty-five feet square with a stove in the middle of the floor to keep the boys warm in the cold of winter. Crude wooden benches ran around the four sides of the room. These were for sleeping. As bleak as the surroundings appeared, the alternative was nights spent sleeping in the alleys or deserted hallways of buildings, sheltered momentarily from the severity of the night.

Their work day began at 7:00 a.m. and continued until later afternoon when the final editions of the newspapers were all sold. At night, following a light supper and evening prayers, lights were extinguished. Forty children sheltered, but many hundreds more were left in the streets.

With a small endowment of $177, Dr. George E. Shipman, in the days after the Chicago Fire, placed a small basket outside the doors of a lodging house at 54 S. Green Street, where he rented living space after losing his home and belongings in the conflagration. Shipman attached a note to the basket bearing the following message to desperate mothers. "Those having babies of which they wish to dispose whether of sin or poverty, have but to leave them in the basket and they will be cared for. No questions will be asked." The next morning Shipman found an infant boy left on the doorstep, then a girl a few hours later. Within two months Shipman cared for fifteen babies in rooms he had rented for thirty-five dollars a month. This necessitated a move into larger headquarters. The Chicago Foundlings Home provided care and feeding for an estimated forty-five thousand babies and mothers over the next hundred years of its history.

A similar effort to provide education and impart the lessons of temperance, probity, and respect for the law were expended by the founders of the Ladies Industrial School Association in 1854, when, through private subscription, four schools opened, one in the West Division district a second in the South Division on Liberty Street, a third at Indiana and Fourteenth Streets, and a fourth location (with less successful results), in the heart of the Sands vice district.

The secular teachings of the association often encountered a storm of opposition from intemperate households where liquor consumption was rampant. In his report of February 26, 1860, A. S. Farnam, president of the association, noted that while some children had left the school "to wander in idleness and vice about our streets, yet we feel assured that the lessons of morality, economy and industry they have been taught will eventually lead many of them to the path of virtue and religion. Our Temperance Society continues to exert a good influence. Two of our boys were the means of getting their intemperate fathers to sign the pledge. Another went to visit his wretched mother in Bridewell and there pleaded until she was compelled to make a vow on her knees to forever abandon liquor. The same boy was sent by his father to purchase some whiskey, but he would not go. The father insisted and he produced his temperance card and said, 'Father, I will not do that!'" Alcoholism presented a tragic, but all too common, picture of Chicago families devastated by liquor consumption. By the 1880s the city had more saloons than every state south of the Mason-Dixon line.

Other boys born and bred into Chicago immigrant ghettos, often to drunken and vicious fathers who inculcated in them the culture of the saloon life at an early age, fell into a bad way if not otherwise properly schooled. They were taken under the wing of the Newsboys' Home, the Ladies Industrial School, or gainfully employed. A Pennsylvania jurist, in an opinion piece published in the *Chicago Tribune* on August 28, 1880, noted with disdain "that among their associates a successful burglary is a deed to be proud of—so much as a victory to a military chieftain; and a convict 'cracking a crib' or for manslaughter is a hero whose acts are to be emulated. The tales of "Dick Turpin" and "The Rover of the Sea" excite in their young minds a spirit of ambition to become equally criminal and notorious. They owe society nothing for society has done nothing for them. Modern philanthropy has almost entirely overlooked them."

Incarcerated in the Bridewell, boys of an impressionable age learned the criminal way from older, hardened felons, and the argot of the streets, the "thieves dialect," uttered in their everyday conversation.

1. Cracking a crib—burglary or home invasion
2. Lushing ken—a saloon
3. Boosing-ken—a place to hide thieves and stolen goods
4. Wipes—stolen pocket handkerchiefs
5. Fogie hunter—a pickpocket
6. Beak—a judge or police court magistrate
7. Prig—a thief
8. Scragged—executed on the gallows
9. Run the flimsy—pass counterfeit money
10. Can rushing—filling a pail of beer at the saloon and delivering it to the boy's father or guardian at home
11. Lagged—arrested
12. Kinchin-lay—stealing from children
13. Slop lush to the pals—sell drinks to the boys

Nineteenth-century judges frequently showed little common sense with the discretion they had available to them in dealing with juvenile offenders in a compassionate manner because legislators could not decide whether or not the reform school was an institution to reform or to punish. The inevitable decision of the justice of the peace or police magistrate boiled down to the Bridewell or the city's first reform school. It was granted its charter on November 30, 1855, with a broad mandate to care for children "growing up in a state of mendicancy, ignorance, idleness or vice." It began operations at the county poorhouse in the Town of Jefferson (a rural community incorporated into Chicago as a city neighborhood in 1889) under the direction of the Illinois state legislature. The city provided initial funding and the directorship of the reform school and assigned the Reverend D. B. "Goodman" Nichols and a board of guardians. Prior to this time boys in trouble with the law were ordered locked up in tiny basement cells of the same courthouse that drew the ire of the lager beer rioters in April 1855.

After a fire gutted the poorhouse at Jefferson, a new building opened north of Hyde Park, a half mile south of the (then) city limits on the Chicago branch of the Illinois Central Railroad. As the population of youths deemed incorrigible by the courts grew, the city added a two-story building with a basement used for the storage of clothing and other supplies, with an attached hospital and workhouse in 1862. A small library with a collection of zoological specimens, and grounds adorned by flowers by all outward appearances, provided the illusion of paternalistic warmth, friendship, and humanity. In the public eye at least, the city reform school could not be compared to the villainous and brutally cruel English workhouses described by Charles Dickens in his popular novels of the day. However, public image and the reality of daily living at the reform school were two different things.

The reform school, theoretically a place of confinement and correction designed to segregate delinquents between the ages of six and sixteen from adult criminals, stood outside the jurisdictional purview of the municipal courts. In December 1868 accusations flew that innocent boys, guilty of no specific crime other than suffering homelessness or neglect from their mothers, were being sentenced and illegally detained at the reform school. The parents of Dennis Grandfield, a lad whose freedom was denied on legal grounds by a judge of the superior court and the city attorney, were informed that the decision was conclusive and irrevocable. The board of guardians wielded absolute power and control over the inmate population, and did not subscribe to the prevailing belief that no child should be released to the outside world until they had attained the age of sixteen. Thus, due process was denied the heartbroken parents, who demanded his release into their custody.

"It is called by the pleasant name of school, but is in reality a prison," recorder's court judge William McAllister told the *Tribune* on December 11, 1868. "It is essentially a prison as the State Prison at Joliet. The inmates are subject to the coercive system of labor for the benefit of the institution or [the] Superintendent and it is as rigidly enforced as at the State Penitentiary.

"As a prison for juvenile offenders who have been indicted and convicted, it is preferable to the jail or bridewell but I deny the authority of any man or set of men to seize boys who are innocent of crime and subject to involuntary servitude."

The majority of the nonviolent offenders sent off to the reform school were adjudged guilty of crimes of petty larceny, the theft of scrap metal for which junk dealers and manufacturers paid them a commission, and other acts of mischief. The average age of the reform school offender was thirteen and a half. The majority of youthful inmates were of Irish extraction (581 out of a total of 1,284 who lived there between 1855 and 1872 were Irish). They were the sons of canal immigrants, and the paupers of Kilgubbin and Conley's Patch. Upon arrival at the school, they were assigned to a "family" of thirty other children (there were seven such families) and assigned to factory work, weaving baskets, constructing chair bottoms, making shoes, and performing other required duties in the greenhouse, the farm, or doing tailoring. A six-hour work day accompanied classroom schooling. Escapes were common, averaging twenty to thirty per year.

Violence and severe punishment were endemic to the institution. In December 1869 enraged watchman John Beeston struck inmate George Miller, a boy of thirteen, over the head with a leaded whipstock after the boy was pushed out of formation in a moment of clowning by another lad as they stood in a single-file line. Miller died from the injury. Beeston, who had previously served as a watchman at the Soldier's Home and whose "good character" was attested to by Seth Hanchett, superintendent of the home, was found guilty of manslaughter but sentenced to just one year in prison for his brutal action. The jury agreed with the defendant's legal counsel that he had exercised the "proper amount of force" to "preserve discipline." After Reverend Nichols left the institution in 1860, a succession of superintendents followed, none exhibiting the same degree of kind regard and compassion as Nichols. Between 1855 and 1872, thirty boys died while in the "care" of the home.

McAllister, who advanced to the state supreme court, called the reform school an illegal institution with no authority in law. Under a writ of habeas corpus, McAllister ruled the Reform School Act unconstitutional when there was no commitment of crime after circuit court judge Frastus Williams incarcerated one DeWitt C. Wallace without apparent cause or due process. "Parents may knock at the door of this prison for their children in vain; nothing but the writ of habeas corpus will restore them," McAllister said. "Is it that the spirit of the Cromwellian Age invested with these austere powers has descended upon the shores of our lake to interfere with domestic relations and cast its chilling shadow on the spirit of childhood, the pleasures of youth and upon hearth and home?" The *Tribune* applauded the decision, commenting in a December 2, 1870, editorial, "The destitute widow of today; unable to properly clothe her boys and keep them out of the streets and from association with vicious companions may be the millionaire of next year. Can it be said that the children taken from her in the days of poverty cannot be reclaimed but must remain prisoners of forced labor until they are twenty-one years of age?"

The Chicago Fire of October 1871 and the McAllister decision hastened the closing of Chicago's infamous South Side reform school. The school grounds and buildings were ordered sold to Cook County for the sum of $50,000. In turn, the grounds were subdivided and the lots sold for residential development with a handsome profit returned to a consortium of Hyde Park capitalists. The decision was hailed as a victory by a handful of socially progressive citizen reformers.

The remaining inmates were transferred to the State of Illinois Reform School, created by an act of the state legislature in 1867. After nearly five years of delay, the school for boys ranging in age from ten to sixteen opened in Pontiac, Illinois, on May 21, 1872, with an inmate population of just 165. In 1891 the legislature changed the name of the Illinois Reform School at Pontiac to the Illinois State Reformatory, and established a system of indeterminate sentences with parole granted to inmates "who in the opinion of the Board of Managers may be safely granted conditional liberties." The young inmates were divided up into two classes, boys between the ages of ten and sixteen, and those between sixteen and twenty-one. Although the rigorous industrial training program provided for career instruction in glazing masonry, broom making, plastering, tailoring, carpentry, blacksmithing, painting, and gardening, conditions were severe and discipline harsh. By 1895 the inmate population had swelled to 812. For all intents and purposes the intended "reformatory" at Pontiac had evolved into a penitentiary.

A minority of concerned citizens urged the city and state judiciary to embrace more enlightened methodologies of turning troubled street youth into productive citizens through humane treatment rather than the upraised truncheon of the watchman and the grind of workhouse toil. Over time other reform schools would open in the Chicago environs, including the John Worthy Manual Training School, completed in June 1894 at a cost of $80,000. Bureaucratic fumbling and delays in constructing three special dormitories for the "younger and best behaved" boys postponed the formal dedication until June 30, 1899.[16]

The Juvenile Court Act of July 1899, establishing the first court of its kind dedicated to youthful offenders in the United States, mandated that children in detention "shall be treated as children in need of aid, encouragement, and guidance." With naive hope that the letter of the law would be respected, Judge Richard S. Tuthill, a Chicago jurist and the divining light of the campaign to build a school for juvenile prisoners incarcerated in the city's Bridewell, expected that the facility would prove most satisfactory to philanthropists interested in prison reform and would be a credit to the city.[17]

"Boys, prepare to be good men," Tuthill urged 131 underage Bridewell detainees as they were marched to their dormitories and cell rooms of the new John Worthy School. "Tell the truth always. Abraham Lincoln and Benjamin Franklin had not better chances than you. But you must be earnest and try to do right."

At night the boys were herded into the dormitory and placed under the care of the jail guards armed with guns. In the morning they were returned to the jurisdiction of the Chicago Board of Education. It soon became apparent to Chicago educators that a reform school for boys theoretically promoting learning over punishment could not be successfully maintained on the grounds of the house of correction. Boys whose eyes had been blackened the night before by enraged guards appeared in class dazed and unprepared for school. Eighteen-foot-high stone walls encircled the building and the young boys placed in the care of the bridewell administrators were subjected to the same brutal treatment as the adult inmates.

It was later determined that Worthy School classrooms exploded into violence as teachers used their fists to inflict discipline. Bareback whippings were frequent.

Corporal punishment was counter to board of education rules, but Principal George Masslich, fired in 1905 for permitting his teachers wide latitude in their disciplinary methods, defended the old way of doing things. "I have been obliged to listen to all kinds of abuse," complained Masslich. "When a boy curses me I am able to do nothing but fold my arms and smile complacently. The boys think I'm a sissy because I don't knock them down." These sentiments were echoed by a generation of teachers who lamented the passing of corporal punishment. At the urging of Jane Addams of Hull House, and other socially conscious reformers, the State of Illinois closed the John Worthy School in June 1914, amid reports of continuing physical abuse and mismanagement.

A new facility, the Chicago and Cook County School for Boys, described as a "semi-correctory institution," opened in 1909 in Riverside, a western suburb of Chicago, with the belief that clean air and a rural setting would cure the scourge of juvenile delinquency. The city and county built the reform school on surplus farmland seized as restitution from the thousand-acre estate of former city treasurer David A. Gage after Gage defaulted the city treasury after losing his reelection bid in 1873. The home operated until 1931when state funding ran out.[18]

The sprawling countryside proved to be no more of an effective cure for the lingering social ills, wrought by hardship and poverty put upon the young, than bridewell integration. The segregation and isolation of the immigrant poor into decaying neighborhoods rife with saloons, gambling hells, bordellos, and jails, progressed in the confident belief that bad boys will always ripen into hardened criminals. They were convinced that punishment and incarceration remained the best remedy to cure the contagion of crime. The festering attitude and benign indifference to reform movements helped to spawn the gangs of Chicago and the poor crime districts they inhabited.

2

DOWNTOWN AND NEAR SOUTH: VICTORIAN VICE, GAMBLERS, CARD CHEATS, CHINESE TONGS, AND THE RISE OF CHICAGO'S ORGANIZED CRIME GANGS, 1870–1920

No one was safe from the lawless elements that were set loose in Chicago after the Civil War. Criminal gangs controlling vice and gambling and committing mayhem in the streets frustrated the police, the courts, and the beleaguered but determined social engineers hoping to shield the young from the pernicious forces encircling the Chicago business district. The gangs made a mockery of the police and the civil authorities.

A new and evolving breed of organized criminals oversaw the dissolute pre-fire vice districts, which were dimly recalled by the *Chicago Inter-Ocean* in June 1872 as "low ranges of dingy buildings, dirty men slouching on the walk and slatternly women lounging out the windows—Wells Street was a street fallen out of Hogarth of as bad repute of any in the city." They shifted operations south of the central business district that by now was given over completely to commercialized vice.

The Custom House Place Levee, a wicked sin strip encircling the Polk Street train station between Dearborn and Clark Streets, existed for two reasons: Pragmatic nineteenth-century politicians believed that segregating the world's oldest profession into a compact, tightly controlled district would spare "respectable" business and residential areas from an invasion of streetwalkers and their pimps; and, two, the traffic in women, gambling, booze, and dope made these same pragmatists and their gangland consorts overseeing the trade a whole lot of money.[1]

"Custom and precedent has established in Chicago certain restricted districts where the laws and ordinances of the state and city are practically inoperative in suppressing houses of prostitution," observed author Wallace Rice. "Because of this condition certain public officials have given a certain discretion to the police department and have allowed police rules and regulations to take the place of the laws and ordinances of these districts."[2]

During the "wide-open years" (that period of time spanning 1870 and 1920), there were four concentrated Chicago vice districts catering to the desires and prurient fascination of free-handed western stockmen and drovers coming into the city with carloads of cattle bound for slaughter at the Union Stockyards. Others followed a well-beaten path to forbidden fruit and free abandonment. Lumbermen, grain and wheat speculators, traveling salesmen, and "slumming parties" of thrill-seeking young men from respectable city neighborhoods ventured into the darkest heart of the city to sample the salacious pleasures frowned upon by Victorian sensibility. Drink and women were the principal objects of these slumming expeditions into the city's segregated brothel districts.

Pamphlets and "sporting house directories" advertised the wicked attractions of the Custom House Place Levee (and its Whiskey Row extension, a block due east) from Chicago to St. Louis and points west. The South Side Levee rose to prominence after the Custom House operators were driven out; a West Side "tenderloin" adjoining the impoverished Maxwell Street ghetto also took root; and the cabarets, gambling dens, and nightclubs were coming into prominence on Clark Street, north of the Chicago River in the 1870s. To the south, the West Hammond / South Chicago resorts straddled the Illinois-Indiana state line.

Whiskey Row grew up on the west side of State Street between Van Buren Street and Congress (the present location of the Harold Washington Public Library) and it bumped up against the Custom House Levee.

This curious rialto facing architect William LeBaron Jenney's majestic Siegel Cooper & Co. department store was a criminal lair in miniature likened to the worst sections of the Bowery in New York. "Why this one block which under normal circumstances would be one of the most valuable for business purposes in the city should be given over to dives and cesspools of infamy is one of the mysteries of the municipal administration," the *Chicago American* wondered.[3] Here in Whiskey Row conniving barkeeps concocted the "Mickey Finn"—the famous elixir spiked with knockout drops capable of disabling a victim long enough for his pockets to be picked clean, and his limp body rolled out into the alley. "A callous rounder who knows better [than] to drink the stuff served to patrons in these dives will see evidence enough in a few hours to convince him enough that the town south of Van Buren is wide open," the "slumming" *American* reporter commented of an all-night tour of the cabarets and dives.

In violation of the midnight closing laws, the revelers carried on into the early morning hours inside the Senate, Jake Weiss's State Street drive where fourteen young women barely past the age of twenty hustled male patrons to fork over a sawbuck for a bottle of Hennessey brandy. Unattached women that congregated in saloons for the purpose of soliciting men for drinks represented an affront to rigid Victorian sensibilities. If a woman entered a public house without benefit of a male escort, there existed the very real possibility of police arrest for the crime of vagrancy and prostitution.

Whiskey Row, protected and secured by a succession of Chicago mayors and influential politicians for over three decades, advertised twenty-two wine rooms, concert saloons, and illicit dens, including Tuck's Place, the Berlin, the Missouri, the Aurora, "Mushmouth" Johnson's place, the Klondike, Mickey Finn's Lone Star Saloon, the Boston, Andy Craig's Tivoli, and Bennett & Baude's. Girls and upstairs gambling were the main draw. As the *American* reporters exited Tuck's Place, a "capper" (working the room to lure patrons into the gambling den) called out: "Game running upstairs boys! Everything wide open!"

In the center of the block, men and boys of all ages elbowed their way into a penny arcade for the chance to deposit their Indian head pennies and liberty nickels into a "mutoscope," a 3-D viewer promising the patron a glimpse of a scantily clad woman. Whiskey Row was both a carnival show and a rialto.

Fat Andy Craig, the "King of the State Street Levee," managed the saloon action. Craig was a First Ward politician, gambler, vice purveyor, and keeper of the Tivoli resort—the epicenter of Whiskey Row decadence. In the basement of his place he operated a gambling handbook.

The first floor was given over to wine, whiskey, and bawdy ragtime music. Overhead, the lodgings of the women who directed their besotted customers into private assignation rooms stood at the ready. Swinging doors, not unlike the entrance way to the Old West saloons depicted in Hollywood movies and television of a later era, opened up onto the street and provided the public with a bird's-eye view of the illicit doings inside. From the sidewalk one could hear music of the "jangling, metallic variety," as one newspaper called it. The feathered plumes of women's hats were visible over the low doors. Loud laughter and occasional profanity of the female consorts punctuated the music of the automatic piano. To the churchgoing Protestants unable to curb the excesses of drinking and gambling in their once-cherished city of white picket fences, these scenes were highly offensive in an era when a glimpse of stocking, as Irving Berlin noted, was still quite shocking.

"Craig is the worst offender on the street and shows more boldness in one hour than the rest of the owners of places of that character allow to crop out in a single day," sighed Police Chief George Shippy on January 19, 1908, during a public hearing investigating the link-up between Craig's operation and police officials.[4]

Andy Craig provided the necessary bail bonds for sneak thieves, gamblers, pickpockets, and female thieves. He spent much of his business day inside the nearby Armory Police Station (an imposing red-brick fortress towering over the neighborhood) swapping ribald stories with the lockup keepers, the desk sergeant, and the detectives who shared their secrets. Saturday night was the peak night for Craig's bonding enterprise.

In an interview with a *Tribune* reporter, published August 25, 1901, veteran police officer Patrick Walsh recalled his fifteen riotous years running the criminals and their weekend revelers into the Armory for booking. "I'll never tell all the wickedness I've seen on the Levee. I'm too old. I wouldn't live to tell it all," he admitted. "But in the old days when Saturday night came around and often on other nights when the head man needed the money from bail bonds the wagons would be sent out and all within reach would be brought into the station. The room would be filled to suffocation with the prisoners lined up for booking and with curious spectators who had come down to see the excitement. Behind the screen and behind the desk sergeant stood the professional bondsman, securing his dollar, two dollars, or even five dollars from each prisoner for release. A good-sized pool, from $100 to $500, was easily collected this way in less than an hour's time, to the financial benefit of those who those who were able to take advantage of it—Andy Craig."

With a wide-open checkbook and a smirk on his face, Craig happily signed the recognizance bonds for his gang of pimps and pickpockets and hustled about among the incarcerated women and their customers, and put up the money to satisfy their fines as well. "The police magistrate got his income from fees then and these fees swelled his receipts into the tens of thousands of dollars," Walsh related. It was a criminal racket until an ordinance passed awarding the magistrate a yearly salary with the proviso that receipts would be deposited into the city treasury.

Craig's whole play was to be the "all around good fellow," charming, glib, and likable. The boys in blue never wanted to give him offense, even though his "Pickpockets Trust" criminal gang robbed many a law-abiding citizen of their cash, their gold watches, and other valuables. "Pass Craig's place anytime between three and 7:00 p.m. and you can see a half dozen or more pickpockets hanging out in front," testified John Risden, special agent of the Chicago & Western Indiana Railroad, in sworn testimony, December 10, 1903. "Enter, and if you look like a detective, as many more will scatter like frightened rats. Craig looks after the pickpockets and when they get into trouble they make his place their headquarters. Craig's people they are called."[5]

John Rafferty, a former Chicago police officer gone over to the dark decay of the underworld, taunted the cops by opening a notorious saloon directly across the alley from the Armory Police Station during the 1893 World's Fair. The proprietor ribbed the bluecoats walking past the dive every day by his familiar expression, "I love a good thief!" Indeed. Rafferty and Craig shared responsibility for protecting Levee criminals. Craig administered to the thieves and pickpockets while Rafferty took care of the bunko men. Said one Levee insider, "When confidence men are out on the road and need help on a job they send to Rafferty and he sends them the kind of man they want. When a thief is in trouble he goes to Craig and gets help."[6]

In his 1910 crime-fighting memoir, Clifton Rodman Wooldridge, a capable but vainglorious and silly police detective guilty of exaggerated self-promotion, wrote: "The Chicago police have encountered the confidence man in a hundred varieties of con games. They have found him in league with politicians and other persons of influence, and waging a war against him has been a task which required the most skillful work."[7] Wooldridge provides no explanation as to why the bravehearts of the Armory Police Station permitted Rafferty to direct his gang of thieves and tricksters without interference for so many years.

Mayor Edward Fitzsimmons Dunne, praised by Chicago historians and scholars of the period as an incorruptible social reformer during his one term of office from 1905 to 1907, turned a blind eye to the mushrooming vice districts of Whiskey Row, the Rafferty and Craig saloons, and the adjoined Levee controlled by Craig and the other criminal gangs during his administration. Dunne wore the mask of the reformer exceptionally well, but could never extricate himself from entangling political partisanship in order to give the town a real cleanup.

Despite spasmodic police raids that managed to close down a handful of the most vicious Whiskey Row dives over a ten-year period (1895–1905), Craig's place was never touched. "Whether the mayor is aware of the power of these men or not is unknown," the *Tribune* remarked on January 26, 1906, "but the fact remains that their power has grown greater during the last two years and that at present no man in the First Ward levee opens a saloon, starts a handbook or a poolroom and no woman opens a disorderly house without first gaining the consent of a least one of the members of the syndicate." Dunne's inaction was thus explained.

The Democratic-controlled district was a sprawling open-air market of vice, gambling, and crime; and sadly for the Civic Association who failed to deliver the legislative knockout blow, the First remained the most flamboyant and important Chicago ward organization for years to come. For the eternally ambitious Mayor Dunne, whose personal drive landed him in the governor's office in 1913, giving offense to the political gangs of the First Ward by curbing their influence would be tantamount to committing political regicide.

How was it possible in this emerging city of commerce, industry, and with a defining architectural style that was soon to spread across the continent to wallow in the company of tinhorn gamblers, pikers, and crooks? The city was an oasis and safe haven, extending its leisurely comforts and the easy availability of bail-bonding money to a dizzying assortment of panders, confidence men and "black leg" southern gamblers (sponsoring cockfights, horse races, prizefights, and all forms of crooked "bunko" games, faro, keno, roulette, and whist).

By the time Andy Craig sampled the abundant harvest of illicit profit stemming from criminal enterprise available to him, the city was already awash in every known vice and temptation offered up for sale by a generation of confidence men and tricksters whose ranks increased tenfold after the Civil War.

Craig was a callow lad of the streets when the principal architect and planner of the underworld unified the gangs of Chicago and the politicians as the fastest way of grabbing on to and holding the first rung of the ladder of economic attainment and upward social mobility.

In his lifetime, this man of discriminating taste, who delighted in the plays of Shakespeare, fine imported liquors, the piano concertos of Ignacy Paderewski, and the pleasures of "the Store," his lush downtown gambling casino, held no elective office. But his formidable abilities as kingmaker made it possible for him to elect three Chicago mayors and to sit in private consultation with two presidents, Chester Alan Arthur and Grover Cleveland, inside the Oval Office of the White House.

The son of potato famine Irish immigrants who settled in the poorest section of Niagara Falls, New York, rose up from despair, and lacked social prestige built an empire of dice and cards from next to nothing. His name was Michael Cassius McDonald, and if you happened to live in Chicago during the "elegant 1880s," you would know of his exploits in the world of liquor, dice, cards, and politics, and perhaps be in awe of him.

In an inspired moment, Arthur Conan Doyle, the creator of the fictional Sherlock Holmes, might have crowned McDonald the "Napoleon of *Chicago* Crime" had he observed the wily trickster cooking up brazen schemes, bribing police, and amassing a fortune from inside his downtown lair. McDonald settled in Chicago prior to the outbreak of the Civil War. He had toured the "Cotton South" absorbing the antebellum world of gentlemen gamblers, copying their gaudy attire, and professing admiration for their great sagacity operating crooked lotteries, games of draw poker and faro banks in hotels, saloons, and paddle-wheel steamships. Years later he expressed his personal code of ethics. McDonald, a man of goodwill, declared: "Stick to your friends and keep your word once given." But in the same breath he sniggers, "There's a sucker born every minute!"[8]

During the war, McDonald established a profitable business running the bar privilege inside the Richmond House hotel, near the foot of the Chicago River. In the upper floors of the fashionable hostelry favored by Confederate spies and southern sympathizers, he sponsored card games and established friendly dealings with the sporting crowd along Hairtrigger Block and McCormick's Block. George Trussell and Cap Hyman were well known to him, but their profligacy and lack of enterprise were duly noted. Trussell and Hyman were the worst kind of fools, and they were destroyed by bad habits.

McDonald keenly understood that as the son of an Irish Catholic immigrant in a city ruled by Protestant Yankees firmly opposed to the liquor and gambling business, he could earn trust, respect, and political power through close interaction with the common people in the saloon setting. A 1875 article in the *Nation*, William Phillips Garrison's influential news and opinion periodical, recognized the saloonkeeper/politician as a self-made success story, well-positioned for advancement and always willing to extend aid to the newly arrived foreign born and society's down-and-outers. Working-class immigrants admired the boss for the jobs he provided and confidence he inspired that the fruits of life were attainable. "He sees them more frequently and familiarly than anybody else and is more trusted by them than anybody else, and is the person through whom the news and meaning of what passes in the upper regions of city politics and reaches them."

The saloon and the men who operated them represented much more to the common people than just conduits to jobs in city hall, the police, and the fire department. In times of economic hardship, panic, and recession, the saloon saved many of the destitute and homeless from starvation. Of the estimated six to seven thousand licensed and unlicensed saloons in Chicago during the late 1890s, approximately half provided a free lunch every day at no cost or obligation to the patron. The *Chicago Herald* estimated that Chicago saloons fed an estimated sixty thousand people every day for nothing, and at five cents for a single lunch, it cost the barkeeps $18,000 a week. During extreme winter weather, saloon owners often allowed the ragged poor free shelter in the basement of the saloon. Political loyalties were forged, Prohibitionists and Republicans scorned, and elections easily won. Joseph Chesterfield Mackin, schemer, ballot-box stuffer, and both friend and foe to Mike McDonald during his free and easy years, was said to have started the practice of the free lunch in the 1880s by serving his barroom patrons free oysters with their beer.

McDonald also recognized that mastering control of the police and the political process was essential to beating back the prejudices of scornful, disapproving bluebloods, the conservative press, and the intrusions of the police. To a Sister of Charity seeking a one-dollar donation to aid the family of a fallen police officer, McDonald handed over five and snorted: "Now go bury five more!"

He intuitively sensed that the protestations of the church counted for little because Chicagoans *enjoyed* their vices and he aimed to give them card games, horse races, illegal boxing matches, dice, and liquor but resolutely refused to traffic in prostitutes. The moral vagaries of the trade rubbed up against the grain of his sacred Catholic belief system, and he steered away from it. But he also knew that in order to succeed in integrating the mechanisms of city government with the rogue "sporting world" it would be occasionally necessary to cooperate with the vice mongers, provide them bonds to them if necessary, and bump up members of the armed gangs to positions of status in his embryonic organization. Such actions were needed to build the foundation of Chicago's enduring Democratic machine.

McDonald was not the first big-city politician-gambler to empower rowdies and toughs to in order to break the political grasp of the mercantile class and the Prohibitionists—avowed enemies of the proponents of the "liberal" form of government. In New York City's dismal Five Points neighborhood of Lower Manhattan, Tammany Hall recognized the practical value of utilizing street gangs in its malevolent conquest of the city tenements. Tammany engaged the most brazen and brutal criminal malefactors of the age—the Dead Rabbits, the Plug Uglies, the Chichesters, and the Shirt Tails. New York City gangs were deeply entrenched by the 1830s, becoming standing armies in certain quarters of the city.

The history of Chicago's political gangs do not extend back in time quite as far as New York's criminal organizations, but with equal measure they engaged in the same brute force and thuggish behavior, particularly during riotous electoral seasons. "Politically, most gangs are opportunistic, conservatively oriented," writes Dr. George Knox, a gang authority and sociologist from Chicago State University, "in the sense that they have as their ideal type a function as a business organization, and their attachment to the legitimate social order through politicians tend to be characterized by lower-level field functions. They are not likely to be used as strategy and policy makers in a political campaign; rather their function is, like their lifestyle a street function."

Mike McDonald received his political baptism just after the Civil War at the Hatch House, a three-story hotel at Wells and Kinzie, north of the river and due east of "Little Hell," the emerging North Side crime district that spawned the Market Street Gang—rowdies, confidence men, and election-eve "sluggers."

The original 134-room Hatch House was an unpretentious dump brushing up against the Galena and Chicago Railroad depot. John T. Corcoran, with his brother, Michael, acquired the building in 1859, spent $25,000 on general repairs and rented rooms to the public for two dollars a day. The Corcoran brothers had no illusions about the quality, character, or reputation of the place. Travelers to Chicago checking into the Hatch House found out real quick that the place was a "tough joint," and if their pleasure was liquor and cards while passing time in the frontier city, this was the place to be. The Corcorans built one of the many Chicago ward dynasties inside their "clubhouse"—an early city headquarters given over almost entirely to political activity, integrated with the leisurely pursuits.

Elected to the first of two aldermanic terms of the Twentieth Ward in 1872, Corcoran ran illegal "brace" faro (crooked, rigged) games all over town. Police Superintendent Michael Hickey admitted to a *Tribune* reporter on May 12, 1877, that "his officers had been all over that building looking for the 'traveling' games—in the washrooms, kitchens and found nothing. They are too sharp for the officers, because I am told by a reliable man that the game, run as it is said, by Johnny Corcoran, has never been broken up. I don't believe that. The officers go there regularly and can see nothing. If any game is played there or elsewhere it is by stealth, and doesn't last long because the officers are around all day up until 1:00 and drop in when they are not expected. Well the men have followed the gamblers all over and they can find nothing." Chief Hickey's professed ignorance of Corcoran's racket was not surprising. A notoriously corrupt demagogue who rose up through the ranks by dubious means, Hickey's partnership with a brothel madam eventually drove him from the force in disgrace.

"Boss" John Corcoran died unexpectedly in 1878, leaving to Mike McDonald his legion of oily bunko men, "cappers and steerers" (assigned to roam the trains stations and hotel lobbies for the purpose of luring gullible travelers into Mike's gambling dens). Harry Martin, "Appetite Bill" Langdon, "Snapper" Johnny Malloy, "Kid" Miller, Snitzer the Kid, "Dutchy" Lehman, Tom Wallace and his brother John, "Hungry" Joe Lewis, who clipped the famed Irish author and playwright Oscar Wilde for a couple thousand in 1882, "Dutch" Hendricks, Tom O'Brien, the "King of the Bunko Men," Matt Duffy, Jim Parrish, "Red" Jimmy Fitzgerald, and the notorious gold-brick swindler George "White Pine" Martin were either in McDonald's direct employ or frequent overnight "guests" in his wife's, Mary Noonan McDonald, Palace European hotel rooms on the upper floors of "the Store" while hiding out from the law. John Rafferty, a Chicago police officer before turning to crime, was one of Mike McDonald's inside men at the Armory Station, in the heart of the Custom House Place Levee.

These practitioners of downtown deception were McDonald's "revenue earners." Equally important to the organization were his street enforcers tasked with punishing deadbeat gamblers, keeping a sharp eye for card cheats inside the casino, and occasionally "freelancing" as stickup men, burglars, criminal fences, garrotters, and pickpockets. For Mike's burly enforcers, the most important day of the year was of course Election Day.

"Illegal voting was not new in Chicago," wrote Bruce Grant in his 1955 history of Chicago's Union League Club. "Lawlessness, scenes of violence, interference of *bonafide* voters, repeaters, ballot box stuffing, colonization and all manner of frauds had been practiced since the early days of the city. Candidates printed their own ballots. Judges of elections counted ballots by tossing those not meeting with their approval into the Chicago River."

The Union League Club battled McDonald and pushed the electorate and the courts for reform, but their headquarters and for that matter the entire business district and retail corridor was surrounded on all sides by gambling hells, bawdy houses, saloons, and vicious dives. For a period of twenty years the Garrity Gang—Hugh, John, Mike, and Tommy—faithfully carried out McDonald's directives at the city polling places but took no personal interest in either strategy or policy making.

Chicago "has suffered the existence and flourishing abundance of the dirty, cowardly and infamous gang of thieves, thugs, bruisers and woman-beaters named Garrity," the *Tribune* reported on November 14, 1877. "If they had their deserts they would not be alive or at liberty one moment. There is not a crime on the statute book they have not among them committed. The origin of this remarkable family of beastly and brutal criminals has nothing remarkable in it, except perhaps it be that they came from comparatively decent parents." Hugh was a "bunko steerer." Arrested in March 1875 for cheating one P. T. Putnam out of $300 in one of Mike's Clark Street dens, Garrity was acquitted by a packed jury after the victim turned down a $300 bribe not to prosecute. It was said of Hugh that he could drink harder, hit harder, and swear harder than any other member of the notorious family.

The unrefined John Garrity, called many foul names in his time by the *Tribune*, including a "bastard son of Satan," robbed fellow gambler John Dowling of $500 one night in November 1877 while Dowling was in his cups inside a downtown saloon. Dowling and Garrity, loyal street soldiers of McDonald, who together assaulted Mayor Joseph Medill's brother, Samuel, in an ugly street attack outside the Store one night in 1872, had a falling out. Garrity fled to Memphis with his loot in hand, but after Dowling regained sobriety and realized his old pal had cashiered him out of his bankroll, he sent a police detective to track down the fugitive and return him to Chicago. Dowling recovered his money but did not utilize the police or the courts to receive justice and paid the price for it. John, Mike, and Hugh extracted their revenge by committing an act of revolting brutality. In front of a hundred eyewitnesses drinking at the bar inside McDonald's Store, including police lieutenant William McGarigle, Hugh struck Dowling over the head with a champagne bottle after the victim had allegedly spit in his face. Driving the diminutive gambler to the ground, John nearly bit off his nose, stood up, then stomped on him with hobnail boots.

The Garritys were granted a change of venue and then tried for criminal assault in Geneva, thirty miles northwest of Chicago. Eyewitnesses were browbeaten and threatened with vengeance. "There will come a dark night pretty soon after we get out of this scrape and then you'll get it!" It is not hard to imagine the understandable terror of street crime committed by raffish thugs in the nighttime shadows of the darkened city.

The gang escaped with minimal two-year sentences. The other indictments against John remained on the docket but in some mysterious way the cases were nol prossed and stricken from the docket. No reasonable explanation could be given other than the firm grasp of Mike McDonald reaching into the Kane County's prosecutor's office. The Garritys resumed their duties of providing "private security" inside McDonald's faro banks up and down Clark Street, but when public pressure mounted against the city administration to raid the illicit dens, the gang initiated a fresh reign of terror in the streets.

They held up a bank in Galesburg. They swindled the "granger" element arriving in Chicago from the rural countryside; they smashed crockery and gouged the eyes of victims in bloody downtown saloon fights; created disturbances in houses of ill fame—a favorite amusement—by choking the life out of unfortunate strumpets.

By 1880 McDonald finally had had enough of the Garrity Gang antics. They had become a personal embarrassment, and their methods were no longer vital to the embryonic Democratic machine. He refused to post any more bail money or provide free legal counsel, because by now the wily gambler gained status and had become a force in city politics after employing every election fraud he could conjure in his successful bid to elect Carter Henry Harrison mayor of Chicago. The Garrity Gang was on its own now.

The brothers drifted north to Minneapolis, where for a brief and violent period they confounded the local police with acts of violence and trickery. But without the backing of a powerful political benefactor, these roughnecks and shoulder hitters ended up in the penitentiary or dead. The Minneapolis and Chicago press reported the death of Hugh Garrity on February 3, 1891. "He was a bad man," commented Sergeant Louis Haas of the central station in an interview. "A few days ago he was picked up in the streets dead drunk. He was a total wreck and had changed greatly in the past few years, drink ruining his health."

The poor illumination of Chicago's gas-lit street lamps provided cover and safe haven for gangsters and sluggers. At dusk the downtown streets, given over to the nighttime vices once the business day had ended, were unsafe and dangerous. The criminal element ruled the city streets, the saloons, concert halls, and gambling dens dotting Whiskey Row, the Custom House, Clark Street Gambler's Row, and much of downtown. The *Chicago Evening Journal* of March 8, 1873, described a typical but deadly after-hours saloon affray at Clark and Jackson Boulevard in the Custom House involving a burly gangland thug named John Houlihan. While making his patrol rounds, Officer Michael Cudmore attempted to intercede in a brutal bar fight involving Houlihan a well-known hoodlum. With no police backup, Cudmore entered the dive and wrestled Houlihan to the floor.

"Taking him into custody, he [Cudmore] was conducting him to the [First Precinct] Armory Police Station, followed by a crown of Houlihan's sympathizers," the *Journal* reported. "When near the corner of Van Buren and Pacific Avenue [now LaSalle Street], he [Cudmore] was surrounded and attacked by them, knocked down and brutally kicked and otherwise maltreated. The gang, having recovered their pal, dashed off westward along Van Buren Street." Moments later, police reinforcements arrived. In hot pursuit, Cudmore fired a shot, striking Houlihan in the shoulder. With the protection of a half dozen officers at Cudmore's side, Houlihan was escorted through Whiskey Row to jail without further incident. In August that same year, this same Officer Cudmore was ambushed and shot in the thigh in an alley between State and Wabash by the same Whiskey Row criminals he had interfered with earlier in the year.

Such nocturnal free-for-alls occurred in the vice districts and saloons after hours with deadly regularity. The highly politicized, woefully paid, often demoralized and undermanned police department formed a thin blue line of protection that afforded little protection from holdups and common street assault by the likes of the Garritys and Houlihans.

Innocent pedestrians out for a pleasant canter on a horse-drawn sleigh down Clark Street on a Sunday afternoon in December 1872 were not immune from the dangerous presence of gangland criminals. "The weather yesterday rendered sleigh riding an enjoyable amusement," the *Tribune* reported, "and a large number of persons took advantage of the improved temperatures to indulge in this delightful pastime. During the afternoon a parcel of roughs of all ages from quite young boys to grown men indulged themselves in a pastime more to their depraved tastes, but scarcely as innocent in its nature as sleigh riding. Their amusement consisted in suddenly rushing out of ambush, seizing the reins and upsetting the sleighs to the imminent peril of the occupants and the boundless merriment of their companions who in turn waylaid other unfortunate persons. Officer Cobb, on learning the circumstances, went to the spot and endeavored to arrest two men he caught in the act. Their pals, ready to relinquish the sport for a more exciting, and to them, agreeable amusement, turned upon the officer, beat him with clubs and wounded him badly."

Putting a stop to petty street crime, saloon fights, malicious vandalism, and harassment of citizens proved daunting for the bluecoats.

"Chicago, it is true, has given to the rest of the world a great many criminals who have held exalted positions in the circles in which they moved. The average detective as a matter of fact, has had much more experience solving murder mysteries than getting at the bottom of lesser crimes," wrote John Flinn and John Wilkie, authors of a fawning, entirely self-serving departmental history of the Chicago police published by private subscription in 1886. "Capital offenses are more difficult of solution than the ordinary run of offenses against property. There was more or less crime of a desperate nature recorded daily; garrotings, highway robbery, and sand-baggings were becoming a little too frequent to be novel or interesting."

In the post-fire period, Mike McDonald's oyster on the fork was downtown Chicago. His domination of the disparate ward organizations, the liquor trade, and gambling spanned Chicago's most remarkable period of growth, 1870 to 1900. In the world of Gilded Age politics he was neither unique nor alone in his ambitions to become a hybrid "boss" lording over the underworld *and* upper world. The rule of politician-saloon-gambler bosses in league with gangland operatives was nearly universal and strongly rooted in the development and evolution of urban America up through the mid-twentieth century.

In Washington, D.C., Edward Pendleton was the sporting man with the important city hall connections. John Morrissey, a former prizefighter and strong-armed brute, directed New York's Dead Rabbits Gang in the 1850s. Morrissey wound his way through the labyrinth of Tammany Hall politics to two terms in the U.S. House of Representatives and ownership of the Clubhouse, a casino in Saratoga Springs. George B. Cox, another self-made city boss, operated keno games inside his brother's Cincinnati saloon before his election to the city council and domination of Hamilton County, Ohio, politics for nearly a quarter century. Christopher Augustine Buckley, the "Blind Saloon Boss of San Francisco," drove city politics at the turn of the nineteenth century, although like McDonald, he never held public office. Buckley and McDonald were pilloried in the local press in their respective cities for bribery, corruption, and felonious crime. Yet at the same time, both were respected and looked upon kindly by the down-and-outers they looked after through the jobs they offered and the food baskets provided.

Commenting on McDonald's influence in a blistering October 22, 1874, editorial, the *Tribune* excoriated the grand jury for failing to indict him for complicity in one of the many Garrity assaults. "This is no ordinary case. This man is confessedly a criminal of no ordinary degree. He is at the head of an organization of gamblers, thieves, pickpockets and receivers of stolen goods in Chicago. His conviction for crime would have a salutary effect upon the large class of which he is the chief. When any of his gang are arrested and fined he appeals their cases to a higher court and there the matter ends. He is not only exempt from prosecutions himself but in one form or another interposes his protecting arm between justices and his associate criminals and there seems to be no authority which dare oppose him. Mike McDonald is the head of the political association composed of the gamblers, thieves, confidence men and their followers. But for their political affiliations Mike McDonald would have been in the penitentiary years ago, his [gambling] hells broken up and his associates dispersed."

As the years rolled by, McDonald grew wealthy through astute real estate speculation, politics, and his substantial gambling holdings, but he did not desire to see his legacy tainted by bad associations and profligacy. Gradually he recused himself from day-to-day involvement with the criminal syndicate he once directed in order to devote his energies to electing John Peter Altgeld governor of Illinois, and repairing his scandal-ridden private life.[9]

Crafty and all-knowing in the affairs of the great city, "King" Mike proved unlucky in love and ended up brutally betrayed by the passions of his two tempestuous wives. The unhappy Mary Noonan McDonald ran away with Father Joseph Moysant after Mike provided the down-on-his-heels priest with free shelter and board in his Ashland Avenue mansion. Recovering from the humiliation, McDonald married Dora Feldman in 1895. The daughter of a Jewish rabbi, Dora was a childhood playmate of his son Guy years earlier. This twenty-five-year-old temptress married the aging gambler for his money then betrayed him for Webster Guerin, a teenage boy who lived across the street. In February 1907 Dora shot the young man through the back in a fit of jealous rage.

The final tragedy played out. McDonald, the cuckolded multimillionaire, political kingmaker, real estate developer, and gambling overlord responsible for weaving together the denizens of the Chicago underworld in a compact with lawmakers, died an emotionally broken man in July 1907. He left a probated $2 million estate to his greedy, cloying sons and ex-wives, and control of the gambling syndicate to a new generation of sporting men carving up the spoils into geographic spheres of influence on the North, South, and West Sides.

Chicago's First Ward, from State and Madison Street running all the way to Thirty-First Street on the South Side, spanned the great mercantile houses, hotels, theaters, department stores, and restaurants in the city center, to the lowest cribs of vice along Whiskey Row and points further south. The gambling syndicate organized and suffused with machine politics and police protection by McDonald, linked to the sprawling vice districts controlled by gangland, formed a "three-legged stool" of organized crime in the turbulent closing decades of the nineteenth century.

At the dawn of McDonald's thirty-year reign, the Custom House vice district, three blocks west of the Row along Federal Street, had already earned a reputation as a baleful den of depravity, vice, and criminality. Brushing up against Gambler's Row on the southern exposure of downtown, Fourth Avenue was not always the thoroughfare of vice and crime that English investigative journalist William T. Stead decried in his censorious 1894 book-length exposé, *If Christ Came to Chicago*.[10] Stead counted thirty-seven brothels, forty-six saloons, and eleven pawn shops in this, the Nineteenth Precinct of the First Ward.

"The lost women, those poor sisters of Jesus Christ, the images in which we have fashioned a womanhood first made in the image of God, are as numerous in Chicago as in any other great city," wrote Stead in a sense of religious fervor. "The silent vice of capitals abounds here at least to the same extent that it prevails in other cities of the million class. Where there are a million inhabitants it is probably an under estimate if it is assumed that there must be at least a thousand women who make their living not intermittently but constantly by means of prostitution. The inmates of the sporting houses, so called, are probably not one-tenth of the total number of women who regard their sex as legitimate merchandise."[11]

In antebellum days, before the vice gangs established a presence on Fourth Avenue, the name of the thoroughfare was Buffalo Street, a pleasant setting. Some of the finest families in Chicago maintained homes with small front yards and floral gardens surrounded by white picket fences. The Civil War occasioned tremendous social upheaval as thousands of southerners, criminal transients, and resort (brothel) keepers invaded the street south of Harrison to form a large and expanding vice district that pushed northward to downtown. The Chicago Fire leveled Buffalo Street and drove the few remaining decent people away. The appearance of hastily built tenements and low-slung commercial structures suitable for saloon occupancy, gambling hells, and drug dens on old Buffalo Street dashed the hopes of utopians and reformers that the Chicago Fire might have cleansed the "social evil."

The few brick-and-stone structures occupied by prostitutes and owned by madams of a more fashionable class, the buildings lining the east and west sides of old Buffalo Street, were cheaply built post-fire lodgings notwithstanding; one- and two-story frame shacks, all of them, were cheap, combustible firetraps. The unpaved streets reeked with filth, horse droppings, and noxious sewer odor. The city council did little to appropriate funds for a crackdown and cleanup but, in their great wisdom, simply changed the name from Buffalo Street to Fourth Avenue.

William Stead described Fourth Avenue, between Harrison and Polk, the "wickedest block in the world" and it formed the nexus of the "Custom House Place Levee," so named because of its proximity to the imposing U.S. Customs House bounded by Adams, Clark, Jackson, and Dearborn Streets.

An unbroken line of wooden dwellings, each sheltering a gang of criminals, pimps, and prostitutes was organized to assault and rob anyone they could lure into the premises. Visitors to Chicago, alighting at the Dearborn Street train station (at Polk Street) and walking north along Fourth Avenue were likely to be seized from behind, pulled into an entrance hallway, and robbed. Vice districts of this magnitude often congealed near the train stations and wharf districts of American cities to prey upon a transient population of out-of-towners and immigrant arrivals.

Twenty-six door-to-door saloons lined the West Side of Fourth Avenue where murders, suicides, and robberies inside the "panel houses" were reported on an hourly basis to the Armory Police detail. A panel house, according to Detective Wooldridge who called upon many such evil dens of vice during his career, "is the invention of thieves of both sexes, and in them hundreds of thousands of dollars have been stolen from the unsuspecting victims of vicious women." Wooldridge estimated that the Fourth Avenue vice gangs netted $1,500,000 annually in 1892, 1893, and 1894. In a variation of the old "badger game," the victim accompanies his consort to the upper floors of the bordello. The man eagerly strips down and places his clothing on a sofa chair nearest the sliding "panel" wall. While in the throes of passion, the sexually distracted man is oblivious to the thief lurking on the other side of the wall. The panel quietly opens, and the thief rifles through the man's trousers removing cash, jewelry, and other valuables, before placing the garment back on the chair. Detective Wooldridge describes what happens next.

"When the poor dupe discovers his loss, he is confronted by a mystery he cannot solve." Fearing embarrassment, the poor dupe rarely filed a police report. But on the off chance they might report the swindle to the police, the panel-house owners stationed young boys assigned to duty outside the dive as "trailers" to intercept the victim and bring him back to the panel house with a promise of assistance in recovering the stolen goods. The resort keeper apologizes profusely and offers a small settlement, often the cost of a train ticket back home to Davenport, Iowa, or wherever else the hayseed might have come from. The panel-house thievery was a protected racket, sponsored by a "certain class of politicians," according to Wooldridge, "who participated in the profits of their highway robbery."

Violence lurked nearby in every dark corner and back alley. The May 21, 1883, murder of Anthony Connolly, proprietor of an all-night saloon and orgiastic panel house at Fourth Avenue and Harrison Street, by Robert Bruce, aka "Harry Curtis," ended in an acquittal the next day by the coroner's jury despite four eyewitnesses who swore to the fact that Bruce fired upon the victim without provocation. "It's too bad," said one police officer, "that they didn't kill each other. It would have been a gain for the public."

Connolly's place was one of the toughest resorts on the street, and robberies and assaults were commonplace. The dead man and his sidekick and henchman, "Jimmy the Tough," ruled a gang of street sluggers hired by Democratic First Ward alderman Jimmy "de App" Appleton to "do up" certain individuals the politicians had it in for. "Connolly . . . bears a bad reputation and is reckoned as a bad man," the *Tribune* reported. "Tales of his ability as a slugger and his brutal and uncalled-for assaults are almost without number."

Bruce, a man of striking appearance with a big white sombrero hat covering a shock of jet-black hair and outfitted in a checked suit with a turned down collar, advertised his services as a private detective. Chicago police called him a "crank," and he was a crank, and a drunken one at that. In his gun belt, artfully concealed by his frock coat, were a pair of six shooters that belonged to Jesse James, or so he said. From time to time Bruce contributed news tips to Shang Andrews, publisher of the *Sporting Life*, and the *Street Gazette*, gossip sheets, and scintillating "tour guides" of the Custom House brothels. In one edition of the racy *Street Gazette* news digest, Bruce had torn into Connolly, calling him a vice monger. The insult precipitated the shooting. An annoying presence in the Armory lockup, Bruce had numerous run-ins with the law for rowdyism, but was saved by skilled attorney Jeremiah Dunn who produced no witnesses to back up Bruce's self-defense alibi. Dunn won over the jury but his client could not stay out of trouble. A few years later Bruce added yet another notch to his gun in the pursuit of dangerous malefactors.[12]

A consortium of criminals, aided and abetted by youthful gang boys, saloon keepers, political sponsors, and brothel madams, controlled the rookeries and imported young women from the rural districts, often by force, to work as prostitutes in the Custom House. It was a syndicate comprised of all races and nationalities. A small colony of

African Americans living among the fallen women on Pacific Avenue patronized the Fourth Avenue gambling den operated by Dan Scott, who owned a dozen racehorses. Blacks were also active in the 1870s vice trade. Dan Webster, a shady bail bondsman, counterfeiter, and criminal fence, paid $3,500 to Superintendent Michael Hickey for the privilege of maintaining a whorehouse at Harrison and Pacific— the street known at various times as "Biler Avenue" because of the grime and dirt of a nearby boiler factory. In 1901 the politicians attempted to sweep away the ugly reputation of Biler Avenue / Pacific Avenue by cleansing this boulevard of vice with a more dignified and historically important new name: LaSalle Street.[13]

The era of open vice, gambling, and drug dealing along Fourth Avenue and the Custom House Place Levee waned as the twentieth century approached. As an economic depression overtook the city and the entire country following the windup of the 1893 World's Fair, the commercial interests of the city, finding the business district too constricted, slowly took back the district block by block. Towering monuments to capitalism and the commercial printing industry arose on the bones of the old Custom House Levee along South Dearborn Street in a ten-year period, from 1889 to 1899. The Pontiac Building, the Plymouth Building, the Fisher Building, the Manhattan Building, and the Monadnock Building—all architectural treasures of late nineteenth-century Chicago—define the city's South Loop skyline, bearing silent testament to the transformation from commercialized dissipation to industry and capital that overtook the southern fringe of the metropolis.

The campaign to close the remaining strongholds of the vice gangs in the Custom House continued through the early years of the new century. In July 1901 Mayor Carter Harrison revoked the license of Ike Rosen, a powerful saloon politician who listed thirty-four alleged "voters" as residing in his two-story frame hovel in the 1900 election season.

Police Superintendent Francis O'Neill, one of only a few departmental heads above reproach, ordered the barkeeps and brothels to nail wooden boards across all rear doors in order to cut off avenues of escape, thus ensuring that patrons would not be able to flee into the alleys, on the theory that illicit doings inside would be diminished. Inside the dives, ground-glass partition walls and the doors to private rooms where assignations took place were battered down and removed.

In 1903 Mayor Carter Harrison restricted further expansion of the Fourth Avenue red-light trade south of Harrison Street. With a stroke of the pen, old Fourth Avenue officially became Federal Place (then Federal Street) in the new city directory, and soon the memory of its many murders and suicides began to fade.

Harrison's successor, Mayor Edward Dunne, struck the final hammer blow in 1906, ordering state's attorney John J. Healy to close up the remaining dives and order the relocation of their businesses to Twenty-Second Street and Dearborn, nearly two miles south of the old Custom House Place. His decision was a matter of expediency. The directive was not carried out for moral, altruistic purposes. In the name of furthering city commerce and benefiting Chicago's burgeoning printing industry (in particular), the Union League Club and civic boosters demanded the restoration of dignity and decorum to the troubled Custom House in anticipation of the coming real estate windfall they expected to reap from the mayor. Accordingly, the remaining rookeries, numbering twenty-five to thirty-five structures, were left to poor immigrant Italians for temporary occupancy until they too were forcibly evicted and ordered to relocate as wrecking crews descended upon the street in June 1909.

The titans of business were not the only ones to reap the whirlwind from the Dunne decrees. "That it was a prosperous time for the enumerated houses is shown in that many had moved from less desirable localities and places not so commodious," noted journalist Wallace Rice. The vice syndicate and criminal gangs from the Custom House grew in power and reach after completing their move to the South Side "Levee," one of the largest segregated districts of any city *on earth*.

For the political powerbrokers governing this enormous economic engine—fueled by illegal kickbacks and payoffs and sponsored by the saloon protective associations, criminal overlords, and police district captains, inspectors, and beat officers regulating the traffic in women—vice relocation easily trumped vice eradication.

This most renowned red-light district in the United States thrived from 1893, when the first disorderly house disturbed the peace of the community, up through 1914, and it is a saga written in blood and money. Vivien Palmer, wealthy socialite and resident of Prairie Avenue, Chicago's boulevard of millionaires situated three blocks to the east of Levee, recalled the shocking arrival of the first Levee brothel during the World's Fair. "Pleasant little cottages" dotted Armour Avenue, Dearborn Street, and Nineteenth Street, to Palmer's best recollections, but these buildings were purchased by the Custom House vice lords and built out with glazed brick and second-story additions to accommodate the crush of the disreputable, represented by commercial realtors in direct negotiation with building owners eager to lease the properties at much higher rental rates than they had been receiving from single-family dwellers.

Many of the properties were privately owned by the well-to-do living miles away from the district. Ownership deeds revealing the identities of individuals collecting rental monies from the suffering of young women, often the unwilling victims of white-slave gangs, were later discovered in the files of Chicago Title & Trust Company.

By 1910 the Levee's (bounded by Twenty-Second Street on the south, Eighteenth Street on the north, Wabash Avenue on the east, and Clark Street to the west) 119 houses of ill fame thrived, housing 686 "inmates." Across the city, the police estimated that 1,012 women earned their livelihood through prostitution. Citizen reform groups pegged this figure in excess of five thousand. The 1910 Vice Commission, appointed by Mayor Fred Busse, who followed Edward Dunne, pegged the rental of properties to the keepers of the brothels, and profits netted criminal vice gangs the sum of $8,476,689, with liquor sales in the illicit saloons accounting for $4,307,000. A prostitute earned $1,306 a year, but her value to the house, capitalized at twenty times earnings as a "chattel," was $26,000 per annum.

Looking back on the wide-open Gaslight Era debauchery in a 1936 retrospective, a *Tribune* reporter recalled that "Any lively night the scene along the Levee streets would have had its resemblance to a tawdry orgy. Noise blared from the pianos. The red lights gleamed. Men, young and middle age reeled from saloon to bawdy house. Girls led their customers from the dance halls to the ever-ready hotels."[14]

Roy Jones, Ike Bloom, Harry Cusick, James Colosimo, and Johnny Torrio comprised a "Big Five" syndicate of vice panders that regulated the sex trade and working conditions for the young women there by personal choice, destitution, or enslavement through the close of World War I, until a young up-and-coming gangland overlord imported from New York's Five Points completed his criminal apprenticeship: Al Capone.

Political power flowed through the offices of the First Ward aldermen—the cartoonish "Bathhouse" John Coughlin and Michael "Hinky Dink" Kenna. The unlikely pair protected and regulated the action continuously from 1892 to 1938. Coughlin, a boisterous, tongue-tied, unabashed grafter and a living caricature of the kind of boodling, stuffed-peacock politician lampooned by illustrator Thomas Nast in the 1870s, partnered with the nimble, closed-mouthed Kenna, whose Workingman's Exchange saloon in the old Custom House served as the clearing house. Kenna and Coughlin, creatures of the street, were mentored by Mike McDonald and subscribed to McDonald's sacred belief that "politics is business." Coughlin operated the Silver Dollar Saloon and Turkish bath on Madison Street.

"Coughlin has been for years the supporter of all the genuine boodle measures ever put before the City Council, the enemy of the honest people and the true representative of the colonized tramps, the grafters, and the haunters of the vice holes of the Levee, among whom he finds his most enthusiastic constituents," the *Chicago American* bitterly noted on March 12, 1902. "He took his seat at a time when the Chicago City Council had sunk to its lowest depth of infamy and its corrupt methods had become a by-word current throughout the country."

"Hinky-Dink," a mite of a man, expressed his belief to writer Jules Huret during the Frenchman's celebrated June 1905 visit to Chicago. "This is where we make voters," Kenna continued. "They drink 12,000 glasses of beer a day in my place." Noticing a continuously flowing thin stream of water trickling down the bar, Kenna, with a faint smile and a satisfied air, informed Huret, "The running water makes them thirsty and that makes business better."[15]

Others in Chicago took a more benign view of the picturesque Coughlin. The admiring reporter James Doherty rhapsodized that Coughlin "was everything a politician of those days should be, ponderous, yet affable; loud-voiced, and stupid. While he did not ordinarily wear the mountain green dress suit which won him international attention, he was still Chicago's best-dressed burgher. Coughlin was considered a good family man, personally virtuous. Yet he was the companion and protector of prostitutes, pimps, barrel-house bums and saloon keepers. Altogether the Bath had the very worst possible reputation but that didn't bother him. Through the aid of Hinky-Dink, the brains of that partnership represented the world's richest ward with a constituency of some of the city's leaders in finance, industry, the arts and sciences as well as the scarlet sisterhood."[16]

Coughlin and Kenna formed an unshakeable alliance during the 1893 World's Fair, and as a consequence, these two artful wheeler-dealers made it possible for the Levee vice gangs to flourish for the next twenty-five years through an intricate "protective system" extending from the docket of the magistrate's court in the Armory Police Station to the Twenty-Second Street Police Station. In the captain's office, the district command maintained an index-card file listing the names and addresses of the brothel inmates and the amount of bribe money collected per woman from the keeper of the bawdy houses.

Control of the political destiny of the ward through the system of "protection" spelled large Democratic pluralities at election time. First Ward votes very often exceeded the number of residents in the ward, and as such the Kenna-Coughlin cabal penciled in its hand-picked candidates to the municipal court and the state legislature during Democratic slate-making caucuses. Police officers assigned to the district refusing to "go along" with the protective system were transferred and "exiled to the woods"—distant precincts in the city—by order of the Big Five through their sponsors, Kenna and Coughlin.

Restaurateur and showman Ike Bloom (née Isaac Gittleson), a Levee potentate standing on the edge of two worlds, maintained outward respectability but assumed the mantle of day-to-day supervision of the gang of pimps, white-slave procurers, gamblers, and barkeeps from his pleasure palace, Freiberg's Dance Hall, 18 East Twenty-Second Street. This is where the decisions were made, bribes taken, assignations arranged, and the ways and means of organizing "white slavery" rings were formulated.

For twenty-two uninterrupted years, Freiberg's, according to one account, was a favored haunt for "those Chicagoans who seek diversions in the after theater hours and to thousands of travelers who speak of Freiberg's as one does of the Moulin Rouge of Montmartre or did of Tait's of San Francisco or of Bustanoby's in New York before Prohibition swept those places into oblivion."

Ike Bloom and his brother Sam purchased the German dance hall and *winestube* from old Frederick "Fritz" Freiberg, the jovial, fiddle-playing host, whose music popularized the reel and square dance with South Siders from inside his old-world cabaret. Freiberg built the famous show spot in 1888 and maintained it for a dozen years until the Custom House Levee swept south to engulf Twenty-Second Street. Freiberg wanted no part of that kind of business, but Bloom, an easygoing, genial man-about-town, recognized an opportunity when he saw one. Politicians, stage performers, after-hours society "slummers" from Lake Shore Drive comingled with the dregs of the Levee once the downtown theaters closed. It was all so daring for them to observe jeweled courtesans and their benefactors gliding across the polished floor doing the "Grizzly Bear," a Barbary Coast dance deemed morally objectionable and called obscene by the reformers.

Smooth and slick, Bloom greeted his patrons at the door and personally escorted them to their tables. The evening's gaiety did not begin until after midnight, and it lasted until the wee hours of the morning. Bloom—who gained early notoriety managing the career of prizefighter Abe Attell, identified as one of the crooked "fixers" accused of bribing eight White Sox players to throw the 1919 World Series—insisted that the young women in the hall show the utmost decorum. However, this man of outward propriety and gracious manner required that the bejeweled courtesans roaming about the hall pay him a percentage of the drink money they hustled from the male patrons. Monies received were paid to local hotels for the rental of assignation rooms, clothing manufacturers supplied elegant gowns to the house, and there was a general fund to suborn police and politicians and judges.

Reform groups assailed Freiberg's as the "dance of death." Behind its sparkling facade and artificiality, it was no better than the less pretentious neighboring resorts along the line. Mounting public pressure to enforce the city's 1 a.m. closing law resulted in the revocation of Bloom's liquor license but the intercession of the aldermen succeeded in opening the padlocked doors. In return Bloom delivered his precinct by pluralities from two hundred to three hundred votes with only token opposition. Efforts to implicate him in voter fraud inevitably failed because he always managed to succeed in squaring up the tally sheets one step ahead of the Municipal Voter's League investigation.

A framed portrait of Bloom hung conspicuously above the desk of Captain Michael Ryan, one in a long line of ineffectual police commanders assigned to the Twenty-Second Street Precinct.

Nothing escaped Bloom's watchful eye. As the major domo of the Levee, he suborned judges and easily defeated justice at every turn. Although he traded in flesh and violated the liquor laws, he was a stickler for outward propriety, insisting that the young women maintain sobriety on penalty of expulsion from the hall.[17]

Bloom enjoyed the fruits of his rising political status in the Twenty-Second Street district by forming alliances with criminal entrepreneurs from foreign lands, including "Big" Jim Colosimo, a brothel keeper and pimp who started out modestly as a water boy on a railroad section gang, before marrying Victoria Moresco in July 1902, taking over the management of her one-story whorehouse in "Bed Bug Row" (a particularly vile, twenty-five-cent-admission den) while advancing himself in the street sweeper's union. Brothel master Colosimo organized his fellow "white wings" (broom-pushing clean-up men) into a social-athletic club to aid and assist Coughlin and Kenna in their election campaigns while his wife kept the books of the family business—the bedraggled Saratoga at Armour Avenue and Twenty-First Street featuring the tuneful airs of piano maestro "Izzy the Rat," and the Victoria, named in honor of its proprietor, at Archer and Dearborn.

Big Jim was a natural organizer, and over time Alderman Kenna and Coughlin recognized his abilities and reassigned Bloom's tasks as "collector of the street tax" to Colosimo. Remembered for his wry sense of humor, Colosimo was vain, ambitious, and proud. "Someday I'm going to run this ward!" he boasted, "and I'm going to build a club that will be the talk of Chicago."[18]

Through his control of opium dens, brothels, and illegal gambling, his annual earnings were said, by the local press, to exceed $500,000 a year. With his accumulated riches he moved Victoria and his immigrant relatives out of his cheap flat on Twenty-First Street, bought a fashionable abode on South Vernon Avenue far from the blare of the police whistle, the screams of the harlots and the hoi polloi, and threw open the doors of his "talk of the town" showplace—Colosimo's Restaurant. The walls were decorated in a green hue with painted palms. Belying the sinister reputation of the place, drawings of angelic nudes cavorting in clouds on a blue-sky ceiling soothed the patron's senses.

Located just around the corner from Freiberg's, Colosimo's served sumptuous Italian fare. Chicken Vesuvio, Big Jim's own invention, was the house specialty. The finest musicians in the country performed to packed houses. In the basement, an enormous still produced Prohibition liquor. Wine served from vintage cobwebbed bottles flowed easily.

By 1911 the opera-loving Colosimo had grown rich, fat, and lazy, but he was never oblivious to omnipresent threats. Big Jim harbored grave fears for his life from repeated Black Hand extortion threats. Although he much preferred the company of "the better element"—Maestro Giacomo Spadoni of the Lyric Opera frequented the café—sensing his vulnerabilities Big Jim sought the help of the baser element he had turned his back on.

Under the cover of anonymity, Colosimo traveled to New York to recruit a bodyguard to protect him from multiple Black Hand torture and murder threats. He found in twenty-nine-year-old Johnny Torrio, a street gang leader of Five Points, "no ordinary ruffian . . . he had executive ability, business sagacity and a practical imagination. He was skilled in the duplicity of politics. He was proficient in the civilities—smooth of tongue and adroit in manner. He had a plausible front and he was ambitious."[19] Torrio, sometimes called "Turrio" by members of the Chicago press corps, was a distant cousin of Colosimo's wife, Victoria, the fat, unlovely brothel madam who managed the girls and kept the books while her husband contrived to become the "Italian Ike Bloom"—showman and nightclub impresario.

Torrio, a complex man both dark and forbidding, put Jim's affairs in order and put a stop to the Black Hand extortion by leveling a sawed-off shotgun at three of the extortionists who had come to collect $25,000 underneath the railroad viaduct on Archer Avenue. Colosimo rewarded his nephew's unswerving loyalty by setting him up in business. The former Five Points gangster opened a restaurant at 2126 South Wabash Avenue.

Within the confines of this repellent vice district, the Big Five took advantage of the depth and breadth of its ironclad rule and sowed the seeds of a criminal gang that would spread its wings across Chicago during Prohibition and redirected their enterprise after the Volstead Act was repealed in 1933. On the eve of Prohibition, Torrio and Colosimo imported Alphonse Capone, a puffy-faced wharf rat from an Italian tenement at Broadway and Flushing Avenue in Brooklyn, to Chicago in 1919 to attend to their expanding empire. The son of a barber who had emigrated from Naples, young Capone collected scrap wood from the streets he would peddle in the neighborhood for pennies on the dollar. The boy surrendered the loose change to his parents to help them in their life's struggle to put food on the table and pay the rent.

Alphonse Capone ran with a tough and virulent crowd of boys but managed to stay out of the crosshairs of law enforcement in his early formative years. He danced with the girls at the Broadway Casino and kept company with poolroom slickers. With a cue in hand Capone established a reputation as a pretty good nine-ball player, but rarely did he touch a drink. He took on all comers in his Greenpoint neighborhood and one night clipped Arthur Finnegan, an Irish tough from the White Hand Gang, for $950 in a game of pool inside a saloon. The unhappy loser came at the twenty-one-year-old Capone with a shiv but the stocky Italian boy flattened Finnegan with a devastating right hook. The Irish gangster fell to the floor unconscious and would languish in the hospital for weeks to come. The White Hand Gang swore vengeance.

Capone's cousins in the Five Points Gang operating on the other side of the Williamsburg Bridge in Lower Manhattan conferred with Frankie Yale, owner of the Harvard Inn at Coney Island where Al had been employed ever so briefly as a bartender. Yale, a seasoned killer, made secret arrangements to hustle Al out of town for his own good. Through his underworld connections, Yale reached out to Johnny Torrio in Chicago, the former Five Points captain and organizer who had merged his James Street Gang with the Five Points mob before receiving the summons from Big Jim Colosimo.

Yale and Torrio agreed. Chicago was the best place for a boy with Al's untapped abilities and ambition to properly learn the ropes, knowing he would benefit from Torrio's mentorship. Wearing his best new suit, Capone reported for duty. Sizing up his brawn and a sinister-looking scar inflicted by a knife-wielding assailant on his left cheek, Torrio dispatched Capone to work as a bouncer inside one of his suburban whorehouses in Burnham, Illinois. His appearance would strike fear into the deadbeats, card cheats, and red-light patrons who might think of skipping out on their bill.

In less than a decade Al Capone emerged as a household name, the most famous gangster in America, whose reputation and exploits are known worldwide. Tracing his meteoric rise to power from a Brooklyn slum, Chicago police labeled him "the field marshal of the Torrio forces." In 1919, a year after his betrothal in 1918, Capone's wife, Mae, delivered a son, Albert Francis, a reticent young man nicknamed "Sonny." The boy suffered early hearing loss, believed by many to be the result of the father's untreated syphilis infection. Johnny Torrio became Sonny's godfather.

With Colosimo, Torrio, and Bloom steering Levee business operations in the early years of the partnership, a multiethnic ensemble cast of hoodlums, brothel keepers, professional gunmen, and gamblers comprising the Chicago "Outfit," a Windy City organized crime faction that endures into the new millennium, hatched. This well-oiled, predatory gang of hoodlums who had grown up in the urban slum districts of Chicago, New York, Sicily, and Eastern Europe were mostly devoid of moral conscience.

The Big Five employed hundreds of young men promising virtuous young girls romance and marriage, but after winning their hearts through devious manipulation and broken vows, delivered them to the brothels as "white slaves." They formed the backbone of a Levee "cadet system." Polished and urbane, the cadets (or procurers) trolled the dance halls, hotels, railroad stations, department stores, and even the excursion boats traversing Lake Michigan in the summertime, for girls easily seduced.

"After a victim is procured, the next step on the part of the perfidious combine is to dispose of her to the highest bidder," according to a searing 1911 exposé titled *The Vice Bondage of a Great City*.[20] "Investigation has shown that the prices for women sold into bondage of crime run from $25 to $500. If the girl is ruddy with the glow of health, well-formed of limb, and innocent of deep crime—the price soars."

Many of the cadets worked independently and paid the customary tribute to the Vice Trust and the standard protection rates to the Twenty-Second Street police in order to ensure noninterference. "One night in the South Side Levee a cadet caught one of his women on the street in front of a resort, cursed her for small earnings and proceeded to beat her into insensibility," the author of *Vice Bondage* reported. "Bleeding from his inhuman blows, she reeled and fell to the sidewalk. Standing in the glow of the arc light, the man's face and hands were smeared with blood. Two policemen approached and stopped. The cadet held up his blood-stained hands and laughed. The policeman pushed him ahead and one of them said: 'Fred, you better move on. Go and wash your face and hands.' A woman came from the resort, kicked the prostrate form of the unconscious girl with her foot, then grasping her by the hands, dragged her into the hell chamber from which she had emerged to breathe a little of God's air." [21]

In a two-month period in 1907, 278 girls under the age of fifteen were rescued from Levee dens. The forcible abduction of young women for servitude in a Levee brothel drew national attention, and was a motivating factor in the final elimination of the district. Maurice and Julia Van Bever ran one such interstate ring from their "Paris" resort at 2101 Armour Avenue and the White City. They employed Mike Hart and Dick Tyler, two thugs working in their saloon as bartenders, to travel to St. Louis and the Missouri hinterland to make a connection with David Garfinkle, a local connection who procured farm girls to come to Chicago for the usual stated reasons: a promise of romance, adventure; a career on the stage, or at the very least a secure employment situation. Trusting the word of the Chicago slickers, the girls boarded trains bound for the Englewood station in Chicago where Julia's carriage and a life of sexual slavery awaited.

Harry Balding, a white slaver accused of imprisoning one Mona Marshall in a brothel at 2553 South Wabash Avenue adjacent to the saloon and future headquarters building of the Torrio-Capone syndicate (later known as the Four Deuces), told federal authorities the ease by which he "recruited" young girls into the life. "The majority of them were girls we met on the streets. We would go around to these penny arcades and nickel theaters and if we saw a couple of girls—we could always tell what they were by looking at them—we would go and talk to them. I never took any girl away from her home and took her down there. The girls I took down there I met in the stores or on the streets."

Just sixteen, Mona Marshall worked in a department store when Balding first approached her. Marshall later told authorities that she was attracted to him because of his good clothes, engaging manner, and evident wealth. He escorted her to theater, fine downtown restaurants, and promised marriage. She accompanied him to a furnished bachelor apartment he shared with other Levee "cadets" for the same brutal purpose. In time, he promised marriage—until that morning in 1907 when Marshall awoke in the brothel, her clothes removed, and her jewelry missing. She had been drugged the night before. Months later, a police raid freed Marshall from bondage. The ledger revealed that the young girl had been sold for fifty dollars to the madam. Her street clothes had been concealed, and the skimpy chemise the slavers provided was impossible for her to wear in public should she have a chance to escape. "I couldn't have gotten away possibly and if I could have done so I would have been ashamed to go home!"[22]

The apartment-flat Balding lured his victims to was a white-slave clearing house. Federal agents produced evidence that fifteen young women had been "processed" through the flat and forcibly shipped to Beaumont, Texas, to work in a local brothel.

"There is enough to indicate that no other city in America holds and harbors the evil of white slavery as Chicago," declared U.S. attorney Edwin Sims on July 25, 1908. Sims and assistant U.S. attorney Clifford Roe, working with Cook County state's attorney John Wayman formed an incorruptible triumvirate that rarely consulted with the Chicago police, knowing the frustration and futility of interagency cooperation. "I'll close these places but the let the cops keep it closed!" he snapped.[23] His words carried a powerful message.

Roe personally broke up the vicious Maurice Van Bever Gang on October 13, 1909. Van Bever, a fashionable dandy seen about town in an elegant touring brougham, built an opulent lifestyle on the backs of countless young white slaves before law enforcement effected his arrest outside the Chamber of Commerce building. "I have always lived up to the order of the police department in having all the girls registered at the station!" he protested.[24] Mollie Hart, wife of Mike Hart, Van Bever's cadet, turned state's evidence and revealed the extensive midwestern white-slave network. The husband and wife brothel keepers were sentenced to just one year in prison and ordered to pay a $2,000 fine.

The syndicate survived spasmodic reform crusades and the efforts of the Committee of 15—the local arm of the National Vigilance Association—and the "Clean Chicago" campaign to close the district. The war against the Levee gangs, fought in the streets and in the judiciary system, dragged on for a period of ten years. A religious revival and citizen's march south to Michigan Avenue and down to Twenty-Second Street in September 1912 drew the "social evil" into sharper focus in the media, but marches alone did not bring an end to the prolonged struggle that would continue through the World War I years. In July 1914 the accidental shooting of Stanley Birns, a Chicago cop, by a member of the Morals Squad, a zealous handpicked plainclothes vice detail permitted to operate outside the governance of the Chicago police, more or less brought the curtain down on the era of segregated vice.[25]

The passage of the Mann Act (or white-slave law), a congressional measure sponsored by Representative James Mann of Chicago prohibiting the interstate transport of women for immoral purposes, went into law on June 26, 1910. Between passage of the bill in 1910 and January 1, 1914, the Mann Act resulted in 1,014 convictions, 159 acquittals, and 145 dismissals. Opponents criticized the measure as draconian and unconstitutional, but it succeeded in its original intent by curtailing the white-slave menace and driving the last remnants of the trade underground.

Moral indignation, coupled with unrelenting press indignation, the frontal assault of Messrs. Wayman, Roe, Sims, and the weight of the criminal code, tilted the scales of justice against the Levee gangs. But more pragmatic considerations, namely land values, improved modes of transportation, and easily bribed suburban police officials, hastened the final downfall of the district. As it turned out, the land underneath turned out to be more valuable to the railroad companies than the prostitution businesses occupying the storefront dens.

One by one, the old red-light haunts of Twenty-Second Street were abandoned to the elements, providing occasional shelter to squatters and homeless tramps until the wrecker's ball reduced the decayed structure to heaps of rubble on the eve of national Prohibition. The railroads claimed the land, driving the vice gangs for cover. By the end of World War I, they had dispersed southward and were clustered near the Indiana-Illinois state line. The automobile and paved roads made it possible for thrill seekers to find their pleasure in the outlying areas without fear of police interference.

Building upon his earlier alliance with Big Jim Colosimo, Ike Bloom opened the Arrowhead Inn in Burnham, Illinois. The inn enjoyed the nurture, comfort, and protection of its "Boy Mayor," Johnny Patton, who got himself elected village president in 1907 at the age of twenty-two so that he could protect his saloon from enforced midnight closings. Burnham, with a population of twelve hundred souls in 1916, is named in honor of Daniel Burnham, Chicago's most esteemed and respected architect. Despite its connection to a revered public figure, Burnham was home to more brothels and prostitutes per capita than any comparable town in the world, according to the *Chicago Tribune*. The local residents seemed to have no problem with the arrangement and heaped steady praise on the "young feller" in charge of their town's destiny.[26]

Thirty-five Burnham vice dens operated around the clock in 1918. John H. Lyle, a Prohibition-era Chicago judge, civic reformer, and mayoral candidate, reported that "Attendants at gas stations, diners and other establishments on roads leading to the dives were hired as lookouts. An electrical system linked the watch towers and the brothels. After a spy detected on-coming raiders a button was pressed sending inmates and customers scurrying for cover out of the barracks and into the woods." Johnny Torrio exported the elaborate escape system from the Levee, where underground tunnels connected the Twenty-Second Street resorts to the back alleys and a means of fast escape from infrequent police raids.

An investigation by the South Chicago police that year turned up some old familiar Chicago names holding title to the new "roadside" brothels: Maurice Van Bever (released from prison), James Colosimo, and Harry Cusick (or Guzik). Nearby, in West Hammond, Mayor Paul M. Kamradt aided and abetted Patton by hiding the working girls of Burnham when county law enforcement moved on the resorts.[27]

"I've been in the saloons and saloon business since I was fourteen," Patton declared in a May 1916 interview. "This town is wide open and why not? We make our own laws about it. We like it open!"[28] Patton went on to boast that a drop of liquor had never touched his lips. He never gambled, swore, smoked, chewed, or spit. What a model citizen he appeared to be.

As the Levee vice district slowly receded into the memory of old-time reporters and bon vivants, an increasingly mobile crime syndicate went to work carving up suburban fiefdoms with obliging politicians, Chinese "tong" gangs (secret societies or sworn brotherhoods ostensibly promoting mutual assistance programs and cultural identity) migrated south from downtown to Wentworth Avenue running south from Twenty-Second Street, forming a wedge between Irish Bridgeport to the south and the brothels controlled by Colosimo, Bloom, and Torrio to the north.

As it was in other city neighborhoods immersed in the grind of poverty, vice, and crime, the well-worn streets on the southern edge of downtown and the adjoining Near South Side could never fully escape from the stranglehold of a continuing criminal enterprise. After one dominant crime group dispersed another stepped in to perpetrate grievous offenses against the populace. Next came the Chinese into this maelstrom.

The ceaseless warfare between the On Leong and the Hip Sing tongs are lesser-known episodes in the city's violent gang history because of the secrecy that shrouded the community and its inner workings for so long a time. These two rival associations fought a violent and protracted trade war for territorial control of their Chicago community spanning five decades. The origin of the conflict is believed to date back to seventeenth-century China when a member of the society of On Leong was murdered with a hatchet. The killer was Hip Sing. According to folkloric tradition, a blood feud, not unlike the Hatfield-McCoy affray in the hills of Kentucky in the nineteenth century, ensued. It spanned three hundred years and crossed international borders.

Chinese railroad workers organized tong gangs in the 1850s to fend off enraged miners and laborers in California unable to find work because the newly arrived Asians had accepted wages for jobs at a fraction of what white workers were willing to accept. The tongs moved east. In Lower Manhattan along Pell and Mott Streets they organized a "gambler's trust" using intimidation tactics and life-and-death threats to force gamblers to pay protection to police officials through Chee Kung, the city's first tong.

The On Leong of New York absorbed Chee Kung into its ranks and grew rich through illegal gambling and prostitution operations. However, by 1900, its hegemony was challenged by Mock Duck, one of America's most fearsome tong warriors, described by historian Herbert Asbury as "a bland, fat, moon-faced man—a curious mix of bravery and cowardice" who had broken ranks with Tom Lee, criminal boss of the On Leong. Mock Duck turned informant, furnished the police with addresses of On Leong's secreted gambling dens, and organized the Hip Sing to do battle. Warfare between the tong gangs in New York was bloody and exhausting, and the conflict quickly spread into other cities. Tong wars between these rival groups erupted in Chicago, San

Francisco, Washington, D.C., and Philadelphia with deadly regularity between 1900 and 1935.

The mysterious, artfully concealed criminal activity of the tongs underscores Daniel Bell's compelling thesis that crime provided "a queer ladder of social mobility" for men of natural instinct and ability seeking prestige and power. However, their ethnic background and unwillingness to assimilate and conform to the rules of the host society were predictors of patterns of bombings, violence, and terror.

Sam Moy, recognized as the "King of the Celestials" and founder of Chicago's colorful and picturesque Chinatown, arrived in San Francisco in 1872 from a central province in China. He was a callow youth of eighteen who mastered the art of Chinese cooking for American diners from Elias Jackson "Lucky" Baldwin, sportsman and owner of the Baldwin Hotel and Theater. Moy saved his money and moved to Chicago in the 1880s where he leased a building at 319 South Clark Street and introduced a new cuisine, chop suey, to the native population. The location was proximate to the Custom House Levee, and the ideal setting to open legitimate business fronts shielding illegal gambling (games of Fan Tan and Bung Loo) and the opium trade. Sam Moy understood the rules of the game.

A man of quiet dignity, but a forceful leader possessing both depth and complexity in the fashion of Johnny Torrio, Moy, working closely with Hip Lung and Chow Tai, functioned as an interpreter and counselor to the immigrant colony that helped to establish the underpinnings of Chicago's Chinatown. In the 1870 city census, eight laundry men comprised the sum total of Chinese residents in the city.

Moy, described in a *Tribune* account "as the first Chinaman on Clark Street to wear boots, store clothes and play poker," encouraged friends, family, and associates to join him in Chicago, legal or otherwise. In September 1892, customs officials in Detroit arrested and charged Moy with subornation of perjury in connection with the smuggling of Chinese nationals through Windsor, Ontario, into the United States.

By 1895 he owned the leasehold on two-thirds of the buildings on the east side of Clark Street between Van Buren and Harrison and owned a stake in every Chinese lottery game and joss house (restaurant) in the city. The King Joy Lo restaurant in the 400 block of South Clark Street and the Canton Tea Garden drew in the tourist trade, but gambling and opium provided the real meal ticket for the criminally inclined.

"On both sides of Clark Street, down in gloomy basements or up creaking stairways to lofts were opium joints, lottery offices and gaming resorts," reporter John Kelley reminisced in a 1927 story. "On Sundays when Chinese laundrymen came to Clark Street for recreation, to purchase another week's supply of groceries, the Fan Tan and Bung Loo games were crowded with devotees."[29]

Opium dens operated around the clock at 110 Federal Street and in the basement at 508 South Clark. U.S. revenue agents estimated in January 1912 that the district was awash in the manufacture of opium. On average a single proprietor grossed a hundred dollars a day. Moy easily covered the usual and customary "tribute," for the privilege of operating the drug dens and Bung Loo games in violation of local statutes, to the Harrison Street police on behalf of the Tong gangs. His fortune was conservatively pegged at $350,000.

As the dictatorial ruler of the On Leong (ostensibly promoted by its followers as a Merchant's Association), Moy was a revered figure and looked up to as a deity during his twenty-year reign in Chicago. Regarded as the unofficial "Mayor of Chinatown," he managed to maintain a shaky and uneasy peace with the rival Hip Sings and mediated disputes between contentious factions in the other cities when war threatened to erupt. Moy's quarter-century reign ended in Milwaukee on April 19, 1902, after the great leader succumbed to pneumonia. The body was removed to Chicago and placed in state inside Rafferty's Saloon—one of the famed Custom House Levee dives. Thousands of mourners came to pay their respects.

"In front of the joss-house was a wooden platform," the *Tribune* reported on April 20th. "Chinese masons gathered on the other end of the platform, bowed before the solid silver joss at the foot of the coffin and, before which were placed a roast whole pig, a whole lamb, and many bowls of stewed duck, chicken and rice." Unfamiliar as they were with Chinese custom, rituals, hierarchy, and tradition, the press described the "weird rites" and, with mixed curiosity and amusement, reported on the large funeral cortege of a hundred carriages as it wound its way northward to Rosehill Cemetery many miles away from the Custom

House. Andy Craig, bail bondsman, gambler, and vice merchant with John Rafferty and other Levee disreputables, served as pallbearers, fulfilling Sam Moy's dying request.

A struggle to establish power and authority over Chinatown followed. The Hip Sing maintained headquarters at 354 South Clark and the On Leong ran its operations at 337 Clark. A rash of shootings and assassination followed, but secrecy prevailed. In a case that attracted national attention, Hip Lung (aka Moy dong Chew, the sixty-year-old "King of Chinatown") stood trial in 1908 for the murder of Chin Wai on South Clark Street. Wai, a member of the rival Chin family, had refused to join the On Leong and had cut into their profits. He paid with his life.

Chicago police translated a circular denouncing Hip Lung, one of the wealthiest Chinese citizens in the community. "Hip Lung is a bloodthirsty hound," the document read. "All good Chinese should do all in their power to rid the world of such a man."[30] On June 17, 1908—amid charges of jury tampering—Hip Lung and his brother were acquitted of a murder the Chinese likened to the assassination of Julius Caesar. The acquittal of Hip Lung established the dominance of the Moy leadership faction of Chinatown. Their influence over the community would extend for decades to come.

When approached by police detectives in murder cases such as this one, tong members and community residents, distrustful of government and the police, offered a stock response: "No can say."

By 1912 the population of Chinatown had swelled to five thousand. With it came a chronic housing shortage. The City of Chicago, basking in the recent success of having shuttered and demolished the Custom House Levee a decade earlier, signaled its intention to relocate the burgeoning Chinese community to Twenty-Second Street and Wentworth, bordering the empire of vice governed by Bloom, Torrio, and Colosimo.

The decision to shift the Chinese settlement nearest to the city "badlands" was a historic watershed event but it seemed to be grounded in the racist belief that the Chinese of Chicago, primarily a bachelor community due to restrictive immigration quotas, belonged there.[31] After all, the city fathers reasoned, had these people with their strange rituals and bizarre customs (by American standards) lost their souls through dope smuggling, prostitution, gambling, and contract murder?

The city council and a consortium of developers eager to reclaim the South Loop and remove the Chinese appropriated the sum of $200,000 to fund construction of forty, three-story buildings along the northern strip of Twenty-Second Street, South Princeton Avenue, and South Archer. Dragon designs in terra-cotta ornamented the exterior with fifteen storefronts reserved for commercial and retail establishments.

The buildings, constructed of sturdy brick, were ready for occupancy in November 1912, and it was expected that they would easily accommodate five thousand residents. The On Leong put its stamp on the community in 1928 by engaging the architectural firm of Michaelsen & Rognstad to design an imposing "city hall / temple" at 2216 South Wentworth Avenue. When completed, the building featured a crown of distinctive twin pagodas, lustrous glazed ceramic tile and delicate terra-cotta flowers. The On Leong Building became a focal point of community life for job placement, lodgings, and, over time, various assorted illegalities.

But not all of the Chinese were willing to abandon Clark Street, the neighborhood that had been their Chicago home for close to thirty-years, so quickly.

Frank Moy, the new "Mayor of Chinatown" and his On Leong followers moved their operations to Twenty-Second Street with the intention to build and expand in the new surroundings while remnants of the Hip Sing held on as long as they could. The last holdouts in the Chinese quarter resisted the impulse to move, until orders of forcible eviction drove them out of Clark Street in February 1927.

John Kelley mourned the passing of custom. "The Chinese new year lasted from one to two weeks. Clark Street was a gay place during these celebrations. There was a mingling of the Tongs—the On Leongs and the Hip Sings—and during the festival season guns and hatchets were laid away. Great quantities of high-powered rice wine were consumed, the Fan Tan, Bung Loo resorts never closed, and special programs were arranged by Chinese musicians for the proper observance of New Year."

In Chicago in the fall of 1928, less than four years after the close of the most violent period of tong warfare in the United States, guns blazed anew on the South Side. The wounding of an On Leong in October was avenged with the murder of Eng Pak, a Hip Sing sitting in a

Yellow Cab outside of the Toy Den Quay Theater at 2113 Archer Avenue, by two On Leongs who approached the automobile from the rear and thrust pistols through the window. Pak fell dead. Two hours later, two Chinese Hip Sings burst into Willie Took's restaurant at 430 East Forty-Third Street. Eight shots were fired. Took was killed; an African American man and a waitress were wounded by errant shots. Retaliation murder and assassination were de rigueur in the worst years of the tong violence on the South Side, but never did this kind of gang warfare attract the attention of the press to the same degree that Al Capone and his rival minions did during Prohibition.

In April 1929 the Hip Sings, ruled by Lester Lee, opened a three-story mixed-use clubhouse, restaurant, and retail center on the southwest corner of Wentworth, Archer, and Twenty-First Street. The detective bureau puzzled over this incursion into On Leong territory at a time when the ranks of the Hip Sing had dwindled nationwide. Police estimated that the Hip Sing numbered only 125 men in June 1930. The defection of many of its most prominent and wealthy members to the On Leong (2,250 strong in 1939) was seen as a catalyst for the renewal of hostility between the two gangs. With this new building an escalation of the violence seemed inevitable.

Frank Moy, the "benevolent despot" and final arbiter of all Chinatown disputes ranging from business matters to private vendettas between families, died of cerebral hemorrhage on September 17, 1937. Moy, no stranger to violence, wore a bulletproof vest after years of receiving death threats. He was well aware that a tong leader's life expectancy was often counted in days and months, never years. The period of mourning for Chinatown's "mayor" ended on November 1st when an assassin pumped three shots into the chest of millionaire restaurant owner and former On Leong national president Chin Jack Lam.

Regarded as one of the most powerful behind-the-scenes Chinese leaders in America, Lam ruled his people tyrannically and was greatly feared in several cities. In Chicago local merchants and residents ducked into storefronts and disappeared into their homes when Lam approached. The On Leong deposed Lam in 1923 after he was accused of absconding with $70,000, precipitating his defection to the Hip Sing in 1923 and the tong war that left seventy people dead from coast to coast.

Police believed that the motive for murder was his refusal to donate $750 to Frank Moy's relief fund to aid war-torn China.

The era of the tong war pitting Chicago's two dominant tong gangs against one another receded following the climactic murder of Chin Jack Lam. Years passed. On Leong members and Hip Sing, setting aside long simmering differences, served their constituency as benevolent societies, and a period of relative calm ensued. The Hip Sing migrated to the far North Side of Chicago, beginning in 1972, as a new and emerging pan-Asian community of Vietnamese, Hmong, and ethnic Chinese evolved in the uptown neighborhood along Argyle Street.

Old problems with familiar characters reemerged during the 1970s in Chicago's South Side Chinatown. The Chicago "Outfit" muscled its way into the insular, but cash-rich, world of Chinese gambling, requiring Wilson Moy, the On Leong's liaison to the English-speaking world, to pay $8,000 a month in "street tax" (protection) to organized crime figures. Moy's payoffs to corrupt police officers dated back to the 1960s.

Government informant Robert Cooley told the feds that Moy funneled $100,000 in cash to pass along to mobbed-up alderman Fred Roti of the First Ward and his henchman Pat Marcy to "fix" the 1981 murder trial of three Chinese gang members accused of killing a rival in Chinatown. The bribe money was allegedly paid to Judge Thomas Maloney, a notoriously corrupt Cook County jurist in the 1970s and 1980s.

The somber, cathedral-like On Leong building shielded a sophisticated, organized crime-gambling operation. The extent of it amazed federal authorities after the place was raided in April 1988 under the leadership of U.S. marshal Edward Scheu, armed with federal antiracketeering statutes. Escape tunnels, not unlike the maze of tunnels that honeycombed the Levee brothel district before World War I, were discovered in the basement. A black altar topped by six urns, thought to be a religious shrine, contained slips of paper with the names of local merchants and the amount of "protection" money they were assessed by the gangsters. The feds seized $320,000 in cash and $76,000 worth of gambling chips, closed the building, and compelled a more suitable name change to the Pui Tak Center and lawful pursuits.

Wilson Moy of Chinatown's dynasty family owned a gift shop. Although he wasn't seen as a grave threat to society and was pitied by the remorseful Judge John Nordberg, Moy was handed a two-and-a-half-year prison sentence in May 1995, concluding a complex gambling and racketeering case that had dragged on for nearly seven years.

Although Hip Sing and On Leong members, by now conservative and graying around the temples, had long ago set aside simmering disagreements, dangerous new tong gangs from the Far East emerged in the late 1970s, according to a San Francisco investigator who said that "Their tactics are the same as the Mafia; terrorize the people in the community then extort money from them for protection."[32] A network of youths smuggled in from Hong Kong called the Ghost Shadows established a base of operations in the North Side Argyle Street community. In an ironic twist, Chicago police responded to a complaint from the once-fearsome North Side Hip Sing after their association headquarters was robbed and a member pistol-whipped by the newly arrived thugs. Other Ghost Shadow factions organized in New York and San Francisco.

The wounds inflicted by the vice merchants of Chicago's original "badlands"—scarred, torn, and bloodied by decades of violence, treachery, and political skullduggery stretching from the southern tip of downtown through the near South Side and Chinatown—were slow to heal. The area from Van Buren Street to Cermak (Twenty-Second Street) degenerated into a slum pockmarked by abandoned weed lots, low-income housing, fast-food hangouts, and auto parts stores in the few remaining shabby Levee buildings that in time succumbed to the wrecker's ball.

In the early 1990s urban renewal erased the last visible reminders of Levee debauchery. Rows of brick townhomes designed for the upper-income gentry desiring an urban experience in secure gated communities featuring small gardens and patio decks arose on the contaminated brown fields of former vice. Only the decrepit Blue Star Auto Parts Store at Twentieth and State Street withstood the ravages of time and survived into the new millennium.

Once it was the Cullerton Hotel, an assignation house, gambling den, and likely white-slave prison. Today the sagging red-brick structure, opened in 1884 as a genteel South Side hostelry, is an out-of-place relic amid luxury townhomes and condominiums. The third and fourth floors are utilized as a storage area, but a closer look at the sagging floorboards reveals impressions of vanished bedroom walls that were taken down long ago. The walls divided rows of oppressively narrow rooms measuring twelve feet in length and eight feet in width until the hotel reopened as a retail store in 1939. Gazing at the upper floors of the building from street-level barred windows suggests the possibility of white-slave imprisonment in a forgotten age.

Nearby, Chinatown remains one of Chicago's important tourist destinations. Gambling operations linked to organized crime, if it exists at all, are conducted furtively and cleverly concealed from the swarm of tourists browsing the souvenir gift shops and the Cantonese restaurants.

3

GANGS OF THE SOUTH SIDE: POLITICS, PATRONAGE, AND BARE-KNUCKLE BOYOS, 1860–1930

By 1870 Chicago had nearly caught up to St. Louis as the fourth largest city in the nation. Growth succumbed to urban sprawl, as the residents from foreign lands descended upon the city and filled in remote sections that only a generation earlier were uninhabited marshlands occupied by packs of wolves. Horse-drawn streetcars extended southward to Bridgeport, the emerging Irish district situated three miles southwest of the central business district along the South Branch of the Chicago River. Originally named Lee's Place after Charles Lee, one of the city's "old settlers" who owned a farm on both sides of the river, the community was called a variety of other names. In 1848, when the Illinois & Michigan Canal (built for navigation purposes) opened, the river traffic frequently stopped near Ashland Avenue and the canal. It was claimed that this station was called Bridgeport. Canal commissioners duly christened this remote settlement near the locks the "Bridgeport Addition to Chicago" or simply Bridgeport so there would be no confusion with Canalport, an adjacent area of the South Division nearby.

In 1850 the city census listed 6,096 residents of Irish descent. By 1870 their numbers exceeded forty thousand and continued to grow thereafter. Impoverished immigrants of the 1840s crowded into squatter patches on the North Side, but more settled into Bridgeport, forming the Hibernian

Benevolent Society and other lodges and societies to build fraternalism and preserve cultural linkage to the old country.

Confronting the religious and ethnic intolerance of the Whigs, the Know Nothings, and the Protestant elites, Chicago's Irish settlers gravitated to the Democratic Party. The party of Andrew Jackson was perceived as sympathetic to the plight of the new arrivals washing ashore during his presidential administration. The Democrats endorsed the right to socialize and congregate in saloons and built political strength on a "liberal platform" of anti-temperance. Irish barkeeps and others connected in some way to the liquor trade protected their business interests and the inclinations of their patrons to drink and gamble by winning municipal elections and championing these issues in the city council. In a letter to his sister in LeRoy, New York, Henry Denison, a traveler passing through Chicago in 1840, commented,

> In regard to politics, a majority of the American citizens here are Whigs, but the votes of the Irish turn the scale in favor of the Loco Foco party.[1]
>
> By the laws of Illinois, every foreigner who has been in the country six months is entitled to a vote but the Paddies are not at all scrupulous about voting half a dozen times over if they haven't been here six weeks.

Through the nineteenth century and into the twentieth, a collection of political dynasties, and autonomous neighborhood machines, governed Chicago. Although Chicago ward "bosses" in the main were Democrats, the city's vast geography precluded a single-party leader, or "strong mayor / weak council" form of government, from marshalling control of the entire city until the midway point of the twentieth century. Factionalized, divisive, and feudal in every way, the confounding "mini-machines" and their whiskey-soaked bosses ruling the North, South, and West Sides schemed, connived, and contrived with one another to hoard the bountiful harvest of graft, while managing to frustrate and thwart reform movements every step of the way. Lincoln Steffens (1866–1936), noted muckraker and social crusader said, "Minneapolis has cleaned up, Pittsburgh has tried to, New York fights every other election, Chicago fights all the time."[2]

Originally a mile square and lying between Twenty-Second Street and Thirty-First Street (east to west) and Halsted and Ashland (north to south), Bridgeport was an incubator for crime, although anti-Irish prejudice must be taken into account when reading the florid descriptions of the locale found in the prose of late nineteenth-century reporters. "Reached by a laborious journey down the Archer Road, now Bridgeport has become a generic term for smells, for riots, bad whiskey and poor cigars," derided the *Tribune* on May 21, 1882.

The foul odors of refuse from the Schuenemann cattle yards, the livestock rendering plants and factories near the polluted south fork of the river, and the low marshy terrain can all be blamed for the rancid smells. Sewage and sanitation was nearly nonexistent.

Residents who first settled Bridgeport in the 1840s to dig the canal and find jobs in the industrial businesses clogging the waterways were laborers—men of no particular skill or trade. They had fled Ireland against the backdrop of potato famine, disease, and poverty, and arrived here with little money and few prospects. To subsist in this harsh new environment, Irish families grew cabbage—poor man's food—in vacant lots and the backyards of wooden cottages. In the daily toils of the grinding manual labor available to them in the earliest stockyards at Madison and Ashland and Cottage Grove Avenue and Twenty-Ninth Street, the lumber yards, rolling mills, railroad-car repair shops and manufacturing plants, they attached a more ominous name to the character of the Bridgeport community: Hardscrabble. Irish laborers working in the slop and bloody entrails of the slaughterhouses were derisively mocked as "Pig Irish" by slightly more upscale socioeconomic strata of society. The deprivations, high infant mortality, street crime, and overall dissolute quality of life in the shantytown work camps where cabbage was the primary food staple made for a truly hardscrabble existence.

The Irish immigrants settled in Bridgeport's frame-and-brick cottages and scattered two-flats and mostly worshipped at St. Bridget's, the oldest Catholic church in the district, opened in 1847. In the afterhours, the men of the community patronized the saloons and groggeries. The drinking establishments provided the stage for violent crime committed by aggressive young buckos reveling in brutality, arrogance, and drunken swagger. "To such an extent has this lawlessness been extended that there is not a single policeman in the City of Chicago—and there are many brave and fearless ones—who has the courage to go there alone to make an arrest, well knowing that if he did so he would be carried home in a coffin," the *Tribune* reported on December 29, 1863. By 1867 the earliest known street gang had formed on Ashland Avenue for the purpose of robbing the stockyard workers on payday. Two Irish gangs conducted a twenty-year reign of terror against the German, Jewish, and Polish immigrants up through the 1890s. These two gangs united, calling themselves the "Mickies."

Chicago's high-crime districts were inevitably carved out of large bachelor communities such as Bridgeport with the saloon a natural setting for socialization among restless young men eager to gain status and respect among their peers through boasting taunts, insults exchanged, and fistfights—often a precursor to murder.

Illustrative of the frequent acts of bloodshed and brutality within Bridgeport's "tough" saloons was the fate of twenty-one-year-old James Townsend inside John Zimmerman's place at 768 Archer Avenue the night of December 8, 1871. After consuming much wine and beer, Zimmerman and four companions were playing a game of "pigeon-hole billiards" when a local rough named Jefferson Cating drew a revolver on another youth who had interfered with the placement of balls on the table. Townsend sarcastically remarked, "I guess someone else can have some of that too!" Whereby Cating, peeved by the insulting remark, rushed at Townsend and discharged a single shot into his head at point-blank range. Townsend slumped over the table dead. Cating, an Englishman in his early twenties with a lengthy police record, was seized by the South Branch police detail as he attempted to flee. Interviewed later by a *Tribune* reporter, the accused murderer was unconcerned.

Reporter: How long had you been in the saloon?

Cating: I had been in there since eight o'clock.

Reporter: Where had you been before you went there?

Cating: I was into Murphy's saloon, number 803 Archer Avenue. I had a couple of drinks in there.

Reporter: Had you any difficulty with Townsend?

Cating: I never had any difficulty with the boy.

Reporter: Are you in the habit of visiting saloons and spending your evenings in drinking and playing pigeon-hole?

Cating: Yes, pretty often.

Reporter: Did you make threats two or three weeks ago to kill someone?

> Cating: I said the reason I bought this revolver—I have had it only three weeks—it is the first time I ever carried one. There have been parties that have threatened to lick me—a whole mob of them and I told certain fellows that if they did anything I would do the best I could with them. I was told that if I didn't look out there was a mob going to tackle me. I can get a half-dozen to prove the same thing.
>
> Reporter: Did you have any words with Townsend before you pulled out the revolver?
>
> Cating: I do not remember anything at all about when I pulled it out and how I was standing or anything else. I was out of my head altogether. I had about seven or eight drinks—Sherry wine and lager beer.[3]

In his examination of patterns of violence in nineteenth-century Chicago, author Jeffrey Adler reveals that in Bridgeport, Kilgubbin, Conley's Patch, and other impoverished settlement neighborhoods, the city's drunken-brawl homicide rate and the proportion of homicides resulting from drunken brawls reached their high-water marks in the 1871 to 1900 period. Only after the turn of the nineteenth century, when the marriage rate climbed steadily, did the level of violence shift from the saloons to inside the home, although incidences of armed robbery in the streets continued to escalate.

Criminal gangs, a by-product of intense ethnic rivalries, tribalism, residential squalor, and economic hardship, quickly formed and became a natural extension of urban strife in the chaotic city streets. They terrorized the district, with saloon owners and barkeeps frequent targets. "The cheap saloons that infest the locality, well-known under the sobriquet Bridgeport, rarely have on hand no more than a quart of liquor at any time. This is supplied to them chiefly by peddlers, who, owing to the wickedness of Bridgeport's inhabitants, are greatly troubled with the depredations of young thieves who prey upon their [saloon owners] goods while they are supplying their trade," the *Tribune* noted on January 1, 1876. "Their thefts have so much annoyed the peddlers that frequent threats have been made to by them to fix the thieves by mixing some violent purgative with the liquor."

By the 1860s, South Side residents from the lumberyards, manufacturing plants, and stockyards, looked beyond the hopelessness of factory work to a brighter future in municipal government as an opportunity to achieve upward mobility. The Irish filled a widening gap in the electoral affairs of the city because they enjoyed an important advantage over the Italians, Croats, Lithuanians, and Poles who populated the neighborhoods: command of the English language that assimilated them into the civic affairs of the city. But there were other important considerations, the gangs and the saloons.

The Protestant elite accumulated wealth, acquired status, and fashioned a midwestern high-society social set that eschewed public service as unrefined and proletarian. Banking, the law, finance, the investment world, commerce and trade, retail, shipping, and real estate speculation beckoned the sons of the prairie aristocracy. The saloon was left to the politicians; the anteroom of the exclusive private club admitted the poised, soft-spoken man of affairs. Class divisions were never so much apparent as in the widening chasm of municipal governance and city commerce.

Bridgeport was the birthplace and childhood home of more politicians and clergymen than any other neighborhood in Chicago. Six Chicago mayors, plus generations of municipal and state employees, political factotums, and ward "heelers," who owed their allegiance to the ruling Democratic political machine that controlled the city's destiny for 130 years, were born here.

Politics was often interwoven with the rogue element of street gangs that sprouted in the nineteenth century. The Irish gangs of the late nineteenth century up through the Great Depression were more deeply engaged in the political process than their law-breaking counterparts in other areas of the city.

Bridgeport and the surrounding communities of Canaryville, Back of the Yards, and the "Patch" and its Italian immigrant community at Indiana Avenue and Fourteenth Street became the battlefields for dozens of street gangs representing narrowly defined "turf" boundaries that were often reduced to one or two contested blocks zealously protected and fought for in the militaristic tradition of feudal estates in the Middle Ages. Although mostly an Irish settlement, this South Side community filled in with Poles, Lithuanians, Italians, and Germans, with scattered pockets of immigrants from the other corners of Europe. In its earliest history, fierce ethnic rivalries between the Bridgeport Irish and the Bridgeport Germans spilled over into gang warfare and violence. "Rows are not infrequent. The Germans have been attacked in the most cowardly manner," the *Tribune* reported in December 1863.

There were myriad holdup gangs and cop killers scattered across the greater South Side in the decades following the Civil War. The Vincent Briscoe Gang gained a measure of notoriety in May 1902 with the murder of Officer Patrick Duffy of the Stockyards Police Station. Briscoe, a professional criminal by his sixteenth birthday, evaded capture for nearly nine years. Blunders and missteps by the police detective bureau left the department open for ridicule and censure after Inspector George Shippy traveled to Mobile, Alabama, to bring back to Chicago a man believed to be Vincent Briscoe. When Shippy and his prisoner reached New Orleans, he realized he had arrested Briscoe's brother instead. Briscoe was finally captured outside San Quentin Prison in 1909, extradited to Chicago, and sentenced to fourteen years, but the charge had been reduced to manslaughter.

Over time, Wentworth Avenue, a major north-south thoroughfare, divided white and black Chicago. East of Wentworth Avenue, the city's "Black Belt" was firmly established after 1900. The "Great Migration" out of the Jim Crow South brought thousands of blacks escaping the persecution of southern whites. However, dreams of achieving equality in the industrial North evaporated in the face of fierce residential and institutional segregation.

Over one half of the city's expanding African American population concentrated in substandard, post-fire housing stock stretching from Michigan Avenue on the east, Cottage Grove Avenue on the west; Thirty-First Street on the north and Fifty-First Street on the south. By World War I, Chicago's African American population had swelled to 92,501—nearly tripling in size from 1900. Shabby, dilapidated buildings lacking proper plumbing and sanitation were rented by white landlords, contributing to rising tensions within the African American community. To the west, ethnic whites feared the incursion of blacks into their domain. The loss of jobs in the munitions plants and in the Stockyards District to nonunion replacement workers (during World War I when the young men of the community were sent overseas), contributed to festering resentments based on patterns of institutional racism. Overcrowding, restrictive racial covenants barring blacks from home ownership in all-white neighborhoods, and physical retaliation directed toward people of color attempting to move from the Black Belt to better neighborhoods contributed to the growing unease permeating Chicago.

The Bridgeport gangs were legendary and known by reputation throughout the city. Others remained obscure and mostly forgotten with the passage of time, but all of them flourished. Boyhood friendships born out of childhood playgroups coalescing in the streets over time contributed to a high degree of neighborhood social organization and self-esteem gained through the acceptance of peers. With minimal opportunity available to escape the grind of poverty, and a lack of positive reinforcement from the school administrators and parents, boys congregated in alleys and parks. Petty theft, the bullying of weaker children, and acts of vandalism were seen as ways to gain acceptance and court the favor of the gang leader.

Political organizers often employed the most fearless of the lot to run "errands" on behalf of the party organization. Chicago park attachés, working with the alderman, would attempt to organize the boys into "social-athletic clubs" and schedule sporting events with rival leagues and other parks and clubs. State charters were applied for and issued through the auspices of the South Side Associated Clubs (SSAC), first convened on November 16, 1901, as a governing body with a stated mission of "promoting amateur athletics." The SSAC formally sanctioned the right of each AC to exist.

Operational funding often came from the deep pockets of obliging political sponsors willing to absorb the rental costs of the clubhouse or public meeting room in return for a pledge from the ACs to support their electoral ambitions and the other party candidates through all available means. This could mean driving out undesirables, a code word for blacks, who might be looking for better living arrangements in all-white neighborhoods or simply using the parks.

Influenced by the changing racial dynamic of the South Side after 1900, the gangs that were formerly divided by tribal identity (e.g., Germans vs. Irish; Poles vs. Italians) united in common purpose to redirect old ethnic hostilities toward a new common denominator—reservation of territorial boundaries separating races.

The Hamburg AC, the Our Flag Club, the Aylwards, the infamous Ragen's Colts ("Hit me, and you hit 2,000!"), the Old Nationals, the Marylands, the Old Roses, the Barefoots, the Wallaces, the Crowns, the Cornells, the Delawares, the Malt Marrows, the Dvorak Club, the Mosspratters, the Crescents, the Carnations, Alhamaries, the Cortlands, the Dirty Dozen from Sixty-Third Street, Favis Grays, Mayflower, the Pine Club, Sparklers, the Dashiells, the Plumrules, and other Bridgeport and Canaryville toughs advertised themselves as social-athletic clubs, thus assuring law enforcement of their good intentions, community spirit, and unflagging respect for authority. Their stated purpose was to organize competitive team sports for the enjoyment of all and as a means to "get the boys out of the saloons" and engaged in more productive activities. Each year sponsored athletic tournaments against clubs from other parts of the city, picnics, parties, and dances drew thousands of spectators. Citywide, there were an estimated 302 social-athletic clubs organized from 1900 to 1930. John M. Hagedorn states that 243 of the 1,313 gangs identified by Frederic Thrasher were SACs and 192 were "mixed adult or youth."[4]

The ACs often assisted favored local political candidates at election time in expectation of the usual perquisites for services rendered. This often meant immunity from police arrest for tearing down a rival's campaign posters at election time, falsifying or stealing ballots, and breaking the windows of storefronts—tasks freely performed in return for job appointments to agencies of municipal government, overcoming problems encountered in the criminal justice system, and other police troubles adjudicated to their satisfaction.

Bridgeport gangs, a natural extension of a vast political patronage army, profited from a stronger, much tighter association with Democratic ward bosses, city departmental heads, and fire and police officials than rival clubs from other areas of the city. The inbreeding of the predominantly Irish South Side ACs with the ward leaders of the party meant the attainment of influence, more commonly understood in Chicago terms as "clout." The waning decades of the nineteenth century through World War I was rough and tumble in Chicago political history when the city still had thirty-five wards and two aldermen per ward.[5] Under the old system of electoral politics, mayoral terms in Chicago were two years instead of four. The ACs were pivotal to the outcome of each campaign, forming a candidate's private army. Their tactics of intimidation were mostly ignored by police.

Election Day on Archer Avenue (Bridgeport's most important thoroughfare, angling southwest and dividing the Fourth and Fifth Wards of the city into two armed camps during aldermanic races in the 1890s and early 1900s) brought out the political brawlers from the saloons and ACs to settle old scores and personal differences in the streets.[6] "If you are looking for a fight you can find it anywhere along 'Archey Road,'" the *Tribune* commented on February 20, 1921.

Archer Avenue was nominally policed by members of the Deering Street Station, but the detail was challenged to maintain the peace of the community against a rising tide of mysterious murders in the 1870s along Butler and Salt Streets intersecting with Archer, a state road lined with deep ditches and shadowed by tall trees that provided excellent cover for highwaymen and armed robbers. Not until the pouring of asphalt and the addition of street lighting and other modernizations in 1901 did the crime rate on the long, twisting street slowly diminish.

In 1921 John J. "Jawn" McKenna, politician, and confidante of author Finley Peter Dunne's and the inspiration for Dunne's fictional Bridgeport seeing-eye sage "Hennessey," nostalgically reflected on the "good natured quality" to Archer Avenue election-day voting in the years leading up to national Prohibition.[7] McKenna reveled in the bluster, the violence, and the general disorder. "Oh boys, we used to have the grand fights on Election Day in olden times. The moment the polls opened at 6:00 a.m. the fight was on. And we kept it up until 11:00 at night and so we did! Ah man dear, but those were happy days! Those were the days of real sport! Now wasn't it nice to fight with your fists and give a fellow a black eye or a fractured jaw than to bore a hole through his liver with a bullet? I was never strong for that gun stuff. Wouldn't it be grand if history would repeat itself and we'd have a real old-fashioned election with broken heads and black eyes and ribs caved in? Oh boys, wouldn't it be grand?"[8]

In its formative years, the Hamburg Athletic Club (named for a residential area in Bridgeport west of the Chicago White Sox baseball park) ran its operation next door to Frank "Stub" McQuade's saloon, a tough joint at Thirty-Fifth Street and Wallace Avenue where person or persons unknown murdered fur thief Joseph Hurley on March 18, 1920, in the presence of twenty-four sworn-to-secrecy barroom onlookers. Hurley and his partner, "Slippery Sonny" Dunn, quarreled over the proceeds of a $15,000 burglary of Brown's Fur Company. Did Dunn and his gang kill Hurley over a rancorous division of the cash splits? Deering District police detectives never bothered to inquire after the fact. McQuade's was a "protected Hamburg place," and the cops knew better than to interfere in "neighborhood matters." Saloon culture was the common element knitting together politics and gang life on the South Side.

The Hamburg AC furnished precinct workers who were much stronger and more physically imposing than the brigade of downtown payrollers that supported the opposition candidates. It was not unusual for ballot boxes to be stolen in precincts where the "Hamburgers" were influential, if it could help their man gain an advantage at the polls.

Thomas A. Doyle's career path is illustrative of the political rewards awaiting ambitious and resourceful AC leaders moving up in the world. In 1914, at the comparatively young age of twenty-eight, Doyle, president of the Hamburg AC, declared his candidacy for alderman against twenty-year incumbent Charles "Cull" Martin, one of the old "Gray Wolves" of the Chicago City Council.[9] At stake: control of the Fifth Ward. Doyle, who strutted around town with a holstered pistol concealed under his coat, emerged the victor in the kind of knock-down, drag-out political contest favored by "Jawn" McKenna and Doyle's old gang, the Hamburg AC, now in complete control of the patronage, the zoning, policing, saloon licensing, and the fortunes of the ward. Journalist Mike Royko said that Doyle "won because 350 young men from the club went out in teams of ten every night and 'campaigned' for him."

Doyle occupied a seat in the Chicago City Council until 1918 when he won a state senate seat. In 1922 Bridgeport voters sent this former gang leader to Congress where he was appointed to the House Committee on Agriculture. Doyle lived in the family home at 3537 South Lowe Avenue—only a few doors down the street from 3602 South Lowe, where fellow Hamburg AC member Richard J. Daley, mayor of Chicago from 1955 to 1976, came of age. Doyle left Congress in 1930 to resume his old aldermanic post, a position he held until his death in 1935.

Sports, politics, and violence were conjoined in neighborhood life, the upper world of athletic contest to disguise the underbelly of gang life. The city parks, gymnasiums, and playing fields obscured the more ominous political, street-fighting activities and intimidation of people of color by the Hamburg AC during its years of greatest influence. It was commonly understood that the express purpose of club life revolved around the amateur sports leagues promoting football, basketball, and baseball.

In 1900 County Mayo native John L. Groark Sr. opened a saloon at Thirty-Third and Wentworth. He sponsored a football and basketball team in Cornell Square, a small park and playground, and named his team the Groark AC. Before World War I the teams were merged with the Hamburgs to become the Cornell-Hamburg AC, a powerhouse in the city's neighborhood sports scene, receiving widespread media coverage in the Chicago newspapers for nearly thirty years.

Joseph P. McDonough, the corpulent, three-hundred-pound former newsboy and prairie football star from Canaryville (that adjoined Bridgeport), succeeded Doyle as president of the Hamburg Club. A menacing brute force on the football field but pleasantly disposed toward "his people" off the field, he had coached the Cornell-Hamburgs in 1905 and played halfback for them before moving over to politics. McDonough was a poor stump speaker and a feeble elocutionist, but nevertheless he built a steadfast and loyal following and was called "the man with the big heart" by his constituents.

Born in the same Canaryville home on Thirty-Seventh Street that he would eventually die in, McDonough served seven terms in the council and four years as Cook County treasurer. The old-timers guffawed every time Joe recited his familiar mantra over a schooner of beer: "Canaryville is so tough, the canaries sing bass!" McDonough's japery reflected the brutal realities of neighborhood living and the grease and grime of the stockyards underfoot with the unending stench of cattle manure hanging in the air. It was often said that in Canaryville the career choices were few for the young men and it boiled down to priest, bum, or politician.

As alderman of the Fifth Ward (beginning in 1917), then later as ward committeeman, McDonough, personable and much loved by the Bridgeport faithful, furthered the interests of the ACs by establishing eight athletic fields leased by the city. However, public parks on the South Side of Chicago were never intended by McDonough, his constituents, and the white aldermen in adjoining wards to become inclusive public spaces for the benefit and enjoyment of all. Access to the open space was jealously guarded and "protected" by the Hamburgs, Ragen's Colts, and the other ACs. African Americans knew better than to cross over the invisible Wentworth Avenue race line and venture into these parks, especially after sunset.

Robert S. Abbott, founder and publisher of the *Chicago Defender* (the city's oldest established newspaper for African Americans), decried the continuing violence and intimidation aimed against his people by the ACs. Commenting on "Ruffianism in the Parks" on July 12, 1919, just two weeks prior to the outbreak of the worst race riot in the city's history, one that claimed thirty-eight lives, fifteen white, twenty-three blacks, he wrote:

> Following closely upon the heels of the recent bomb outrages in which the homes of a number of our citizens residing in Hyde Park were blown up, comes a report of an exhibition of ruffianism in our public parks. Gangs of young hoodlums from the district west of Wentworth Avenue have been making it a practice of attacking our people under cover of darkness and, so far, have been able to elude the police. Most of the young men come from the so-called athletic clubs that are so numerous in the territory aforementioned. These clubs are nothing more than hangouts for gangs of young toughs. The records of the police department show that much of the banditry now prevalent in the city is due to the activity of this class of young men. These young hoodlums, many of them not yet in their teens get their inspiration from what they read in the yellow press. It is there that they receive suggestions for their lawless acts. Added to this, is the influence of bad home surroundings and the ill-advised counsel of their elders. They listen to the evil judgments of the family circle. Single-handedly they lack the moral courage of their convictions, but when acting in gangs they are a positive menace to the peace of any community. The parks are public property, open to all citizens, black and white alike. The attention of the park boards has been repeatedly called to this situation, and blame for whatever happens under their jurisdiction rests with them alone. A few strong measures resulting in the arrest and punishment of the miscreants with stiff fines will do more to stamp out the trouble than all the newspaper agitation possible. Judiciary leniency is responsible for much of the existing lawlessness in this city.[10]

Boss McDonough mentored a generation of Hamburgers aspiring to political life. One of them, Richard J. Daley, a political neophyte from 3603 South Lowe Avenue who had worked menial jobs in the yards, rode Joe's coattails to power as a precinct captain, ward secretary, then later clerk in the Chicago City Council. Young Daley closely studied Joe's organizational wizardry. He allowed his superior to take credit for many of his good ideas. Playing the waiting game, Daley understood that his obsequiousness would gain him acceptance and entrée into prominent Democratic circles. He climbed the first important rung on that ladder on April 24, 1934, when Daley solemnly served as one of Joe's pallbearers after McDonough ate and drank himself into an early grave.

Saloon politician Hugh B. Connelly took over McDonough's committeeman job and then replaced Doyle when Doyle passed on in 1935. By default, Connelly became the undisputed kingpin of the Eleventh Ward until Daley's apprenticeship was complete. Before attaining citywide political prominence as the most powerful big-city machine boss in twentieth-century America, Daley learned the "Chicago way" by serving as a Hamburg AC president in 1924. Shrouded in mystery are Daley's whereabouts during the four days of rioting and civil disturbance that spread from the Black Belt to downtown and parts of the North Side from July 27 to August 1, 1919. Tensions had been building throughout the war.

The entire city had become a powder keg of racial resentment. Earlier that year bombs were thrown at the homes of African Americans in Hyde Park who had breached the color line and moved into the white neighborhood. Genteel Hyde Park, home of the University of Chicago, a bastion of intellectual thought and the home of many future Nobel laureates, contended with its own gang problem during World War I, a time when blacks first began their migration to the outer edges of the community. Criminal activity centered around the Illinois Central Railroad tracks and in the heart of the commercial business districts along Fifty-Fifth and Fifty-Seventh Streets. The Bat Eyes, the Kenwoods, and the Dirty Dozen were most active during the riot period, and they stashed stolen and looted goods in the basements of local retail stores.

The triggering incident that engulfed the city in four days of looting, murder, and mayhem began on the Chicago lakefront when fourteen-year-old Eugene Williams and his friends floated their homemade raft into the restricted Twenty-Ninth Street beach area—a "whites only" bathing area. From the shore, George Stauber, an angry white racist, hurled rocks at the raft. The boys thought nothing of it initially. This dangerous game had been played out many times before by black youths goading white segregationists nearest the boundary line. This time though one of the airborne missiles struck and killed Williams. The Cook County coroner later ruled that the stone that struck Williams was not responsible for the young man's death. Stauber had been arrested and was held on a $50,000 bond.

A black police officer standing on the beach summoned Officer Dan Callahan from the Cottage Grove station to assist in the arrest of Stauber. But in the presence of hundreds of eyewitnesses, Callahan refused the request. By his actions, angry blacks attacked the rock thrower as indignant whites rallied to Stauber's defense. Callahan raced down the beach, in full retreat to the Cottage Grove Avenue Police Station to call out armed reinforcements. Pursued by a mob of black men, Callahan reached the station in time to put in a call. Within minutes of the arrival of police, gunfire broke out. The riot was on. In the downtown district throngs of angry whites besieged hotels singling out blacks employed as porters, waiters, and elevator operators.

Men were beaten on the street outside of the department stores and restaurants. One man was shot through the chest and another pulled out of a Thompson's Restaurant on Randolph Street, beaten and left for dead. On the South Side, in the heart of the Federal Street slum near Fifty-First Street, a mob of blacks dragged a white taxi driver and an operator of a truck delivering candy from their vehicles and beat them to the point of death. Violence committed by both whites and blacks in the stricken city threatened to spiral into a wider race war. Washington, D.C., and other cities experienced spasms of racial violence that summer, but in Chicago much of the blame for the rioting was borne out of fear, ignorance, and the provocation of "hoodlums" of both races, the ACs, and especially politics.

Cook County state's attorney Maclay Hoyne traced the blame to the politicized, demoralized police department for failing to uphold the law by their reticence to control the hoodlum element. "I know that police officials in the district are afraid to prosecute before the civil service commission subordinates who should be discharged from the force because some politicians may get after them," commented Hoyne to the *Tribune* on July 29th.[11]

The department, deeply woven into ward politics, graft, and influence peddling from the superintendent's office down to the lowliest patrolman owing his appointment to the alderman or committeeman, showed natural reticence in arresting white provocateurs linked to the ACs. Hoyne, a Democratic office holder in the administration of Mayor William Hale Thompson, Chicago's last Republican mayor, had been elected to the first of three terms of office in 1915. Thompson, a larger-than-life showman, part demagogue, and thoroughly corrupt politician who had vowed to "bust King George in the mouth" if the British monarch ever set foot in Chicago, rarely went to city hall except on city council days when he gaveled the meetings to order.

"Big Bill" employed a police lieutenant as his private cook. He turned a blind eye to the Capone mob and other Prohibition-era bootleggers, and often greeted the gentlemen of the press from his suite in the Hotel Sherman, directly across the street from city hall, clad in pajamas and a bathrobe.

In a moment of pique, Edward R. Litsinger, a member of the board of review who had broken ranks with the mayor in his failed 1927 electoral bid said that Thompson "had the hide of a rhinoceros and the brain of a baboon." Thompson fired back a broadside of his own at his former political angel, calling Litsinger "a donkey." The mayor and his spoilsmen coddled the gangland elements and wealthy bootleggers while playing rough with opponents. The atmosphere in Chicago was highly charged in those days and as one political wag observed, "politics in the Windy City ain't bean bag."

The mayor's personal songwriter, one Milton Weil, composed the lyrics to "Big Bill the Builder," a sonnet to a ridiculous man ruling the nation's second-largest city through the wild unpredictable 1920s. In moments of high humor, Thompson ordered corporation counsel Samuel Ettelson to warble the tune as best he could during the many drinking bouts with "the boys" held inside the Sherman. For his troubles, Milton Weil was awarded a $5,000-a-year job as an assistant commerce commissioner on the payroll of the State of Illinois.

Thompson was ill-suited to the task of restoring order to a riot-stricken city. Until it was no longer politically expedient to do so, Maclay Hoyne battled corruption and exposed the myriad of frauds and bribery schemes he traced to the Thompson coterie, but stopped short of vigorously prosecuting members of the ACs responsible for much of the violence on the South Side. To do so would antagonize a partisan political base of voters, offend South Side aldermen, and turn an estimated seven thousand AC members whose loyalties were aligned with the Democrats against him.

Early on in the rioting, the police raided gambling dens and jazz clubs in the bailiwick of Alderman Robert R. Jackson, an important ally of Thompson in the Black Belt. Guns were seized inside the Ranier Club, Mexican Frank's, the Pekin Club, and the Pioneer Club—all black-owned jazz establishments. African American gambling bosses who ran the "policy rackets" up and down the Black Belt were held responsible for inciting rioters, and scores of operatives were arrested.

"State's Attorney Hoyne it seems is of the impression that Colored gamblers started the race riots in Chicago," bristled the *Defender* on September 6, 1919. "Much of the trouble can be laid at the door of the so-called athletic clubs west of Wentworth Avenue, from which it appears, raiding parties were sent out into the territory of our people attacking old and young alike. Bands of these gangsters had swept through Washington Park and adjoining neighborhoods. Several months ago we had occasion to call attention to these clubs as breeding spots for crime. And we believe we are safe in saying that much of the trouble leading up to the riots might have been avoided had these gang rendezvouses [sic] been closed. If our fighting state's attorney would push his probe in the direction of these clubs, he would go far toward striking at the real source of the race rioting in this community."

For self-serving political reasons, not the least being Hoyne's higher ambition to unseat Thompson as Chicago's next mayor in the coming election, he did not. Though notoriously corrupt, and flagrantly so, Thompson's administration had at the very least cultivated and built a strong alliance with Chicago's African American community.

Through the onset of the Depression, the Republican Party clung to its Reconstruction Era reputation as the party of Lincoln, emancipation, and ensuring equal rights for all races. Memories of the Jim Crow South, Democratic sympathies with the Confederacy through the Civil War, and the post-Civil War Ku Klux Klan terror period were not easily dismissed or far removed from memory at election time by black voters. Klan recruitment and membership in 1920s Chicago was the strongest among all of the northern cities.

The Hamburgs, the Sparklers, Ragen's Colts, the Aylwards, the Our Flag Club, the Lorraine Club, and other athletic associations, by their political entanglements with the Democrats and by their actions, struck fear in the Black Belt.

Richard J. Daley, just seventeen years old and a recently minted graduate of De La Salle commercial high school when the rioting broke out, remained close-mouthed to the press through the duration of his life concerning the culpability of the Hamburg AC during the violent days of July 1919. "Its purpose was social and athletic and some of the finest priests and citizens of Chicago have been members!" And that was all that "Hizzoner," the mayor, would have to say about that. When asked about the Hamburgs, the old political warhorse William Lynch, Daley's former law partner and legislative spokesman in the Illinois General Assembly, sheepishly added: "It was a great debating place. We talked about the issues of the day, national affairs, local politics and of course sports."[12]

Bombings, arson, and automobile "raids" into the Black Belt committed by the ACs west of Wentworth in the summer of 1919 escalated on July 29th after the two Hamburg stalwarts Fifth Ward Alderman McDonough and State Representative Doyle demanded that Chicago Police Superintendent John J. Garrity swear in one to two thousand special police to protect the South Side. Garrity resisted, deeming it inadvisable to recruit an army of untrained volunteers and arm them at this dangerous moment when their judgment and reliability were not "thoroughly known." Rising to his feet, McDonough loudly denounced the administration and urged upon his fellow aldermen the need for swift action during an impromptu meeting of the city council.

With his customary South Side Irish banter and bluster, McDonough told of an incursion into Bridgeport he had personally witnessed by armed black men riding in an automobile the night before at Thirty-Fifth and Wallace—by no coincidence the target of the gunmen happened to be the Hamburg headquarters where the boys held court at McQuade's saloon. In breathless excitement he spoke of a woman and her little boy standing only a few feet away from him who were struck by stray bullets. "I was lucky I didn't get it too," Doyle solemnly affirmed.[13]

"As the guns spurted fire, the muzzles looked as if they were aimed straight at me. That corner is half a mile from where colored people can get to work. What will happen when they go home at night? Remember that 35th and State Street is the heart of the most thickly populated section of colored folks in the United States! They are all well armed and the white people are not. *We must defend ourselves if the city authorities won't protect us.*"

Alderman McDonough warned the council that Chicago's black population had enough ammunition and weapons stockpiled to launch a guerilla war that could drag on for a hundred years.

In a rage, McDonough accused the Garrity-Thompson police of laxity in their prosecution of black gunmen. His demand for the immediate arrest of the auto raiders who allegedly fired upon him was ignored. McDonough was furious, and by his spoken word, the alderman roused the Colts, the Hamburgs, and the other ACs into action. If the cops could not safeguard the lives of Bridgeport and Canaryville citizens to their satisfaction, the ACs would, he reasoned. The next day the *Chicago Herald & Examiner* printed the verbatim transcript of the alderman's incendiary comments. The press had unwittingly aided and abetted a mobilization of armed thugs—many of them boys in their early teens.

The ACs quickly fanned out across the stricken riot zone. A black man who owned a candy store in the Black Belt at Thirty-Fifth and State told investigators of a verbal threat made against him inside his shop. "Remember, it's Ragen's Colts you're dealing with! We have two thousand members between Halsted Street and Cottage Grove Avenue, Forty-Third Street and Sixty-Third Street. We intend to run this district! Look out!"

Automobiles loaded with white men cradling army rifles sped down State Street firing into a crowd of black people. The marauding parties carried flasks of benzene and lit them with matches and hurled these homemade bombs at African American homes at Wentworth and Forty-Third Street in retaliation for a fire that leveled the frame homes of white stockyard workers in Canaryville and Back of the Yards. The arsonists were recruited from the ACs, and evidence of their involvement was handed over to Illinois attorney general Edward J. Brundage by deputy state fire marshal Matthew White after uniformed soldiers armed with bayonets from five Illinois regiments were ordered into the district, finally putting a stop to the mayhem on August 1st.[14]

As law and order broke down in the City of Chicago, Superintendent Garrity issued a general order to police closing all saloons, jazz cabarets, social-athletic clubs, and poolrooms where men of both races east and west of Wentworth congregated. In defiance, the Pelican Club, another well-known Bridgeport AC at 468 Wallace, tacked up a sign outside the door reading: "Pelican's Open! Please come over and arrest us!" The cops never showed up. The Our Flag Club petitioned Mayor Thompson for permission to open, but when the mayor refused them an audience, William Cannon, club vice president, said to hell with it and defiantly threw the doors open. As the jazz piano beat out a lively tune and the Our Flaggers guzzled their beer, a detail of Stockyards police finally showed up at their clubhouse at 613 West Forty-Seventh Street.

Six of the "Flag" leaders were marched to the lockup, but they were quickly released because there was no statute on the books police could charge then with. Following that latest embarrassment, the other clubs cautiously reopened one by one. By now it was August 1st and relative calm was just about restored to the South Side, until Brundage's investigation laid bare the deeper inner workings of the clubs in criminal activity, arson, and wholesale looting.

A midnight raid on the clubhouse belonging to the Sparkler's AC at 215 West Nineteenth Street had revealed the existence of an arson plot and evidence the ACs were responsible for the incendiary destruction of at least fifty-eight homes of African Americans in the riot zone. A new weapon of terror turned up—the "hand grenade torch": bricks thickly wrapped in waste paper and saturated with oil before being set afire and hurled through the front windows of the wood-frame slum houses. Gasoline torches stolen from the railroad tracks was another infernal device used to touch off a blaze. "One favorite trick was for the white mobs to start fires underneath the rear porches of Negroes' homes and call the fire department," White told reporters. "When the firemen would arrive the whites would follow them into the houses and carry off furniture, bric-a-brac and other articles. We have traced these goods to certain athletic clubs and also to the homes of white people."[15]

After receiving a reliable tip from an informant on August 3rd, soldiers from Company J of the Illinois Reserve Militia did the job the police either could not do or refused to do, by seizing five members of Ragen's Colts at Fifty-Fifth and Halsted as they raced north in an automobile, calling out to passersby, "We're going over the top at 5:00 in the Black Belt! Come watch us!" The Ragen men were pulled over and taken to the Stockyards Police Station for processing before they could carry out their threats.

Nineteen other youths ranging in age from fifteen to twenty-one were also arrested, including seven from the Sparklers AC, who provided police and arson investigators with enough information to implicate Polish and Lithuanian ACs in the Back of the Yards community, along with members of the White Rocks, the Murderers, and the Lorraine Club, who had terrorized black residents in the vicinity of Wentworth and Forty-Seventh. The Our Flag A.C, a white gang at 613 West Forty-Seventh Street holding a state charter since 1899, and the Aylward Club at 417 Racine stood accused of beating blacks coming to and from their jobs inside the Stockyards—a flashpoint of racial hostility and labor unrest throughout the tense summer months.

Superintendent Garrity, an ineffectual ex-military man, had been thrust into an uncomfortable, embarrassing position as a result of these volatile disclosures. He ordered his South Side commanders to padlock fifteen ACs, including the Colts, the Hamburgs, Our Flag, and the Lorraines, until such time as "the riot is thoroughly crushed and countermanding orders are issued from City Hall." [16]

Garrity famously threatened to ask Illinois governor Frank Lowden to revoke their club charters, but these were desultory, largely meaningless moves that stood little chance of being enacted. Garrity declared that any police officer that was found to have discriminated against blacks in the discharge of his duty would be brought before the trial board and his dismissal sought. But as an uneasy peace settled over the Black Belt and white Bridgeport, neither Garrity nor Hoyne could convincingly explain that of the first sixty-seven indictments voted against the rioters only seventeen of them were white men. "It is indeed a sad commentary on Chicago that a number of howling mobs pursued colored persons through the Loop District, two of whom just lost their lives at the hands of the mob without an arrest being made for these murders," Brundage noted.

An exhaustive report filed by the Cook County Coroner's office, and the *New York Times*, pointed to the white gangs as the major perpetrators of the arson fires. It is believed that the planning for the arson attacks originated at 5142 South Halsted Street—headquarters of Ragen's

Colts, who were a veritable army of two thousand whose reputation lived on and superseded the other long-forgotten South Side ACs.

A large but tightly knit organization, the Colts were organized as the Morgan Athletic Club in 1900 by twenty-six-year-old Frank Ragen, a tempestuous, often polarizing South Side political-spoils man elected to the Cook County Board of Commissioners in 1908. The Morgan Athletic Club, under Ragen's stewardship, claimed legitimacy through competitive team sports.

Each year the Colts sponsored an annual athletic tournament featuring track and field events at Santa Fe Park that drew upwards of twelve thousand spectators. In the summertime the Morgans played baseball games against teams from the Chicago City League and all other corners of the city. The arrival of autumn meant prairie football matchups in the city parks between the ACs and their opponents on Sunday evenings.

The "Tower Ticker," a popular, long-running *Tribune* column devoted to all things Chicago, nostalgically recalled the excitement of the leather-helmeted gridiron action as the AC "boyos" commenced battle with their opponents in a retrospective article published August 26, 1949, long after the amateur sports scene receded into the collective memory of the former athletes, their wives and sweethearts.

> It happened on the South Side with the Ragen Colts, the Polar Bears and the Hamburgs; on the West Side with the Marquettes and Austin Bullets; the Northwest Side brought out the Mozarts, the Cragins, the Logan Square Clippers, and the Titans. The Sunday afternoon games on the local prairie were reward enough. Along the sidelines the highly partisan crowds pressed closer and closer to the play, sometimes even running interference for a particularly favored local boy. The team's girlfriends passed through the crowd with collection boxes and tags for the benefit of injured players, and if the take was big enough, the visiting team would get at least carfare home. The battle was on! Those were the nights!

Veteran *Tribune* reporter George Bliss took a more sobering, less heroic look at the Colts, their rivals, and their exploits over the years in his July 15, 1955, look-back. "When the Ragens were the dominant gang on the South Side some thirty years ago, other clubs were formed as a means of protection from the Ragens and similar groups. They had definite leaders and whether they continued their activities along the lines of athletic clubs or branched off into crime groups depended much on the leaders. Many of the Ragen gang later became model citizens and outstanding civic leaders. However a good number followed the root of such members as Danny Stanton, a gangster who was shot in a saloon."[17]

Frank Ragen, a striking, and nattily attired figure who combed and parted his greased hair down the middle and elegantly draped himself in three-piece suits, conveyed an easygoing manner and pleasant smile, but when provoked he became a loud and hot-headed bully. In one incident, on September 8, 1913, after fellow commissioner Avery Conley of Evanston, Illinois, introduced a resolution to censure Ragen for conduct unbecoming during a stormy county board session, Ragen hurled a book weighing three and a half pounds at Conley, striking him in the face and breaking his nose. Ragen, a product of the South Side streets demonstrated why he was out of place trying to push his own agenda in this smoke-filled room full of North Shore Republicans. It was an encore performance, because three days earlier, while visiting the Cook County Hospital, Ragen spewed a vile epithet and blackened the eye of Wladyslaw Wieckowski, an investigator on the staff of the county agent probing allegations of widespread bribery and graft in hospital admissions. Ragen and his allies on the board stood accused of sending their friends, their political cronies, powerful business associates, and family to the hospital to receive free health care, food, clothing, shelter, and treatment for their assorted ailments any time they desired. The county commissioners oversaw the affairs of the hospital and held the fiduciary responsibility for the institution. Ragen hotly denied the charges and in a profanity-laced tirade, he screamed at board president Alexander A. McCormick, a former newspaper editor and battling Progressive reformer daring to stand up to the Ragen cabal, and state's attorney Maclay Hoyne, who had demurred from ordering his office to conduct a nonpartisan investigation.

With blistering criticism, Ragen denounced his enemies and singled out the opposition press for bringing on his present troubles. "I have always worked and talked for the underdog, and the *Post* and the *Tribune* and the [Daily] *News* has called me a yellow dog for fighting for the poor! The dirty stiffs of newspapers! They have never endorsed a decent, honest man in their lives! Now they have a man they can't handle, and they can't handle Ragen!" Casting a mean scowl in the direction of

McCormick, who called Ragen a ranked coward, he snarled: "You know what you are, a dirty lousy liar!"

The motion by the board to censure the self-important Ragen passed by a six to four margin. The defiant Colt leader sullenly marched off to the Clark Street Police Station to post a $500 bond for assaulting Wieckowski.

There was little doubt among Ragen's supporters that his edicts to the gang were ironclad, and by his wild and reckless behavior as an elected official of Cook County, he set the tone and manner of conduct for his massive South Side street army to emulate. In 1912 Ragen changed the name of the Morgan AC to the Colts in order to exploit his rising prominence in Democratic Party circles, and as a means to enforce his decrees and intimidate rivals during heated board meetings.

Called the "chief disruptor" of the county board by the Republican *Tribune*, Ragen frequently packed the meeting room with his Colts, who whistled, jeered, and hooted at rival commissioners opposed to the leader's proposals, budgetary allocations, or pet projects. In another Ragen-led contretemps that threatened to spiral out of control, several hundred Colts had to be forcibly restrained from packing the small, cramped county room during its regular meeting on December 20, 1913.

Citing city fire ordinances, board president McCormick barred the Colts from entering the chambers. "I move we let the crowd in!" Ragen screamed. "We have had that fire ordnance for twenty years and never enforced it here! I demand a roll-call."[18] The roll call was read and Ragen's motion failed. His face turned purple with rage.

A year later, Ragen announced his candidacy for board president in order to oust McCormick, his hated rival, in the fall 1914 general election. "Watch me get 50,000 names on the petition!" Ragen boasted. "Didn't I get raises for the scrubwomen, the deputy bailiffs and the elevator men? I've been campaigning for months. Why I never make less than four or five stags [testimonial dinners, public appearances, etc.] a week. I swing the clubs for them and tell them stories and they're all for me! If you want to get in good, go for the big job. I'm for the soft chair and the big roll-top desk!"[19] That was his aim all along of course, and he nearly pulled it off until common sense prevailed.

Tiring of Ragen's bizarre outbursts, Cook County voters wisely elected Democrat Peter Reinberg, the respected former president of the Chicago

Board of Education, to the presidency of the county board. He succeeded McCormick and restored proper decorum to county board deliberations by removing Ragen from his membership on the finance committee because of Ragen's "picturesque arguments against economy." Reinberg went ahead and laid the groundwork for the creation of the vast fifty-five-thousand-acre Cook County Forest Preserve system.

Rejected by the electorate and rival factions within the Democratic Party, Ragen's credibility was further eroded by press reports of the unseemly conduct of his Colts out in the Stockyards District. He ended up in hot water with the Juvenile Protective Association on January 2, 1918, after renting the Chicago Coliseum and throwing open the doors to soldiers, sailors, and the general public for a New Year's Eve revel that turned into an all-night debauch. War-time Prohibition had closed all of the saloons—or so it was said—but Ragen had secured a "special bar permit" courtesy of his downtown political allies.

In his scholarly study of "1,313 Gangs in Chicago" for the University of Chicago, urban sociologist Frederic Milton Thrasher noted that "in the days before Prohibition it was customary for these groups to obtain special bar permits and sell intoxicants at their dances, which on such occasions tended to be unspeakably bad. The liquor produced a complete relaxation of all restraint and the wildest debauchery often followed the dance with no attempt at control by the police, who themselves had often imbibed freely at the improvised bars. Some dances of this type, promoted by the larger clubs were mammoth affairs and were held even in the Coliseum."[20]

The Coliseum box office remained open until three in the morning, and police made little effort to put a stop to the sex party inside the hall. It was reported that boys of twelve and thirteen, consorting with prostitutes, were freely served.

Drunken young women on the verge of passing out were sexually assaulted in private booths, but Ragen answered the stern admonitions of Jesse Binford, superintendent of the Juvenile Protective Association, by threatening her organization with a libel lawsuit. "I do not know who the Juvenile Protective Association is, or who runs it, but if there is any way of making it pay for its false statements I intend to employ it!"[21]

The Juvenile Protective Association produced evidence showing that 5,601 special bar permits were issued in 1914 and 3,650 a year later.

City statutes required that no club would be entitled to obtain a special bar permit more than six times a year, but with the contrivance of politicians and corrupt cops the measure was little more than a "scoff law"—a standing joke. This fact was underscored by the issuance of a permit to a man who had been dead for two weeks. "It sometimes happens that after investigation the police refuse to grant a special bar permit," wrote Thrasher. "For instance, in one case they refused a permit to a certain club because at one of their previous dances two young girls had been outraged. The officers of the club then secured the services of the alderman of their ward who interceded for them with the chief of police, and a permit was granted by him over the heads of the police committee which made the investigation."

During the March 1915 Coliseum "ball," representatives of the Henry Booth House, a social-reform agency, joined with several club women from the South Side to observe the yearly bacchanal. They expressed the opinion that "No Roman saturnalia could have been wilder than that dance. We thought we had improved conditions a little but a glimpse at the revel of the Ragen Colts showed how mistaken we were." The relationship between the Colts and other gangs holding their own soirees and the management of the public halls was reciprocal. The owners of these establishments depended on the proceeds received from the dances as a major source of revenue.

Hostile press coverage of these events underscored the Colts deeper underworld involvement and firmly implanted in the public mind that team sports, social dancing, and other recreational activities masked a more sinister side to the club, despite the usual excuses and denials from Ragen and club president Jimmy O'Brien. "We know that we have a bad reputation," O'Brien alibied to a *Daily News* reporter on August 13, 1919. "And why? Because during the war 500 of our members went to war in the 32nd Division and the gaps they left in the membership had to be filled up, and a lot of young fellows were taken into the club. We know that some of them raised Cain and worse. And the reputation they acquired has made things extremely difficult for us. Now nobody under eighteen years can become a member of this club. Also they must have work and deport themselves decently. Otherwise their membership is taken away."

By 1922 the club was in disarray under Jimmy O'Brien's leadership. Embroiled in interparty political brinkmanship and weary of supplying personal recognizance bonds to jailed Colts locked up in the county stir for their usual Saturday night mischief, Frank Ragen bowed out. Hugh E. Mulligan from South Sangamon Street, and an AC member since 1917, marshaled his resources and succeeded in keeping the club viable for the next five years. Mulligan was one of three AC officers designated as Sergeants at Arms, and a prominent labor union official with the Asbestos Worker's Union and Local 17 of the Heat and Frost Insulators for nearly forty years. An avid sportsman with close ties to Knute Rockne and Notre Dame football, Mulligan provided football players with scarce jobs during the Great Depression.

Despite soothing assurances from O'Brien and Mulligan's honorable intentions, their efforts belied the Colts' treacherous nature and a record of criminality in the post-riot era. Colt activities ranged from adolescent hooliganism to mob action to the close interplay between labor union racketeering and bootlegging.

During the ragged Prohibition period several notable Colt alumni graduated to organized crime. One of them, Joseph "Dynamite Joe" Brooks, a member of the Electrical Workers Union, Local 134, operated a saloon at 5152 South Halsted near the Ragen headquarters. He joined forces with the Klondike O'Donnell gang after leaving the Colts. Brooks became an early casualty of the 1920s beer wars. In the company of Cook County police officer Edward Harmening, the ex-Colt was shot down by rival rum-runner Frankie McErlane in Marquette Park on December 23, 1925.

Nearly thirty years later, in December 1954, Joe's surviving brother, Robert Brooks, told a city council committee investigating labor union racketeering that he was "the boss" of the city Bureau of Electrical Inspections, although at the time he was not listed as an employee on the city payrolls.[22]

A parade of underage Colts, mere adolescents deemed "too young for membership" by Jimmy O'Brien, passed through the boys' court, charged with a myriad of crimes. "The Boys' Court is a clinic for the study of criminals in the making," explained Judge Charles F. McKinley on June 23, 1923. "Every boy who goes wrong is a public liability.

Something is wrong when more than 2,000 boys come into this court in the first six months of the year." Among the two thousand juveniles processed through the system were four Colts arrested on weapons charges. They had positioned themselves as snipers outside of the Stockyards Police Station to take aim on uniformed officers.[23]

With live ammunition in their pistols, they fired upon the bluecoats from the bushes in a target practice exercise. Miraculously no one was killed. The four underage thugs established alibis and were summarily dismissed by Judge Francis Borelli, who issued a stern note of warning. "If you call yourselves an athletic club you should be sportsmen," he said. "Sportsmen don't shoot at policemen from ambush."[24]

Proud of their tribal identity, the Irish-Catholic Colts engaged in periodic mob actions to defend their honor and their religious beliefs. In September 1921 the Colts hung in effigy a white-sheeted Ku Klux Klansman as several thousand Back of the Yards residents looked on. The triggering incident had nothing to do with the sad state of race relations in Chicago, or a sympathetic gesture on the part of the Colts to mend broken fences with the African American community. Rather, it was the long-standing Klan prejudice against the Roman Catholic Church that had incurred their ire.

Not long after, in February 1922, forty Colts primed for action boarded an elevated train bound for the North Side intent upon "invading" the Swedish Viking Sports Club at 3466 North Sheffield Avenue and banging the heads of the hated Protestants. They had been tipped off about a speech scheduled to be delivered by one Eli Erickson assailing the wartime record of the Knights of Columbus, and a sweeping indictment of the Catholic Church and the papacy. The marauding Colts stormed into the hall. They hurled a wooden chair at Erickson on the dais, narrowly missing his head. They hurled bricks and rotting vegetables, and overturned tables. The Colts slugged inoffensive members of the audience—an estimated gathering of a thousand listeners. The Town Hall Police District riot squad rushed in to arrest three Colts and finally succeeded in dispersing the mob. During the wild melee, Erickson, besieged and outnumbered, managed to slip out through the back door, narrowly escaping serious injury and possible murder.

More serious incidents of gun play followed. On March 7, 1926, police raided the Ragen clubhouse after the fatal shooting of James Thomas, an African American man they had lured to the rear of their establishment. Colt members plied him with drinks until he passed out, then shot him three times. Believing Thomas dead, the Colts dumped the severely wounded man at Fifty-Eighth Street and Normal Avenue where police eventually found him—barely alive. Questioned on his deathbed at Cook County Hospital, Thomas supplied police with an accurate description of bootlegger Hugh "Stubby" McGovern, a famous Colt alumnus known to police as the "bad boy of the South Side," and pickpocket Dave "Yiddles" Miller, another hoodlum from the West Side.

McGovern, who would be shot twice in the back inside the Granada Inn at Sixty-Eighth and Cottage Grove Avenue by gangster George Mahoney just two years later on December 30, 1928, never answered for the murder of Thomas although Thomas's blood stains smeared the floor of the clubhouse.

The cautious and conservative *Tribune* headlined a March 8, 1926, story of the Thomas shooting in such a way that would maximize Ragen's embarrassment and discomfort: "Four Morons Kill Negro at Ragen Colts' Hangout." The glorious gridiron afternoons of wholesome prairie football games were coming to end. During the 1920s' bootlegging wars, the Colts had degenerated into a criminal gang of armed brigands; not that they weren't that all along.

It took another eleven months and a second deadly shooting inside the clubhouse to finally break the power of the Colts. When the police showed up at 5142 South Halsted on January 31, 1927, to investigate the shooting of thirty-year-old fugitive Thomas Shields, they located a cache of shotguns, pistols, cartridges with dum-dum bullets, a stick of dynamite, and a length of fuse. Shields had been shot through the neck. The wounded man, a member of the Ralph Sheldon bootlegging gang, staggered out the door and made it as far as a nearby barber shop. An ambulance conveyed him to the German Deaconess Hospital, where, during interrogation, he refused to I.D. the shooters or even admit that the assault had occurred in the Colts' clubhouse. The cops knew better. Fresh bullet holes speckled the walls and a trail of blood led to the back door.

William Emmet Dever, a reform-minded Democrat who had succeeded the scandal-plagued William Hale Thompson into office in 1923, expressed outrage at the state of affairs and the rash of shootings involving club men, and immediately ordered the law department into action. City of Chicago Corporation counsel Francis X. Busch succeeded in taking away the political protection long afforded the Colts and the other ACs by dissolving the numerous injunctions that had previously barred police from conducting periodic raids on the gang headquarters. The strict enforcement of injunctions allowed the clubs to serve intoxicants in violation of the Prohibition laws, and to store weapons and other illegal contraband without the fear of police raiding parties confiscating the stash. "We have been making determined effort since October 1, 1925 to dissolve injunctions of that kind," Busch told the press. "Within the next two or three months we hope to clean all of them up and prevent the issuance of any more except in very extraordinary cases."[25]

For Frank Ragen the political reverberations from the two shootings convinced him that now was the opportune time to disband the Colts, or what was left of them. In August 1927 Ragen announced that his membership base had dwindled from several thousand to only twelve active members, a claim that seems rather dubious. Defending their honor and reputation, Ragen described the Colts as a force for social good. "The Colts strong box was always open to any person in need and they held Christmas festivals for children," he said. "Many of them who were members became famous in athletic fields. One of those was Hugo Bezdik, now coach of the University of Pennsylvania football team. When the war broke out 1,100 members immediately enlisted in the army and navy and the war records of those members is one of high bravery."[26] It is remarkable that the number of Colts called to duty in the trenches of the Western front in 1917 had swollen from the five hundred members cited by Jimmy O'Brien in 1919 to eleven hundred, by Ragen's fuzzy calculations, eight years later.[27]

His reputation and political ambition sullied by the hospital scandal, Frank Ragen left the Cook County Board in 1920 in order to storm the barricades on a new front that seemed certain to keep his name prominent before the public. He appointed himself titular head of the Meter Readers, Billers and Collectors Union Local 17224, founded on February 21, 1920. "Big Tim" Murphy, a towering bully from the Stockyards District who dabbled in bookmaking, armed robbery, and electoral politics (he served one term in the Illinois General Assembly), anointed his South Side pal Frank Ragen as the boss of the newly founded local. Frank Dunn, the brother of fur thief and suspected murderer "Slippery Sonny" Dunn, hired on as the secretary of the local.

Hoodlum labor boss Murphy had blood on his hands, and everyone in the trades knew it. Murphy and three cohorts were jailed on suspicion of murdering Maurice "Moss" Enright, a labor slugger, convicted murderer, and secretary of the Pipe's Trade Council outside his home on Garfield Boulevard on February 3, 1920.[28] A year later Murphy went to prison for a $125,000 mail heist at the Dearborn Street train station. Big Tim and Frank Ragen supplied the necessary "muscle" to advance union causes by force if necessary. In the opening decades of the twentieth century, organized labor was intertwined with the criminal underworld and men of questionable repute.

"Umbrella Mike" Boyle ruled ten thousand city electrical workers with impunity.[29] Despite a 1920 conviction on antitrust charges and six months of jail time in 1923 due to jury-fixing charges in the corruption trial of Illinois governor Len Small, Boyle succeeded in winning high wages for electrical workers. On July 12, 1921, he plunged the City of Chicago into total darkness and virtually shut down the city during a wildcat strike that was broken only after Boyle was threatened with prosecution for murder and manslaughter if loss of life resulted.

Mentored by both Boyle and Murphy in the tactics of divisive labor vs. capital confrontation, Ragen boldly threatened Samuel Insull, president of Commonwealth Edison, with a job action that he predicted would "close down" his company. Ragen predicted that Boyle's Local 134 (four thousand strong) would join forces with his 175 meter readers and his most feared sluggers and brawlers to cripple Edison unless his own local received formal recognition. "It is unfortunate that our boys are being misled by outside agitators," commented Louis Ferguson, ComEd vice president. "We have 90 meter readers and none has come to us with any demands for grievances. If they have any real grievances they can be rectified."[30]

Faced with the impending (but separate) strike of several thousand gas workers, Insull and his negotiators reached a quick settlement to avoid a potential catastrophic situation. In comparison, Insull considered Ragen a minor irritation and of little consequence. Despite dire threats from Ragen, unconcerned ComEd executives mailed circulars to their electricity customers in Chicago providing necessary instruction on how to read a meter. The strike of Ragen's meter readers ended quickly.

After concluding his foray into union organizing with little to show for his troubles, Frank Ragen lived out his remaining years on the South Side quietly and rather uneventfully. After a three-year illness, the ex-Colt leader and force of nature, now seventy-four and mostly forgotten, peacefully passed away at his sister's home on July 1, 1945.

Another year passed. Then a tragedy on the mean streets of Chicago befell his brother James M. on June 24, 1946. Again the Ragen family name became prominent in press circles after James, the owner of the Continental Press, a leased wire service distributing racetrack information to gambling parlors and bookie joints across the United States, was ambushed and cut down by gunmen concealed in a delivery truck while driving his car near the intersection of Thirty-Ninth and State Streets. Before being shot, the aging gambling czar told police and news editors that Jake Guzik, the West Side gang boss and one of Al Capone's successors, had targeted him for death as a way for the Chicago mob to seize control of the lucrative racing wire. Jim Ragen enjoyed a virtual monopoly of the business since purchasing controlling interest from Moses Annenberg in 1939. "I always had a thousand dollars to every dollar Guzik had," Ragen bragged.[31] His business grossed an estimated $60 million a year.

Though seriously wounded, doctors at Michael Reese Hospital gave him a fifty-fifty chance at survival, but hopes for recovery evaporated on August 14th when doctors pronounced Ragen, sixty-five, dead of mercury poisoning in his room. The deadly substance had been found in blood plasma used in normal blood transfusions. There was little doubt in the minds of the police dicks that a person or persons unknown had slipped into Ragen's room and poisoned him.[32] The Continental Press went out of business in 1953. James Ragen Jr., heir to his father's depleted fortune, had already fled to Paris, France, in order to escape the same deadly fate at the hands of the Chicago mob. The Ragen era, bridging the netherworld of gang war, crime, politics, and union activism, ended for good.

Exchanging their knickers and brickbats for voter registration lists and white lapel carnations pinned into their brown wool suits, other former Ragen AC members matriculated into positions of civic importance in their later years. Municipal court judge Joseph A. Graber presided over the boys' court; Al F. Gorman, a lifelong career politician, represented the Back of the Yards in the state senate; and former alderman William O'Toole pledged his allegiance to the Colts and thrived on these connections amid constant criticism from the downtown newspapers of his machine-style tactics in the city council.

Reunions of Bridgeport's politically connected AC / gang members as they and their kin advanced into old age in the 1930s and 1940s inevitably touched upon nostalgic turn-of-the century memories of the rollicking good times they had all once enjoyed; the camaraderie, the dances and picnics, prairie football games, the lifelong "old neighborhood" friendships and the marriages that followed. Indignant and angry denials accompanied the slightest accusation that the old ACs were anything more than an up-and-up group of good-natured lads who loved their sports, their beer, and their roughhousing.

The alumni of the Ragen Colts held their first celebratory reunion extolling their accomplishments at the Saddle & Sirloin Club restaurant in the Stockyards during the winter of 1934. The dinner attracted over three hundred Morgan AC / Colt members, and the success of the evening inspired them to turn this into a yearly affair.

Each year thereafter, the celebratory "Old Timer's Night and Homecoming" reunion at Mark White Square at Thirtieth and Halsted reunited thousands of expatriate Bridgeport, Canaryville, and Back of the Yards residents to the old neighborhood to share fond reminiscences. Amid the hoopla of band music and speech making, the night of September 8, 1939, Robert Casey recalled that Mark White Square was the setting for one of the roughest, most explosive gang fights of the 1890s, pitting the Dashiells against the Bridgeporters in a bare-knuckle brawl.

"Gang fights were different then. You fought with your fists and the best man won," Mike Bozen, pipe fitter and former member of the Croatian division of the Hamburg Club, wistfully recalled in a published interview with a *Tribune* reporter on April 10, 1978. Many of the aging Bridgeporters and Back of the Yards men subscribed to this questionable belief that somehow gang fighting was socially acceptable behavior just as long as guns and knives were kept out of the quarrel. Ethnic differences were usually settled in this customary manner, but guns occasionally came into play. In the late 1940s teenage boys of Polish extraction battled the Italians and Irish in Bridgeport and Back of the Yards. After being shot by a Polish lad in August 1950, fifteen-year-old Ray Houlihan told Chicago police captain Martin Mullin, "I've been in gang fights since I was five. Out here we have to fight."[33] The Cook County state's attorney, in response, attempted to join together boys of all nationalities in an "All-American Gang" that would utilize the resources of the Chicago Boys Clubs and the city parks.

The South Side old-timers steadfastly defended the honor of the ACs and denied that they were street gangs when the historical legacy of race baiting, violence, and gang fighting suggests otherwise.

One of the last visible reminders of Chicago's unsolvable racial divide, and the political legacy of former members of the Hamburgs, the Colts, and the lesser-known AC members who had risen high in public life to enforce segregation in the latter decades of the twentieth century, was the construction of the Dan Ryan Expressway (Interstate 90/94), connecting Chicago to Indiana and points further east.

It was no coincidence that the massive highway carved out of Wentworth Avenue became the traditional boundary line separating white Bridgeport from black Chicago decades after the high tide of the South Side AC era. The Reverend Jesse Louis Jackson and other prominent African American leaders have long contended that the Dan Ryan and the adjacent Robert Taylor housing project hugging the east side of the Ryan (until its demolition in the new millennium) formed a "wall of segregation" to protect white Bridgeport and other communities west of the expressway.[34] They are probably right in their assessment.

Against the tide of history and the profound racial change that overtook the South Side after World War I, pockets of AC culture rooted in the tradition of neighborhood loyalties, parish, and faded glories of the sporting life struggle to survive. The Hamburg AC is a cultural institution in Bridgeport—a multigenerational social club steeped in the tradition of fraternalism, ethnic identity, church, neighborhood pride, sports, and the art of conversation. City workers and some of the Chicago's most prominent men are lifelong members.

"The Hamburg Athletic Club is an institutionalized gang in every sense of the term," wrote a skeptical John Hagedorn. "It has persisted despite changes in leadership; has a younger generation waiting to join; has built an organization with multiple political and social roles;

has adapted to changing conditions of being on the outside to being consummate political insiders to now being in a fierce fight within the Machine with the rising Latino voter bloc."[35]

A vacant lot overrun by weeds, broken sidewalks, and wild grass mark the location of the former Halsted Street headquarters of the Ragen club in the Back of the Yards. It is a rather forlorn, eerily quiet scene of urban desolation. But less than a mile away, on Forty-Seventh Street, due east of Halsted at Wallace, a modest, but perfectly maintained single-story brick building in a racially changing neighborhood prominently bears the name "Flags Club." It stands adjacent to an empty lot that was once the original 1919 "Our Flag A.C" clubhouse. Overhead, the stars and stripes gently flap in the breeze.

Further to the east, the Grand Boulevard community (encompassing Bronzeville—the former "Black Belt" of Chicago) contends with raging gang violence and a spiraling murder rate unparalleled, even in the tense July 1919 days of bloodshed and riot. The community witnessed thirty-eight homicides related to street gang activity during a five-year period from 2009 to 2014. Gentrification and slum clearance has done little to stem a rising tide of gang-related shootings in the city's oldest and presumably most stable African American neighborhood.

4

MAXWELL STREET, THE WEST SIDE TERROR DISTRICT, 1860–1930

Squalor and crime congealed on Chicago's West Side, the fastest-growing worker colony in the city in the years 1848 to 1860. Commencing operations in 1859, the Chicago City Railway and the West Division Railway opened up this sandy wasteland on the West Side of Chicago to the poor immigrant classes segregated from the well-to-do living along the lake shore and the fledgling North Division, just across the river from the original Fort Dearborn stockade. Here, southern and eastern Europe transplants congregated along the western and southern fringe of downtown and nearest the south and north banks of the Chicago River.

Realtors valued the cheap wooden dwellings lying south of Monroe Street and west of Wells at $1,000 on average. They were a powerful lure for the Italians, Jews, Greeks, Poles, Bohemians, and Slovaks coming to Chicago seeking work in the factories hugging the polluted waterway where deposit of animal entrails and waste from the stockyards fouled the river, and the South Side "Bridgeport stench" wafted to the east, west, and southwest. Edith Abbott estimated that in 1870, two hundred thousand people lodged in forty thousand jerry-built wood-frame cottages, constructed two to the lot.

The grimy appearance of the emerging slum sections of the city south and west of Madison Street in October 1871 belied the image of fiscal prosperity, industry, and commerce within the central business district when a sudden firestorm of flame rained down and destroyed nearly all of Chicago. The Great Chicago Fire erupted inside a tiny hay barn belonging to Catherine O'Leary, the "milk woman" of Conley's Patch (who peddled containers of milk supplied by her cows) to the neighbors living along Jefferson Street. Within the confines of this dirt-poor section of the West Division, Patrick and Catherine O'Leary raised their brood of four children in a ramshackle cottage at 137 DeKoven Street.

Survivors and the descendants of survivors of that night of pyrrhic destruction related countless stories and myths, lies and legends about the true origins of the fire in the succeeding years. Whispered rumors gave way to an enduring fable, and while much of that legend traced the blame to a clumsy milk cow kicking over an oil lantern while being attended to by its owner, the apocryphal tale is grounded in actual events. Other bizarre notions that have surfaced over the years, including the theory that a comet striking down from the heavens set the city on fire, have inspired further debate.

When interviewed about the matter in the 1920s, "Big" Jim O'Leary, Catherine's wayfaring son, who ruled a deluxe Stockyards gambling resort in the early years of the twentieth century and commanded an army of handbook operators clocking bets on horse races across the city and in northwest Indiana, blamed spontaneous combustion of the freshly laid timothy hay in the loft. It is widely accepted that the fire had its origins in the Patch. The O'Leary family had gone off to bed at eight o'clock the evening of October 8, oblivious to the presence of several of the neighborhood "youngbloods" dancing and carrying on at a welcome-home party for one Denis Connors in the McLaughlin dwelling, occupying the same lot as the O'Learys. A local character, Daniel "Peg Leg" Sullivan, the one-legged drayman from across the street, known to drink excessively, curse, and smoke, is held accountable by revisionist historians as the perpetrator of the fire. Sullivan, according to the most recent and accepted version of events, filched some milk from inside the shed where Mrs. O'Leary kept five cows and a horse. While doing so, fallen ash from his pipe allegedly ignited the timothy hay.

Late in life, Mary Callahan broke a long silence and admitted that she was one of the young people who broke away from the McLaughlin gathering to steal a pail of milk from the O'Leary barn in order to make punch. The McLaughlins had run out of milk, and grocery stores in those days were scarce. Denis Connors, unfamiliar with milking a cow, fumbled in his attempt and the animal reared back and kicked the kerosene lantern into the hay. Their harmless prank had turned deadly. Fear overtook them. Denis Connors fled Chicago the next day. Mary Callahan departed for Sheboygan to live with relatives until the storm died down, and did not return until the entire city had been rebuilt.

If this is true, then Sullivan is a hero and not a scapegoat. At 9:15 p.m. "Peg Leg," who had been sitting contentedly on the plank-board sidewalk across the street smoking his pipe and enjoying the fiddle music at the McLaughlin dwelling, raced to the rear of the O'Leary property and furiously pounded on the door, alerting the family to the blazing inferno in the back barn. In a signed affidavit Sullivan swore his innocence of the entire matter, saying that he had tried to save the animals after noticing the blaze from across the street. He said he managed to rescue only one calf, before warning the family of the imminent danger.

Within hours, the fire had devastated the gas works, Conley's Patch, the industrial properties hugging the river, the entire downtown Chicago commercial district, and would spill over into the fashionable lakefront residential section of Terrace Row and the emerging North Side before the last ember was extinguished two days later on October 10.

Firefighter Jimmy Reese, one of the last surviving members of Fire Department Engine Company 9, told reporters in a 1934 interview that neighborhood hooligans were responsible. "Why I saw the whole bunch of loafers who started that fire," Reese said nearly fifty years later. "They were all drunk. Those fellows had been drinking all afternoon in O'Leary's barn, and smoking their pipes. Some sparks of burning tobacco—they didn't have cigarettes in those days—got into the hay and set off the barn. The whole bunch was standing there round the hydrant at Forquer and DeKoven Streets and I know because I heard them talking among themselves."[1]

Reese's recollections raise interesting possibilities. Could the young men speaking among themselves have come from the McLaughlin party, or were they a local gang of Irish-American lads up to no good?

"Although we intended no harm, we couldn't tell what might be done to us," Mary Callahan confided, "and when we heard that they were giving away free tickets to get out of town we went."[2]

Mrs. O'Leary, her family, her descendants, and the wretched cow were left to shoulder the blame for the infamy and to endure the attending disgrace brought upon their good name for generations to come.

Within two days of the fire the *Chicago Times* was back on the street and in full circulation. Mrs. O'Leary, the paper described, is "an Irish hag of seventy" (she was only thirty-five at the time of the fire). They held her personally accountable for the conflagration that left three hundred persons dead, reduced to smoldering ash 17,450 buildings (nearly all less than three stories in height)—roughly twenty-one hundred acres of land or 3.3 square miles of city real estate, rendering more than a hundred thousand residents homeless.

Harassed to the point of madness, Catherine and Patrick O'Leary sold their house and moved to 5133 Halsted Street in the Stockyards District where "nobody would know them." They lived out the remainder of their days in quiet solitude, shunning the press and curiosity seekers demanding from them the "real story."

The devout members of the religious community, the Prohibitionists, the Committee of Seventy (a blue-ribbon panel appointed to safeguard the morals of the community by discouraging saloon drinking), the anti-immigration Know Nothings, and the zealous Sunday School / Maine Law crusaders, compared the devastation of Chicago to the destruction of Sodom and Gomorrah. Had not God's vengeance struck down the wicked and immoral elements of the city lurking within the Hairtrigger Block and Wells Street?

The "wastrel Irish" and all other suspicious foreign-born "anarchists" and saloon imbibers that the mercantile class and patricians held responsible for the moral turpitude were surely to blame, were they not? The prevailing view from the pulpit and many mercantile capitalists held that this fire holocaust of biblical proportion would occasion a great rebuilding and usher in a new age of spirituality with a renewal of moral precepts.

"With the saloons closed, the temptation would be removed and the Lord's Day observed as it should be," declared Judge S. B. Gookins to a gathering of the Committee of Fifteen in the Second Presbyterian

Church on October 10, 1872. "Crime would be diminished and the devil's stamp removed from Chicago. The moral and religious people had heretofore been inactive on the temperance question; they recognized that drunkenness was to be deprecated; still did not seem inclined to aid the authorities in carrying out the laws in their spirit. Their inertness was deplorable."[3]

Visionaries confidently asserted that the fire was a hidden blessing to Chicago, a cleansing and healing force to stimulate energetic expansion and summon to the city creative men of talent, drive, and ambition to build a coming "utopia." Sunday closing, as advocated by the Committees of Fifteen and Seventy, seemed the logical first step to instill God into the hearts of the sinners.

Amid the prevailing optimism that the dawn of a new age of purity and spiritual renewal was at hand, there was a shared hope that the holdup gangs terrorizing the roads leading into the city, the "Break a Day Johnnies," the prostitutes of Fourth Avenue and Wells Street, and the tinhorn gamblers and faro dealers plying their trade inside the old Richmond House Hotel on South Water Street or congealed within the upper floors of McCormick's Building would be vanquished forever. No longer, they predicted, would the citizens of the world narrowly view Chicago as the "tough among American cities," as Lincoln Steffens described it in 1904.

A social nirvana, free of saloons, attendant vice and criminal gangs, Chicago would never become. When the sun went down on the 10th of October 1871, two thousand unlicensed establishments were already selling alcohol to the burned-out, homeless victims. Saloon brothels and gambling dens opened for business in hastily built wooden shacks on the edge of Lake Michigan while gangs of men looted and pillaged ruined properties in search of valuables.

Author James O'Donnell Bennett described the "ultimate in human wickedness" unleashed upon Chicago once the fire ended. "Then as now Chicago harbored a ruthlessly tough element, and again then as now, it paid a heavy penalty for its toleration of that element. Savage looting broke out and savage was the punishment of the criminals when they were caught in the act. Some of them set new fires in order to commit robbery in the areas outside the areas already burning." The *Tribune* posted a notice on October 11, 1871, advising that "two men who were caught trying to set fire to the Jesuit church on the West Side were disposed of without ceremony and the lookers-on were pleased to say 'served 'em right.'" Without ceremony meant that the offenders were either lynched or shot.

The sudden and shocking appearance of gambling dens and brothels outraged sensibilities and triggered embarrassing memories of the old Sands District, wiped out by "Long John" Wentworth fourteen years earlier. Near Canal Street and Randolph—four blocks west of the Hairtrigger Block, gaudy burlesque shows drawing the ire of censors were in full operation within two months of the fire.

The rebuilding of the central city with brick, steel, and mortar steadily progressed and the press accounts of the city's resiliency were reported in glowing terms, but the human toll was fearful. The homeless borrowed heavily to construct new dwellings at high prices for labor and material. Several hard winters accompanied the fire. An epizootic outbreak killed off thousands of horses and threw scores of drivers into the ranks of the unemployed. Then at the worst possible moment, the Panic of 1873 swept down upon the nation with gale force. Manufacturing plants were shuttered. Throngs of desperate, hungry people took to the streets demanding relief from an impotent city administration operating under the deceptive moniker of the "People's Party"—a coalition of liquor men and gamblers opposed to Sunday closings and crackdowns on gaming parlors. Mayor Harvey Doolittle Colvin, a tool of the powerful gambling boss Michael Cassius McDonald, had not the vaguest notion of how to run the city's affairs. His one-issue, "liberal thinking" administration was bloated, corrupt, and a scandal-ridden disgrace.

The years 1873 to 1879 represented the worst economic downturn in U.S. history up to that point in time. The nation sank into a wretched six-year depression, and in Chicago the effects of it reduced the value of homes and made it all but impossible for people to pay off their debt and tax obligation. For many owners of scorched land where houses once stood, their properties were sold to developers for far less than what they were originally worth as a desperate measure to reduce indebtedness.

Outside of the central business district the pace of new home building for middle-income wage earners lagged, even as the general population (and immigrant population) continued its upward rise from 334,000 in

1870 to 503,000 in 1880. The effects of the Panic upon the stricken city did not begin to ease up until 1879. During these hard years, thousands of laborers and unskilled working men lacked employment or the means to put food on the table, creating a permanently displaced class with a resulting dramatic escalation in crime. Between 1871 and 1886, the police department more than doubled in size from 451 to 1,036 and the corresponding arrest rate rose from twenty-six thousand to forty-four thousand in the same period.

Poor housing conditions and the want of clean, single-family residences providing proper sanitation and safe streets contributed to the rising tide of lawlessness. The sturdy and impressive commercial buildings arising with pomp and grandeur in the downtown streets failed to mask the plague spots of the West and South Divisions. The naive hope that the new Chicago might live up to utopian expectations and become more than just another segregated city divided by income, class, and ethnicity were permanently dashed. Indeed, in many ways the new city evolved into something far more terrible than the one before it.

Homeless victims had to make due living in the post-fire slum areas that had arisen west of downtown as a consequence of the well-meaning but misdirected intentions of the Citizen's Aid Committee, its shelter subcommittee, and the Chicago Relief & Aid Society (CRAS). The society, the city's oldest private agency distributing food and clothing through local offices, opened in North, South, and West Divisions. In the eighteen months following the fire, CRAS distributed nearly $4.5 million to an estimated 160,000 people. There was natural reluctance on the part of many immigrant poor to appeal directly to the Relief & Aid Society because of the inherent hopelessness of challenging well-defined class divisions. Founded by city elites, the society favored the "better people"—native-born, English-speaking residents and northern Europeans, providing for them accordingly in the belief that they were industrious, churchgoing teetotalers, free of the wages of sin and more likely to remain gainfully employed without becoming a continuous burden on the resources of the society.

Superintendent C. G. Truesdell of the Relief & Aid Society outlined the stated mission, which was to provide only "temporary assistance." He justified his rationale for formally excluding the most destitute in an interview with the *Tribune* on February 14, 1875. "Of course we have to investigate carefully to guard against imposition, and then, besides we have to discriminate between those who naturally belong to us and those who require aid from the County Agents. People inflicted with incurable diseases, rendering them permanently dependent and paupers who are shipped here from other cities are not proper claimants upon the county. We have a number of trained visitors whose duty it is to investigate every application for assistance."

The object of the society was not to support paupers in danger of being classified as vagrants and subject to arrest but to furnish aid to the "worthy poor"—families who under "normal circumstances" would have been self-supporting. The *Chicago Globe* revealed the extent of the society's discrimination against certain ethnic groups deemed objectionable in a January 21, 1889, review of "City Charity." "The Germans, Irish, Americans and Scandinavians head the list of nationalities assisted and the Poles appear at the foot of the list, with no Jews or Chinamen on the list at all."

Truesdell provided the *Globe* with a disturbing profile of the "typical people" the society chose to serve, and those they intentionally ignored.

> Most of our people are plain poor people, struggling as best they can for a decent existence. We have few if any cases of tumble-down tenement-houses, with garrets and cellars swarming with thieves, drunkards, and of course paupers living like beasts; a dozen or twenty men, women and children in a single room reeking with filth, drinking quarreling, and fighting at all hours of the day and night. Some of the applicants are filthy and ignorant and give no promise of improvement. *Relief will only do harm to such persons, and we never do anything for them, unless it is to administer to their immediate necessities and then turn them over to the county agent.*
>
> The recipients of our charity mainly live in little cottages or parts of them, and in flats or clean tenement houses comfortably arranged for four or five, perhaps eight to ten families. Their children attend the public schools and there is an air of respectability about them, in some cases refinement.[4]

Chicago was slow to take the necessary actions to regulate and improve the quality of tenement housing. It was not until 1902 that the city council enacted ordinances to proscribe building codes that established standards and guidelines for heating, ventilation, the addition of fire escapes, fireproof roofing, wider hallways, and more than one stairway.[5]

For many of the ignored, forgotten, and ragged poor on the brink of starvation, the only place to bunk down at night in the bitterly cold winters of 1872 and 1873 were two Relief & Aid lodging houses opened at 14 Union Street and at Clark and Harrison on the southern edge of downtown. These two ill-equipped and drafty buildings accommodated a transient, homeless population sleeping side by side. The alternative arrangement, however unpleasant it might have been, was a ninety-day stretch in the Bridewell for a conviction on a charge of vagrancy. For a number of unfortunates it got them through the winter. William Penn Nixon's *Chicago Inter-Ocean* lumped the homeless and unemployed together with gamblers and flesh peddlers in a series of editorials published in August and September 1873. The Republican paper upbraided the justices of the peace for their perceived leniency in allowing vagrants to roam free.

"They are a vicious set, these fellows and they fare sumptuously off of the earnings of the gaming table or the ill-gotten gains of fallen women," the *Inter-Ocean* editorialized on September 5th. "The city authorities have become fully impressed with the necessity of ridding the city of the useless class of our population which flourishes on the property of our citizens and on the gullibility or rural victims. If the law can be brought to deal severely with these culprits, our community and our visitors will be allowed a comparative immunity from their depredations."

Stern measures and the threat of jail confinement left only the county agent on West Madison Street and the Chicago Good Samaritan Society, with limited resources, to work with those most severely challenged by poverty and homelessness. All nationalities living in Chicago were represented in the books of the county agent. Four-fifths of the applicants were foreign born and had not lived in the city long enough to qualify for assistance. But even the county agent imposed limitations. "Attempted frauds on the part of the shiftless, drunken and dishonest have made the addition of iron-clad rules absolutely necessary, and the deserving poor are in consequences obliged to wait until an investigation into their cases can be made," the *Globe* reported on January 14, 1889.

The long rows of wooden tenements and cottages that encircled the city after the fire represent only a temporary solution to the emergency housing problem. The combined charities confidently believed that as fire victims regained economic status, they would build themselves out of want and abandon these places. That did not happen, and many of the displaced were pushed into economically disadvantaged areas and forced to live in miles of post-fire housing stock on the West and South Sides, destined to become permanent "barracks" of poverty." Cheaply manufactured clapboard homes and residential tenements evolved into "halfway houses" accommodating generations of immigrants and races up to the midpoint of the twentieth century when urban renewal initiatives finally leveled the last of the slum sections.

Looking back on that time, architect and former City of Chicago building commissioner Richard E. Schmidt blamed slum conditions on the curse of the "narrow twenty-five-foot lots that forced people to build high. In some communities settled by the foreign-born, the owners would operate a business on the first floor and live upstairs." Schmidt served as building commissioner from 1934 to 1942. "But the young people as they married were ashamed to live over stores. After the old folks died neglect set it. That is how buildings slipped from family homes to tenements in one generation."[6]

Meanwhile, in the central business district, the grounds were swept clean of fire debris, making it possible for city engineers to raise the grade of the business streets without putting the owners of the commercial properties to the expense of raising their buildings to a higher elevation. This same consideration was not extended to the cholera-infested slums of the near West Side.

In the decades following the Chicago Fire, the Maxwell Street Police Precinct, two miles long and one mile wide, and lying between the Chicago River on the east, Wood Street on the west, Harrison Street on the north, and Sixteenth Street on the south, became one of the toughest police districts in the midwest region, if not the entire country. Bridgeport, extending southeast of Maxwell Street, easily qualified as the second worst nether region in the public mind. However, the many police officers assigned to patrol the streets in the years 1870 to 1925 in their own words called Maxwell the "Terror District," or the "plague spot of the West Division," no better and probably much worse than Whitechapel in London's East End or the Five Points in New York City.[7]

Before the Civil War, Irish, Germans, and Bohemians lived quiet and contented lives here. They provided for their families without strife, disruption, or a discernible escalation in reportable crime. "Peopled by Irish, German and Bohemian Catholics, there was no more orderly region in Chicago," observed John Kelley, "nor was there a better citizenry than the old timers whose homes dotted the prairie." Maxwell Street gave more priests to the Roman Catholic Church than any other similar size district in the world, by Kelley's recollections.[8]

The district fell into disrepute soon after the Civil War ended. The time of horror and blood was soon at hand. Returning veterans; a generation of restless young men jaded by the action and adventure of combat and no longer accustomed to the placid routines of ordinary family living, idled in saloons, engaged in mischief, and formed holdup gangs. The railroad viaducts near Twelfth Street provided both concealment and shadow for "highway men" (as armed robbers were so often called back then) to carry out their crimes, ranging from the theft of gold watches to the snatching of women's handbags. Armed robbery was the most common offense committed in the Maxwell Street Precinct during its rapid descent into misery.

After 1870 the district became a way station for thousands of late arriving Irish and Eastern European refugees escaping from the pogroms of Europe. It was a patchwork quilt of divergent ethnicities and races. Greeks, Hungarians, Magyars, Lithuanians, Turks, Italians, Poles, Slovaks, and Russian Jews lived in a cluster of high-crime, socially disadvantaged, frightfully unsanitary neighborhoods segregated by nationality and religion with only one thing in common: their extreme poverty. The drudgery of low-paying sweatshop work in the low dilapidated tenements provided little incentive for young people to aspire to anything other than escaping the district, or engaging in crime.

The *Tribune* asserted in December 1897 that "more genuine criminals have been brought up in the Maxwell Street District than any other similar community in the United States." The intersection of Halsted Street and Maxwell formed the focal point of community life, but the worst incidents of killing and mayhem occurred along four residential side streets: Henry, Johnson, O'Brien, and Sangamon Streets.

Police estimated that of the four hundred citywide murders committed in the four-year period from 1893 to 1897, seventy-five of them occurred in the Twenty-First Precinct—Maxwell Street, staffed by 416 officers, the largest concentration of police personnel at that time. All through the district there could be found houses standing four to seven feet below grade, surrounded by dark underground passageways formed by low-plank sidewalks. Lurking in these dark caverns of crime were fugitive wife murderers, gang members, holdup men, garrotters, and sexual perverts.

In summer, the season of crime and killing, the intolerable, oppressive Chicago heat and humidity drove residents into the streets where they often found their comfort sleeping in the discarded refuse of old cardboard garbage heaps left behind by itinerant fruit and potato peddlers. Wooden sidewalks that had not been pulled up and carted away by scavengers and burned for firewood during the winter sagged into the mud from years of wear and were covered with filth. The interior rooms of the slum houses reeked with moisture year-round. Plaster, usually stripped away by a succession of families, was discolored and covered with grime. Slum houses without windows and proper ventilation very often accommodated twelve families. Outdoor privies were of course commonplace in the neighborhood. So it was little wonder then that young boys preferred to keep company in the streets or in saloons.

Summertime (in the days when bottled and canned beer was not commercially available by the six-pack in stores) signaled the arrival of the "can rushing" season, when fathers fetched their young sons into the saloon to fill the "growler" with the frothy lager. By this method the most poverty-stricken Maxwell Street man could remain in a state of perpetual intoxication as he beat up his wife, the children, and even the neighbors nearby. Children were society's throwaways. A 1906 estimate pegged the average family size in the district at nine—the struggling parents and their seven undernourished children.

In the saloons, the can rushers sampled the gin spirits where they often met up with older, experienced criminals (the "Fagins" of the district, who prevailed upon boys to commit crimes that would spare them from incarceration were they to break the law themselves), enticing them into the life of the lawbreaker. Boys of six and seven were recruited into the criminal world because their diminutive size worked to the burglar's advantage. They could easily be pushed through tight openings and windows an adult might not otherwise be able to navigate.

"Rushing the can is responsible for a good deal of the crime," a veteran police officer confided to the *Tribune* in 1897. "That is the thing that has come in the last twelve years. It is ruining hundreds of boys, and in my opinion is one of the great breeders of crime."[9] In 1885 measures were taken to prohibit children from conveying beer from the saloon to the parental home without a written permit. The police, their resources taxed and thinly deployed across other areas of the district, simply did not bother to arrest the barkeeps or adults for violating the permitting process. Applications were easily forged by boys in the street.

Barkeeps provided safe haven for boy crooks and often directed their criminal activities from their saloons. In the 1890s, Jack Flaherty's Halsted Street resort served as a clearinghouse for young pickpockets, card sheets, and thimble-riggers of the worst sort that worked county fairs and places of public assembly. The cops knew Jack Flaherty as the "West Side Mayor," and paid him a courtesy call every time something big was about to go down in Chicago—a crowded hotel convention, Derby Day at Washington Park Race Track, or a torchlight political rally. The central station police blotter from November 14, 1892, provided a vivid description of Mayor Flaherty's Maxwell Street con gang during the visit of the Democrats to the city:

> "Red Jim" Crayton, whose right name is William Campbell, is only twenty-two years old but heads a section of the toughest gang on the West Side. He is a disciple of Jack Flaherty and is thoroughly posted in all the tricks of the trade. He can work a con game to perfection and pick your pocket after telling you he is going to do so. The Bridewell register contains his name for temporary lodgings on several occasions.
>
> James Kern, an old confidence man and something of a leader among the younger thieves. He has been an all-around sneak thief for years, and seems to be too old of a bird to reform at this late date. He is fifty-five.
>
> William Morgan is only fourteen-years old, but is credited with being one of the smoothest pickpockets that infest the West Side. He has been to the Bridewell several times in his short career.
>
> James Keefe is twenty-four years old. He is a prominent member of the West Side gang and trains with "Red Jim" Crayton. He can turn his hand to most anything from a safe job to a shell game and has an enviable reputation among brother cracksmen.[10]

With its door-to-door saloons, its filthy living conditions, and reputation for lawlessness, Maxwell Street's crime bosses and crooked barkeeps schooled a generation of nineteenth-century criminals ranging from wife murderers to armed robbery gangs. On April 23, 1898, the criminal justice system executed peddler, thief, gang leader, and street fighter Chris Merry. A sad and pathetic Maxwell Street habitué, the young man was born the night of October 8, 1871, to a stonemason and his wife, just a few hours after firemen had driven the family out of their home on Spruce Street in a mad retreat from the onrushing Chicago Fire.

Merry grew into adulthood a belligerent, violent sot, greatly feared by his neighbors and a nuisance to the police. In a final desperate act of his ragged life, he bludgeoned to death his common-law, invalid wife, Pauline Ballou, inside their cramped lodgings at 50 Hope Street. It happened in the madness of an irrational, drunken quarrel. The tearful Pauline had just confessed to her husband that an hour earlier she had been sexually assaulted by two neighborhood men. Merry, in a wild rage, exacted his vengeance by beating her to death. With the help of a second man, he placed the lifeless body in a wheelbarrow and buried the corpse in an open field.

As a boy making the rounds of post-fire Chicago, Merry never experienced the softer side of life. He observed his father drink cheap whiskey until he was nearly paralyzed and passed out on the door stoop. Merry's Irish immigrant father thought more of whiskey than bread, and these traits were imparted to his son who began consuming liquor at the age of fourteen. Prone to gloomy fits of depression and wild, unprovoked temper tantrums, Chris took on all comers in his corner of the world. After gang member Harry "Butch" Lyons cracked open Merry's skull with an iron pipe, the boy grew more dangerous and became a law unto himself.

"Butch" Lyons, another Maxwell Street incorrigible defeated by misery, poverty, and bad associations, was sentenced to the Bridewell at age nine and at least sixty more times after that. He was subsequently executed in back of the Cook County Jail on October 11, 1895, after being convicted of shooting Alfred Mason, a scenic artist walking along Van Buren Street between Clinton and Jefferson in the course of an armed robbery. His last words before the scaffold dropped: "I never had a chance." And neither did Chris Merry or the victims these two desperate men sent to an early grave.

Commenting on the implications of the Chris Merry case, Dr. John A. Benson of the College of Physicians and Surgeons in Chicago cited the linkage between the saloon and violent crime. Benson had previously served as medical superintendent of the Dunning Insane Asylum and the County Poor House, a walled campus tainted by corruption, scandal, and sadistic practices of its keepers, located ten miles northwest of the central business district.

> Look for a moment at the surroundings amid which this wretched young creature was brought up. His own people and the neighbors and the neighbors of these neighbors by the thousands live in crowded and filthy tenement districts. The houses they inhabit are the breeding places of disease, vice and crime. There is an insufficiency of light and air, a super abundance of dampness and of filth. The smell of sewer gas hung in the air.
>
> Modern improvements are unknown. Within the walls of the tumble-down shanties or larger barren and barnlike structures there is not a single thing to please the eye, cultivate the mind or elevate the soul. There is an unavoidable contact with the low, the base, the brutish and the wicked. The common ambition of the inmates is to satisfy their sensual appetites. In such neighborhoods the saloon is the common rendezvous; the commonest form of social pleasure is to drink.[11]

For years, the Henry Street Gang of thugs, gunmen, and robbers, weaned in the tough saloons, terrorized the district.[12] Organized by John Kavanaugh, alias the "Kid from Troy," a Maxwell Street tough who committed his first assault at age sixteen, Kavanaugh was in and out of jails in Chicago and Milwaukee for the next seven years. He ran with Al Beiter, Joe Slater, Dyer Scanlan, and John Kenney, his constant companions who were with him one night in 1879 when Kavanaugh murdered saloon keeper John McMahon inside his premises at Thirty-Nine and Laurel. Acquitted for lack of evidence, the "Kid" was freed by a criminal courts judge, but died in the Bridewell a few years later.

After Kavanaugh's downfall, John McGrath and William Mortell, with Mortell's kid-brother, John, all habitués of Henry Street, seized control over the gang of ruffians most often etched into the Twenty-First Precinct arrest log. Mortell-McGrath members plotted their crimes at 116 Henry Street, a residential strip between Jefferson and Clinton described by police to be the "toughest place in Chicago." The "clubhouse" was one of the cheaply built post-fire tenement hellholes; a tumbledown frame shanty below sidewalk level standing fifteen feet back from the walk.

McGrath, a brash, and supremely confident young tough who committed his first criminal offense at the age of twelve, brutally murdered Chicago police officer Adam Freyer at Harrison and Clinton on August 9, 1889, after some trouble flared up inside a saloon at Fifteenth Street and Union Avenue. Freyer pulled the patrol-box alarm after spotting the two men running toward him, chased by police detectives. In the struggle to subdue McGrath, a bullet pierced Freyer's carotid artery and abdomen. Death ensued within five minutes. Later, McGrath unsuccessfully tried to kill his own mother, and boasted that "no police officer could take him alive."

His gang staged many daring holdups. The Mortell-McGrath gang committed a range of petty and serious offenses including stealing brass from the railroad coaches of the Chicago, Burlington & Quincy Railroad, looting railroad boxcars on the Fort Wayne Rail Yard near Twelfth Street, and armed robberies against women and the elderly in the West Side streets.

McGrath and Mortell were convicted of the heinous murder of Officer Freyer and sentenced to life, but in a move that stunned the Cook County criminal justice system, the pair was granted a new trial in March 1891 by Judge Murray Tuley on the grounds that the police had suppressed evidence. Returning to his old Henry Street haunts, McGrath resumed his life of crime until January 13, 1893, when he was cornered and arrested at Jefferson and Henry after shooting Officer John Mahoney who had tried vainly to serve an arrest warrant inside the Hayes Saloon. "He [McGrath] has been arrested by nearly every officer in the station and he always shoots if he gets the drop," complained one officer.[13]

Inside Pat Casey's saloon at Henry and Stewart Avenue, a shambles of a place with a billiard table propped up on soap boxes because the legs had fallen off long before, Chicago's oldest barkeep in terms of service and age plied the Mortells with liquor and provided refuge from the law. In better days, Casey, a quiet taciturn man with long white whiskers and a stern demeanor, operated the "Silver Fountain" at Madison and Market Streets and captained volunteer Fire Department Brigade No. 6. Volunteer firemen of the antebellum period in Chicago (as in New York) were inevitably petty criminals drawn from the ranks of saloon loungers. They were roughhousing "boyos" all, who set as many fires as they helped extinguish.

Before the Civil War, thinly disguised criminal gang members formed volunteer firefighting brigades before municipal control and professional training reigned in their activities. The volunteers flocked to Casey's "Silver Fountain," where he served a particularly potent swill that he called "Casey's No. 6," guaranteed to stir up the blood of its imbibers. After the Chicago Fire destroyed his establishment and left him without capital, Casey hired on at Mike McDonald's "Store," the high-toned downtown casino and saloon at Clark and Monroe.

The Store was an important rendezvous for sporting men, politicians, outlaws on the run, and shady characters with favors to trade. At the height of McDonald's power in the 1870s and 1880s, it was the de facto city hall, and Casey, the keeper of the secrets. That ended after 1888, when McDonald disposed of his liquor business and severed his pervasive ties to the gambling fraternity in order to attain "social respectability" as a businessman and behind-the-scenes political power broker. From the redolent, polished surroundings of the Store, Casey's grimy Henry Street dive was a remarkable comedown in life for an Irish immigrant who had worked his way up from poverty to the management of an extravagant Gilded Age palace of dice and liquor after landing in Chicago in 1834.

McGrath's capture in 1893 accompanied the roundup of lesser-known members of his mob and closed out their criminal enterprise. Not long after McGrath's takedown, Casey succumbed to old age and disease and passed on. But there were many other vicious gangs and many accommodating West Side barkeeps that provided them with cover, food and liquor, and the means to operate.

By the early years of the twentieth century, Maxwell Street, comprising the "dark, foreboding, river wards that were the worst in the confines of civilization," according to the *Tribune*, had, in the opinion of cops and reporters, become the most dangerous district in the world.[14] With little incentive for children to grow up in a structured environment of home, religious observance, respect for life and property through regular schooling, the fastest way to acquire notoriety, status among peers, and money was through gang membership.

An estimated fifty thousand Jewish immigrants flooded into Chicago in the last two decades of the nineteenth century.[15] Gentiles living outside the district often referred to it as the "Poor Jews Quarter."

Street gangs invaded the Jewish-owned tailor shops lining Twelfth Street near Halsted, taking what they could and occasionally ransacking the premises. "Silk stealing" involved the theft of clothing, bolts of cloth, and buttons and thread for resale in the open-air markets, or very often the goods were shipped to New York by fencing gangs. The Jews were singled out for the worst forms of harassment and persecution after 1880 when their numbers rapidly increased. Boy gangs and the young rowdies of other nationalities hurled stones at Hassidic peddlers and harassed them in unimaginable ways as they tried to go about their business.

In a February 1905 case that underscored the serious problem of Jewish persecution in the ghetto neighborhood, Judge Julian Mack, president of the Infant's Welfare Society of Chicago, struck the fear of God into twelve-year-old Robert Lambele, accused of stoning and seriously injuring Jacob Provusky of Morgan Street. "I didn't do it Judge, honest," wailed Lambele. "The others lied out of it and put it all on me. And I never pulled nobody's whiskers, hope to die I didn't."

Judge Mack looked at the boy evenly. He threatened him with Bridewell incarceration and enrollment in the notoriously feared John Worthy School. "This business of groups of boys making life a burden for peddlers, rabbis and aged men and women has got to stop," he admonished. "Every gang of boys in Chicago is going to be held responsible for the acts of all its members. There will be no more leniencies and no more lying to avail young rowdies, and I want every boy in Chicago to understand it. Within three months there have been twenty cases in the Juvenile Court where complaints have been made that gangs of boys have maltreated aged men and women."[16]

Judge Mack spared young Lambele a Bridewell term, but instructed the boy to return to his gang friends and warn them all of the dire consequences of any future actions against elderly Jews. They would all wind up in the John Worthy School if they were not careful, the judge cautioned.

Jewish gangs formed for the purpose of protecting shopkeepers and the pushcart street peddlers renting sidewalk space in front of the delicatessens and clothing stores on Halsted Street from the vicious boy gangs. "After passing 12th Street one could well imagine himself out of Chicago," observed newspaper man and humorist George Ade in the 1890s. "Every shop sign is painted in the angular characters of the Hebrew alphabet, and even the playbills in the window are Hebrew."

The Italians, who settled immediately north of the district along Taylor Street, opposed the Jewish gangs in later years, and became the scourge of the district. In May 1908 a frenzy of panic overtook the ghetto when a hundred women—the mothers of the children enrolled at the Washburne School at Fourteenth and Jefferson—stormed into the building demanding protection from Black Hand extortionists rumored to have planted five hundred pounds of dynamite underneath the school. In excited tones, the frightened parents related wild and unsubstantiated rumors that Black Hand criminals had invaded the ghetto demanding $4,000 in extortion payments from the nearby Garfield School. They were described by anxious but overly imaginative children as "men in black coats with large mustaches."[17]

Rumors swept through the neighborhood that the elementary schools filled with Jewish children would soon be blown to bits if the money was not paid. A near-riot of pushing, screaming parents ensued at Garfield School, but no evidence of bombs were uncovered by police. It was the worst years of the Black Hand terror in the adjacent Italian quarter, but in this multicultural milieu, rumor often gave way to unwarranted fears, suspicion, and mutual loathing. In truth the majority of the city's serious gang crime was perpetrated by members of the same ethnic groups against one another, e.g., Italian against Italian, Jew against Jew, Irish against Irish, although factional fights between gangs of Italians, Jews, Bohemian, and Irish boys were widely reported after 1890.

The accidental shooting death of twelve-year-old Stanley Zavadil on March 1, 1906, by his friend and fellow gang member Arthur Heier as they prepared to attack a crowd of Jewish boys stirred grave concerns of a pending "race war" on the West Side. Heier was bound over to the juvenile court after police determined that the shooting was not deliberate.

Coroner Peter Hoffman ordered Captain Edward McCann of the Maxwell Street Station to commence an immediate and thorough investigation, beginning in the schools. "We are going to sift this race and factional war business among these little boys to the bottom," he vowed. But later, McCann admitted that he and his men in the detective squad were stunned to learn that there were "innumerable factions of lads" and not just one or two boy gangs stirring up trouble in the neighborhood. Eight boys from the Walsh School were caught carrying revolvers. According to one published account, the youths in question were "reprimanded" and the guns taken away in the station by police, but nothing more. Tough Irish gangs formed inside the Walsh School, a staging ground for attacks against the Jews, Germans, Bohemians, and other ethnic tribes.

"In most cases, the parents of the lads are anxious to put an end to the dangerous fights," McCann added. "We have had a host of boys in here during the last two days and we have taken revolvers from many of them." The Bohemian gang from Twenty-Second Street in the heart of the ethnic Bohemian settlement of Pilsen was under the leadership of fourteen-year-old Fred McGovern, who was Irish. McCann's men removed a pistol from his jacket pocket.[18]

Though limited in size, the Juvenile Protective Association (JPA), founded in 1900, with a neighborhood center at 468 South Halsted Street, pledged to keep up the fight against juvenile delinquency and gangs working with the courts.[19] Such well-meaning social service agencies administered by men and women from outside the community were common in the slums of Chicago, but their long-term impact was mostly negligible despite their best efforts.

Outlining the many dangers posed by the boy gangs to inner-city residents, the *Tribune* warned the public in July 1909 that "the boy gangs soon pass the limits of mere annoyance and approach the borders of the criminal. Their graduates seek and find places in the corner gangs whose operations frequently figure in police records or enlist the attention of those connected with the Juvenile Court. The safety of society enters into the equation."

Incorrigible boy gangs of this era evolved into burglary and holdup gangs, extortion gangs, and as the 1920s and Prohibition dawned, bootleg gangs with easy access to machine guns, bombs, and other weaponry.

Although the frequency of gangland bombings did not pose a serious threat until the beer wars of the Roaring Twenties, Maxwell Street home invasions and harassment of the ordinary working people were common. The marauding tactics of the gangs frightened shopkeepers and pushcart vendors. They knew that if they "peached" (told the police), there would be serious reprisals including death. To maintain their safety and sense of well-being, powerless residents and business owners observed the code of silence and often made separate arrangements with the gangsters, including the payment of petty tributes and providing temporary shelter from the police inside tenement rooms during a "crackdown" or "dragnet," or more substantial financial payoffs.

Through the maze of twisting, turning alleys and side streets, Twenty-First District police officers easily lost their man in pursuit. Many of the bluecoats detailed to the station at Fourteenth Street and Maxwell had grown up in the district but even these streetwise men could not keep track of, or recognize, a fraction of the people passing through. By 1906 there were an estimated 205,000 people—one-ninth of the total city population—crammed into the district; few were conversant in English, and a hundred thousand residents were under the age of sixteen.

There was little respect for the law and rampant hatred of uniformed police. The arrival of the wagon—the "Black Maria"—filled with vagrants, prostitutes, sneak thieves, and other crooks headed for the toils at the precinct station, brought out swarms of boys and girls and slum residents to jeer and heckle the bluecoats and the offenders. A raucous circus atmosphere attended the arrival of the "paddy" wagon but mostly it left the police unfazed. The men in the station were used to it by now. It was a daily grind and they did their best to hold back the throngs of unruly spectators.

The Maxwell Street Station, a solemn, red-brick fortress built in 1886 and surrounded on all sides by saloons and crime scenes where the spilling of blood was a daily occurrence, stood two blocks from Fourteenth and Sangamon. This was one of several notorious "Death Corners" scattered about the poorest sections of the city. Here, Thomas "Buff" Higgins, a killer whose early career mirrored that of Chris Merry, held sway as leader of the Johnson Street Gang.[20] Raised in the streets by an immigrant Irish teamster and his wife, Higgins robbed fruit stands and hurled stones at wandering peddlers, or through the glass windows of their homes. His first arrest came after police collared him for swiping a handful of grapes from a fruit stand.

Buff—short for "buffalo" because of his imposing physical stature—ran with an older crowd of delinquents congregating in Sangamon

Street saloons and on the nearby corners when he wasn't stirring up trouble inside the Walsh School. The boy became a hardened criminal before he was eighteen and had been sent to the Bridewell over two hundred times on charges of larceny and vagrancy. Up until 1893 the courts had never convicted him of the more serious crimes of murder, burglary, or assault. For fun and amusement, Higgins, with Jack "Red" Gary (his second in command) and the other Johnson Street brigands, targeted police officers walking their daily beat on Sangamon for attack when they were not otherwise breaking into private residences.

Home invasion often spelled death for the intended victim. One night in 1893, "Buff" Higgins, in the company of "Red" Gary and Harry "Itzke" Feinberg, entered the Johnson Street home of Peter McCooey, a common laborer at the Crane Brothers factory, during the early morning hours, in an invasion attempt that netted him the man's entire life savings—$400, recently withdrawn from the bank by Peter's wife, Bridget McCooey.

Higgins brandished his weapon and shot McGooey through the head as he lay sleeping in bed with Bridget before racing off with the loot. He was arrested a short time later, after police found him crouching underneath the sidewalk at Fourteenth Street and Jefferson, clutching his revolver. In the roundup of the usual Maxwell Street rowdies that inevitably followed a crime of this nature, John Mortell of the Mortell-McGrath mob were questioned, detained, and later freed.

Higgins was stripped naked and thrown into a Maxwell Street holding cell and deprived of essential civil liberties. He was refused food and drink over the next four days and the right to consult with his attorney. Only after he was finally given a pint of whiskey purchased with a fifty-cent piece the captain of the district pulled out of the pocket of his trousers, did he confess. The admission of guilt forced out of Higgins came only after he had become thoroughly intoxicated.

The McGooey murder was the final depraved act of Buff's short and violent life. It ended with his execution on the Cook County Jail gallows, May 23, 1894. Standing upon the platform facing his jailers, Higgins kissed a crucifix placed against his lips. Moments before the drop, in the final seconds of life, he mumbled a contrite farewell, minus the histrionics or anguished denials of guilt common among other death row inmates. The *Daily News* reported that he was "very game"—cool and collected. His only objection to the entire arrangement concerned the presence of fellow death row inmate Eugene Patrick Prendergast, the convicted assassin of Chicago mayor Carter Harrison I. Prendergast, a feebleminded and disappointed office seeker who imagined that Harrison had broken a promise to appoint him corporation counsel to the city, awaited his own execution on the same platform. Higgins, just twenty-three years of age at the time of his death, told his jailers that he did not want to occupy the same miserable space on the scaffold as the despised Prendergast, scheduled to die hours later.

Judge James Goggin (1842–1898) of the Superior Court of Cook County reflected on the brutal treatment of Higgins during the incarceration period and the fate of the other young men entangled in senseless crimes. He noted that seventeen hundred underage boys had been arrested and jailed in 1896. He questioned why evidence suggesting that "Butch" Lyons shot Alfred Mason in self-defense had been allegedly suppressed by the police in his unpublished 1896 manuscript detailing police abuses. "When I have finished the book, I shall have no more to do but my duty as Superior Court judge until my term expires," he told a reporter with a sigh of frustration. "Then I shall shake the smoke of Chicago from my head, the dust of Chicago from my feet, retire from public life, go to a little farm 100 miles from New York and live in peace away from the criminal public and the criminal police."[21]

Judge Goggin's overriding frustration with the system—the methods of policing the slum neighborhoods and incarceration of underage offenders, the lack of proper parental responsibility and personal involvement in the lives of their children, and the pervasive feeling of hopelessness in the slum sections of Chicago— resonate down to the modern day in the killing streets of Englewood, Austin, and Auburn Gresham. Maxwell Street, a blighted stain on the map of Chicago for over seventy-five years, offers a stark, but compelling parallel to these twenty-first-century crime zones.

As the nineteenth century ended, the marauding tactics of the West Side gangs worsened. The three Feinberg brothers—Joseph, Harry, and Benjamin Feinberg (aka "Kid Farmer," an aspiring pugilist)—took over leadership of the remnants of the deposed Mortell-McGrath mob, converting the ethnic identity of the gang from Irish-German to mostly Jewish. Synagogues, sweatshops, kosher delicatessens, chicken and feed stores, and bakeries proliferated in the district by 1900. The Jewish Manual Training School was established as a way to educate wayward boys and teach them a useful trade. The transformation of the Mortell-McGrath gang reflected the changing ethnic demographics of the precinct from a mix of European tribes to predominantly Jewish.

Harry Feinberg, Chicago's first important Jewish gang leader, was a violent, impulsive felon, incapable of exercising even a modicum of self-control. He had a long rap sheet dating back to 1893 when the cops arrested and charged him as an accessory to murder. He spent the next twelve years in and out of the state reformatory for juveniles, later graduating to a prison cell in the Joliet penitentiary for hardened criminals. He had served two years in the Pontiac Correctional Center for complicity in the Peter McGooey murder.

Granted his parole on August 7, 1904, Feinberg returned to Maxwell Street to resume his thieving ways. Less than a month later, in the company of Frank Gagen, Feinberg again became a wanted man after sticking up a saloon at Morgan and Henry Streets. The police scoured the district in their search. There was no doubt in anyone's mind that Feinberg was the responsible party. Lieutenant Thomas Meagher of the Maxwell Street Station traced his whereabouts to rented rooms at 86 Twenty-Fifth Place maintained by Gagen's brother, Edward, on the Southwest Side of the city, and dispatched four officers to the home to bring him in—dead or alive.

After surrounding the building, Officer James J. Keefe entered through the rear entrance and made his way through the kitchen, with pistol drawn. He rapped on the bedroom door. Feinberg answered Keefe's surrender demand by gunfire. A bullet tore into Keefe, who collapsed to the floor, calling out to his comrades, "Help me boys! I'm shot! For God's sake come to me!" Within minutes Keefe was dead. Detective Richard Birmingham rushed to his fallen friend's side. Then he kicked open the door but took a bullet in the abdomen from Harry Feinberg.

He returned fire, striking Feinberg in the back. Mortally wounded, Feinberg jumped out the window and flagged down a passing streetcar that conveyed him to Twenty-Sixth and Wabash Avenue on the South Side. Staggering from loss of blood, he pushed on, making it all the way down to the drugstore owned by Charles Walgreen on Forty-Second Street, where he collapsed from loss of blood.[22] While waiting for the police ambulance to take him to Lakeside Hospital, Feinberg asked his police captors if he could dictate a letter to his wife, Minnie Wagner. They granted the dying man his wish.

> *Dear Min:*
>
> *I love you as I always did. This is the last of me I guess. I hope you think the same of me as you always did, and I am sorry to bring you so much trouble. I tried to be good but I was hounded. I am terribly wronged by those who said things against me. Do not grieve for me, but take life as it comes. My love and best wishes, Harry*[23]

When police arrived at 4859 Justine Street to interview Min" they discovered to their chagrin that the girl was missing, and her mother said that she harbored grave fears that Feinberg had already killed her daughter.

Police reconstructed the shoot-out and determined that Officer Keefe's gun had jammed at the critical moment, thus allowing Feinberg to escape. Keefe, a fourteen-year veteran of Chicago policing, who had worked on criminal cases involving gang crime before and was credited with personally "taking down" Edward Lally of the North Side Market Street Gang a decade earlier, was given a hero's burial at Calvary Cemetery.

Guarded by two patrolmen standing adjacent to his hospital bed, Feinberg resolutely refused to answer questions about where his wife might be hiding, or a string of armed robberies in the district he was held accountable for. Smirking, he cast a venomous look toward his inquisitors and snarled, "I fixed Keefe!" Meanwhile, one by one, a parade of saloon owners, junk dealers, and butchers called upon the Maxwell Street Station for the purpose of identifying Gagen and Feinberg as the men who had intimidated and robbed them.

Reporters caught up with the dying killer's prostrated mother, Mary Feinberg, who expressed sad resignation. "All of my children are bad. I feel as if I have nothing to live for." Her son, the cop killer, expired a short time later. Only then did Harry's missing wife put in an appearance. "Oh, why couldn't he reform and be good, as I had begged him to be?" wailed Minnie. "And he had promised me that he would reform and be a good man. And here he's dead—dead from a policeman's bullet!"

Languishing in the Maxwell Street lockup, Gagen refused food and expressed the desire to commit suicide. Lieutenant Meagher, according to a January 8, 1905, report in the *Chicago American*, attempted to unhinge Gagen with repeated taunts. "You're in an unlucky cell Gagen," he said. "A lot of other murderers here occupied that cell and they've all been hanged—'Buff' Higgins and Chris Merry and Louie Thoombs all had that cell. You'd better tell everything." Gagen just laughed.

Although robbery resulting in homicide was Chicago's fastest-growing violent crime activity during a thirty-year period, 1890–1920, not all West Side gang boys graduating into full-blown criminal careers at this time were capable of committing willful murder. Some well-traveled gang members of Bloody Maxwell confined their activities to petty larceny and small-time street activity. William Scully, aka "Scully de Robber," and his boy gang first came to police attention in June 1884 after officers rousted a gang of boys ranging in age from ten to seventeen in a cave situated in a lonesome spot in Lincoln Park on the North Side. Police recovered a lot of clothing, jewelry, and other valuables pilfered from stores and houses. The stolen goods were sold to the denizens of Maxwell Street, and with the money in hand Scully purchased tobacco and liquor and divided them equally among his gang.

Ignoring the tearful pleas of the mother of Scully gang member twelve-year-old Jimmy Conway, Judge Rollin B. Williamson of the superior court sentenced the boy to three years in St. Mary's Training School for wayward youth at Feehanville for his involvement with the crimes of Scully the Robber.[24] "Judge your honor won't you please let him go? He'll be a good boy sure,"[25] the woman begged, dropping to her knees in a praying position. "The law is clear!" he shot back.

Arrested for pickpocketing at age fourteen, Scully, a slim-faced, meek-looking lad, was in and out of Illinois and Wisconsin prisons over the next twenty-years for the crime of larceny, but always refused to give up the life of bandit and swindler.

Working in tandem with John Sterling, Frank "Milwaukee Avenue Dutch" Matusek, Edward McNichols, Frank Dyer, Mickey French, and John Reilly, the Scully robbery gang remained active in Maxwell Street and the fashionable North Side from the mid-1880s through the early 1900s by carefully avoiding the discharge of weapons or engaging in unnecessary gunfights with the police. After Maxwell Street officers arrested the bunch after they had snatched a woman's purse on a Twelfth Street omnibus on December 11, 1900, Captain John Wheeler bragged: "These men have been a disgrace to society long enough. In some manner they always escape to the North Side but this time we have them right. We have witnesses who cannot be induced to remain away from the trial and it is almost a certainty they will be sent to the penitentiary."[26]

In Scully's highest-earning days, police estimated that he commanded a gang of up to seventy robbers and pickpockets roaming the city at will. Scully's father charged police with persecuting his son, claiming that the real "Scully de Robber" was a character from Goose Island named *Gorman Scully*, but central station booking produced a rap sheet of two hundred arrests attributed to *William* Scully. There could be no other.

Frauds and violence and gang terror were institutional. Illegal gambling dens thrived in the shadow of the Temple doors, inviting neighborhood toughs to congregate. Larman's Billiard Hall and Pool Room at 813 Maxwell Street was a notorious dive where on any given night in 1913, a hundred young men gambled at craps and *stuss*, a popular Yiddish card game. One night armed thugs assaulted reporters and shot a *Tribune* photographer through the chest after snapping photos of the dive for the morning paper. Max Annenberg, strong-arm labor slugger and the brother of Moses Annenberg, political power broker and the nationally renowned publisher of the *Philadelphia Inquirer*, was arrested by police and charged with assault with a deadly weapon against the photographer, Alexander Belford.[27]

Although the place enjoyed political protection from the "boss," Twentieth Ward alderman Emmanuel "Manny" Abrahams, Chicago mayor Carter Harrison II promptly revoked the liquor license of Frank Larman, proprietor, and removed the Maxwell Street police commander, Captain John J. Mahoney, for permitting the gamblers, vice peddlers, and extortionists free reign in the ward.

Commenting on these matters on July 18, 1913, the *Jewish Daily Press*, the influential Yiddish newspaper in the district, reported that "In the Jewish quarter—to our shame—an underworld that is indebted for its existence to corrupt Jewish politicians who have the brazenness to pose as representatives of the Jewish population, Thanks to the influence of these politicians, there are on the West Side a large number of poolrooms and other places where poor working men gamble away their wages, the money which should have gone to their wives for bread and clothing for themselves and their children."

Baggy-pants politicians and grafters helped rule Maxwell Street during the treacherous reign of Manny Abrahams, saloon proprietor, alderman, and legislator.[28] Abrahams employed a gang of sluggers to beat up political opponents, while rewarding his loyalists with appointments as deputy bailiffs in the municipal courts and in other city agencies. Police captains desirous of "cleaning up" the district and ridding the neighborhood of its political gangs were "sent to the woods," the term commonly applied to reassignment to a distant district.

Reform-minded police captain James Gleason was transferred out of the ghetto in 1913 in favor of Captain James O'Dea Storen, a "cooperative" police official indicted in January 1915 with two detectives on a charge of obstructing justice by failing to arrest members of a "million-dollar burglar trust" that victimized business owners up and down Twelfth Street. Political fixer Abrahams had demanded Gleason's removal and Superintendent John T. McWeeney, with the mayor's approval, obliged in order to "accommodate" Manny's "request."

It was a pathetic, but all too familiar story. The burglary gang was afforded safe haven in a politically controlled saloon owned by Harry Cohen. It had served as the rendezvous point for the gang. An investigation commenced following the burglary of $6,000 in merchandise from the clothing store of Isaac Stein at 569 West Twelfth Street on September 10, 1913. Stein fingered gang member Max Rovich as the ringleader who had been under surveillance for weeks leading up to the break-in. He preferred charges against Rovich, Isador Wexler, and Nathan Steinberg at the Maxwell Street Police Station, but the charges were summarily dismissed. Undaunted, Stein took his complaint to State's Attorney Maclay Hoyne through his attorney, A. Henry Goldstein.

Wexler and Steinberg were convicted. Gang leader Rovich, boasting of his considerable police influence (known colloquially to generations of Chicagoans as "clout"), was later acquitted. He filed a $50,000 civil law suit against Stein for defamation of character, but the accuser was vindicated by Storen's discharge from the department and eventual conviction. Storen managed to avoid jail time and was assessed a $1,000 fine. He never donned the blue police tunic again, and was killed in an automobile accident in 1929 at age seventy-one.

Others who "had it in bad" with Manny had cause to fear. The "court of last report" was often a desperate plea to Manny's brother, Morris, to intercede. Their livelihoods were in jeopardy. Indeed, the safety of their families and children were at stake.

Maxwell Street was a tough place for boys to grow up. To survive, a lad had to be tough, nimble, and unafraid to fight. Some were very happy to showcase their pugilistic skills before a paying audience.

The annual prizefight (usually held at Maurice Ginsburg's Dew Drop Inn at 91 Waller Street), pitting the toughest kid in the neighborhood against challengers from around the city, marked the biggest social event of the year among the West Side boy gangs. The illegality of the "ghetto prizefight" did not escape police attention. Although patronized by residents of every age and economic status, the Maxwell Street cops raided the saloon and arrested everyone in sight. Three patrol wagons were often needed to take the participants and spectators to the station for processing. Fathers and mothers, mixing Yiddish and English in a way that was incomprehensible to the police, crowded into the station to post bond for their sons.

Recognizing the vital commercial and economic importance of the district to the city, the City of Chicago appropriated a section of Clinton Street between Sixteenth and Twelfth Place in September 1912 and turned it over to the Chicago Terminal & Transfer Company for industrial development. The city preempted the thoroughfare and razed dozens of buildings with the compliance of the two Twentieth Ward aldermen, Manny Abrahams and his arch enemy Dennis J. Egan. It marked the modest beginning of the new Maxwell Street Market, a curious makeover of the entire neighborhood from ghetto into an open-air bazaar that Abrahams helped to engineer in 1912 with the full backing of the Chicago City Council.

Rules and regulations were imposed upon the sellers. One of the new statutes required street peddlers to add wheels to their sidewalk vendor stands. The entire operation was run by the duly appointed "market master" under the thumb of Manny's handpicked operative, A. I. Goldstein, whom the *Tribune* accused of "extorting dimes from men and women whose ordinary currency is pennies and nickels."[29]

After the city decreed that the old ghetto would best serve the city as a wholesale bazaar, a parade of hustlers began to line up each day at Thirteenth and Union Street to await the blowing of the 8:00 a.m. whistle signaling the start of a the business day. Vendors, fish peddlers, fortune tellers, sellers of used clothing and every other item under the sun rushed willy-nilly to occupy the choice spots on the street. "Spot holders" (gang members and the minions of organized crime) accepted cash payments to "reserve" the space. Failure to pay the petty extortion meant that another vendor would claim the location the next day.

That contributed to the general state of confusion and the frequent flare-ups of street fighting and urban rioting until the law was amended and the desired locations formally assigned by the market master and the Maxwell Street Businessmen's Association. Nevertheless the rule of occupancy did not fully deter the spot-holders from perpetuating the shakedowns. Considerable amounts of merchandise offered for sale were goods stolen or hijacked from railroad cars or trucks, but police rarely arrested market thieves for this kind of dubious activity.

Armed with sworn proof of a pattern of systemic graft, Chicago Corporation counsel Francis X. Busch laid out the evidence showing that Maxwell Street merchants were subjected to a general levy of illegal taxation by agents purporting to represent "high politicians" in city hall. The city charged each peddler a dime a day in May 1926 to operate a sidewalk stall. Busch estimated that political pressure from city hall operatives yielded up to $250,000 per annum through "the collector," Victor Cohen, assistant market manager representing the interests of Alderman Dennis Egan and Officer Michael J. Grant of the Maxwell Street Station.

Maxie Eisen, a flabby, doubled-chinned 1920s bootlegger, thug, and labor union extortionist, terrorized Jewish peddlers with the same bullying tactics as the Black Hand preyed upon the poor Italians of Little Hell and Taylor Street. Notorious in union circles as the business agent of the Associated Hebrew Butchers and the Chicago Retail Fish Dealer's association, and included in the first "public enemies" list in 1930, Eisen made it all but impossible for merchants in the Fulton Street Market to operate their business.

A $3,000 "kick-in" demanded by Eisen and his lieutenants had to be paid in advance . . . or else. "I'm a poor woman with three children to support," complained Mamie Oberlander, a fishmonger trying to make ends meet, in a July 1928 letter to Frank Loesch, special prosecutor and the executive director of the Chicago Crime Commission. "For thirty-two years I was in the fish business in Chicago, made a comfortable living for me and my children. But for now for the past year, I've been practically starving on account of gunmen. I went to Eisen and pleaded with him to let me open a store and he agreed on a condition that I give him $3,000. He said he is the boss and is not afraid of anybody or any official in the city or county, that nobody can make him do what he doesn't want to do."[30] Eisen and his henchmen were indicted on conspiracy charges, but making the charges stick were another matter.

The boundary lines of the ward shifted over time. By the end of the 1920s, Maxwell Street and the lawless "Valley District" to the immediate west comprised the Twentieth Ward—the "Bloody Twentieth"—the bailiwick of a new and evolving hoodlum empire controlled by shady politician Morris Eller, a sanitary district trustee and city collector. Eller courted the favor of the local gang chieftains and enjoyed the warm regard of Mayor William Hale Thompson, Thompson's political acolyte Illinois governor Lennington Small, and a statewide Republican machine that controlled all municipal and state patronage up through the 1931 election season.[31]

From the dense cluster of two- and three-story tenement buildings, frame houses below street grade, and saloons of the Valley District in the closing years of the nineteenth century emerged "Heinie" Miller, Jimmy Farley, Cooney the Fox (whose real name was Mortimer), "Nuts" Nolan, Red Bolton, and "Tootsie" Bill Hughes. They organized a gang of burglars, armed robbers, and pickpockets to carry out violent and systemic crime before moving on to more lucrative enterprises in labor racketeering and bootlegging. Paddy "the Bear" Ryan, a stockily built champion brawler in his early twenties took over control of the Valley Gang and redirected his resources to the booze racket once the Volstead Act became the law of the land on January 1, 1920. Ryan owned a saloon—"a real tough joint"—at Fourteenth and Halsted, in the heart of the Maxwell Street District. A *Tribune* reporter ventured into the district one night and made inquiry about the fearsome reputation of the man who fought his way to leadership of the gang with a wicked right hook. "Paddy was a big guy," an informant advised, "handy with his mitts. Powerful. The Bear. Ever been at Paddy's place? Some joint it was! A hangout for thieves they say. Dips (pickpockets), burglars, all that sort. The dips worked streetcars all up Halsted. Others worked at different points. The Bear was boss. He had powerful friends."

Paddy had friends with connections inside city hall. He was employed by Dennis Egan, first a bailiff of the municipal court, then an alderman. The Ellers, father and son, could always count on him for favors. His saloon became a clearing house for desperate crooks seeking divine intervention from the political operatives. Ryan was always happy to oblige.

For Paddy, his friends on the street were less trustworthy and hardly reliable. The gang was just breaking into the bootlegging racket when Paddy was gunned down—shot in cold-blood by professional slugger Walter "Shrimp" Quinlan on orders from the gang's first lieutenant, "Nuts" Nolan. The Valley Gang hijacked 1,350 cases of whiskey from saloon keeper Harris Winsky up on Solon Street on May 22, 1920. The whiskey seizure was enormous and it helped usher in Chicago's "lawless decade."

The liquor was driven to Paddy's warehouse, but when the time came to divvy up the cash after the booze had been sold and distributed, Ryan welshed on his promise and shorted the gang on their promised payback. Less than a month later, Paddy took four slugs in the belly from "Shrimp" Quinlan's .45 caliber pistol inside McElligott's Saloon at Fourteenth and Racine. Ryan staggered to the street and collapsed as the bullets flew. Quinlan was sought by the police for a month before surrendering. He had received private assurances from certain politicians that everything had been "squared up," Chicago "justice" being what it is. State's Attorney Maclay Hoyne and the easily bribed, cartoonish Cook County coroner Peter Hoffman conducted a sham investigation, and a coroner's jury declared there was no evidence against Quinlan and ordered him released. The newspapers looked into the matter and determined that the jury had been packed.

Gangster "Little Danny" Vallo served as a juror. "Sure I was on the jury," Vallo later boasted. "We sprung Quinlan. There were two or three other friends of mine on the jury. But it wasn't a frame-up. They didn't have anything on Quinlan, that's all."

Six years passed. With Prohibition in full tilt, Frankie Lake and his inseparable pal Terry Druggan took over the Valley Gang and gave

Quinlan the boot. The pair recruited new gunmen, Johnny Barry and "Fats" Watkins, to direct hijacking operations. Within two years the Druggan-Lake partnership netted them a cool million dollars. With their ill-gotten earnings, Terry's brother George Druggan bought a house in suburban Long Grove and installed an immense flagpole on the property. Each afternoon his wife ran a large American flag up the pole, visible for a mile, signaling Druggan from afar that there were no federal agents poking around and causing trouble.

Out on his own, Quinlan went to work hustling illegal beer for South Side bootlegger Edward "Spike" O'Donnell. Quinlan made lots of money and an equal number of bootlegging enemies. Justice caught up with Paddy's killer on April 3, 1926. As Quinlan affixed his signature to a paid invoice for three barrels of beer at Joseph Sindelear's saloon at 1700 South Loomis Street, a gunman burst through the doors, firing away. Quinlan, with a pencil in his hand, was dead before he hit the floor. The vengeful killer was twenty-year-old John "Paddy the Cub" Ryan, one of the Bear's seven children. Criminal associates nicknamed the boy the "Fox." Before his father exited the world, he taught John at an early age the proper techniques of bootlegging. By 1926 young Ryan had linked up with the Ralph Sheldon–Danny McFall Gang and had at last reaped his revenge while eliminating an important rival for his bosses.

With each passing year, the Bloody Twentieth became even more blood-soaked. In April 1928 attorney Octavius Granady, Morris Eller's reform-minded opponent in the race for Republican committeeman, ended up the victim of gangland election violence. Granady aspired to become the first African American to represent a growing but underrepresented Twentieth Ward black population. He was a man of honorable intentions but lacked a political organization and had no real voter support. Against all odds, he counted on a primary-day surprise.

Accompanied by two colleagues, Granady steered his green Marmon automobile past the Twenty-Ninth Ward polling place on Blue Island Avenue on Election Day when an assassin's bullet whizzed past his head. He stepped on the gas and attempted to escape a potential ambush, but within a few moments a caravan of four automobiles gave chase in hot pursuit through the West Side. One of the four vehicles bore "America First" and "Morris Eller" banners, according to witness accounts.

As bullets shattered the glass and metal of the Marmon, Granady lost control and crashed the car into a tree at Thirteenth and Hoyne. Gunmen from one of the four hit cars pumped multiple shots into the candidate while Granady's companions managed to crawl away from the shooters. The Democratic press joined with the *Tribune* in a censure of "Thompsonism," a metaphor for escalating gangland mayhem.

An independent investigation led by Frank Loesch identified eighteen West Side gangsters inside the four-car caravan, including "Big" Louis Smith, John Armondo, Sam Kaplan, and Harry Hochstein—all dangerous criminal types on the payroll of Eller. Loesch's diligence exposed the inner working of Eller's formidable control of West Side law enforcement. Chicago police lieutenant Philip Carroll with three bureau detectives manned one of the death cars. Police bullets fired by the plainclothes detectives most certainly riddled Granady's body.

With Loesch's damning evidence laid before them, a grand jury returned indictments against Carroll, four detectives, and three gangsters including Sam Kaplan and Harry Hochstein. All were indicted and tried for murder, and all were quickly returned to the street after Judge Emanuel Eller reduced their bonds by nearly half the original amount. Underworld characters threatened eyewitnesses during judicial proceedings. One of them was killed in the street, and not surprisingly, all of the accused killers were acquitted.

The entire district became a Prohibition battleground for rival bootlegging gangs, labor racketeers, and politically connected shakedown artists like Maxie Eisen. The lucrative traffic in illegal alcohol provided the ways and means for wisecracking Maxwell street urchins forming up kid gangs in the 1890s to graduate from harassing pushcart peddlers, pickpocketing, and terrorizing the weak and vulnerable to organized crime and its attending rewards: a suite of rooms in the Congress Hotel, silk shirts, luxury touring cars, caviar, chorus girls, and the happy clink of champagne glasses.

Following the multimillion-dollar "whiskey trail"—a road that "led into crooked politics, questionable cabarets, gambling houses and disorderly resorts"—the Miller Gang, Herschel (Hershie), Maxie, and Davey, were early kingpins of the Maxwell Street Jewish underworld. Another brother, Harry Miller, joined the Chicago Police Department, but under a cloud of suspicion, he was dismissed in 1933.

By 1920 they had set aside petty stickups in order to chisel in on Paddy the Bear's lucrative rum racket. Davy Miller refereed prizefights on the side, and for his troubles he took two slugs to the belly outside the LaSalle Theater from his hated rival, safe blower and North Side gang mastermind Dion O'Banion. As a boy, Davy's kid brother, Hershie, fought many rounds in the prize ring and was known as "the best man with his fists" on the West Side. Hershie was a real scrapper but he understood the rules of the game: gain political patronage, land an insider job, and cultivate friends in high places. From humble beginnings on Maxwell Street, he acquired all three in due measure.

As a court bailiff in the municipal court during the Thompson administration, Hershie acquired his patronage through Twenty-Third Ward alderman Joseph O. Kostner, a friend, former school chum, and a Democratic wheelhorse on the West Side. Miller operated a string of gambling dens, and aligned his interests with one of the district's earliest and most clever Jewish gangsters, Samuel "Nails" Morton (born Samuel Markowitz), winner of the "Croix de Guerre" from the grateful French government for gallantry in battle during World War I.

First Lieutenant Morton led his 131st Illinois Infantry "over the top" and sustained two wounds in battle before being sent home a hero. Basking in past wartime glory in a postwar world held little interest, not with the possibility of attaining instant riches as a criminal fence disposing of stolen automobiles, high-stakes poker games, and organizing the West Side booze racket in defiance of the Volstead Act. In 1920, at the tender age of twenty-six, Morton clipped Nicholas Andrea "Nick the Greek" Dandolos, famed "king of the high rollers" for a cool $107,000 in a single night's play. That was in 1920. It was in the bootlegging world that Morton made his bones.

Through his East Coast connections, the war-hero-turned-gangster succeeded in importing the "real stuff" from Canadian distillers—not the cheap denatured alcohol swill cooked in homemade stills on Taylor Street and peddled by the Genna Gang. Chicago's emerging speakeasies and cabarets appealing to the Lake Shore Drive swells demanded only the best for their patrons. Morton, considered by many Jewish residents of the district to be an "avenging angel," protecting them from the harassment of the Gentiles, took in O'Banion as a kind of "junior partner" and acted as conciliator among the rival gangs as truckloads of imported booze arrived on the hour. "There is enough money in this racket for us all," he cooed, despite O'Banion's high-handed hot-temper tendencies.

For a time, Hershie, "Nails," and Dean were thick as thieves. Their Irish-Jewish West Side–North Side partnership netted them a fortune during the opening years of America's "Noble Temperance Experiment." Morton and Miller escaped prosecution for a lot of illicit doings, including murder. In a riotous, drunken debauch of jazz music, hard drinking, and an all-night craps game inside South Side undertaker Daniel Jackson's Beaux-Arts Club in August 1920, the pair shot down Chicago police detective sergeants William "Spike" Hennessy and James "Plucks" Mulcahy of the Cottage Grove Avenue Station, both ex-servicemen who saw heavy action during the war—and got away with it.

The Pekin Inn Café and the Beaux-Arts (an after-hours upstairs annex where the high rollers shot craps), were "black and tan" resorts located at Twenty-Seventh and State Streets in the heart of Chicago's burgeoning Black Belt community. The intermingling of blacks and whites in a social setting featuring jazz, the new musical art form matriculating northward from New Orleans during a racist, segregationist era, earned the Pekin Café the familiar sobriquet black and tan. Undertaker Jackson, a political boss, operated the club and ran vice operations in the black community for Alderman Louis Anderson.

On the fatal night, Mulcahy and his partner entered the premises just as Morton and Miller walked toward the gaming table in a private alcove. Detective Mulcahy, drunk and apparently there for no other purpose than to play a hand "with the boys," flashed a thick wad of bills. "Jim, gimme some ice [cash]," Morton demanded of the cop. Morton had come up short in his finances and wanted to be staked.[32]

Mulcahy chuckled and said, "No way, my friend." Words were exchanged; something about a whiskey shipment and an unfair split of the proceeds. Then the smile vanished from Mulcahy's face and all hell broke loose. Eyewitnesses testified that Morton knocked Mulcahy to the floor. Hennessey, accompanied by treasury agent W. W. Britton, assigned to enforce the Prohibition laws in Chicago, raced upstairs to see what all the commotion was about. He found Hershie Miller desperately trying to restrain the enraged "Nails" Morton while the staggering, punch-drunk Mulcahy tried to stand up. "Stick it on 'em!" the prostrated detective called out to Hennessy. In the confusion of the moment, Morton tripped on a chair leg and fell. By now Mulcahy was on his feet and viciously kicked Morton in the head.

Spotting Hennessy's gun, Hershie Miller drew down and fired a fatal shot. Hennessy's errant shot missed its target and splintered a wood pane. Miller then whirled around and turned on Mulcahy, dropping him to the floor with a well-timed shot. The detectives who should not have been there in the first place lived long enough to identify their assailants from their hospital deathbeds. Miller and Morton, along with the waiters, musicians, and patrons, were taken to the station. Alderman Kostner, feigning concern for Miller's wife, was the first to show up at the jail to visit his friend, the murderous Miller. Asked if he would defend Miller in court, Kostner demurred, citing conflict of interest, owing to his official capacity as an elected official.

The double killing sparked an outcry among law-abiding citizens, and was an opening salvo of decade-long gang warfare in Chicago. Speaking for the "business element" of the South and West Sides but stating the obvious, former Assistant State's Attorney Frederick L. Barnett pointed the finger at the raging Thompson corruption. "It goes without saying that the vice conditions which are permitted to exist throughout the South Side are worse today than ever. The police department seems paralyzed. It is my opinion that political protection given to this traffic by persons in high authority is responsible for the present detestable system. Something must be done—but it seems we can't expect it under the present system."

Indicted for murder, Hershie Miller freely admitted shooting both men. He had no fears of the law, but claimed it was an act of self-defense. "They were both kicking him [Morton] in the face when I told them to stop it. 'I'll give it to you,' Mulcahy told me and turned on me with his revolver. Hennessy did the same. We all started shooting then."[33]

Alderman Anderson, anxious to protect his professional reputation—and South Side operations— denied he had anything to do with the Pekin Inn Café and Beaux-Arts. "I am not interested in any way, financially or otherwise in either place," he said. "I have never been in either place. When Chief Garrity issued his 1:00 closing order for cabarets I understood they had closed because their business had all been after 1:00. I was much surprised to hear that either of them was running."

There is nothing more frustrating to a prosecutor than to think the killer might get away with murder, or witnesses compromised.

Amid charges that the entire first trial was a "fix," resulting in an acquittal in 1921, it took a second jury less than one hour and just one ballot to find the defendants not guilty on January 7, 1922. In his published memoir of the *Dry and Lawless Years*, Judge John H. Lyle, citing the case as an example of the influence of the gangs in the courts, called the outcome "a patent miscarriage of justice that injured police department morale."[34]

Succumbing to public pressure, Dan Jackson, assisted by Alderman Anderson, sold the Pekin Inn Café to the city for $35,000. Perhaps it was poetic justice or just a case of strange irony. The former jazz club, awash in bootleg liquor and stained with blood, received a remarkable baptism as the "Pekin Inn Municipal Court." Judge Lyle's bench was mounted on the same mahogany dais where jazz trumpeter King Oliver once performed.

With his fortune now secure, Hershie Miller abandoned Maxwell Street and his former associates for a luxurious home on Sheridan Road on the far North Side lakefront. In a single day, March 24, 1924, rival gangsters fired at him as he drove his car on Clark Street, but Miller dove under the wheel, escaped the gangster slugs and steered the car to safety—for a few hours.

Later in the day a bomb tore apart his place of business, the Acme Cleaning and Dyeing Company at 3332 Clark. "I can't understand it," Miller sighed. "I left the gangs and tried to live quietly, even moving to a new neighborhood. It begins to look like I must do one of two things, leave town or fight it out to the end with some gang that seems to be after me."[35] In 1925 Hershie sold the cleaning and dyeing business coveted by the North Side gangsters and walked away with $250,000 in his pocket, his stormy career in the gangs nearly over. In June 1929 Miller was arrested and sentenced to three months in jail on a bootlegging rap, but thereafter his name disappeared from the police blotters. Having narrowly escaped the wrath of his former gangland associates, Hershie Miller quietly expired of natural causes at his Michigan City, Indiana, summer home on July 12, 1939.

As the gangsters battled one another to death to secure territorial control in the 1920s, profound demographic change resulted in an outward movement of the emerging middle-class residential community into more gentrified surroundings. Further west, along Twelfth Street, the adjoining community of Lawndale emerged as a center of secondary Jewish settlement. Assimilation with the outside world and the desire of the American-born children of the old settlers to shed the customs and trappings of Europe in order to conform to the rhythms of American life rendered the district obsolete.

Maxwell Street shopkeepers and peddlers saved their hard-earned money and advanced themselves out of poverty to become larger-scale merchants, business entrepreneurs, real estate agents, entertainers, and contractors well beyond the confines of the old ghetto. The criminals and the old-time gambling bosses of Maxwell Street likewise followed the steady westward migration as the years rolled on. The splintered bootlegging gangs coalesced in Lawndale and Douglas Park to form a monolithic criminal organization—the "Jewish Faction" of Chicago's organized crime syndicate that took shape and form during the short and violent reign of the Eller Gang during Prohibition. As grown men, many of the street hustlers, pickpockets, silk stealers, and petty extortionists of former times became the bookmakers, bootleggers, professional assassins, and "juice" men of a new and emerging order—the mob, colloquially known as the "Outfit."

By the early 1940s, Jake "Greasy Thumb" Guzik, Maxwell Street gangster and a Levee District brothel master, had ascended the hierarchy of the "organization" to assume the mantle of leadership as a syndicate boss. Small of stature, sad-faced, and baggy eyed, Guzik, the son of a Russian cigar maker, lived near Lytle Street and Taylor as a boy, in the same neighborhood where Chicago White Sox founder Charles Comiskey and federal court judge Abraham Lincoln Marovitz grew up. Guzik ascended from the status of pimp and whorehouse master—working in partnership with his brother, Harry, and devoted wife, Rose—to trusted gambling overseer, political fixer, planner, and financial wizard of the Chicago mob in the latter day.

Old Maxwell, as it once existed, was recognizable to most mid-twentieth-century Chicagoans as an open-air peddler market spanning Jefferson to Morgan from just south of Twelfth Street and Halsted, serving the entire city from a mélange of ramshackle street stands and the buildings behind them. A semblance of political control and fiscal management existed amid the bark of entrepreneurial pitch men speaking a dozen different languages. In moderate weather upwards of eighty thousand people poured into the market on weekends.

In the 1950s African Americans followed newly arrived immigrant Hispanics filling in the former Valley District where Paddy the Bear and Hershie Miller once held sway and displaced the few remaining European ethnics. As the memory of the bootleg wars faded, the old and historic problems of crime and delinquency were never solved of course. In 1949 the entire area had the largest number of delinquency referrals to the family courts. Of Chicago's s(then) seventy-five community areas, Maxwell Street had 146 more referrals than any other area in the city. As late as 1950, 77 percent of the buildings lacked a private bath or were classified as dilapidated, compared to only 19.6 percent for the rest of the city. Sixty percent of the community dwellings lacked running water.

The area remained a dismal slum until the arrival of the neighboring University of Illinois campus. Construction of the university and the opening of the Dan Ryan Expressway eliminated miles of residential housing and pressed down on the remnants of old Maxwell Street. The popularity of the market slowly diminished in the 1970s. Then, as the death knell of a way of life slowly sounded in the early 1990s, what was left of Maxwell Street became a tawdry stretch of urban landscape populated by a handful of remaining junk dealers, blues men, flea-market hangers-on, and car radio and hubcap thieves selling the very same items wholesale that they had purloined from parked cars across the city the week before.

Efforts to achieve historic landmark status in order to save the remaining Halsted Street emporiums from demolition failed as the property values for these ancient, weather-beaten structures declined. The City of Chicago relocated the remnants of the old market several blocks east to Canal Street in 1994 to make way for the expansion of University of Illinois housing and the complete gentrification of the Halsted Street business district. In September 2008 the market was moved again, this time to Desplaines Street. Today the former open-air market is unrecognizable from its days of past glory.

Trendsetting restaurants, coffee shops, and upscale boutiques opened for the residential student population and affluent city dwellers. The retail corridor lines Halsted and crisscrosses Maxwell Street. Nearby, the police station, in its diminished fame (or infamy) has withstood the wrecking ball. In September 1923 the *Tribune* commented on the dingy interior of the building, then only thirty-seven years old. "The grime and damp and mold of ages seem to have settled in these old stone corridors. Behind the iron bars men are lying on the stone floors or on the bare wooden bench which serves as the only finishing. A little stream of water about an inch deep and six inches wide runs along a groove in the back of each cell. This is the only sanitary convenience afforded."

Nowadays the former Maxwell Street station capably serves the University of Illinois police as a headquarters building. It is a forlorn, out-of-time relic to a lost age, surrounded by an expanse of shipping warehouses, factories, and University of Illinois student housing, because the densely backed tenements, saloons, corner groceries, and gambling hells vanished into the vapors of history long ago.

Andy Craig, gambler, flesh peddler, bail-bondsman, and boss of Whiskey Row decadence in the early 1900s. DN-0054349, Chicago History Museum, *Chicago Daily News* negatives collection.

Police detectives examine the crudely fashioned dugout and hideaway used by Chicago's Car Barn bandits near Clarke, Indiana. DN-0001561, Chicago History Museum, *Chicago Daily News* negatives collection.

Car barn bandit Gustave Marx contemplates his scheduled April 22, 1904, rendezvous with the hangman inside the Cook County Jail. DN-0001539, Chicago History Museum, *Chicago Daily News* negatives collection.

County Commissioner Frank Ragen (right), organizer of Ragen's Colts Social Athletic Club in the unlikely setting of the Grand Pacific Hotel during a meeting of the Progressive Party in 1913. DN-0061769, Chicago History Museum, *Chicago Daily News* negatives collection.

Former gang-boy turned murderer "Ammunition" Eddie Wheed escorted to the lock-up following his capture during the siege of Thomas Street, August 31, 1917. Wheed's vicious "kill or be killed" attitude outraged the public and inspired the formation of the Chicago Crime Commission. DN-0068927, Chicago History Museum, *Chicago Daily News* negatives collection.

Death Corner, Milton and Oak Streets in Little Hell during the heyday of the Black Hand terror, 1911. DN-0056708, Chicago History Museum, *Chicago Daily News* negatives collection.

Cook County Jail, March 1915. A product of Little Hell squalor and misery, 16-year-old Elmer Fanter earned the nickname "the Boy Evangelist" for his street-corner preaching. Then he joined a gang, idled away his time in pool halls, and killed August Jantzen during the commission of his first armed robbery inside a delicatessen. DN-0064142, Chicago History Museum, *Chicago Daily News* negatives collection.

Chicago's deadly race riot, July 31, 1919. Brick-throwing gang boys raid the South Side Black Belt. Chicago History Museum, i65495.

ounded in 1903, the St. Charles Training School for Boys in St. Charles, Illinois (shown here in 1926) vas accurately described as a "breeding ground for criminal gangs" although its benefactors, John W. Gates and Cook County judge Richard Tuthill, envisioned an idyllic, pastoral, country setting to give delinquent boys a second chance in life. DN-0080308, Chicago History Museum, *Chicago Daily News* negatives collection.

The wily Maxwell Street political boss Morris Eller, a tool of the William Hale Thompson Machine, and his son Cook County Judge Emanuel Eller regulated the gangsters, street peddlers, gamblers, and saloon action in the "Bloody" Twentieth Ward during the 1920s. DN-0089498, Chicago History Museum, *Chicago Daily News* negatives collection.

William Hale Thompson campaign poster, 1927. Chicago History Museum, i24189.

Vote for Big Bill the Builder
He Cannot Be Bought, Bossed or Bluffed
CUT OUT THIS PICTURE AND HANG IT IN YOUR WINDOW

Al Capone and Chief of Detectives John Stege, an honest and determined crime fighter discharged by Mayor Thompson in 1927 for harassing Thompson's gangster allies. DN-0091506, Chicago History Museum, *Chicago Daily News* negatives collection.

Thomas J. "Buff" Higgins, feared leader of the Johnson Street Gang, had been sent to Bridewell two hundred times before his eighteenth birthday. He was executed March 23, 1898, for home invasion and the murderer of Peter McGooey. *Chicago Times-Herald*, March 23, 1898.

"Buff" Higgins on the gallows of the Cook County Jail. *Chicago Times-Herald*, March 23, 1898.

Maxwell Street gang leader Chris Merry—born on the same night as the Chicago Fire—went to the ga lows on April 23, 1898, for the murder of his common-law wife, Pauline Ballou, in a drunken rage. Merr typified the nighmarish cycle of urban decay, hopelessness, and misery of West Side slum life at the en of the nineteenth century. *Chicago Chronicle*, April 24, 1898. Retrospect by James Diotenry.

Illinois State Senator John F. O'Malley—powerful Democratic boss of the Twenty-first and Twenty-thir Wards bordering "Little Hell." In the 1890s, O'Malley utilized the services of the Market Street Gang—hi henchmen—operating from both inside and outside of the penitentiary. *Chicago Tribune*, September 13, 195

John Stevens, otherwise known to the denizens of Little Hell as Major John W. Sampson, led the Market Street gang of thieves, pickpockets, and political enforcers during the 1880s and 1890s. Later in life he turned to politics and counted on his allies in the Twenty-third Ward to elect him alderman, but fell short. *Chicago Tribune*, November 17, 1904.

The trial conviction of 15-year-old Clement "Cookie" Macis in July 1955, for the murder of 17-year-old Kenneth Sleboda in a drive-by shooting occurring in Chicago's Bridgeport community, signaled a dangerous turn in street gang activity in the not-so-tranquil 1950s. *Chicago American*, February 16, 1956.

Looking NE toward Cabrini Green Housing Project, Green Housing Project, North Halsted Street at right. West Division Street at left, and Goose Island at the bottom of the frame. North Halsted Street Canal Bridge, spanning North Branch Canal at North Halsted Street, Chicago, Cook County. Courtesy of Library of Congress; reproduction HAER ILL, 16-CHIG,148.

Corner of Maxwell and Halsted Streets, Chicago, known as "Bloody Maxwell." Courtesy of Library of Congress; reproduction LC-DIG-fsa-8a29866.

5

THE GOLD COAST AND THE GANGS: NORTH SIDE AFFLUENCE, LITTLE HELL, AND GANG CRIME, 1860–1930

The North Side became the last permanently settled region of Chicago. Before the Civil War the Chicago River was choked with cargo boats and schooners distributing goods to the lumberyards and produce merchants of South Water Street, a noisy, congested open-air market hugging the river from Michigan Avenue south to Market Street. For much of the day, the drawbridges spanning the river could not be crossed because tall-masted vessels, coal barges, and freighters blocked pedestrian vehicular access as they eased in and out of their moorings. Commerce, foot traffic, and the carriage trade between downtown and points north suffered as a result. Unpaved roads minus horse-drawn street railway cars presented commuting hardships for people desiring to travel north from the business district.

West of Clark Street and north of the river, the isolated and dismal shanties of Kilgubbin, located on Goose Island, offered cheap but affordable housing to early arriving, threadbare Irish immigrant squatters laying claim to the land in the 1840s. But a colony of the ill-fed, unwashed poor tended to discourage residential and economic development nearby.[1]

Beginning in 1860, the Common Council, in a concerted effort to stimulate North Side development, rectified an immediate problem by passing the first in a series of measures to encourage growth. New and improved bridge crossings lightened the load of the old Rush Street Bridge. Significantly, William Butler Ogden, millionaire real estate entrepreneur and Chicago's first mayor, acquired the rights to lay track for the North Chicago City Railway traversing Clark Street, Clybourn Avenue, and Division Street to Sedgwick. With this significant step, desirable residential lakefront homes sprouted on the prairie.

The city desperately needed a park system and green space for public recreation. In 1865 the city council appropriated the old city cemetery extending from the (then) city limits at Diversey Avenue south to North Avenue for that purpose. The beautifully landscaped park on the Lake Michigan shoreline became a catalyst for residential and commercial growth in the postwar period. The acreage was once owned by a German gardener named Milliman who died intestate in the mid-1840s. The grounds were sold to the city by the public administrator for the sum of $2,500—monies the Milliman family required in order to liquidate the debts of the deceased patriarch. In 1868, following three years of landscaping, road grading, the excavation of 1,685 graves, and the transfer of the disintegrating coffins from the grounds to other cemeteries directly north, the new Lincoln Park, a place of serenity and quiet repose for all people, opened.

In a letter dated August 30, 1868, a visitor to Chicago, with the nom de plume "Peregrine Pickle," wrote: "Lincoln Park, when I first saw it a week ago was to me a new revelation. It showed me what I had long doubted, that there was taste enough in this city to conceive, and enterprise enough to execute a beautiful retreat out of the everlasting din and wear of business. Chicago is no longer a mere depot for hogs, pine boards, lard, corn and whiskey and a good staying place for those who deal in these articles. She is now going to set her house in order for us to live in. She will beautify it and adorn it and make a home of it, full of attractions which will keep us here in the golden summer days. These are the promises the present makes to the future."[2]

The ballyhooed opening of Lincoln Park represented an important step in the birthing of Chicago's "Gold Coast." Potter Palmer, hotel magnate and the city's most revered socialite and arbiter of good taste and breeding in the Gilded Age, glimpsed the future of the North Side lakefront and established the district east of Clark Street as the epicenter of the city's concentrated wealth. On a patch of swampy soil situated between Banks and Schiller Streets, Palmer personally financed construction of a castellated twenty-three-room mansion with a conservatory and ballroom, elaborate down to the smallest details.

The Canada-gray limestone structure, its design influenced by two European castles, Schloss-Rheinstein on the Rhine near Bingen, Germany, and Castle Lismore in County Cork, Ireland, towered above every other North Side building. The Palmer "residence," if one could apply ordinary layman's language to a building of so much grandeur, featured the city's first passenger elevator to be installed in a private home. The mansion had no exterior doorknobs or locks. Callers could only be admitted by the household servants, who exercised the greatest discretion as to who gained entry and those refused admittance. The castle became the staging ground for Chicago's most lavish and ostentatious seasonal parties, high teas, and evening suppers of the Gilded Age, presided over by Bertha Honore Palmer, then the reigning arbiter of Chicago society, style, grace, and manners.

Palmer hastily bought up a number of other frontage properties along the Lake Shore Road (Lake Shore Drive in the modern day), and encouraged other prominent men who counted their wealth in seven figures to join him. Thus he inspired a speedy exodus of other important social climbers, Union League Club members, and titans of commerce, banking, retail, and manufacturing from Prairie Avenue to move to the quiet opulence of tree-lined arteries of Gold Coast streets: Ohio, State Parkway, Cass Street (now Wabash Avenue), Dearborn, Rush, Banks, Goethe, Bellevue, Scott, Division, Astor, and Schiller. The South Side "millionaire's row," threatened by the arrival of heavy industry, an army of immigrant poor, and the menace of the Levee, an encroaching brothel district three city blocks to the west, contributed to the decline of Prairie Avenue in the late 1880s and 1890s.

The Gold Coast remains to this day a privileged, sequestered world unto itself—sheltered and guarded. A short walk to the west from the palaces of the rich, prosperity gave way to an entirely different social and economic milieu—the squalor and decay of the slum district known as "Little Hell."

From the foot of the Chicago River at Wolf Point (near where Mark Beaubien opened his Sauganash Hotel), west to Market Street and north to North Avenue (until 1889 the northern city limits), this crime-stricken, impoverished region inspired the hostility of the press and law enforcement. In the days of Beaubien and "Long John" Wentworth, the lowly regarded district of Kilgubbin was known as "the terror of constables, sheriffs and policeman," according to one 1865 newspaper account.

Long before the Chicago Fire, the neighborhood east and south of Kilgubbin (hugging the river on Market Street between Kinzie and Erie Streets) was mostly featureless open prairie until the great conflagration of October 1871 opened up the district to the immediate north for settlement.

The Relief & Aid Society, accountable for the formation of ghetto neighborhoods and the herding of an unstable heterogeneous population into tenements on Maxwell Street, installed thousands more displaced immigrant Irish into hastily built "relief cottages" and the "Barracks of Poverty" north of the Chicago River after the fire. The Barracks, a long, low-slung wooden tenement constructed on the west side of Crosby Street across from the city gas works, reflected the politics of ethnic and class segregation of nineteenth-century Chicago. One room was allotted per family—not quite the idyllic image of "home and hearth" working people from foreign lands dreamed of in their rush to escape famine and old-world political repression.

Inevitably the subpar living arrangements on the North Side (or North Division as it was then called) spawned drunkenness, vice, gambling, street gangs, and cycles of crime. The consequence of Relief & Aid policies set into motion during the 1870s established the underpinnings of an economic and corrosive social structure whose echoes still exist in the modern day. Lincoln Steffens said that in Chicago "class, race, religions, regions are the background against which the play is built."

"Their food and lodgings and much of their clothing came from the Relief and Aid Society," recalled one old timer recalling the plight of the North Side refugees in an 1890 interview. "The citizens of the Hell were comfortably fixed for social enjoyment. They found themselves each week with a surplus on hand and nothing to do with it unless they devoted it to the pleasures of the cup that cheers. It was thus that Little Hell began."[3]

Gangs formed early. Mickey Barry, a tough Irish lad, nearly killed several Chicago police officers with bricks. "Foreigner" Sweeney and

"Bull" Ryan ran with the most dangerous gangster of a bad lot, "Fighting" Jimmy O'Neill, an ex-union soldier captured by the rebel army and confined to Libby Prison during the war. With the South in tatters following surrender, Jimmy crept back into Chicago to anoint himself the "King of Little Hell." It was O'Neill's habit to trail his coat behind him and to challenge local toughs to tread upon it—and test their pugilistic skills in street-fighting brawls. The "King" lorded over Wesson Street, from Chicago Avenue to Oak Street. The neighbors called this section of the North Side badlands "Big Hell."

Little Hell drew in a mix of working-class Irish, Swedes, and Germans. The Swedes worshipped at the Evangelical Lutheran church and monopolized the cloth trade and tailoring industry in the 1870s and 1880s, but as Neapolitans and Sicilians began arriving from southern Europe in the 1890s and 1900s, the small Scandinavian shops were undercut and driven out of business by enterprising Italian women willing to pick up and deliver their customers' needlework.

Suspicious and fearful of darker-skinned immigrants arriving from Italy, the Swedes migrated further north along Clark Street to escape the inevitable clash of ethnic culture and religion. The Germans formed a pocket of settlement in St. Michael's parish of Old Town, to the immediate north. That left the Irish and Italians to do battle with one another for control of the city blocks and to settle old scores—a fight with no clear-cut resolution, but one that had a direct bearing on the formation of the beer-running gangs and the outcome of the decade of Prohibition mayhem.

Although the boundaries were not always clearly defined and tended to shift over time, the vicinity west of Larrabee Street and north of Division Street extending to Goose Island encompassed much of the Little Hell post-fire settlement. In a January 1895 story, the *Chicago Sunday Herald* traced the origins of the name to the frequent rows and disturbances the paper attributed to "the belligerent temperament of the people who were temporarily housed here." The Little Hell name took hold in the public imagination c.1873, but it was not original nor was it unique to Chicago. Reportedly the inhabitants of the district borrowed it from one of the poorer sections of London.

Describing the chaos of Little Hell on November 27, 1875, an *Inter-Ocean* reporter wrote: "Two years ago Little Hell began to acquire general fame by reason of frequent rows and disturbances that occurred within its borders. Scarcely a day passed without some knifing or shooting scrape. Numerous, have been the burglaries traced to their lairs in its precincts. As many of the men wore heavy boots, it was not infrequent to hear of noses being crushed, or bones injured by boot heels. Sometimes by way of variety ears and fingers would be bitten off."

Pockmarked by winding alleys and tumbledown one-story wooden dwellings lining narrow unpaved streets filthy in the extreme, Little Hell paralleled the squalor of Maxwell Street by the dawn of the twentieth century. Sidewalks sagged and were irregular in size and rarely ran twenty yards on the same level. Alleyways were cramped and dangerous affairs that barely allowed for the passage of a horse-drawn wagon; rats and vermin routed around in piles of uncollected garbage. "Children are abundant in Little Hell," the *Inter-Ocean* continued. "In fact they are about the cheapest commodity in that market. The streets are overflowing with juveniles, ragged hatless noisy, dirty juveniles as they deport themselves in little groups along the gutters."

The word on the street among the criminal gentry: "no lights, no police." In a letter to the *Tribune* on May 15, 1887, a resident of Market Street complained of "a crowd of loafers, young men from fifteen to 20 years old, [that] occupy the sidewalks, and if a single person, man or woman should venture to pass by, he or she will certainly be insulted by offensive remarks, if not roughly handled. Usually these loafers are consulting about the best method of stealing or fighting. The writer has been residing at Market Street for nearly three years and always saw a policeman patrolling there until since [sic] four or five months ago. Are our policemen afraid of making their beat on Market Street or are they only visiting streets where there is nothing for them to do?"

The Women's Society of the Unity Church opened the Eli Bates social settlement house on Larrabee Street in 1876, with a mission of providing sewing classes and a nursery for young mothers as a means of escape from the O'Neills, the Ryans, and other violent men of the district, including their own husbands. In 1884 wealthy Chicagoan Eli Bates funded the construction of a larger building at 621 Elm Street and broadened the objectives of the charity in order to better address the deprivations of slum living, saloon dependence, and juvenile crime. An industrial training school, kindergarten, and various clubs for both children and adults offered positive alternatives to street life but there were few playgrounds, public baths, or other social amenities in the surrounding area to serve the divergent ethnic groups that lived there.[4]

Until it passed out of existence in 1938, the Eli Bates House received much of its charitable funding from conscience-stricken Gold Coast society philanthropists. But as Harvey Warren Zorbaugh ruefully noted in his landmark work *The Gold Coast and the Slum*, "The ward committee of the Women's City Club conducted tours in Little Hell—instructive slumming parties for society's social minded during which large motor coaches brought the Social Register into fleeting and horrified contact with the 'submerged tenth.' At the same time, an organizational scion of an old family was bringing back from Harvard or Princeton that first flush of enthusiasm for social uplift which was soon to become a fashion and later a profession." One well-meaning millionaire opened the doors of his Lake Shore Drive mansion to the poor of Little Hell, and offered free lodging in unused rooms to the extreme examples of want and despair. However, as Zorbaugh demonstrated, the concerns of the upper world were mostly viewed with mistrust and scorn by the immigrant poor and their political benefactors.

"Somehow the neighborliness that had been anticipated as the result of this mingling did not materialize. Mothers from the slum thought they were being patronized. Petty politicians, unable to comprehend this startling phenomenon, thought their host must be intending to run for office." Despite good intentions, vice, prostitution, gangs, and drugs compounded the misery of the slum dwellers.

In Little Hell, 386 saloons were open for business in 1906, but only twenty-one police officers and six plainclothes detectives from the Thirty-Eighth Precinct of the East Chicago Avenue Police Station were on hand to prevent the habitués from killing one another. Clark Street, a major thoroughfare running north from downtown all the way out to the city limits, comprised the "buffer zone," a kind of no-man's-land separating the heart of the Gold Coast aristocracy from the darkest corners of the tenements and slums.

Chicago police monitored forty-five cheap Clark Street rooming houses occupied by thugs, rowdies, prostitutes, and "dope fiends" (as substance abusers were commonly referred to in those days) who committed armed robbery and burglary by night, shooting their victims without rhyme, reason, or provocation. Storefront chop suey restaurants operated by immigrant Chinese fronted upstairs opium dens. Opium and morphine addiction were commonplace in big-city vice districts before World War I. The passage of the Pure Food and Drug Act of 1906 and the Harrison Narcotics Act eight years later outlawed opiates, cocaine, morphine, and other recreational drugs that previously could be procured from neighborhood pharmacies and apothecaries. Before 1914 only twenty-nine states had laws in place outlawing opium. Prostitution was endemic.

"Walk up Clark Street any night between 8:00 and 1:00 a.m.," the *Tribune* reported in March 1906. "Immediately on crossing the bridge [over the Chicago River], you will feel the atmosphere of the vice district. Brilliant electric signs mark the endless succession of saloons; from the concert halls come harsh notes of a piano sadly out of tune and floating on the evening breezes are the strident and uncultivated tones of the lady warbler who is doing things to that ever popular ditty 'Everybody Works but Father.' The resorts in the district are frequented by the younger girls of the half-world; graduates of the dance halls and fruit stores, both nurseries of vice."[5] Twenty uniformed patrol officers were deployed along north Clark Street to bar juveniles from entering dancehalls and keep close watch on barkeeps attempting to sell liquor after prohibited hours.

The 386 saloons and the rooming houses were hangouts for known criminals, North Side politicos, panders, streetwalkers, and the gangs of Little Hell courting their favor. Police detectives—mostly clever, nimble men, the few of them that remained uncorrupted—roamed freely in the vice dens and groggeries. In the first three months of 1906, 872 arrests were recorded during a fifty-nine-day period. The gaudy burlesque of the concert saloons where pimps arranged assignations inside the rooming houses drew scarce police resources away from the daily grind of violence and social disorganization of the slum lurking behind the Clark Street "curtain" of vice.

Here in the North Side ghetto spanning three generations dwelled a shiftless, parasitic population of safe blowers, pimps, barrel-house bums, thieving con artists, grafters, roustabouts, and Chicago's oldest enduring criminal organization up to that time, the Market Street Gang, a byword for violence and murder from the 1870s through the early 1900s. "They are not brave, but they are vicious and unforgiving," cautioned the *Tribune*.

The alliance of gangdom and ward politicians as the game played out in Bridgeport—over on the West Side, in the bowels of Little Hell, and in other city districts where the poor congregated—manipulated the socioeconomic life of communities. To collect votes and build up the organization to ensure Election Day success, the local district leadership recruited the lads of the street. On this side of town, the Market Streeters enjoyed the protection of their own "silk-hat" political potentate, John F. O'Malley, the redheaded Democratic leader of the Twenty-Third Ward for nearly three riotous decades.

Tall, smooth-faced, and well built, O'Malley (aka "The Red Fellow") was born in Little Hell in 1859 at Superior and Kingsbury Streets. As a young man he entered the political fray at a time when physical prowess, a gun, and a set of brass knuckles trumped mediation when serious matters required resolution. All were essential tools of the trade for a politician rising up from the streets. The scion of a North Side political family steeped in nepotism, John sponsored his brother Martin into the police department, while a cousin, the quiet and withdrawn Thomas, entered the plumbing trade and worked in the city sewers as a master plumber until John coaxed him into politics as an aldermanic candidate. The family motto and battle cry reverberated across the Twenty-Third Ward: "O'Malley forever!"

With the full support of the Market Street voters rallying behind him, Tom O'Malley easily won his aldermanic seat in the Twenty-Third Ward at the same time his cousin ran the state senate district from his offices in Springfield and Chicago. Under such an arrangement as this, the red-light district operatives and the gangs of the North Side enjoyed unlimited mobility, immunity from arrest, and all the protection they needed to run their rackets with minimal interference, just as long as they demonstrated obedience and a willingness to take on the "heavy" work when called upon.

John O'Malley was an unrefined old-school brawler, not the kind to put on fancy airs or fine graces. During one political season, he even refused an invitation to run for the U.S. Senate because he said he did not own a silk hat. But he was a kingmaker in his own right, answering to statewide Democratic boss Roger Sullivan, a political acolyte of Mike McDonald in the closing years of the Gilded Age, and undisputed kingpin of the electoral process spanning the opening decades of the twentieth century.

O'Malley owned a saloon inside the old Sid J. Euson Theater building at Clark and Kinzie Streets where red-hot burlesque queens cavorted to ragtime piano and carried on with their men all night. The clubhouse-saloon remained his active home base of operation for nearly a quarter century. It was the quintessential Chicago "political saloon." Through the lens of flawed memory, James Doherty, a grizzled press veteran who undoubtedly enjoyed John O'Malley's unique blend of 1890s hospitality and the abundant free lager provided, showered exaggerated praise upon O'Malley in a 1953 look-back that belied the true facts surrounding the near fatal shooting of four-term state representative William R. Lyman inside his sample room on May 23, 1900.

> The Red Fellow . . . had so much pride in his reputation for keeping a promise that he felt compelled to shoot his intimate friend Alderman Billy Lyman. "Keep out of my saloon when you are drinking," said O'Malley to Lyman, "or I'll shoot you when you sit down." Calmly he went to a drawer, took out a pistol, walked over and without malice shot Lyman through the seat of his trousers inflicting a painful flesh wound. Theirs' was a beautiful friendship for the rest of their lives—O'Malley dying in 1921; Lyman in 1928.[6]

In truth, Lyman had sustained a life-threatening wound, and that "beautiful friendship" (if one could seriously describe it that way), turned murderous. O'Malley and Lyman were bitter antagonists representing rival factions within the Democratic Party battling for supremacy of the Twenty-Third Ward. It was an election season and the "Red Fellow" touted the candidacy for alderman of his protégé and protectorate, John Stevens, aka "Major" John Sampson, a treacherous Market Street gorilla, thug, and suspected murderer.

As the divided-party factions strove to resolve petty differences and unite behind an acceptable slate of candidates, Billy Lyman casually strolled into the saloon hoping to talk some sense to O'Malley's business partner and henchman, James Lyons. A hot exchange of words, the trading of insults, and the inevitable crack of a gun from the saloon politician sent Lyman sprawling to the floor with two slugs embedded in his thigh. Doctors feared that the injured man might expire at any moment from blood poisoning. O'Malley, hiding his pistol in a drawer, hastily retreated to the theater adjoining his saloon to watch the boxing matches already in progress when Captain Luke Colleran, no stranger to Market Street violence himself, arrived to escort him to jail. "Why Captain, it was an accidental shot, that's all," alibied O'Malley.

"The feeling in the ward has been bitter," Colleran told the press. "We have been fearing trouble of this kind for several days. I am glad it is no worse, but this talk of accidental shooting is foolish."

At the center of the vicious feud, the polarizing presence of "Major" Sampson, notorious confidence man, counterfeiter, swindler, and unchallenged leader of the Market Street Gang, tilted the scales of power on the North Side in favor of the organization he commanded. On the West Side there was Manny Abrahams and Morris Eller, with their divergent careers, and the thugs they commanded. While on the South Side, Frank Ragen and his race-baiting Colts in Bridgeport and Major Sampson in Little Hell mastered gangland organizational strategy in the decades before Al Capone first spied Chicago from the coach car of a westbound Pullman in 1919.

Within every precinct in the city, Democratic Party bosses (looking to establish political hegemony) courted the favor of underworld characters of the worst stripe who had signaled a willingness to exchange their street smarts, bullying tactics, and intimidation in return for guaranteed patronage jobs to dispense downward to the rest of the gang. "Democrats in the ward were as clouds of locusts compared with the Republican handful," commented the *Tribune*. The paper extended its withering support to Michael Francis Garrity, a bloviating Republican politician whose ward-heeling antics were viewed with skepticism, if not benign amusement, by the editorialists.

"Sinator Moike," as the G.O.P. ward operatives addressed him, was narrowly viewed as a Democrat in a Republican's suit of clothes.[7] He "had a masterful bunch to fight, and when the opposing gangs came together a Donnybrook fair was a crossroads prayer meeting compared with it," commented the *Tribune*. "When Garrity was in his prime, and each saloon had a water trough in front . . . and when bands of political opponents clashed or luckless voters did not cast their pasted ballots right, these troughs were filled with offenders, or such of them were not beaten up [by the Market Street Gang], to show them the error of their ways."

"Sinator Moike" operated his own saloon at Clark and Kinzie, replete with water trough for horses and brawlers. During election days he presented a fully stuffed ballot box to the vote counters, just as his Democratic rivals were known to do in their own grog shops down the street. In those days no one held an exclusive monopoly on the business of filling up the troughs with political enemies with broken heads.

Garrity exchanged hot words with Major Sampson and his men. Inside his saloon one night in November 1887, the senator accidentally shot Michael Kennedy through the left lung when the bullet was really meant for the good major. "By the love of God, it was an accident!" Garrity gasped when Captain Michael Schaack came calling. "And by the way, can you keep it out of the papers?" Schaack replied he would do no such thing. In the hospital, Kennedy told reporters that it was just an accident, an unfortunate beer-soaked spat and nothing more. But when a doctor advised the wounded man that he might suffer death from pneumonia or pleurisy, he quickly changed his mind and said it wasn't an accident after all. However, no prosecutions were forthcoming.

Garrity had no chance of conquering the entrenched O'Malley machine, although this mostly forgotten political creature had one minor claim to fame: He occupied the governor's office for exactly one day while the incumbent governor and the lieutenant governor were traveling out of state.

Within his own party, O'Malley frequently sparred with a smaller contingent of head-knockers loyal to the "Redhead's" bitterest of all political foes—James Aloysius "Hot Stove Jimmy" Quinn, alderman of the adjoining Twenty-First Ward, stretching from the Chicago River to Lincoln Park. Quinn, owner of a North Side haberdashery, protected the gambling rackets and sold protection for fees ranging from twenty-five dollars a month for poker games to a hundred dollars a month for the Clark Street brothel keepers. Saloon wags said that if only Quinn could get away with it, he would steal anything that wasn't nailed down, including the hot stove in the kitchen.

"Hot Stove" Jimmy Quinn, in the pocket of North Side gambling boss "Mont" Tennes for nearly two decades, sized up his constituency and played all the angles. On rare occasions, he happily sipped afternoon tea with Mrs. Bertha Palmer on the overstuffed settee in her drawing room. Call it nerve or call it genius, Quinn ingratiated the silk-stocking crowd by slating Honore Palmer, Bertha's benighted first son, for the city council. Society was simply agog when young Palmer won his 1901 election bid—on the Democratic ticket. But then, had not the elder Palmer declared allegiance to the Democrats by sponsoring illegal games of faro with Mike McDonald inside his plush hotel in the Gilded 1870s? Mrs. Palmer's endearments and all the Clark Street muscle Quinn could muster was never the equal to forces the Redhead commanded. And while the rival factions shot at each other during pitched gun battles in the back alleys, when the smoke cleared the O'Malley faction maintained control of the North Side patronage.

Appointments of low-level Cook County and city hall government factotums and official sanctions from the politicians awaited Market Street higher-ups. The perpetuation of the Clark Street girly shows, brothels, concert saloons, and neighborhood clip joints belied the enormous sense of unease and fear among the peasant classes of Little Hell to the west. Despite his protestations, everyone knew the character and less-than-stellar reputation of Sampson. The Republican newspapers around town recoiled at the thought of this scoundrel taking his place in the council and warned the voters in no uncertain terms that in his "previous life" the boisterous and arrogant "Major" had been:

- Arrested, convicted, sentenced to one year in the Bridewell in 1881 for passing counterfeit money;
- Summoned as a witness in the 1893 trial of former police detective and accused murderer Daniel Coughlin; indicted for the May 1889 abduction-assassination of Irish nationalist Dr. Patrick Henry Cronin in a conspiracy hatched by the Clan Na Gael. Sampson testified that he had been offered a contract to kill Cronin.[8]
- Arrested on fourteen counts of perpetrating mob violence and encouraging other members of the Market Street Gang to commit criminal acts during the 1894 fall elections. Sampson was tried on several counts and acquitted each time.
- Arrested numerous times in different parts of the country for running confidence games and other swindles upon the unsuspecting.

By day, Sampson earned an honest keep as a mechanical inspector in the employ of the Northwestern Elevated Line and Charles Tyson Yerkes, the powerful American financier, traction magnate, and monopolist who bought up a number of street railways in Chicago before his plundering tactics were rejected by the "Gray Wolves" of the council. They had demanded a sizeable share of the "boodle" Yerkes claimed for his own. In 1900 negative public opinion drove Yerkes into permanent exile in London. Never again would he interfere in the affairs of the city or dare to attempt to steal from the "Gray Wolf" aldermen that which they had *already* pilfered.

By night Sampson ran with a rough crowd of holdup men, oily conmen, and tricksters—the dregs and roughs of Market Street. With the "Major" directing the thieving enterprise, Eddie Hall, the dapper, quick-thinking shell-worker and pickpocket, charted the criminal misdeeds of the Market Street Gang.

Early in his young life Hall held down a legitimate job in a Michigan Avenue millinery store before reverting to a life of crime. Honest work held no special appeal for Eddie and his associates, who acquired a fine cut of clothes and easy style of living by trimming "suckers" in rigged games of three-card monte and fantastic confidence schemes that bilked unsuspecting rubes out of their cash. Hall, always glib, quick with a joke, sharp-eyed, and persuasive, convinced greedy "suckers" that he alone held title to the Masonic Temple and was offering the majestic downtown office tower for sale to "investors" at an attractive, too-good-to-be-true price. Another clever ruse involved peddling bogus stock certificates granting "ownership" of Lincoln Park land to the purchaser. Everyone, it seemed, wanted an in on that one.

Hall came up through the ranks of Chicago gangdom and was a charter member of the old Hatch House Gang of thugs, Mike McDonald's street muscle during the formative years when he was building his empire of dice and cards at Clark Street and Monroe in the 1880s. Later, after the Hatch House Gang dissolved, Hall pooled his talents with Sampson and received his reward—a political appointment as a sidewalk inspector during the mayoral administration of George Swift in 1895. He later acquired a saloon of his own, providing a rendezvous and hideout for North Side criminals taking it on the lam.

"Clabby" Burns, another Market Street ringleader, had no peer as a pickpocket of great sagacity and aplomb. James "Kid" Murphy held a position of city water inspector during the regime of Mayor Carter Harrison II, but had to be removed by the Civil Service Commission when it was found that he had exceeded his sixty-day temporary-worker status. Harrison, a friend to "Hot Stove" Quinn and enemy of the O'Malleys, undoubtedly had a say on that decision.

The city was better off without the "Kid" of course, and the taxpayers most certainly were spared a funeral expense after he was shot down inside a Clark Street saloon belonging to William Donahue on January 6, 1898. The gunplay resulted from a blood feud surrounding the proprietor's brother, Martin, and the Kid for the usual stated reasons. An old insult demanded satisfaction. Satisfaction received once "Kid" Murphy staggered out of the saloon mortally wounded. He dropped to the sidewalk, gasping for air, uttering a plaintive, dying message to his boss, Major Sampson. "I'm done up, John!" Sampson removed the pistol from Murphy's grip, but was promptly arrested and hauled in for questioning.

Chicago police were naturally reluctant to take on the entire Market Street Gang, let alone tangle with them in back alleys, lest they suffer the pain of death or a crippling injury such as nearly ended the career and life of their colleague Officer Luke Colleran on the Randolph Street viaduct on December 13, 1887. For years Hall, Burns, "Slick" Davies, Dickie Dean, the Major, "Kid" Murphy, and "Smoky" Gorman gathered under the viaduct to swindle all comers out of their hard-earned change by means of the old pea and shell game.

The gang deployed scouts, lookouts, and utilized hand signals to warn of an impending police presence, but had failed to spot Luke Colleran, who had been keeping a close vigil. Colleran had waited for the opportune moment to swoop down and escort them singly or in a group into the East Chicago Avenue lockup.

Disguised in plainclothes, Colleran spotted Jimmy Davis working the skin game on a farmer. A pile of money, presumably belonging to the farmer, rested on the ground. Cradling his gun, Colleran approached cautiously, but close enough to grab Eddie Hall by the collar. At the site of the revolver, the gang momentarily scattered. As Colleran crossed the bridge, pleased that he had the worst of the lot in custody, suddenly Burns, Sampson, and the others rallied to their friend's defense and jostled with the officer. A crowd assembled to cheer on the Market Street boys, following their arrest. It was standard police protocol for police officers to escort prisoners on foot to the precinct station, providing a comedic spectacle for pedestrians who inevitably sided with the offender.

Colleran brandished his service revolver at the Market Street boys, and for the moment, Burns and Sampson cautiously stepped back. The officer crossed over a carriageway spanning the railroad yards twenty-five feet below, and for a scant moment turned his gaze away from the gang closely trailing him—long enough for "Kid" Murphy to sneak up from behind and whack him over the head. Colleran lost his balance and tumbled over the side, landing on top of a railroad boxcar. His injuries were serious, but not fatal.

The incident was retold down through the years from one cop to another. Police have a way of never forgiving or forgetting when one of their own is placed in harm's way, injured, or killed. Nor would they rest easy until "Kid" Murphy was placed in custody, prosecuted, and sent off to prison. Other Market Streeters fled to Canada, but finding the northern climates not to their liking, they returned hat in hand and pled guilty, receiving jail sentences ranging from six months to one year.

Hardened criminals all, the Market Street toughs clashed with police and rival politicians numerous times, drawing no distinction between the lawmakers and those tasked with upholding the law. Election violence was second nature to the "political gangs" of Chicago, and the fatal shooting of Gustavus Collander, a thirty-five-year-old precinct worker assigned to duty inside a polling place at 117 West Oak Street on November 6, 1894, was a serious matter drawing too much unwanted attention. It had all the earmarks of Market Street Gang treachery. It was their most serious criminal action to date.

All day long, the club-wielding thugs from Market Street had threatened, and in some cases attacked, Twenty-Third Ward residents as they went out to vote. The rowdies drove from one precinct to the next while police looked on, seemingly unfazed and unwilling to intercede. Collander, an important man in ward politics, owned and operated a saloon at Oak and Sedgwick Streets—one of the last in the district to serve the diminishing numbers of Swedes. He managed a theatrical company and was himself a candidate for North Town collector on the Democratic ticket until he bolted the party to become a Republican. Collander had unwisely opposed John O'Malley—the Swede versus the Irishman—and never passed up the chance to denounce him publicly. The dead man held in his hands Swedish votes, many of them in fact, but they were lost to John and his cousin Tom O'Malley and their Democratic stalwarts. Major Sampson did not take kindly to the affront.

Collander had left his saloon at noon and walked a half block to the polling place where six men armed with revolvers and lurking in the shadows, awaited his arrival. "Throw up your hands!" one demanded, while another attempted to remove a ballot box stuffed with votes from the room. The theft of three or four ballot boxes in the ward would be enough to tilt the election odds in John O'Malley's favor. His was a closely contested affair.

Police officer Nicholas Michaels, as was his custom on Election Day, had been dozing contentedly in his chair. Suddenly awakened by the intruders, he blindly fired four wild shots, one of them extinguishing a gas-jet lamp. In the darkness more errant shots rang out as men scuffled and cursed. After the gas jet had been relit, Collander lay on the floor groaning, a bullet lodged in his abdomen. He died in Alexian Brothers Hospital not long after. Three other men, including Officer Michaels, were wounded.

Police Inspector Michael Schaack, the scourge of the North Division, gained dubious notoriety for his relentless pursuit and roundup of alleged "anarchists" following the explosion of an incendiary bomb in Haymarket Square that killed seven police officers during a May 4, 1886, labor rally. In a different role, he oversaw a two-and-a-half-year investigation into the Collander shooting. Leaving nothing to chance, Schaack presented to the grand jury the names of Alderman Thomas J. O'Malley, Major Sampson, "Kid" Murphy, John Santry, Dickie Dean, and Jack Bingham of the Market Street Gang as those responsible for the outrage. Implicating a political insider of O'Malley's stature, however, was a bold, if not sensational stroke—and it brought upon him the wrath of the Chicago Irish and the O'Malley clan in particular. Schaack, an immigrant from the Grand Duchy of Luxembourg, was detested by the Irish and made no bones about his dislike of the Hibernians. He had been active in the prosecution of Clan na Gael separatists during the Dr. Cronin murder investigation five years earlier.

Sampson, Bingham, and one George "Dice Box" McGuire, realizing that Schaack and his men were on to them all, fled the city—Sampson to New Orleans, McGuire to England, and Bingham to Milford, Illinois.

However, the vigilant New Orleans detectives noted the presence of Northern "sharpers" and conmen in the Crescent City and immediately took the tall, well-dressed Sampson (disguised and traveling under the alias "John J. Shaw") and two cohorts into custody. After receiving notification, the Chicago detective bureau dispatched Captain Herman Schuettler, another German officer unsympathetic and hostile to the Irish, to New Orleans with extradition papers in hand.

"There is not a man in Chicago more wanted than Sampson," the burly, hard-case detective told New Orleans reporters. "He has figured in the criminal annals of that city for years, ever since he was a boy, in fact. He has two indictments hanging over him with others yet to be heard from, doubtless. Besides this, he has been guilty of almost every crime under the sun from murder to stealing a pocket handkerchief." Locked up in a holding cell of the parish court, the Major expressed astonishment after glimpsing the Chicago cop, a rising departmental star, who, over time, rose through the ranks to become superintendent of police. "Great Heavens!" exclaimed the surprised Sampson. "There is Captain Schuettler. I am a goner!" The usual denials followed. "I was at work all day long in my own precinct, the Third, and any of the people around me can tell you I was!"

Ever vigilant and often zealous, Schaack assembled an impressive list of cooperating witnesses and neighborhood people to positively identify the fleeing assailants, and several who swore to the fact that Alderman O'Malley had authorized the polling place rampage. O'Malley laughed at the charge made against him and said Collander was one of his closest friends. Worse, Cook County state's attorney Charles Kern upbraided Schaack and told him "there was nothing to the charges." The tables swiftly turned on Schaack though defense counsel did its best to discredit witness testimony and challenge the jury to come up with the hard evidence proving Sampson or Murphy had fired the fatal shot.

It was claimed that the sleepy police officer, Nicholas Michaels, and not Sampson, accidentally shot Collander with his service revolver inside the darkened room. Gang member John Santry had also been hit by a bullet, and this, the defense charged, was also the work of Michaels. Witnesses from the Twenty-Third Ward had a change of heart about naming O'Malley after being threatened with their lives. Several others sold their homes and fled north into the Lakeview community rather than encounter the wrath of the Market Street Gang on a dark corner at night. Charged with the crime of assault with intent to kill, the case against Sampson was shaky from the beginning and the jury acquitted him on all fourteen charges on February 2, 1895, for want of hard evidence. In the case of "Clabby" Burns, a noll prosequi was entered.

The O'Malley revelations were startling, and the trial memorable in its time. Tried separately in February 1897, the alderman lined up an array of men of high public standing. They attested to his honesty and strength of character and all agreed that clean-shaven, soft-spoken Tommy O'Malley was not the sort of man who would sanction, let alone participate in, a drunken raid. The prosecution therefore had only the testimony of a few nervous witnesses claiming to have observed the alderman fleeing the crime scene. One of them, policeman Michaels, refused to buckle under the pressure put upon him to recant. Although half asleep at the time of the attack, he had been sitting in a chair when the gang burst into the polling place. The jury did not buy Michaels's story and acquitted the alderman on the first ballot on February 13th. It took a little longer to decide the fate of gang member John Santry, but after four ballots, he too was exonerated.

Before the ink dried on the acquittal documents, exhilarated Democratic aldermen had already drawn up a formal resolution to censure Inspector Schaack on the floor of the city council. Their delight in publicly shaming Schaack was tempered by an illness that had prevented the inspector from attending the trial. He was at home in bed struck down by paralysis and would die within the year.

Alderman O'Malley, his eyes glistening with tears and suffering the tortures of seven weeks of anxiety, fell on the shoulder of his attorney, William S. Forrest, and kissed him on the neck. "God bless you sir!" he gasped. "God bless you!" From the audience seated in the courtroom came a strange intermingling of cheers and laughter at the expected outcome that should not have come as a surprise to anyone familiar with the local "justice" mills, Chicago jurisprudence being what it is. Presiding judge Murray Tuley exited the courtroom, shaking his head and refusing all interview requests. His face registered disgust—understandable among the robed gentry of jurists clinging to the naive notion that they could still maintain their political independence.[9]

Major Sampson's skill in running elections and backing winning candidates finally misfired in 1900, after the Redhead's cousin, Tom O'Malley, came up a loser in his bid for reelection. It was the Major's overriding ambition to share the power with the Redhead, and with his announced intention to run for the office and keep it under Market Street Gang control, he had boldly defied Mayor Harrison. Angered by the challenge to his leadership as the titular head of party, Harrison slated Captain Thomas J. Ford, drillmaster of the Chicago Police Department, as the regular Democratic candidate. An independent on the ballot, scheduled to run against the duly elected party candidate, was a first in the crazy, surreal world of Chicago politics.

Incensed, Harrison called out Sampson's criminal associations and ticked off his previous arrests. "We cannot have this man in office!" Undeterred, Sampson came up with a catchy 1900 campaign slogan, printed on business cards and placards and distributed amongst voters in the Twenty-Third Ward, proclaiming his "independence" from the city hall bosses. "I ain't what I used to be; it's what I am today!" bellowed the Major, amid the guffaws and sly winks of his Clark Street cronies. The line had been directly borrowed from a popular ditty, sung in a popular Chicago vaudeville review, and Sampson decided that the chorines were really singing about him.

Why revive the unpleasantness of the past, Sampson reasoned, his many one-way excursions to the city Bridewell and courtroom appearances notwithstanding. He threw down the gauntlet to his adversaries by reminding them that he had won the primary foursquare, and would go to court if necessary to defend his ballot spot. "Let bygones be bygones!" he pleaded. Sampson received crucial support from the Board of Elections by their ruling against the party regulars in a petition to knock him off the ballot, because, they claimed, as a felon with prior convictions he had been voting without legal right. The board's decision stirred hot protest among a group of truculent politicians who had themselves been implicated in a myriad of graft scandals going back twenty or more years, but this time their blocking moves were to no avail. Sampson would remain on the ballot.

"The council chamber is not a house of correction," implored Mayor Harrison to a gathering of thirteen hundred Twenty-Third Ward voters in Phoenix Hall at Division and Sedgwick on May 30th. "He is as rotten as the machine that made him and good voters will break him and the [O'Malley] machine together!" Moments after uttering those censorious remarks, two bricks crashed through the glass windows of the room—a "campaign message" from the Market Street Gang to the mayor and the voters.[10]

Unfortunately for Sampson, he was a poor speech maker. Standing in front of a public throng was not exactly to his liking. He much preferred the back room of the O'Malley saloon to conduct ward business. Following one uninspiring talk during that election season, one Chicago attorney turned to another and said: "What kind of speech did he make anyway?"

Replied the second attorney: "I'm not sayin' much about its eloquence, but it is certainly the longest speech the Major ever made in his life."

"How was that? He certainly didn't talk long did he?"

"No, but you know the speech the Major usually makes is just 'Not guilty Your Honor.'"

Harrison's angry denunciation eventually turned the tide of public sentiment against the Major. He lost his 1900 electoral bid but made two more attempts to win a seat on the council, failing each time. "It was never meant for Johnny to die like peaceful people," his North Side friends lamented to one another on October 20, 1903, after a hot-tempered Italian laborer assigned to a work gang on the South Side struck the Major over the head with a pickax. Sampson, acting as foreman on the construction site, berated the man for not working fast enough or hard enough. Gus Panabas, the ax-wielding assailant, delivered a glancing blow that landed near the base of the brain. Sampson was a tough old bird, and did not die. Instead, he swore vengeance. Panabas prudently fled town.

Over the next few months the debilitating injury forced the Major to retire from his job and lead a quieter, more orderly life. Sampson dabbled in politics, but in a cursory way, for only a few more years. He lived out the remainder of his days quietly and behind the walls of his Chestnut Street mansion not far from the Gold Coast aristocrats that had abhorred the very idea of him. "Johnny's not a bad fellow. He never forgot a favor," said one of his associates.[11]

By 1906 the rule of the Market Street Gang had run its course, and the name of the poorly regarded avenue that they borrowed their name from was changed to Orleans Street by order of the city council, for the same reasons it changed the name of Pacific Avenue to LaSalle Street in 1901—so that future generations would forget the scourge of the criminal presence. The old-time Market Street leadership and rank-and-file members had dispersed.

Senator John O'Malley, the obdurate politician that Mayor Carter Harrison once castigated "as dangerously irresponsible as a madman when drinking," died in Grant Hospital on August 3, 1921, at age sixty-two. "I've made a good hard fight of it—but I've got to quit," were the last words heard from the old redhead. At the time of his passing he had reached the pinnacle of power, sharing the mantle of Democratic Party leadership in Illinois with George E. Brennan. It was a kind of "heritage" passed down to them by Roger C. Sullivan, a canny, behind-the-scenes boss who molded the party machinery in the image of his organizational patriarch, the gambler-boss Mike McDonald.

Former Market Street members languished in prison. Others had left Chicago for fresh opportunities in the American West, while a few lingerers moved on to other local pursuits once Major Sampson retreated behind the doors of his mansion. "Black Jack" Gallagher, the last of the old gang, died of consumption.

The gang never fully evolved into a social-athletic sports club participating in organized leagues or tournaments as did its dangerous South Side counterpart, Ragen's Colts. In the main, this was a criminal-political gang whose livelihood stemmed from thievery, con games, and the support of candidates favorable to its survival. The legacy of the Market Street Gang spilled over into Prohibition and could not be easily dismissed or forgotten. Several of its better-known alumni continued to draw press attention through bootlegging or gambling activity. One who lived on in legend was Dickie Dean of "Smoky Hollow."

The residents of this Irish settlement occupying the lower southern terminus of Little Hell dispensed with any pretentious illusion of flattery by calling their corner of this tough, working-class neighborhood "Smoky Hollow" (Ontario Street to Chicago Avenue, east to the river and west from Market Street past the railroad tracks). The nearby gasworks dumped cinders into the low, marshy depressions in the earth. After a hard rain the refuse sent up a cloud of noxious steam and smoke to further the misery of the immigrant families from County Mayo living here.

The neighborhood men worked twelve hours a day in the dismal factories and got paid once a month. McHale's grocery dispensed beer to the pails of the "can rushers," and to keep matters legal in the eyes of the law, the sale of intoxicants was recorded in McHale's credit book as the sale of a bar of soap. Born and reared in Smoky Hollow, Dickie Dean chose a different path in life than that of a working stiff subsisting on pennies a day in a factory job. As a confidence man, shell worker, saloon keeper, then later as a self-appointed "constable" executing writs and arresting all who gave offense or attempted to cut into his protection rackets, Dean was unique. As a young up-and-comer, the Market Street Gang afforded him the means to perfect two of the most dodgy and artful swindles of the day, the "explosion on the lake" and the "turning around" of the Masonic Temple by mechanical means. It worked this way.

Dean or one of his confederates accosted strangers on a downtown street and asked to be directed to the Chicago lakefront. The stranger, fingered as an out-of-town tourist, farmer, or cowpoke from the stockyards by his manner of clothing, would be stopped on the street. The stranger would say no, and Dean would reply: "Oh, I see. I just thought that you might have heard about the big explosion about to go off in a half an hour down by the water. I understand everyone is going there to observe it. It's really something to see, or so I heard. Why don't you accompany me? I think if we head off in that direction, we might be able to find it. What do you say?" It was always surprising to the police that so many visitors to Chicago acquiesced and followed the trickster down to the Randolph Street railroad viaduct where three of four members of the gang busily engaged in a shell game or some other rigged game of chance invited the sucker to join in.

In the 1890s and early 1900s, Chicago's tallest building, the twenty-one story Masonic Temple at Randolph and State Streets, inspired suicide jumpers and con artists galore to utilize the building in unimagined ways. Dickie Dean made a sport of cheating gullible victims out of five dollars by promising them an unforgettable engineering spectacle: a complete 360-degree rotation of the entire Masonic building on its axis.

By "special arrangement" with the engineer, Dean would first proceed to the basement office and give the order to crank up the machinery and spin the building around . . . then disappear down the alley with the ill-gotten fin burning a hole in his pocket.

Realizing that it was to his advantage to work both ends of the law, Dickie, now older and wiser, secured a nomination for constable of the North Town, an elected position the public knew little about and paid scant attention to. Not surprisingly, it was under the regime of Cook County state's attorney Charles Deneen when Dean, as a duly elected constable serving justice of the peace writs and claiming to head up a private detective agency, ended up in a world of trouble.

Deneen filed three indictments charging Dean with conspiracy and larceny, while at the same time he was accused of collecting bribes and protecting slot machines. In his capacity as a constable, he had "seized" twenty-eight slot machines belonging to the Charles Scannell Company on the South Side. Scannell could no longer afford to pay Dean "protection" money to look after his slot machines as Dean had demanded of him, so on the pretext that an illegal gambling game was in progress inside the storage warehouse, Dean and his men transferred the machines to the Mills Novelty Company where they were resold.

"The greater part of these lawbreakers who masquerade as constables get on the ticket in the West and North Towns," complained one official on September 5, 1901. "In several cases they have used assumed names. There has been so little attention paid to this class of men who sneak into these offices. Nearly all of the Dean crowd got their tin stars in the North and West Divisions."[12]

The abolition of politically controlled justice courts and the elimination of the outmoded justice of the peace, a judicial officer whose income derived from the fees paid by the defendants he convicted, did not happen in Cook County until the mid-1960s.

The influence of politically sponsored street gangs like Ragen's Colts and the Market Street boys, which burrowed deep into the agencies of city and county government, the police, and even the administration of the courts, belied the viciousness and depravity of unaffiliated gangs of youths who passed into young manhood, robbing and murdering at will. The residents of Little Hell knew both kinds and contended with the two varieties of criminal in different ways; the polished and urbane political variety and the uneducated, rampaging thugs.

The forever infamous corner of Milton and Chicago Avenues in Little Hell "for a long time . . . had been infested with thieves and robbers," the *Chicago Globe* reported on July 6, 1891, after four men robbed and murdered an eighty-two-year-old Swedish man of all his money. Largely responsible for the carnival of crime in this vicinity were members of the McCarthy Gang, local hoodlums that swarmed their victims, emptied out their pockets, and left them dead on the sidewalk in a series of midnight robberies. Jerry, Dennis, and Cornelius McCarthy all had long prison records, and all hid out in a "robbers roost" located at 60 Milton Street, with "secret passageways and secret stairways such as Dickens described in *Oliver Twist*," the *Tribune* commented.

On three consecutive nights in the summer of 1891, the McCarthy gang brutally murdered two Swedes and shot Lieutenant Charles Barcal of the East Chicago Avenue Station through the chest at close range as he tried to break up a burglary in a dark alley near Milton and Chicago. Barcal, who made his mission to drive out the McCarthy marauders, survived the gunman's bullet. Inspector Schaack and his men rounded up the gang one by one and raided the clubhouse. The police claimed a victory.

"This will be a quiet neighborhood now," Schaack promised. "The old house wasn't as mysterious as it has been described, but it was a queer place to get into just the same. The doors had no catches and shut with springs so that if pushed, the boys could run through a door and let it slam in the pursuer's face. There were no doors in the basement at all and if the thugs were chased in one way they would run out the other side like so many rats," he angrily added. "All the fences around had loose boards and there was no place around the whole outfit where one of the officers could have cornered one of the toughs in a chase."[13]

Schaack's hopeful prediction offered a stirring of hope but yielded no tangible result in curbing the scourge of North Side crime. The Edward Lally Gang, another source of irritation to Schaack, and the police detailed to the East Chicago Avenue Station added to the miseries of slum living. A thief and all-around crook and a former member of the Market Street Gang, Ed Lally, branched off and organized his own gang with Ed Burns, George "Shakespeare" Simpson, and Fred Jones, alias "Sam Ritch," inside a Canal Street saloon for the purpose of getting some "easy money." The Lally Gang crossed neighborhood borders and traversed several city neighborhoods and spread into west suburban Oak Park, holding up saloons and robbing citizens on the street.

Saloons were an easy target for the Market Street Gang in its early years. After branching off on his own, Lally continued the tradition with one important difference. While most gang members avoided the gunplay in favor of cheating their victims with daring and guile, Lally was a stone-cold cop killer. In January 1895, while in the course of breaking up an attempted residential burglary on Division Street near Townsend, officer Edward Duddles fell to the floor with a bullet to his head. John Carey, twenty-one years old and of slight build; John McCormick, a seasoned criminal whose photo hung in the police "rogues gallery"; and teenager Billy Roach—all members of the Lally Gang—were encircled and trapped inside their Green Street hideout before they meekly surrendered. Lally slipped through the hands of the police.

He had succeeded in avoiding prosecution for the Duddles murder, but three years later, on January 5, 1899, Lally and his gang again trained their guns on another Chicago police officer, murdering Edward J. Wallner in the Maxwell Street District after burglarizing the Henry Bormann grocery store on Twenty-Second Street. Lally and three cohorts fled to Minneapolis, but they were easily captured and extradited back to Chicago. "I shall do my best to hang every one of them!" indignantly exhorted Captain John Wheeler of Maxwell Street. "Every one of this gang should be given the extreme penalty as a warning to others who would like to follow in their footsteps!" The jury, with three venire men who could neither write nor read, showed surprising leniency. Lengthy penitentiary sentences were handed down to Fred Jones, Thomas McFadden, and George Simpson for the Wallner murder. Edward Lally, unflinching in his refusal to confess, earned a surprising reprieve.

The criminal exploits of older, streetwise criminal gangs inspired youthful imitators belonging to embryonic neighborhood "play groups" thirsting for adventure and finding it in the "romance" of crime. Frederic Thrasher observed that the "organization of the gang is non-conventional and unreflective . . . detached and free from the mechanisms of inter-action in social situations."[14]

Members of the boy gangs residing in the slums witnessed lawlessness all about them: in the poolrooms, the commercialized vice resorts, the shady hotels, the saloons, the alleys, junkyards, and the dealings of criminal fences paying cash for stolen goods. An attitude of fatalism prevailed among youthful lawbreakers; in other words, today the reform school and tomorrow the gallows. Resigned to his fate, Nick Romano, the fictional Italian-American altar boy in Willard Motley's novel *Knock on Any Door*, expressed the belief that early death awaited all good men trapped in the grind of slum living. As Romano commented with bitter resignation, it is far better to "live fast, die young and have a good looking corpse."

Teenage gang boy Jimmy Formby provided police with a blueprint example of one who lived fast and damned the consequences of his actions. Formby bragged that his specialty was killing—not robbery. Jimmy and his brother William launched their criminal collective as a play group in the park with friends Peter Dulfer and David Kelly, taking by force small items from other children, throwing stones at policemen, and eventually graduating to armed robbery. They were particularly adept at sticking up drugstores and shooting streetcar conductors. Formby, with John Palm and Carl "Curly" Terry, boarded a streetcar and killed the motorman, George Beckler of the Western Avenue Electric Line, on February 5, 1904. "I pulled a revolver and covered him at the same time commanding him to hold up his hands," Formby freely confessed to police after their crime spree grounded to a halt. "As I said 'up with your hands' the conductor leaned to one side and with his left hand reached into his hip pocket. I thought he was going to shoot so I fired a bullet into his heart. Then Curly, Palm and I ran down an alley."

Safe from the police for the time being, the Formbys plotted the robbery of the streetcar barns on the city's West Side, but at the last minute cancelled the plan and trained their guns on the barkeeps.

On the fourth of July 1904, Dulfer, in the company of his three companions, entered the saloon of Gustave Riegel at 150 North Kedzie Avenue, declaring a holdup. John Lane, a theater carpenter, eating a sandwich at the counter on that bright summer morning, glimpsed the clean-shaven boys and laughed. He picked up a plate at the free-lunch counter and hurled it at Dulfer, ordering him out of the establishment. Clutching two revolvers in both hands, the enraged Dulfer discharged two shots, killing Lane and mortally wounding Riegel. Calmly and coolly, the gang strolled out of the saloon in an air of unconcern. Dulfer bragged that "I didn't even have to take aim to hit him! I saw 'em fall, that's all I wanted!"

"These young robbers left behind them a record during the few months they operated that long will be remembered," the *Tribune* commented. "The gang began the way of all gangs, by gathering together in a hidden corner and playing bad."

After the boy bandits were taken down and hauled in for arraignment, they each made detailed confessions to Assistant State's Attorney Fred Fake. Murder suspect William Formby stunned law enforcement by showing them his personal scrapbook of newspaper clippings describing the exploits of another youthful Chicago street gang they hero-worshipped and sought to emulate: the Car Barn Bandits, famous in the pages of Chicago history and forever known as the Automatic Trio.

"We read all about the exploits of Peter Neidermeyer, Gustave Marx and Harvey Van Dine," bragged Will Formby. "We wanted to out-do them, and that's why we became what we are. My brother Jim kept a scrapbook containing the accounts of the doings of the Neidermeyer bunch and the pictures of the trio were pasted in the book."[15]

Schooled in crime through bad associations, the three Car Barn felons attended the Hamilton School adjoining Monticello Avenue and the Northwestern Railroad tracks, but that ended by their own volition after only a couple of years. Born to working-class parents of modest circumstances, Van Dine, their leader, Niedermeier, the tall, raw-boned boy Gus Marx who made twenty-five dollars a week working as a housepainter, and a dull-witted youth of menial abilities named Emil Roeski showed few redeeming qualities despite their parents' best efforts to prod them into leading respectable lives. As for Roeski, he would later explain, "I wasn't getting much wages so I quit my job and they fixed me out with guns."[16]

There was a manic, homicidal coldness to the three ringleaders. Rejecting societal conventions, their hero and role model, or so they claimed, was Jesse James. The boys met up in the streets and joined up with the Monticello Pleasure and Athletic Club, a quasi-North Side SAC whose principal activity was mischief making unrelated to participation in competitive sports. According to Herbert Asbury, the Trio "dominated the Monticellos and led the young ruffians on innumerable thieving expeditions, raiding fruit and vegetable stands, clotheslines and unattended wagons, and stealing practically everything they could carry away."[17] As they advanced into young adulthood the crimes became more serious.

Between July 9 and November 27, 1903, the Trio killed eight men, including two Chicago police detectives. They openly bragged to police detectives that they had mowed down thirty-three persons, but their claim was far-fetched and easily discounted. But even by the low standards of Chicago crime, the barbarity of these relentless killers shocked the city and inspired a continuing fascination with this barbaric case that continues even today.

Their most sensational foray into the criminal world and the one that drew them into national prominence began in the wee hours of August 30, 1903, with an attempted holdup of the Chicago City Railway car barns at Sixty-First and State Streets on Chicago's South Side. Conductors and motormen dropped off their daily receipts and departed for their next run at this location. It was 3:00 a.m. when three strangers, their faces concealed by old underwear cloth that extended to their shoulders, entered the waiting room, brandishing a new type of weapon—the automatic, or magazine pistol, unfamiliar to police up to that time.

Armed with a sledgehammer, one of the hooded bandits confronted clerk Francis Stewart who had been tallying up the night's receipts and placing them in a strongbox drawer. "I want that money!" he demanded. Stewart put up no resistance, but was fired upon anyway and dropped to the floor dead. The holdup men grabbed at the cash and continued spraying bullets recklessly inside the office, wounding two others. Aroused by the sharp report of a gun, a dozing motorman, James Johnson, bolted upright in his chair, and a second later took a bullet to the head. He too fell dead. The bandits stuffed all the money they could carry into a sack, a sum of $2,250 mostly in coins, and raced out the door, still shooting wildly as they fled the premises.

Emboldened by the ease of the heist, the boy bandits boarded a train bound for Cripple Creek, Colorado, to purchase sticks of dynamite they were unable to procure in Chicago. The dynamite was to be employed in a series of railroad holdups under consideration. However, an attempt to rob a Northwestern train in Jefferson Park on the far Northwest Side failed, and further attempts to blow open boxcars, and a second wave of planned robberies against the North Side car barns, were called off.

What these young criminal geniuses failed to realize is that they had carelessly left behind a trail of clues, including the hammer bearing the inscription of the Chicago & Northwestern Railroad and copper cartridge shells different from standard issue but similar to what had been retrieved by police investigators in a previous shooting that left two people dead inside a saloon up on the North Side.

Chicago police detective William Blaul of the North Side Sheffield Avenue Station took a personal interest in closing out this case after receiving a tip from neighborhood watchman Paul Karkut. The man had observed three young men taking target practice in a vacant lot at Belmont and Robey Streets (now Damen Avenue)—certainly a most unusual thing to witness on a crowded North Side thoroughfare. Karkut instantly identified the three toughs as Niedermeier, Marx, and Van Dine. The hammer was easily traced back to the Northwestern Railroad, where Van Dine had previously been employed.

The cops soon received another important tip-off. The Automatic Trio would be meeting up inside Manny Greenberg's saloon at Addison Street and Robey (now Damen Avenue) the night of November 21st. Police learned that from there the boys would proceed to a neighborhood social event—the annual ice-man's ball. Staking the place out, they spotted Gustave Marx leaning up against the bar, passing time and sipping a glass of lager. Blaul and Officer John Quinn decided to split up and converge on the killer from opposite sides. Quinn, after being cautioned by his superiors to exercise extreme caution, replied in a brash moment, "Well I'll bring him in on a stretcher if he makes a move toward me!"

As directed by Detective Blaul, Quinn entered the saloon from the side door. Blaul rushed through the rear door of the establishment and drew down on Marx, but Marx whirled around and shot Quinn twice. Blaul steadied his aim and discharged two bullets, wounding the killer, but the shots were not fatal or considered serious. Marx still had some fight left in him, but before he could get another round off, Blaul leapt on the boy and battered him over the head with a pistol butt.[18] Marx was taken to the Sheffield Station in the Lakeview community due north of

Little Hell, where he freely confessed. "I killed Quinn and I'll be hung for it!" he snapped. "But you'll get no more out of me!" Marx badly underestimated the ferocity of the Chicago Police Department.[19]

The next few days were telling. With one of their own lying in the morgue, the cops showed no mercy in their ruthless interrogation of the boy. Marx, twenty-one years of age, was beaten and tortured in a way we can only imagine today. The "third-degree sweat" was standard in police interrogation procedures for decades until civil libertarians forced sorely needed reforms through civil and criminal litigation. His eyes swollen shut from repeated beatings, he had completely lost track of the time of day. He did not know if it was morning or evening. On November 25, Marx finally gave in. "All right," he gasped, after many hours of around-the-clock torture. "Those rats haven't kept their word with me, and I'll talk about them. Van Dine and Niedermeier were with me in the car barns. I shot Johnson and Van Dine carried away the money which we divided in Jackson Park. They were with me when [Benjamin] LaGross and Adolph Johnson got killed in the saloon." (Ben LaGross and Johnson were slain inside the LaGross tavern at 2621 Ashland Avenue on August 1 during a holdup).

Marx was angry over the betrayal of his companions, who had made a pact to storm the jail lockup and rescue any captured gang member. Roeski later revealed that Niedermeier and the gang contemplated blowing up the police station but the plan fizzled, and Marx believed he had been sold out.

Reading Marx's jarring police confession in the morning newspapers, Niedermeier and Van Dine, with Roeski in tow, fled to their crudely fashioned dugout near Clarke, Indiana, in the wild wilderness of the Indiana Sand Dunes. A suspicious storekeeper at Clarke's Station on the Baltimore & Ohio line, noting the presence of three disheveled young men not from those parts, alerted police. Eight detectives were dispatched to the Indiana shoreline and located the earthen dugout. The hovel was empty, but the snow-covered grounds revealed footprints that led to a second dugout near Calumet Heights. Detective Sergeant John Sheehan ordered the boys to come out and surrender. "Come carry us out!" Niedermeier retorted.[20]

A furious gun battle followed. Detective Joseph Driscoll took a bullet to the stomach and died. For the moment, it appeared to be a stand-off. The fortified, well-concealed Trio, plus their hapless companion, gave no indication of their intent to surrender. Seventy-five additional police officers were summoned from Miller, Indiana. As they awaited the arrival of reinforcements and attended to the stricken Driscoll, Niedermeier and his pals quietly slipped away and walked four miles to Tolleston, Indiana. Roeski, who played no role in the killings, deserted. He was later arrested in Aetna, Indiana, near the yards of West Hammond where he answered to the alias "George Hayes."

Escorted to the Harrison Street lockup south of the downtown Chicago business district for questioning, Roeski was sullen and spiritless. "I was working in the Northwestern Brewery when Van Dine and Marx asked me to join them in holdups. I was in the job in Jefferson Park when we tried to rob the train but Marx made a fool of himself and we didn't do the job. I never got much. They used to buy me something to eat and give me a few nickels once in a while. Then afterwards they got sore at me."[21]

While Roeski spilled gang secrets, Niedermeier commandeered a Pennsylvania Railroad freight train, ordering the brakeman, L. J. Sovea, and the fireman, Albert Coffey, to uncouple the cars. Sovea hesitated and was shot to death. "Get out on the mail line and go like hell!" ordered Van Dine. Coffey had no choice but to comply.

The plan of escape failed miserably however, after just two miles. A locked switch stopped the locomotive in its tracks near the cornfields of Tolleston. Unable to unhinge the lock, the fugitives raced into the surrounding countryside. Coffey related his story to the farmers and local residents in the town. Posses quickly formed up and marched into the cornfields, armed with weapons loaded with birdshot. The men fired blindly into the cornstalks striking the fugitives and breaking their resolve once and for all. Van Dine and Niedermeier, stung by birdshot, at last gave up and walked out of the frozen Tolleston marsh and into the clearing, hands raised in surrender. "I thought it was no use fighting anymore," Van Dine told his captors. "We could have killed every farmer in front of us but what would have been the use? We would have been got before night."

The trial of the Car Barn Bandits stirred national comment and it opened in the courtroom of Judge George Kersten in January 1904. Before it ended, the entire proceedings would cost the State of Illinois

$60,000—a staggering sum in those days. Given the age of the defendants, the case sparked renewed debate about the morality of executing such young offenders. Assistant District Attorney Harry Olson led a blistering attack against sentimentality, and never once doubted the wisdom imposing the supreme penalty. "Kill first and rob dead men? Kill the witnesses of your robbery and the law will reward you?" Olson was incredulous at the defense's demand for mercy.[22]

"It had been planned out like a military campaign. Do we find any dullness, stupidity or insanity in this?" inquired Assistant State's Attorney Fletcher Dobyns in reply to the defense's closing argument that the boys were deranged and therefore incapable of making a sound judgment.[23]

Niedermeier, smirking and indifferent, remained stoic and unrepentant to the end and offered his jailer a $25,000 bribe if he would set him free. Van Dine appeared very solemn and reserved. Roeski was uncomprehending, with only Marx freely admitting guilt.

"We want to see that cowardly Marx hanged and hanged first!" snorted Van Dine to Assistant Chief Herman Schuettler. Van Dine did not know that Schuettler, who commanded the Sheffield Avenue Station, was a personal friend to the parents of Marx. He had known the family from a personal association within the German immigrant community. "If you hang that dog of a preacher we'll forgive you everything," he added. The obstreperous Niedermeier said that he wanted to kill Marx all along. He always suspected him of being a yellow dog and a "preacher to law enforcement."[24]

"The four men, Marx, Van Dine, Niedermeier and Roeski are young savages; the degenerate offspring of decent parents," opined the ever-vigilant *Tribune* on November 26. "Each of these thugs deserve the penalty of death." The jury delivered the guilty verdict on March 12, 1904. The *Tribune* and all who agreed with its opinion had only to wait until April 22, 1904, when Niedermeier, Marx, and Van Dine were escorted to the Cook County Jail gallows, one at a time, in the mid-morning hours. "I'll die game," Niedermeier avowed. "I don't need any priest to help me die! Tell them to keep them away from me!"[25] His bold words were betrayed by his actions. Three days before his scheduled execution he swallowed sulfurated ends of matches and attempted to sever the arteries in his left arm with a lead pencil. The suicide attempt failed.

Accompanied by priests from Holy Name Church, Marx kissed the crucifix and begged for God's mercy. Moments before being led from his cell he shook hands with Van Dine, who apparently had forgiven his fellow robber. "I hope we will meet above. I feel God will forgive us because we have repented."[26] Shortly before the executioner came to fetch him from his cell, Van Dine received word that Governor Richard Yates Jr. had refused his final appeal for clemency. Van Dine and Marx were buried in Mount Carmel Cemetery after both men accepted the ministrations of the church.

In death Dr. Joseph Springer and Dr. G. F. Lydstron measured the heads and faces of the three Car Barn Bandits in a posthumous effort to determine if they were "morons." In less sensitive times than these, it was common practice to label an offender (especially a sexual predator) a "moron."

Examiners determined Niedermeier to be the most "deficient" of the three. But Van Dine "possessed leadership qualities." However, it was conceded that all had exhibited signs of acute degeneracy. Emil Roeski, just nineteen and diagnosed mentally ill, was found guilty of murder and sentenced to life in the state penitentiary at Joliet. In 1916 he was adjudged insane and transferred to the Chester, Illinois, prison where he later died.

Interviewed inside his cell by reporter Arthur Sears Henning before his march to the scaffold, Gustave Marx offered a chilling, fatalistic view of life and the common motivation that drove gang boys to commit such extreme and violent acts. "What's life anyway? To enjoy yourself till you die isn't it? And you can't die more than once can you? I knew they would get me sooner or later but I made up my mind I'd have a good time as long as it lasted, then take my medicine."[27]

A horrendous crime wave Chicago police laid at the doorstep of sensational newspaper publicity surrounding the Car Barn Bandits swept over the city in December 1903. "In the majority of cases the bandits have been young men," the *Inter-Ocean* reported. "Saloons have been held up and patrons robbed in a manner that has startled Chicago's oldest police officers. Other places of business have been visited by the criminal gangs and proprietors and patrons forced at the muzzles of revolvers to deliver up their money."

The murder of prominent Chicago attorney, clubman, and churchgoer James A. Fullenwider by holdup men at Forty-Second and Wabash on the South Side the evening of December 2nd galled clergymen and members of the judiciary, who blasted police for their culpability with crime syndicates and their investigative inertia. Experts expounded on the matter with all kinds of interesting theories for the pervasive lawless conditions. Through the World War I years, crime only escalated.

Chicago's intolerable conditions exemplified by "Ammunition" Eddie Wheed, a former gang boy turned murderer, stirred outrage and inspired a desperate call to action. Wheed, a stoical, cold, natural-born killer known in the Northwest Side streets of Chicago as "Sure Shot" Logan when he organized the Wheed-Westcott counterfeit gang, murdered two men in a daring daylight payroll robbery of the Winslow Brothers plant, 4600 West Harrison Street, on August 28, 1917. The holdup climaxed an appalling crime spree that left behind six dead men and a trail of blood. Police surrounded his wooden cottage at 2633 Thomas Street three days later demanding his surrender.

Wheed blasted away and threatened to dynamite the entire block if they took a step closer. His bullets felled three detectives, while holding 250 police officers at bay. At the end of the block three thousand spectators witnessed a furious "Wild West" shootout. No attempt was made to cordon off the area. The situation was desperate and there was no time. On the rooftops across the street, sharpshooters in prone position fired down at the windows of the frame structure where the killer was holed up.

Five hundred shots were exchanged before Wheed finally surrendered, ending the drama. It was the insolent comments he made to the press and to police that angered the civic leaders of Chicago who by now had become ever so weary of gang holdups, Car Barn Bandits, shoot-outs inspired by their imitators, the easy availability of weaponry, and incorrigible youths advancing into the ranks of dangerous felons.

"When I order a man to throw up his hands he ought to have sense to do it," snapped Wheed. "If he makes the mistake of not obeying orders I kill him. He is plainly a fool and the world is well rid of him. If I have to kill a man in doing my work my conscience does not bother me. I regard robbing the rich not only as not wrong but perfectly right. It is sort of a duty I owe to myself."[28] In a shack sitting on an open prairie at Fifty-Ninth and Kedvale on the South Side, police recovered a cache of five hundred steel-jacketed cartridges, burglar's tools, jimmies, and saws—Wheed's "working tools." The nickname "Ammunition Eddie" accompanied the discovery.

"Ammunition Eddie," found guilty of killing the two bank express messengers from the payroll robbery, marched to the gallows mumbling contrite prayers on February 15, 1918. Wheed, a man coming out of a world of petty depredation, inspired the founding of the city's most important and reliable civilian watchdog crime-fighting agency, the Chicago Crime Commission. Newspaper man Henry Barrett Chamberlin, with the full backing of the Chicago Association of Commerce, galvanized the business community and recruited civic leaders from their ranks to lead a crusade to aid law enforcement, while bolstering and maintaining the public vigilance.[29]

"Crime is business," Chamberlin patiently explained. "It is an organized business, and must be fought with business methods. Criminals go about the business of robbing, burglarizing or safe blowing just as other men attend to their ordinary business affairs. They know the business. They have police connections, their sources of information in the offices of prosecutors. They know the judges to avoid." Chamberlin's statement marked the first time that anyone of high-profile stature had formally recognized the existence of gangs of criminals organized around a hierarchical reporting structure. Edwin W. Sims, who as U.S. attorney had led the successful judicial and law enforcement crusade to close the Levee in 1912, was chosen to serve as the commission's first president.

The mission as it was presented by Sims and his team were met with stiff resentment among old-guard law enforcement. Judicial heavyweights resented a cabal of LaSalle Street financiers telling the city how to manage the crime problem. In a speech to the Hamilton Club on May 14, 1920, Judge William N. Gemmill conveyed a strong message of dissent. "The statements of the Chicago Crime Commission as to the prevalence of crime in Chicago are an unwarranted attempt to tarnish the fair name of our city." Gemmill dismissed the recent crime wave to the disruptions brought on by the tense postwar world. The judge assailed liberal parole policies that turned loose hardened criminals, and called on the commission to address the tertiary issues of juvenile crime contributing to rising gang membership and adult crime.

"There are many boys who will not go to school," he said. "The labor unions will not let them become apprentices until they are seventeen-years-old. They will not even go to the manual training schools. Many of them would not work if they could. They spend their time concocting crime. They are hyenas at heart. When they come into court so serious are the offenses of many of them. So desperate their character, that the judge is forced to hold them to the grand jury. The grand jury is the loophole through which they escape."[30]

Chamberlin defended the commission and his honest assessment of the dangers of the crime wave. "The crime business is as stable in Chicago as the banking business," he shot back, citing statistics indicating that the city was home to ten thousand criminals or one-third of 1 percent of the total city population.[31] At the same time, Chamberlin pledged the support of the commission to investigate and report on the root causes of juvenile delinquency and effective remedies.

Judge Joel Longnecker, a former city prosecutor, called for the courts to take a tougher stand against youthful offenders. "I believe than an amendment to the parole law is needed. It should be made possible to send minor offenders to the penitentiary for a fixed term. Bad home influences and the placing of evil literature in the hands of children is to be considered as tending to produce crime."

Chicagoan Samuel Beard and others agreed with Longnecker that the purveyors of contemporary popular culture, including the tabloid (yellow) press and cheap novels, influenced young boys to commit crime. "Too many children are brought up on the streets," Beard said.

"In their homes they are not taught to have respect for their parents. The yellow papers and the dime novels encourage boys to emulate the deeds of thieves and murderers," Frank E. Johnson said. "The saloon dives and extensive advertising of criminals by the yellow press encourage a great deal of crime. The yellow journals make the criminals appear like heroes. By closing the saloons where criminals hide, the hold-up men would be without refuge."[32]

Others suggested that the Chicago Public School System was to blame because of its secular approach to instruction. Without teaching lessons in God and morality, public school students could not be expected to distinguish between right and wrong. Statistics showed that parochial students from Catholic and Lutheran schools committed far fewer crimes, but the data was unreliable and open to interpretation.

As vigilant as they may have seemed, the powerful LaSalle Street banking and commercial interests making large donations and attending speaker luncheons in the Palmer House Hotel to further the mission of the Crime Commission demurred about the issue of gun control.

Cook County coroner and former sheriff John E. Traeger called for the passage of strong gun control measures—an impossible dilemma for a gun-crazy city such as Chicago, as history has shown down through the years. "I am strongly of the opinion that a great many of them [homicides] are caused by the indiscriminate carrying of concealed weapons. Men have resorted to the use of firearms at the slightest provocation and the most trivial quarrels have often resulted seriously on account of the combatants being in possession of revolvers."[33]

The gun-control debate in Chicago has since intensified, even with the passage of local statutes curbing ownership of automatic weapons. The same vexing problems of gun violence in 1903 continue today. Conceal and carry is permitted by law in Illinois and regulated by the state police.

At the same time the Automatic Trio and "Ammunition Eddie" terrorized North Side neighborhoods, the police made excuses, and the preachers postulated about cause and effect, Little Hell was rapidly filling in with thousands of new arrivals from Sicily and mainland Italy. Industry demanded a cheap, available labor force, and the *paesani* from the villages and countryside emerged as the dominant ethnic group in the river district of Little Hell, particularly during the years 1903 and 1904.

The boundaries of the original "Little Sicily" formed in the 1890s along Grand Avenue beginning at the foot of Milwaukee Avenue. On the north side of Grand, east of Milwaukee, stood a wooden tenement building adjoining Frank Morici's saloon, a clearing house and headquarters of the dreaded Black Hand, a secret society of Sicilian extortionists and killers prominent in the United States from the 1890s through the 1920s. Members of the Black Hand were known to meet in a back room of the Morici saloon or in the house next door.

"Policemen never go into the territory except in couples, and more vendettas have been satisfied there and more mischief done than in any of the other parts of Chicago which at one time or another have been called plague spots," the *Tribune* commented on March 3, 1901. "From the patrol box at Grand and Milwaukee Avenues, the ambulances and police wagons have taken away many wounded men to hospitals but in not one case has a conviction been secured of the man who injured the man. It is simply impossible to get Sicilians to testify against Sicilians." Down the street from the Morici dive stood the "House of Blazes," a labyrinth of twisting alleys and sunken walks providing an elaborate escape route for Black Hand extortionists.[34]

In Little Hell the imprimatur of the old Market Street Gang and the Collander murder were part of the historical record. The Swedes had already fled from the district. Dwindling numbers of Irish remained, but they were being eclipsed by newly arrived Italians and Sicilians. By 1910 the Sicilians had succeeded in erasing the original boundary lines of the Irish Kilgubbin settlement, and with resettlement came a new and even more deadly crime peril—the trail of blood left by small cells of Black Hand extortion gangs and the "Shotgun Man," an unknown killer preying upon fearful Italian residents. Four incredible years of mayhem in the streets redefined the earlier barbarity of daily living in Little Hell, and its nearby environs.

- 1911: forty murdered
- 1912: thirty-three slain
- 1913: thirty-one killed
- 1914: forty-two homicides

Sicilians from the western tip of the "boot" opened businesses along West Division Street. Fruit and vegetable stands dotted Oak Street. The residential settlement centered around Townsend Street, nearest the worst areas of Black Hand activity. The corner of Oak Street and Cleveland Street (previously Milton Street) was the most prominent "Death Corner" among several locations in the big city claiming that dubious notoriety. For a dozen years leading up to World War I, the West Chicago Avenue police logged more recorded homicides in their ledger book than any other comparably sized district in the country. At least three of the murders occurring near Death Corner were attributed to the Shotgun Man. Curiously there were no demands for extortion money put upon the victims of this savage killer, leading police and community leaders to speculate that the shooter was not a Black Hand assassin at all.

Old world "vendettas" (feuds) were private matters between families, often settled by gunplay and deadly reprisals. Fearful Italians were extremely reluctant to go to the police due to an inherent mistrust of law enforcement, the notoriously poor closure rate in homicide investigations involving Black Hand offenders, the certainty that local politicians extended certain "courtesies" to Black Hand criminals, and the pervasive belief that it was no one else's business but their own. In his scholarly study of Black Hand crime in Chicago, Robert M. Lombardo writes, "Southern Italians and Sicilians traditionally did not go to the police when wronged because that revenge was their personal responsibility *sangu lava sangu* (only blood washes blood)."[35]

Between January 1, 1910, and March 26, 1911, seventeen men were assassinated at Death Corner, mostly immigrant Italians shot by the Shotgun Man, who took down four people in a three-day bloody rampage. The unsolved Black Hand killings compelled desperate police officials to incorporate a countervailing "White Hand Society" on December 6, 1907. The Italian-American lawmen assigned to duty to neutralize the threat were fearless and incorruptible—handpicked by a delegation of prominent Italian businessmen, attorneys, and merchants. The White Hand dispersed its officers throughout the district at frequent intervals and achieved some tangible results, although the Black Hand would not be completely eradicated by police action alone.

During a daylong dragnet of Little Hell on November 22, 1916, a "flying squad" of detectives scoured the pool halls, saloons, and known hideouts of Little Hell in search of Black Handers. While the cops questioned four hundred residents of Little Hell, the crack of pistol shots at Hobbie Street and Milton Avenue sent police patrol wagons scurrying from Chicago Avenue in the early evening drizzle. There they found two Italian immigrant women mourning their dead husbands, likely victims of an extortion plot inspired by the bloody Pietro "Silver King" Catalanetto–Michael Locascio neighborhood feud.[36] "Who did this?"

the police demanded. In teary-eyed anguish, the women averted their gaze and shook their heads no.

Although anonymous to the police, it is likely that the residents, the shopkeepers, and the street people knew the killers well, but out of fear of reprisal they kept silent. White Hand detectives doggedly pursued Black Hand criminals and uncovered numerous assassination plots, kidnappings, and bombing attempts. In March 1912 detectives Gabriel Longobardi and Anthony Gentile received an anonymous tip in the form of a letter that neighborhood candy maker Giovanni Fiannesca had accumulated a stockpile of black powder and dynamite bombs concealed in the shanty of his Milton Avenue home.

The Black Hand was indiscriminate about the targets of its threats. Peasant, policeman, and even federal judge Kennesaw Mountain Landis were targeted for assassination at one time or another. While investigating the abduction of six-year-old Angelo Mareno in front of his parents home on Gault Court in August 1911, Detective Gentile received the usual "letter of warning:"[37] "Dear friend, we let you know that you must go no further in the investigation of the Mareno case. This is the first notice we will send you. If you go further you will receive harm from the Black Hand." The detectives suffered no harm at the hands of the terrorists, but Mareno's wife suffered a fatal stroke after months of anguish and nervous exhaustion following the abduction. Day laborer Antonio Moreno paid the $500 extortion demand and the boy was returned safely, but the trouble did not end there.

For cooperating with the police, Mareno lived out his days in abject terror after convicted kidnappers Joseph and Carmelo Nicolosi, owners of a saloon on Oak Street, were released on bond in May 1914. The politically connected brothers served only three years of a seven-year sentence and were released on reduced bonds thanks to the intervention of Alderman Johnny Powers, a "Gray Wolf" politician whose business interests were over on the West Side. "Alderman Powers is a saloon keeper who misrepresents the 19th Ward," complained Reverend Elmer Williams of the Grace Episcopal Church. "He recognizes the political value of a neat little organization like a Black Hand Society. The blackest hands are not in Little Italy. The blackest are the hands that put out to sign bonds for such characters as the Nicolosi."[38]

A brass band greeted the two extortionists upon their return to the city. An automobile drove them slowly past the home of Antonio Mareno, followed by a procession of laughing and cheering men and boys. In the days that followed, Mareno maintained a sleepless vigil behind his locked front door, clutching an armed pistol awaiting a Black Hand attack that never materialized. However, public exposure of the criminal-politico tie-up with Powers, the West Side Irish Democratic boss christened "Johnny de Pow" by friend and foe, contributed to the inevitable decline of the Black Hand. Successful federal prosecution of Black Hand criminals checkmated attempts of shady Chicago politicians to intervene on their behalf during judicial proceedings.

The Italians of Little Hell, the "backyard" of the Gold Coast, contended with recurring patterns of violence through the Depression years—and beyond. A 1931 map of Chicago gangland identified Locust and Sedgwick as the latest "Death Corner"—the location of fifty homicides.

Years passed but the chokehold of crime never disappeared. The entire area remained vulnerable to chaos and misery and a breeding ground of juvenile delinquency for the next six decades. In July 1934 the Lower North Community Council (formed during World War I) partnered with a number of local social services agencies to deploy trained workers into the neighborhood to work with community and religious leaders to affect a solution involving organized recreational programs and classes aimed at improving the quality of life for youth.

"This district has always had a reputation for being unmanageable and from it has come a large percentage of the court cases of juvenile delinquency. With eighty-five percent of the families on relief the problem has become acute," explained Joseph D. Lohman, director of the project and a future sheriff of Cook County. "The natural resources of the district—the leaders, institutions, social, civic and church groups—are being used to make this community active on behalf of its own welfare. Seven vacant lots have been cleared for playgrounds; churches, schools and halls are being lent for meeting places and trips are being taken to parks, beaches and to a Century of Progress." [The Century of Progress was the name given to the 1933 Chicago World's Fair.][39]

The long overdue initiative succeeded in treating the symptoms of crime and decay, but offered no palpable, permanent solution. The area built upon its legacy as a troubled high-crime area, unchanged until another ethno-demographic change overtook the community. The resettlement of blacks from the impoverished rural sharecropper regions of Georgia, Mississippi, and Alabama began at the foot of the Chicago River between Wells and Franklin shortly after World War I, and then quickly spread northward, displacing the Italian colony in Little Hell. There is little supporting evidence of black street gangs prior to the 1930s.

Useni Eugene Perkins, a former executive director of the Better Boys Foundation Family Center in Chicago, suggests that blacks living in Chicago before the Great Depression were not fully acclimated to "urban lifestyles and values which most often foster anti-social behavior." Perkins believes traditional behavioral patterns of "second and third generation southerners . . . clung to those values and mores that governed socialization of black youth in the South."[40] Those values slowly eroded in the industrial north as the demands of inner-city living, the breakdown of family life, and racial and economic discrimination contributed to rising juvenile delinquency, and hastened the formation of street-corner gangs, especially after 1950.

African Americans, navigating the painful social adjustment from life in the feudal, backwater South to the harsh realities of the urban, industrialized North, paid exorbitant rents for rear flats and basement apartments in recycled post-fire tenements lacking central heating and plumbing. Backyard privies were the standard in plumbing for the poor.

The prevailing racial hostility between white and black on the South Side crystallized in Little Hell in subsequent years. Just as the Irish had fled the South Side, so did the Italians of Little Hell give ground and retreat north and west, managing to stay one step ahead of the Great Migration. The continuous pattern of "white flight" from Chicago's inner-city neighborhoods fully crystallized and continues into the modern day.

A plan to clear the slums of Little Hell to relieve residential overcrowding and lessen the appalling evil of street crime commenced with Mayor Edward Kelly's June 1, 1934, announcement of the city's urban renewal and community revitalization program. The Metropolitan Housing Council (MHC) and its successor agency, the Chicago Housing Authority (CHA), began work in February 1941 tearing down the old buildings to pave the way for the Mother Cabrini Homes, 586 two-story row houses located on the empty lots of the former Little Hell tenements.

At the urging of Reverend Louis Giambastiani of the St. Philip Benizi Church (the neighborhood parish serving the religious devotions of the Italian community), the CHA named the first phase of the public-housing project after Mother Frances Xavier Cabrini (1850–1917), a sanctified Catholic nun who provided medical care and relief work for immigrant Italians. Cabrini founded sixty-seven missions in New York, Chicago, and elsewhere across the country.

In the name of urban renewal, slum clearance, and the spirit of Mother Cabrini's charitable benevolence, CHA envisioned an end to poverty by providing affordable alternative housing to lower-income people of mixed race and ethnic origin—the same common goals the Relief & Aid Society had failed to achieve in the years following the Chicago Fire. The CHA, by its actions, inadvertently sowed the seeds of the gang menace that would devastate this community from the 1960s into the New Millennium by creating a *perpetual* slum.

The Cabrini Extension North and Cabrini Extension South added 1,925 residential units in 1957. Four years later the William Green high-rise buildings opened up 1,096 more apartments. By that time, 80 percent of the residents were African American.

Envisioned as an antidote to squalor, Cabrini, as a social experiment, ended in spectacular failure for many of the same reasons the Relief & Aid "Barracks" failed in 1872. In the early years, the CHA project served a mixed-income multiracial housing market. Families applying for housing had to first be fully vetted, and strict rules of occupancy were enforced. Residents were expected to maintain their properties as best they could, and attend to the small flower beds and the grass growing outside of the low-rise dwellings. There was a semblance of community pride and social organization . . . at first.

By 1981, however, the rules had been flaunted, or simply cast aside. Cabrini registered a population of fourteen thousand (mostly African American) with an estimated six thousand undocumented residents. The cluster of high-rise buildings dotting the landscape of the former Little Hell continued an old and failed policy: herding the displaced into overcrowded, poorly constructed, decrepit properties; but this time the slums had risen skyward and were no longer congealed in densely packed, twisting, narrow lanes and back alleys.

In her landmark study of urbanization, *The Death and Life of Great American Cities*, published in 1961, sociologist and author Jane Jacobs censured post–Depression era urban planners for failing to understand the "vicious circles" (slums ringing the commercial business district) or the means of easing conditions. "Our present urban renewal laws are an attempt to break this particular linkage in the vicious circles by forthrightly wiping away slums and their populations and replacing them with projects intended to produce higher tax yields, or to lure back easier populations with less expensive public requirements. The method fails. At best it merely shifts slums from here to there, adding its own tincture of extra hardship and disruption. At worst, it destroys neighborhoods where constructive and improving communities exist and where the situation calls for encouragement rather than destruction."[41]

In 1981 six hundred Cabrini residents were listed as active gang members, and two thousand more were peripheral, or "wannabees," according to police estimates.

Urban renewal, aimed at the reinvention of communities, was a form of social engineering embraced by a liberal coalition of reformers in the 1940s and 1950s challenging the wisdom of preserving old neighborhoods, their housing stock and infrastructure. The Cabrini plan invalidated good intentions. The apartments evolved into a living nightmare of gang shootings, poverty, and drug dealing after the industrial and manufacturing plants that were an important source of jobs and income shuttered. Courtyard terraces overlooking the street below had to be sealed off with metal screens in order to prevent garbage and other objects from being hurled to the ground. The malfunctioning elevators and stairways invited rapists, drug dealers, pimps, and armed robbers. The terraces served the gangs as an open-air drug market and as a haven for snipers.

High-profile shootings, including the 1970 sniper murders of Chicago police officers Anthony N. Rizzato and Sergeant James Severin as they walked their beats, occurred with numbing frequency. The men were targeted by gang members while patrolling community housing for an all-volunteer "Walk and Talk" project. In response, the city poured more than $22 million into long-overdue repair work, the remodeling of apartments, and the refurbishment of the elevators. Peace was momentarily restored but the killing resumed. Thirty people were murdered between 1978 and 1981. The press, the public agencies, and the mayor held the cash-strapped CHA accountable.

In a stunning March 1981 announcement, Chicago mayor Jane Byrne announced her intention to move into one of the dismal 3,607 slum apartments in the sky—3,607 self-contained apartments crammed into twenty-three buildings occupied by fourteen thousand poor, uneducated residents stacked on top of one another. Whatever the motive, the finely crafted publicity stunt and the rhetoric of police and members of clergy that she hoped would galvanize the community into a cohesive plan of action yielded few positive results. Still, one had to admire the mayor's chutzpah. Charles Glass, deputy director of the Department of Safety, described the diminutive Byrne as "a gutsy, blond-haired blue eyed lady."[42] That much everyone could agree upon.

After Byrne moved out and media coverage of the stunt withered, the gangs resettled and the cycle of violence resumed under the domination of the Gangster Disciples. Security guards and police were powerless to stop the sniper fire, a persistent problem.

The 1992 shooting of seven-year-old Dantrell Davis, killed by a stray bullet while walking to the Jenner Elementary School with his mother, defined the Cabrini-Green area to the eyes of the world. The gunman, a known gang member, had fired down from a tenth-story window in a presumed "act of retaliation" against a rival gang member. An errant bullet struck Davis in the head. It was a senseless, tragic affair underscoring the failures of public housing and its devastating impact on youth. The Reverend James Fleming of the Fourth Presbyterian Church, a Gold Coast community landmark since 1874, noted that the children of the projects he had personally tutored were "very street wise. They've seen a whole heap of more problems than other kids. They've seen violence and they know how to survive it, but they still need love and friends." A Fourth Presbyterian Church task force report on racism, completed in 1992, concluded that few African Americans from Cabrini-Green were unwilling to cross "the social distance" between the projects and the Gold Coast in order to attend religious services, because blacks "had to resist the dominant white culture and maintain their own sense of social and cultural identity" and "boundaries were important for both sides of the conflict."[43] Segregation, based on class, race, and religion, no longer acceptable after decades of hard-fought Civil Rights struggle, continued to prevail as a result of polarizing economic forces and, as the church report stated, by choice in some instances.

Five years later the January 1997 "Girl X" rape case became a watershed community event. Girl X, later identified as Shatoya Currie, had been blinded, paralyzed by insecticide sprayed down her throat, and left for dead in the seventh floor of a Cabrini stairwell.[44] The case hastened adaption of the Near North Redevelopment Initiative, a master plan calling for immediate demolition of the projects and redevelopment. Following years of inertia, the CHA's Plan for Transformation, in 1999, moved things forward from the drawing board to implementation. The federal government mandated the razing of eighteen thousand units of public housing in Chicago, signaling the end of one era and a closing chapter to 140 unbroken years of crime history in this one corner of Chicago.

By May 3, 2011, the last of the infamous high-rise apartment buildings were demolished, leaving behind only the vacated, boarded-up low-rise Francis Cabrini row houses from the 1940s as a visible reminder of the intractable resilience of urban crime districts.

The affluent Gold Coast, extending from the luxury boutiques and hotels of Michigan Avenue (the "Magnificent Mile") north past Lincoln Park, is still a playground for the rich, although no longer bound by the dictates of the prominent families whose names were emblazoned in the social register. The Palmer mansion, a symbol of decadent wealth and nineteenth-century noblesse oblige, succumbed to the wrecker's ball in April 1950. Its deserted, ghostly rooms were caked with fallen plaster, and dust obscured the beautiful murals in its final days.

Honore Palmer, the silk-stocking political acolyte of "Hot Stove" Quinn who went "slumming" into the city council chambers for two undistinguished terms of office in the early twentieth century, lived to the ripe old age of ninety. He died in Florida on March 4, 1964, far removed from the gala cotillions and afternoon teas of his lost Chicago youth and the wealthy gadflies from the Blue Book directory he once ran with.

The archbishop's mansion, the last remaining symbol of that splendorous era, stands amid a congested landscape of luxury high-rise apartments, condominiums, upscale restaurants buffeted by Lincoln Park and Lake Michigan. It is a vintage 1874 Victorian relic on Dearborn

Parkway owned by the Archdiocese of Chicago. The Catholic Church would love to extricate itself from the costly maintenance and repairs of the drafty old home, but there are no buyers.

For the moment, an eerie stillness engulfs the killing grounds of Little Hell and Death Corner. Prairie grass grows on the vacant fields where the dismal dwellings of the Market Street Gang, the McCarthys, the Black Hand, and the latter-day Gangster Disciples had stood. But all that is soon to change.

"The skyline's going to change really quick over there," exclaimed Matt Edlen of Gerding Edlen Development, an Oregon firm, in July 2014. "There's so many possibilities for that neighborhood and how it comes together."[45]

Urban planners look to a brighter, more hopeful future of residential resettlement and retail malls for upper-income millennials that would push the wealth and density of Gold Coast affluence westward. It began in 2014 with the arrival of the first construction crews and the drilling of holes in the foundation of the deluxe, eighteen-story, 240-unit Gerding Edlen apartment building at Division and Howe Streets. Chicago's booming post-recession real estate market fueled the build-out on affordable former brown fields of crime.

The CHA has committed its resources to adding 1,786 public-housing units to replace the demolished Cabrini buildings and has pledged to keep the neighborhood racially diverse. In the interest of providing housing "flexibility" for CHA following the demolition of Cabrini-Green, the agency has expanded its program to place its lowest-income residents into the most luxurious high-rise apartments dotting the Gold Coast. The CHA calls the controversial taxpayer subsidy to fund $3,000-per-month market rental units for each occupant as "exception payments." Quite understandably, this policy has stirred exceptional criticism among taxpayers and politicians. In August 2014 the U.S. Department of Housing and Urban Development launched an investigation and audit of the questionable CHA subsidized "super-voucher" (or higher-dollar-amount housing-choice voucher to cover rental cost) program.

Whether or not poor "Section 8" (voucher program) minorities and their upscale white neighbors from the professional classes can coexist in such an arrangement as this is a great sociological experiment with an outcome that is yet to be determined. Will the chaotic patterns of vandalism, graffiti, gang behavior, all-night parties, criminal assaults, and drug dealing take root along the Gold Coast and drive away the anchor tenants and thus replicate yet another Cabrini-Green? Or might it not foster better understanding between the races and elevate the lives of the disadvantaged so that they too may be inspired to lead wholesome, productive lives? History suggests that the evolutionary cycle of residential infill and resettlement within this North Side neighborhood will be complicated and difficult to achieve.

6

THE GANGS OF PROHIBITION-ERA CHICAGO

Frances E. Willard, president of the National Women's Christian Temperance Union (WCTU), marked the solemn observance of "National Temperance Day," October 6, 1894, with words of impassioned optimism to her followers that a new day was soon to dawn in America. The social evil of debauchery equated with the excesses of social drinking would soon be abolished through providence and the faith of good men and women everywhere.

The nation, Miss Willard was convinced, would find its comfort and rescue from temptation through the divine path of alcohol abolition. A temperate nation would be a productive nation, a nation with family life fully restored, a nation unshackled from its sin. Frances Willard of north suburban Evanston, Illinois, was a dreamer, an idealist, and a utopian but to her eternal misfortune she was on the losing side of history.

"We believe in prohibition by law, prohibition by politics, and prohibition by ballot in the hand of women as well as men," she exhorted a cheering throng of Ohio White Ribboners in Cincinnati. "We believe there should be no sectarianism in religion, no sectionalism in politics, no sex in citizenship. We believe that only the Golden Rule can bring the Golden Age."[1]

The WCTU's national membership ranks swelled to two hundred thousand by 1890, and with the expectation of receiving a five-dollar donation from each member in good standing, it was predicted that the financial obligation of building a "temple" headquarters in the heart of Chicago's central business district would be met. "There can be no further doubt in the public mind in regard to the purpose, erection, and final ownership of the temple building," beamed Matilda Carse, president of the WCTU building association on May 3, 1890.[2]

John Wellborn Root, distinguished architect and a member of the first "Chicago School" of architecture, designed for her a majestic temple of marble and stone masonry. When the WCTU headquarters opened in 1892, the building towered high above the mere mortals traversing the streets below at LaSalle and Monroe just three blocks north of the "capitol" of sin, sleaze, and wickedness, the old Custom House Place Levee. For the next six years it represented a stolid, implacable citadel against the institutional evils in Chicago's underbelly.

The temperance crusaders were confident in the belief that with their allies in the clergy, Congress, and through ballot box measures, a lasting Prohibition was an attainable outcome. There was one big problem however. The WCTU could not afford to pay its rent. The building was erected on leased grounds owned by retail baron Marshall Field I. The $40,000 rent had to be paid for 188 years without the possibility of reevaluation. There were not enough nickels and dimes in the pledge envelopes of the good Christian ladies to overcome such a heavy debt obligation as this and it trumped all other considerations, including Frances Willard's hoped-for "attainable outcome."

Although sympathetic to the aims of the movement and desirous of cleaning up the rottenness of Chicago, Marshall Field was not a man to forgive so huge a debt. By a vote of 174 to 22, the WCTU in national session decided on December 20, 1899, that it would have to vacate its "citadel of virtue" and shift operation to the Frances Willard's Rest College in Evanston, a wood-frame private residence in this dry North Shore suburb twelve miles north of downtown.

Forced into temporary retreat, the temperance crusaders and the Anti-Saloon League of Illinois reaffirmed their vow to convert Chicago into a Prohibition stronghold. With each election fresh petition drives placing the Prohibition question were placed in public referendum. In

December 1909 Anti-Saloon League delegates poured into Chicago for their national convention to launch a renewed drive against the saloons. A number of downstate Illinois cities had already voted in the dry law under local options, and these early victories emboldened the league to press forward. However the attitudes of downstate Illinoisans toward God, neighborly respect for the Sabbath, and temperance were more southern than big city.

A long and bitter fight to save the soul of Chicago followed, pitting the WCTU, the Anti-Saloon League, and allied organizations against the political might of the United Societies for Local Self Government, a coalition of saloon owners, brewers, distributors, ethnic Germans, Bohemians, Irish, Italians, Poles, Scandinavians, and their political sponsors. In a city like Chicago where social drinking was inbred in the culture of its European immigrant residents, denying the right to drink on Sunday, or any other day for that matter, was a heretical notion. From the time of Levi D. Boone, and his Know Nothing movement, attempts to legislate morality during municipal elections failed dismally.

The United Societies membership, a hundred thousand strong, demanded that "the useless expenditure of money by public authorities to enforce such laws be stopped." At a massive meeting of the societies held in the First Regiment Armory on February 9, 1908, the officers and board issued a formal proclamation decrying attempts of Cook County state's attorney John Healy from closing saloons on Sunday. The manifesto asserted the right of local self-determination and decried the revival of antiquated blue laws.

> The United Societies believe in always maintaining the peace and good order of society. They also believe in the doctrine of temperance in all things and excess in none. They are opposed to vice and crime in every form. They favor strict police regulation of dram shops as well as other places where people gather, but they know that Prohibition never prohibited and that sumptuary laws have not made men good. They accept the principle declared by Daniel Webster, "The less restraint we impose upon others; the more liberty we have," and they insist upon Constitutional rights of civil liberty guaranteed to every citizen.[3]

The United Societies' Political Action Committee, acting through its secretary and spokesman Anton J. Cermak (mayor of Chicago 1931–

1933), endorsed or turned thumbs-down on aldermanic candidates based on "the record and reputation of the candidates as friends of our cause." Secretary Cermak, a powerful political boss and an alderman from the predominantly ethnic Bohemian Lawndale community on the West Side, explained the standards by which candidates were to be evaluated in a May 26, 1910, interview. "Any alderman who will vote for a Prohibition district or who is not right on the bar permit question is not in accord with the personal liberty for which we stand."[4]

The temperance debate clouded Chicago politics for the next two generations, leading up to the passage of the Volstead Act in 1920. There was no halfway solution or possible compromise between opposing sides. Wrapping their mission around religious and moral dogma, the "drys" naively attributed the city's decaying moral fiber and inherent social ills exclusively to the evil of drink.

The "wets" refused to acknowledge that the highest percentage of city homicides occurred in saloons, or were tangentially related to domestic disputes and alcohol-induced quarrels. Economic self-interest motivated their opposition to the drys. Their mantra of "personal liberty" was a meaningless code word for the protection of the career politician's outside business interests in the manufacture, distribution, and sale of intoxicants. The earnings of Chicago's ruling cadre of saloon politicians were imperiled by the demands of the Prohibitionists.

In 1907 the State of Georgia set in motion a chain of events culminating in the passage of the Volstead Act of 1920 by enacting legislation to outlaw the sale and distribution of alcoholic stimulants. A rural, mostly Protestant grassroots movement that gained strength in Ohio, Kansas, and across the Midwest, the South and the Great Plains states, Tennessee, North Carolina, West Virginia, Mississippi, and Oklahoma enacted prohibition laws. By 1913 thirty-one other states voted local-option statutes into the books.

Although numerous attempts to force Chicago to yield to the dry movement had failed, elsewhere in the United States the national push gained traction. In the belief that federal legislation would reduce or severely curtail the per capita consumption of liquor, Congress passed the National Prohibition Act, also known as the Volstead Act, on October 28, 1919. The measure provided enabling legislation to implement the Eighteenth Amendment, commonly known as the Volstead Act after Republican congressman Andrew Volstead from Yellow Medicine County, Minnesota. Volstead, strictly a "backbencher" in Washington politics until his moment in the national spotlight, had actually collaborated with Wayne Wheeler, the zealous head of the Anti-Saloon League, to draft the original legislation. But even Volstead harbored reservations. In subsequent public statements that drew the ire of the drys, the congressman said he never considered the consumption of 3 percent beer as intoxicating.

Congress ratified the Eighteenth Amendment on January 16, 1920. Nationwide prohibition took hold January 17, 1920, ushering in a period of national lawlessness unprecedented in American history. Heralded by President Herbert Hoover as a "great social and economic experiment, noble in motive and far-reaching in purpose," Chicagoans went on a madcap drinking binge unparalleled even in the "come hither" days of Mike McDonald.

Cabarets with floor shows and chorus girls, comedians and jazz bands opened all over town, some of them beginning at four in the morning. Commentator Will Leonard recalled that "in residences and drug stores, at cigar stores and secret barrooms which had never seen a floor show, the rough, raw booze and the rank green beer went gurgling down gullets."[5]

Ike Bloom's Midnight Frolic (formerly Freiberg's), Colosimo's, the Cotton Club in Cicero, the College Inn at the Hotel Sherman, the Rendezvous at Diversey and Clark, the Vanity Fair Café at Grace and Broadway, the Green Mill Gardens further north, the fabled Moulin Rouge at Wabash and Van Buren were among the whoopee spots served by gangsters in that decadent era.

"The South never has respected the amendment proclaiming the Negro equal," snorted Alderman Cermak. "More than 83,000 stills have been confiscated in the South. Why should the South tell us to respect the Eighteenth Amendment?"[6] There was logic to Cermak's words.

The last of the legal beer and wine disappeared from the shelves of Chicago grocery stores on January 20, 1920. Just two days later, treasury agents under the direction of Major A. V. Dalrymple raided a big still in the heart of Chicago. It marked the first official act of Prohibition enforcement by the government against individuals who would subvert the law of the land. "We want convictions and violators in prison. That's the only sure cure for violators." Dalrymple was a humorless Texas cowpoke—old school, incorruptible, and completely out of his element in Chicago.

Dalrymple's raiders ruffled the feathers of Chicago's "smart set" on February 1st by staging a daring raid on the chic Red Lantern nightclub at Kinzie and Clark—a North Side "whoopee spot" catering to only the best clientele. The Red Lantern, once John F. O'Malley's saloon headquarters and a clubhouse of the Market Street Gang, had become a gaudy show palace by Prohibition. O'Malley was a name from Chicago's yesteryear, and thirty to forty society slummers in tailcoats, ascots, and formal gowns, believing they were immune from the indignity of federal raiders, suffered the "pinch" during a predawn raid.

It was an animated scene. Bail bondsman Tom "Spike" Hennessey, a creature of the police court half-world, posted a $1,000 Liberty Bond for each of the high-struttin' prisoners. The shame-faced detainees, begging that their names be kept out of the papers, were allowed to go home. Banker Charles Neil Thomas was formally charged with carrying a flask of Scotch whiskey into the establishment, but the case was later dismissed. Bondsman Hennessey came away with a tidy $4,000 commission from the evening's adventure, demonstrating that there were other ways to make a fortune from Prohibition than distilling a homemade brew from second-floor tenement flats lining Taylor Street in Little Italy or risking a hijacking by smuggling in the real stuff from Canadian distilleries.

Far from crafting a better and happier world for people, Prohibition proved to be a ridiculous farce. Dalrymple, its local upholder, didn't last very long in Chicago. Sensing the futility of trying to enforce the "national Prohibition scofflaw" he quit his position and returned to Texas to strike it rich in the oil business. His successors, if not outright corrupt, were at best indifferent, overmatched, and impotent against the rising surge of criminal gangs in Chicago battling each other for territorial supremacy in the bootlegging racket.

"The American masses enjoyed Prohibition but the criminals married it," quipped author and playwright Ben Hecht who was present in Chicago to witness the entire gaudy spectacle. "Crooks all over the world hearing the great news of the Eighteenth Amendment headed with or without passport for the U.S.A., which had become again the promised-land. Some of them got side-tracked in New York, Detroit and Cleveland but the cream of the crop reached Chicago in triumph. We were the big time. Our town was the Maypole upon which the nation's lawbreakers capered."[7]

Mayor William Hale Thompson, the puppet tool of the Capone Gang, and his shady number two man, Cook County state's attorney Robert Emmet Crowe, tolerated malfeasance at all levels of city government. *Tribune* publisher Colonel Robert R. McCormick, the bitterest of all Thompson enemies, minced few words when he wrote: "For Chicago, Thompson has meant filth, corruption, obscenity, idiocy and bankruptcy. He has given the city an international reputation for moronic buffoonery, barbaric crime, triumphant hoodlumism, unchecked graft, and a dejected citizenship. He nearly ruined the property and completely destroyed the pride of the city. He made Chicago a by-word of the collapse of American civilization."[8]

Thompson was a buffoon and much worse. He sowed the seeds of Chicago's international reputation for unchecked lawlessness and effectively destroyed what was left of the two-party system in Cook County, surrendering the city to the evolving Democratic machine. Chicago voters never again sent a Republican candidate to the fifth floor of city hall after Thompson staggered out of office one last time in 1931.

In one ludicrous example of the municipal clowning that made Chicago a national laughingstock, Mayor Thompson appeared on stage before a crowd of five hundred voters jammed into the Cort Theater for a political rally and to hear speech making and rabble-rousing on April 6, 1926. On the table in front of him were two caged rats named "Doc" and "Fred." "Some of my friends have advised me against doing this," Thompson chuckled, pointing to the two small wire cages on the table before him. "They tell me it is a political blunder, but I don't think so. This one," pointing to the rat named after Doctor John Dill Robertson, former city health commissioner, ex-friend and one-time mayoral ally, "is Doc. I can tell him because he hasn't had a bath in twenty years until we washed him yesterday. But we did wash him and he doesn't smell like a Billy goat any longer."

The second rat, named after Fred "the Poor Swede" Lundin, Thompson's former political strategist, campaign manager, and spin doctor, he called a traitor.[9]

"Fred, let me ask you something. Wasn't I the best friend you ever had? Isn't it true I came home from Honolulu to save you from the penitentiary [from a scandal involving the Chicago Public School Board]?"[10] Then Thompson went off on a pointless harangue about his dislike for the King of Britain (whom he threatened to punch in the nose), and other enemies real or perceived.

Newspaper editorialists and Swedish community leaders were incensed. A resolution of censure from Andrew Ringman of the Swedish Club circulated in the corridors of city hall. "Mr. Lundin is of Swedish birth, but also because in my opinion, no man is fit to be mayor of Chicago, who, instead of submitting sane arguments on public questions, stoops so low as to exhibit rats on the public platform and to call them by the name of human beings, especially by the name of a man in whose home for years he accepted hospitality and was treated with kindness."[11]

"Thompsonism," a metaphor of greed and graft, was a decade-long descent into near chaos. The only clear-cut winners from the scandals, murder, and mayhem of the era were lawbreakers, crooked cops, and the mayor's friends. An estimated 60 percent of the Chicago police rank and file were on the take to bootleggers, by admission of Superintendent Charles Fitzmorris, a surprisingly capable and mostly honest political appointee in a decade of unchecked dishonesty and malfeasance.

Thompson's wobbly Republican "machine," a loose coalition of beguiled political hacks and gangsters bridging the underworld, city hall, and the wards and legislative districts they purported to represent, danced on a volcano. Russian-born Morris Eller and his leering son, the municipal court judge Emanuel Eller, ruled the West Side with the connivance of Thompson and Crowe, never really bothering to conceal their lengthening ties to the Capone mob. Father and son were indicted in 1928 on a raft of conspiracy charges ranging from the protection of gambling and prostitution to conspiracy to murder opposition candidate Octavius Granady. Eller was acquitted and charges against his son were dropped.

The Ellers mentored a generation of up-and-coming West Side political climbers whose alleged ties to the gangs were constantly scrutinized and called to account by the *Tribune*, the Municipal Voter's League, and the Chicago Crime Commission. Eller protégé William V. Pacelli, spokesman for the Taylor Street Italians from the end of Prohibition up until his death in 1942, had a knack for cashing checks from several city payrolls simultaneously while serving at various times in the state legislature and as alderman of the Bloody Twentieth.

Pacelli and his cousin Daniel Serritella rapidly ascended the rungs of the Thompson machine through Al Capone's patronage. Serritella also enjoyed the added support of municipal court judge Bernard Barasa, one of the few Italians to accede to the bench in those years. Both men worked menial jobs as First Ward newsboys at the dawn of Prohibition but that was about to change. Capone, rising fast in gangland circles, was busy pimping his girls inside the Four Deuces in the Levee District, but he quickly recognized the abilities of these two young Italians and put them to work on Taylor Street in the Italian end of the ward.

The Jews of Maxwell Street were a vibrant political force in the 1920s and Eller was still the man to see, but after the stench surrounding the Granady murder, his grip loosened. For the time being, Pacelli took his orders from Eller without protest. After Capone consolidated his interests and marshalled control of Taylor Street, Serritella became the Republican committeeman of the First Ward, with Pacelli holding down the same position in the Bloody Twentieth. As a local patronage boss, Pacelli took secret orders from Capone. It has long been whispered that Pacelli had intimate knowledge and may have even sat in on the planning sessions of the 1929 St Valentine's Day Massacre, convened in Capone's Northwoods compound in Corduroy, Wisconsin.[12] The resulting bloodbath of February 14, 1929, is Al Capone's calling card for posterity, the signature crime of the decade and a symbol of Chicago in the eyes of the world.

Dan Serritella, the former head of the Newsboys' Union until he began keeping company with Capone and a livelier crowd, won appointment to the office of city sealer after Thompson clinched his third and final mayoral victory in April 1927. "Serritella was boss and was in a position to say who could open joints and who could not and to give orders as to whose beer and booze was used and the dealers all say they had to take Capone's brands," the *Tribune* reported.[13] Serritella's word, from the mouth of Thompson and Capone down to the masses in the street, was absolute.

Prohibition made criminals out of otherwise law-abiding citizens, and millionaires and political bosses out of criminals. "Gangsters rode to power and riches under the dry law, corrupting police, politicians and plain citizens on the way," reminisced reporter James Doherty, who took in the floor shows and slurped bathtub gin with the same mobsters he wrote about. "They fought gang wars for the profits in the illegal liquor trade. They double-crossed one another and they shook down the public. Some enforcement agents were earnest and honest but many of them were little czars, not much better than the hoodlums."[14]

This was not a game of Cowboys and Indians, or the good guys in white hats rescuing maidens from the dark forces. As Ben Hecht keenly observed, "Good and evil did not meet in a head-on collision. They met only for the payoff. The forces on law and order did not advance on the villains with drawn guns, but with their hands out, like bellboys."

Who were these gangsters and where did they come from? Generally speaking they were defiant and opportunistic young men in their twenties and early thirties (some older), former juvenile offenders born into poverty in the 1890s in the slum sections of the inner city emulating the behavior of more experienced hoodlums. Sociologist Frederic Milton Thrasher categorized these seed-bed districts of crime as the "West Side Wilderness," the "North Side Jungles," and the "South Side Badlands."

"In Chicago the empire of the gang divides into three great domains, each of which in turn breaks up into smaller kingdoms. In some respects, these regions of conflict are like a frontier, in others like a no-man's land, lawless, Godless, wild. Gangland stretches in a broad semi-circle about the Central Business District (the Loop), and in general forms a sort of institutional barrier between the Loop and the better residential areas," Thrasher wrote in his landmark 1929 work, *The Gang*.[15]

The north and south branches of the Chicago River and the physical geography of the city formed natural barriers protecting downtown and the pricier areas of the lakefront from a residential invasion of the disenfranchised poor and destitute immigrants. In the aftermath of the Chicago Fire, the Relief & Aid Society effectively segregated classes of people by economic and ethnic status and herded them into tenement housing in the Wilderness, the Jungles, and the Badlands.

The inability of local government to formulate a fair and equitable housing program for the poor in the 1870s and 1880s in many ways contributed to the extreme brutality of the emerging criminal gangs of the twentieth century. For the young brigands, the price of escape from slum life was not to be found in the Golden Rule or the proselytizing blather of the "luck and pluck" Horatio Alger novels, but with a gun, a shiv, and an instinctive ability to advance from street-corner troublemakers to roles of leadership of formidable criminal organizations patterned after modern business principals, and a top-down structural command model.

Chicago's Prohibition gangsters gained local and national infamy in a celebrity-obsessed media culture that reported their exploits in magazines, radio broadcasts, and newsreels. Everyone, it seemed, wanted to become party to the public spectacle. The violent death of a gang leader often attracted a thousand spectators flocking to a funeral home, hoping to catch a glimpse of the widow, the pallbearers, and mourners. The sport of it was guessing the identity of the hoods and the criminal outfit they associated with.

For many, gangland funerals were enjoyable spectator pastimes in Chicago after 1921.

The Chicago Crime Commission tallied Chicago's year-by-year homicides of criminals that had been "taken for a ride" during the years of the so-called Noble Experiment. An entire generation, in many ways a "lost generation" of young men, risked life and limb to supply an insatiable and thirsty public with what it wanted most, the gin spirits. In 1925–1926, the bloodiest period of open warfare on the streets of Chicago, 133 hoodlums were killed in the battle for control of the liquor rackets.

Under Thompson the police seemed powerless to stop the reign of terror. Most district commanders were tolerant regarding the enforcement of Volstead, as the power and influence of gangs grew steadily. After 1923, reform mayor William Dever unleashed his "cleanup man," Captain John Stege, his most fearless and incorruptible detective boss, to rid the city of its gunmen. In October 1925 Stege laid it on the line to his men: "You must send them to the penitentiary or gallows. You must drive them out of Chicago, or you must kill them." His pronouncement marked the first time a police official issued a blatant shoot-to-kill order. "Whenever you see one of these men, arrest him!" Stege snapped. "If he has a gun in his pocket, kill him without any talk over it. Be tough and let him understand that he if doesn't skip out of our city he is going to land a sorry existence."[16]

William Hale Thompson won a third term of office in April 1927. Stege and two other police captains, unafraid of the political hoodlums and the gangsters they protected, were immediately discharged. Captain Stege was let go because Thompson's lackeys discovered that as a young man Stege had a minor run-in with the law and misrepresented himself by falsifying his name with the Civil Service Commission under his birth name, John Stedge. Reform lasted only four short years—the entire duration of the Dever administration.

The WCTU temple, irrelevant, antiquated, but strangely symbolic of the failure of Prohibition to prohibit, was reduced to rubble. In early August 1926—the deadliest year of open gang warfare in the streets of Chicago—an army of workmen besieged John Wellborn Root's monument to temperance and the ideal upon which it was built, razing it. Slabs of marble inscribed with the long-forgotten names of the "White Ribbon" contributors of 1890 to the construction of the WCTU temple were hauled away on flatbed trucks and the rest of the site cleared in order to make room for the twenty-two story State Bank of Chicago.

Year	*Number of Prohibition-Related Gangland Homicides in Chicago*
1920	23
1921	29
1922	37
1923	52
1924	56
1925	66
1926	75
1927	58
1928	72
1929	56
1930	64
1931	48
1932	39
1933	32

The wholesale liquor industry flourished like never before during Prohibition. In the early years of the Noble Experiment, the gangs established geographic spheres of influence. And just as modern nations fought for control of disputed territories and occasionally engaged in wars of conquest to annex these lands, the gangs of Chicago battled one another in the same way. In the end, it was the old Levee District Colosimo-Torrio-Capone combine declaring final victory in the frenzied decade-long scramble to wrest control of the $60 million liquor racket. Vice, gambling, and the takeover of labor union locals were tertiary enterprises the gangs fought over.

THE WEST SIDE "VALLEY GANG" | TERRY DRUGGAN AND FRANKIE LAKE

Boyhood chums Terry Druggan and Frankie Lake worked menial jobs in the Valley prior to Prohibition. Druggan labored on his father's garbage truck and Lake toiled as a railroad switchman and Chicago firefighter. According to author Robert Schoenberg, "Lake, guided by an older fireman, started selling five-gallon cans of bootleg alcohol to local saloons."[17] Druggan and Lake declared a partnership and took over the remnants of Paddy "the Bear" Ryan's operation, retaining George "Dutch" Vogel, a criminal fence acquitted of killing Detective Sergeant James Hosma inside Ryan's saloon, Walter Quinlan, Heinrich "Big Heinie" Miller, Manny Schreiber, former manager of the notorious Ansonia café, and Sam "Gelish" Hoffman as their street muscle. Politically, Druggan and Lake were Morris Eller acolytes. These pioneering bootleggers entered into partnership with brewer Joseph Stenson and Stenson's brother to distribute a higher grade of beer to their West Side clients from their own brew house at Campbell Street and Roosevelt Road. The Lake-Druggan combination invented "needle beer"—a curious blend of evaporated industrial alcohol obtained from druggists and other sources and injected into the bland but legal "near beer" with a tube resembling a needle. The partners earned a fortune in the early years of Prohibition from "needle beer." Johnny Torrio studied their business practices and applied lessons learned to his own bootleg operation.

Jailed in 1924 for operating the Standard Brewery, Druggan and Lake were accorded special privileges from Cook County sheriff Peter Hoffman. Their weekly furloughs away from the jail culminated in a major scandal in 1925. A prison secretary informed an inquiring reporter that "Mr. Druggan and Mr. Lake are downtown attending to business. They will be back before dinner, and you can see them then." Hoffman was sentenced to serve thirty days in jail. The embarrassing incident inspired playwright Ben Hecht to invent the role of the bumbling Sheriff Peter Hartman in his long-running satire *The Front Page*. "I don't know what all the fuss is about," wailed Hoffman. "I was only accommodatin' the boys."

Lake, the debonair man-about-town and reluctant gangster was never really comfortable toting a gun. He was more at home sampling the pleasures of Chicago's abundant nightlife and was happiest in the company of society swells inside the famous College Inn of the Hotel Sherman. The millionaire beer merchant enjoyed a floor show on the evening of January 27, 1930, when Detective Andrew Barry rousted him and three companions as they sipped their mint juleps. "Why don't you dicks go after real racketeers and stick-up guys and leave us business men alone," he complained. "I travel with white-collar gents that carry fountain pens and pencils!"[18]

Named "public enemies" in 1930, Lake and Druggan were in the sights of government prosecutors. The feds levied an income-tax indictment against Lake for evading taxes in 1923, 1924, and 1925. A $200,000 I.O.U. came due. Lake served fourteen months of an eighteen-month sentence in Leavenworth (where he joined his boon companion and friend Terry Druggan) on February 4, 1932. On his release, Frankie Lake returned to Chicago where he swore off the beer racket. After failing to impugn the character of U.S. attorney George E. Q. Johnson, who had sent Capone to prison in a false accusation that Johnson accepted his offer of a bribe, Terry Druggan joined Lake in prison. Druggan enjoyed catered meals, fine linens, and other special privileges while an inmate in Leavenworth. On release, he retired from the rackets and fought his greatest battle, with illness and disease, in his final years, passing away in 1954. Terry's brother George ran a bootlegging operation in distant Lake County, Illinois, sixty miles north of Chicago. Twice wounded in the Prohibition beer wars, George owned stock in the Huntley Brewing Company until bankruptcy closed the beer plant in April 1935. Lake moved to Detroit to run his ice business and lived out his remaining days in the Motor City, dying in peace in 1947.

THE WEST SIDE O'DONNELL GANG | WILLIAM "KLONDIKE," BERNARD, AND MYLES O'DONNELL

The three brothers dominated liquor trafficking between Madison and Grand Avenues from McElligot's Saloon at Fourteenth and Blue Island in the heart of the Valley District. Myles co-owned a saloon in West Suburban Cicero with James Doherty, and Klondike, a disturbed criminal sociopath, led a gang of bootleggers allied with, and later in opposition to, Al Capone, whose South Side gang took over Cicero in

1923 after Thompson's corrupt reign was temporarily interrupted by reform mayor William Emmet Dever. The O'Donnells and the Capone Gang forged a temporary alliance for reasons of expediency and self-preservation following a 1923 "gang summit" to establish treaties and territorial boundaries to end the cycle of violence. The brothers were restricted to the neighborhoods north of Cicero, but boldly violated the shaky agreement by undercutting "Scarface" Capone's retail prices. Myles killed Cicero saloon owner Eddie Tancl, a friend and ally of Capone, but was found not guilty of the crime of murder when fearful eyewitnesses changed their stories. The Capone Gang quickly retaliated on April 27, 1926. Gunmen waited in ambush outside the Pony Inn on Roosevelt Road. Assistant State's Attorney William McSwiggin, a young and ambitious prosecutor with a bright future (but linked to the O'Donnells in friendship), with James Doherty and Thomas "Red" Duffy, a precinct captain and political hack from the Thirteenth Ward, were killed instantly in a blaze of machine-gun fire. Ownership of the Thompson machine gun traced back to Capone who had purchased it from a Cicero hardware dealer, Alex Koracek, but no indictments were forthcoming. Capone modestly explained that he "liked the kid McSwiggin," nicknamed "the Hanging Prosecutor" by the press, before he inexplicably left town. "They made me the goat," Capone said. "McSwiggin was my friend. Doherty and Duffy were my friends. Why I used to loan Doherty money. Just a few days before the shooting, my brother Ralph, Doherty, and Myles and 'Klondike' O'Donnell were at a party together." Who killed McSwiggin? The unanswered question echoed across time.

"Klondike" O'Donnell was sentenced to Leavenworth for siphoning whiskey out of the Moran Brothers' warehouse in Chicago—a minor charge for a Prohibition murderer. Myles and Klondike survived the beer wars and branched out into labor racketeering following repeal. In an era of hoodlum domination of trade unions, Klondike seized control of the Elevator Operators and Starters' Union, Local 66, and bled the coffers dry. During congressional hearings convened in Chicago in 1948, committee members grilled the Capone-era hoodlum about his role as the mastermind behind an extortion racket worked by a union and contractors' association shaking down construction workers of initiation fees and annual dues. The O'Donnell name remained prominent in the press through 1962 when the *Tribune* reported the arrest of Myles

J. O'Donnell, a nephew of Klondike, operator of a Cicero gambling den for the murder of one Gus Vivirito, a police informant. On his deathbed, Vivirito fingered the youthful offspring of Myles O'Donnell, but a Cook County grand jury refused to return an indictment.

THE SOUTH SIDE O'DONNELL GANG | EDWARD "SPIKE," STEVE, WALTER, AND TOMMY O'DONNELL

After serving time on a bank-robbing charge, Illinois governor Len Small (a cog in the Thompson machine who handed out paroles to felons as candy to a child) paroled "Spike" O'Donnell. Returning to the South Side from his stretch in the Joliet Penitentiary, "Spike" organized a bootlegging gang with his three brothers, and George "Spot" Bucher, George Meeghan, and Jerry O'Connor, an associate from the Kerry Patch neighborhood. Their business was beer, and the preferred method of growth and expansion was simple. Upon entering a speakeasy, one of them would flash a holstered gun at the bartender and inquire, "Now who are your buying from?" For all their bluster and swagger, the O'Donnells were not the big shots they imagined. Hemmed in on all sides by the Joe Saltis Gang to the north and the Capones to the east and south, theirs was a battle for survival. On ten different occasions his blood enemies in the rival booze gangs tried and failed to kill Edward "Spike" O'Donnell, and ten times bullets failed to pierce the target. Gunman Frank McErlane was a top triggerman for the Saltis gang. He murdered O'Donnell's top men, Meeghan and Bucher, on the West Side on September 7, 1923. Jerry O'Connor was shot through the heart by Danny McFall, ex-Cook County deputy sheriff and triggerman for Saltis in the saloon of Joseph Klepka on Lincoln Street. In that same gunfight on September 8, 1923, "Spike" O'Donnell's brother Walter fell dead. These separate shootings ushered in the long and infamous period of open warfare between rival liquor profiteers in Chicago and spurred Mayor William Dever, just six months in office, into action. Dever revoked the licenses of two thousand so-called soft-drink parlors, and promised action on all fronts: "This guerilla warfare between hijackers, rumrunners and illicit beer peddlers can and will be crushed." The mayor's vow was futile. Matters only got worse.

"Spike" had already lost a business partner and a brother. Six members of his gang were taken for the proverbial "ride" by the late 1920s, but he gamely fought on in order to hold on to his shrinking South Side liquor stronghold in the Chicago Lawn and Gresham Police Districts. The rangy, jocular, and often sarcastic beer runner appeared before grand jury hearings smoking expensive cigars and attired in checkered suits, yellow gloves, and high hats. He was always good for a printable quote with reporters. "They tried to kill me often enough," he complained to chief of detectives William Schoemaker in 1926. "But I'm not crazy enough to tell you about it. The racket is no good. I ought to go in for the Reverend Williams' [a church reformer] line. Reformers make more than beer runners and don't work near as hard for their dough." In the same breath he declared that he could "whip this bird Capone with his fists." He said he would do the same, and much worse, to the depraved and vicious McErlane, the first to deploy the deadly Thompson submachine gun on the streets of Chicago.

On a warm early autumn afternoon of September 25, 1925, McErlane opened up on O'Donnell outside the J. J. Weiss drugstore at Sixty-Third and Western as O'Donnell chatted amicably with a police officer named Reed from the Chicago Lawn station. A slow-moving automobile with McErlane in the front and two in the back approached from Western Avenue and were headed south. The kickback of the Thompson machine guns caused the bullets to fly harmlessly over O'Donnell's head. Bullet holes are still visible on the exterior brick of the building today. Less than a month later, on October 11, 1925, "Spike" and his brother Tommy, who had just gotten out of jail in Milwaukee, were driving near Thirty-Fifth and Western when a carload of gunmen opened up on them, riddling the vehicle with bullets. Miraculously neither man was hurt. With characteristic gallows humor, "Spike" joked: "Life with me is just one bullet after another!" The O'Donnells prevailed in their war of attrition with the Saltis/McErlane Gang, but wisely made peace with Capone who allowed "Spike" to retain a small slice of his territory—but nothing more.

After Prohibition ended in 1933 life wasn't all that exciting for Spike but he enjoyed his time in the spotlight nevertheless. An English theatrical troop offered him $15,000 to portray a Chicago gangster in a London musical. In 1933 O'Donnell staged an impromptu press conference outside the ballroom of the Palmer House, discussing the means of getting away with crime after he was refused admittance to a Senate subcommittee where he had asked permission to testify. O'Donnell's charmed life ended quietly and with little fanfare on August 26, 1962, when a bad ticker cashed him out at the age of seventy-two.

JOE SALTIS / FRANK MCERLANE GANG

As a boy, the rustic-appearing "Polack," Joe Saltis, worked in the Chicago stockyards for ten cents a day. Born in Austria-Hungary, the burly, six-foot, two-hundred-pound beer baron operated a saloon in Joliet, Illinois, at the onset of Prohibition and rose to affluence by setting his sights on becoming a beer chieftain on Chicago's populous Southwest Side. Saltis was a plodding, malevolent force—a killer without peer. He made a fortune in the beer racket and owned 220 acres of prime farmland resort property in the town of Winter, Sawyer County, Wisconsin. He called himself a "gentleman farmer" and summer resort manager when the facts suggested otherwise. Saltis joined forces with Frankie McErlane, the inventor of the "one-way ride," and a compulsive killer and torturer with a police record dating back to 1912. A true sociopath, McErlane scared even the most hardened Chicago criminal. In 1924 rival bootlegger Morris Keane was the first gangland figure to be taken for a ride by McErlane who had shot him to death in an automobile.

McErlane dispatched former Saltis loyalist John "Dingbat" O'Berta and his chauffeur, Sam Malaga, to the afterlife on March 5, 1930. O'Berta, the Republican Thirteenth Ward committeeman, paid the price by defecting to the "Spike" O'Donnell Gang. "Look for 'em in a ditch," McErlane advised Chicago police when they came to question him about the shootings. "That's where you'll find 'em. They were a bunch of cheap rats using pistols. I'll use something better. McErlane takes care of McErlane." O'Berta's lifeless form was pulled out of a frozen ditch on 103rd Street and Roberts Road. A swanky dresser who, when arrested, often wore expensive evening clothes, O'Berta operated the Southwestern Floral shop, and while in the employ of Joe Saltis, he had slain gangster John "Mitters" Foley, a crime that went unpunished despite indictments against him and Saltis.

Labor racketeer "Big" Tim Murphy tagged John O'Berta with the sarcastic nickname "Dingbat" during O'Berta's failed political campaigns for alderman and state representative. The gangster-florist had a unique way of expressing himself in the public forum. "I am for subways. We need rapid transit," he said. "It makes for easier getaways." Concerning juries, O'Berta quipped: "The present jury system is alright as far as it goes. But it should go further away." His campaign slogan: "An open town with bigger beers." O'Berta took a chance and married Murphy's widow less than a year after Big Tim was mowed down in one of Chicago's labor wars. Florence Diggs Murphy-O'Berta very quickly became a widow for the second time. Questioned by police afterward, Saltis bragged, "I picked him up as a newsboy and made a man out of him."

Regarded by law enforcement as the most vicious of all the 1920s killers, Frank McErlane died of pneumonia in the Schmitt Memorial Hospital in Beardstown, Illinois, October 8, 1932, just one year after shooting Marion Miller, his common-law wife, to death, and killing her two dogs. In his final hours McErlane leapt out of his bed, and with a powerful blow, he slugged the night nurse in the mouth. Four loaded pistols were found underneath his pillow.

Joe Saltis, shot twice in the neck by "Spike" O'Donnell in 1926 and feeling threatened by Al Capone as Prohibition drew to a close, quit the rackets and retired to his Wisconsin estate, abandoning his former territories to his nemesis. His wife, Anna, charged him with physical and mental cruelty after he had threatened to kill her and the children in 1939, and divorced him. He was prosecuted for gambling violations in the Badger state. He lost his brewery in Thornton Township and squandered what was left of his hidden fortune on assorted vices, although he claimed that his estranged wife, Anna, "had taken it all." At the end of his life the impoverished bootlegger lived in a grimy Clark Street flophouse. He died in Cook County Hospital on August 2, 1947, with only a few dollars to his name.

RALPH SHELDON GANG

Just eighteen years old at the start of Prohibition, Sheldon headed up a small Southwest Side bootlegging gang nominally allied to Capone.

Sheldon and his youthful brigands constantly engaged in a series of pitiless, futile wars of attrition against "Spike" O'Donnell and Joe Saltis. As he slept inside his South Side home on February 5, 1926, a bomb blast demolished his car. "I haven't an enemy in the world!" he told Chicago Lawn police. "It must have been some kids playing around the gas tank with matches." Hearing this, the cops just rolled their eyes. Meanwhile, other gang leaders were busy negotiating a temporary truce. A citywide amnesty initiated by Maxie Eisen, an emissary to the North Side gang, and Tony Lombardo, head of the Unione Siciliana, the twenty-five-thousand-strong Italian-American fraternal society, in October 1926 in the belief that "there is enough money in the racket for us all" ended when Saltis gang members murdered Sheldon's ace triggerman, Hillary "Heddy" Clement, who vanished from sight on December 18, 1926, after hailing a cab outside the Ragen's Colts clubhouse on South Halsted Street. Retaliation killings inevitably follow in gangland. Sheldon, closely allied with former Ragen alumni Danny Stanton and Danny McFall retaliated against Saltis in the March 11, 1927, slayings of Frank "Lefty" Koncil and Charley "Big Hayes" Hubacek at Thirty-Ninth and Ashland Avenue. "I'll give $5,000 to one policeman or private citizen who will tell me who killed my friend Koncil!" an angry Saltis threatened, while attending the inquest. Saltis claimed sovereign rights over the Southwest Side and there was no room for Sheldon in the territorial alignment. "The truce of last August is ended. There will be plenty of murder from now on," sighed a Chicago police detective. Sheldon had no hope of winning a war against either Capone or Saltis. Driven out of the Windy City by Capone, he resettled in Los Angeles in 1930, but ended up in jail on an assault charge after attempting to murder a Long Beach police officer in 1931. Sheldon returned to Chicago and faded into obscurity.

MARTY GUILFOYLE

A minor figure of the Prohibition period, Guilfoyle owned a Wabash Avenue cigar store adjacent to the Four Deuces, where the old Levee Gang and Capone operated at the end of World War I. In September 1919 he shot feared labor racketeer Peter Gentleman four times in the back inside the store. He freely admitted the murder, but said it was purely a matter of self-defense. Gentleman was a hired gunman and labor racketeer sent in to kill Marty Guilfoyle, but Guilfoyle knew he was coming. The state's attorney believed him and no indictments were forthcoming. During Prohibition Guilfoyle ran a small and inconsequential bootlegging operation on the Southwest Side. He survived the mayhem of the period and operated a North Avenue cigar store business front concealing a blackjack game in the back room during the 1940s.

THE "TERRIBLE" GENNA BROTHERS

The six Sicilian Genna brothers, Peter, James (the admitted leader of the clan), Michael, Angelo (the toughest and most-feared of the bunch), Tony, and Sam (the political fixer and "connection" man to the politicians), controlled liquor-distribution activity from their warehouse at 1022 Taylor Street in the heart of Little Italy. The manufacture of the stimulants was strictly a "homegrown" affair. In the early years, their government permit to distill industrial alcohol provided the legal means and opportunity. Italian immigrants living in the Taylor Street tenements cooked the "bathtub" variety from crudely fashioned homemade stills in the basements and upper floors of their property for eighteen dollars a day per family. The Genna technique of mass-producing this swill had been taught to them by their brother-in-law Henry Spingola. Violent when provoked, unforgiving, and utterly ruthless, the Genna Gang organized their business as a cottage industry, receiving early guidance and political support from "Diamond Joe" Esposito, business agent of the International Hod Carrier's Building and Construction Laborers' Union, and the proprietor of the Bella Napoli Café, where important men of the city gathered. Esposito, an influential old-time West Side boss presiding over the Republican Club at 2215 West Taylor, also owned the Milano Café in Chicago Heights, and that would soon become a big problem for him. He suffered only one indictment for violation of the Volstead Act during his reign.

The picturesque Italian leader had dared to defy the Thompson-Crowe stalwarts by running for ward committeeman of the old "Bloody Nineteenth" Ward against their approved candidate, former assistant state's attorney Joseph Savage. The silver-haired Esposito unwisely flaunted his wealth and position in clothes and jewelry and the lavish lifestyle he had become accustomed to. He sported a prized diamond-encrusted belt buckle bearing his initials "J. E." and that was the first thing noticed by police the night he was cut down in a volley of shotgun pellets by assassins outside his residence on Oakley Boulevard on March 21, 1928. "Get out of town or get killed. You ought to go down to that farm of yours [in Cedar Lake, Indiana] and raise chickens!" He received the last and final warning by telephone the morning of his death but refused to bend to the threats. "I can't go. Just this morning my boy Joe was taken down by scarlet fever. I promised [U.S. senator Charles] Deneen I would run for committeeman," he told his advisors one day earlier. Esposito skirted both sides of the law and protected West Side gambling and booze rackets (as well as overlooking the assorted misdeeds of the Terrible Gennas). A shadowy figure conducting his affairs in the tradition of the old-fashioned Italian "Mustache Petes" of the 1890s and 1900s, nearly all leading Illinois politicians from Senator Deneen, Mayor Dever, the governor on down to municipal court judges and minor Cook County factotums receiving city hall appointments warmly embraced "Diamond Joe." All sang a chorus of praise to his friendship, support, and leadership of the Italian-American West Side.[19] It was a morally ambiguous era, when political figures were criminals and criminal figures became beloved community leaders and politicians. Who killed "Diamond Joe"? The question was asked all over town. At first the speculation surrounding the death of the genial politician centered on Ralph and Joe Varchetti, the two bodyguards flanking Esposito as he strolled down the sidewalk, waving his cigar and sharing a jest with the boys. Had they plotted the death of their boss? Investigators later surmised that Capone's Chicago Heights faction, led by rackets boss Lorenzo Juliano, took care of the matter. The ranks of the Genna Gang were severely depleted by eight years of continuous warfare with police and rival booze gangs, leaving Joe vulnerable to attack from outside gangs in the spring of 1928.

The history of the Genna reign begins in 1921 with the opening round of hostilities directed against former Mike McDonald protégé Alderman Johnny Powers in an Irish-Italian struggle for control of the Nineteenth Ward. After municipal court bailiff Paul A. Labriola, a northern Italian loyal to Powers, ended up in a casket on March 8, 1921, at the hands of the Gennas and their political ally, aldermanic candidate Anthony d'Andrea, Powers lamented, "What is this country coming to if a man may not go about his business on election morning working and voting for the man of his choice without dying from assassin's bullets because he dared to exercise his rights given to him by the Constitution?" John Powers's indignation belied his own selfish motivations to run his ward without interference from the Italians who had displaced a majority of Irish voters that had faithfully sent him to the city council in every election since 1888. Powers's opponent and political enemy Anthony d'Andrea did not receive these same constitutional protections. He was felled by an assassin outside his home in May 1921. Thereafter Powers's control over the ward slipped as the status of the Gennas and Esposito rose. Over the next few years, the Gennas, steeped in old-world Sicilian traditions of blood oaths and fraternalism, battled the North Side O'Banion-Weiss-Moran gang and challenged the Capones to the south as their wealth and stature grew in Little Italy. Emboldened by their early triumphs, the Gennas encroached on North Side O'Banion territory and challenged Capone to the south. They overplayed their hand in a serious miscalculation of their influence and reach. Angelo Genna, twice acquitted on charges of murdering Paul Labriola, was shot to death May 26, 1925, while driving from his expensive apartment to the West Side warehouse. Dion O'Banion stood accused, but there was never evidence to indict. In June 1925 Mike Genna, known as "Il Diavaolo" (the Devil), took a "one-way ride" in the company of his would-be assassins, Alberto Anselmi and John Scalise, when a police cruiser from the Chicago Lawn station overtook them at Forty-Seventh and Western on the South Side.

The cops sounded an alarm and chased them down to Fifty-Ninth Street, forcing them to stop. Scalise and Anselmi, tied to Capone and then later killed by Capone, opened fire just as Officer Harold F. Olson stepped out of the police car. While fleeing from the clutches of Scalise and Anselmi, Genna was cut down by police bullets. Jim Genna, short, plump, and next on the list, fled to Italy and was out of harm's way for the next five years. He returned to Chicago in October 1929, just in time to be questioned by detectives for possible complicity in the St. Valentine's Day Massacre. "I came back to sell olive oil and cheese," he told Stege. Tony Genna, a home builder and general contractor, came to a violent end at Grand Avenue and Curtis Street when three gunmen rushed him, pistols drawn. On his deathbed Antonio muttered the name "Cavallero" but the police could make no sense of it. Antonio perished in the streets just two weeks after Mike.[20] Fearing he would be next, Sam Genna received a police guard. He died of a heart attack on November 8, 1931. Then Peter announced his retirement, leaving political and criminal operations to city sealer Daniel Serritella, "Wild Bill" Pacelli, and Capone. The Genna killings were carried out by either "Cavallero," the North Side gang in reprisal for the murder of O'Banion, or Capone for their refusal to cooperate and respect territorial rights.

JOE AIELLO GANG

Raised in Milwaukee, Giuseppe Aiello, and his brothers, Dominick, Tony, and Sam, operated a modest neighborhood bakery in Little Hell before branching out to rum-running and expected windfall profits. Not merely content with just obtaining a slice of this profitable side business, the Aiellos had larger designs. They desired nothing less than a takeover of the Gennas' Taylor Street business. With the contrivance of the O'Banion-Weiss-Moran Gang, they went after the prize after the last of the Gennas were either killed or driven for cover. During a busy five-week period in the spring of 1927, nine Italian grocery-store operators and food suppliers working with the alcohol cookers of Taylor Street were murdered by the Aiello brothers in a brutal campaign to seize control of the disputed Genna territory. Joe Aiello's eventual undoing resulted from his misguided ambition and reckless attitude concerning Capone. He coveted the presidency of the Unione Siciliana, the fraternal association that had final say-so in legitimate businesses and the Italian gangs. Control of the organization would mean subservience from Capone and power over liquor trafficking and related food-supply industries operated by Italian merchants. Denied the opportunity to move up in the leadership cadre after the previous head, Mike Merlo died of natural causes. Aiello and Louis La Cave, his second in command, saw the potential for unimagined riches and instigated an alliance with the North Side Irish gang to plot a takeover of the society by eliminating the next in line for succession, the tall and striking Anthony Lombardo of Cicero. In the presence of thousands of downtown shoppers, Lombardo was executed on September 7, 1928, at Madison and Dearborn Street, a block away from State Street, often called the "World's Busiest Corner." At first police believed the crime was carried out in retaliation for the murder of New York gangster Frankie Uale, who held the same position in Manhattan as Lombardo in Chicago. There seemed to be little doubt however, that it was an Aiello plot from beginning to end.[21] The *Tribune* reported that Capone had gone into hiding and "the Aiello Gang were gone from their usual haunts." Aiello had tried and failed on other occasions to dispose of Lombardo.

A plot to spike the soup of Lombardo and Capone with prussic acid as they dined in style at "Diamond Joe" Esposito's Bella Napoli restaurant failed after the nervous chef decided his life was worth more than the $35,000 promised by Aiello. Capone later remarked, "If I had known what I was stepping into in Chicago, I would have never left the Five Points outfit!"[22]

That night Aiello's wholesale pastry shop at 431 West Division Street was sprayed by machine-gun bullets. Unafraid but still determined to claim what he believed to be rightfully his, Aiello next offered a $50,000 bounty to the kid Ralph Sheldon to do the job, but Capone found out, forcing Sheldon to leave Chicago or die. Aiello and the North Siders refused to scrap their plan despite impossible odds. Pasquilino "Patsy" Lolordo, former bodyguard of Lombardo, succeeded his former boss without trepidation or fear. He lived with his wife, Aliena, in a three-story flat at 1921 West North Avenue in the middle of O'Banion-Weiss-Moran territory. A meeting was arranged between Aiello and Lolordo at the North Avenue flat, ostensibly to settle differences, collect a $1,500 rental payment for a liquor depot on Kinzie Street that Moran had allowed Lolordo to use for the time being, and to affect a peace agreement that everyone could live by. Aiello and three other men, believed to be James Clark and Frank and Peter Gusenberg of the Moran Gang, appeared at the front door on January 8, 1929, and were served wine by Aliena in the front parlor. Before a proper toast could be offered, the gunmen emptied their guns into Lolordo. Although she would not name Joe Aiello as her husband's slayer, her loud, piercing scream after being shown a photo of Aiello provided the cops with all they needed to know.

Daniel Serritella, always willing to demonstrate his civic responsibility by helping out law enforcement, tried to coax the information out of the woman at detective headquarters.

Aiello managed to evade the wrath of Capone and his gunmen for the next two years, that is, until October 23, 1930, when he stepped into a carefully laid trap. Gangsters lying in wait machine-gunned him from concealed sniper nests inside two neighborhood flats on Kolmar Avenue near West End Avenue on the West Side. The coroner extracted fifty-nine slugs from Aiello's body, quite possibly a gangland record. He was buried with great pomp in an $11,800 casket.

THE CIRCUS GANG

Headquartered inside John Edward "Screwy" Moore's (aka Claude Maddox) Circus Café at 1857 North Avenue, directly across the street from Patsy Lolordo's Italian-American Citizen's Club, this gang of Northwest Side toughs and labor union sluggers led by Moore and "Tough" Tony Capezio, a gambler and gunman, supplied armaments to the Capone Gang in return for political protection and influence as they solidified their position deep within O'Banion-Weiss-Moran territory. Moore, who came up through the ranks of Egan's Rats, a St. Louis, Missouri, criminal gang, drifted into Chicago in the early years of Prohibition after serving a year in the county workhouse, and another twelve months for armed robbery. The Circus Gang manufactured and planted homemade bombs the gang planted with deadly effectiveness inside Moran's saloons and soft-drink parlors. Moore, with Capone's authorization, had recently taken possession of the beer distribution rights in the Cragin neighborhood on the city's Northwest Side. And then, just as quickly, he emerged as a key suspect in the St. Valentine's Day Massacre killings.

Police believed the Circus Café served as a weapons depot for the Capone Gang during the planning of the massacre, with Moore acting as the point man in the recruitment of St. Louis killers to come in and do the job. In 1930 Moore shot and wounded Bellwood police sergeant James McBride, who was to be the principal witness against Circus Gang member William "Three Finger Jack" White. After repeal, Moore elbowed his way into Local 450 of the Bartender's Union as a union steward while mentoring young Anthony "Big Tuna" Accardo, boss of the Chicago Outfit for the better part of four decades beginning in the 1940s.

THE "42" GANG

The merciless war between the Prohibition gangs claimed hundreds of victims and spawned an up-and-coming generation of teenage gangsters born and bred in the West Side slums. The "42" Gang, a motley crew of juvenile toughs from Taylor Street, otherwise known as "The Patch" and the adjoining "Valley," organized in 1920. The leadership took in boys as young as six to commence a reign of terror that escalated in the middle years of Prohibition. "Recruits come in when they are only six and seven years old," Captain Phillip Parodl of the Maxwell Street Station explained in a December 1932 interview. "It sounds silly but it's true. The bigger boys teach the little fellows how to open the doors of automobiles with skeleton keys. A big one stands a little way off and when he sees that the doors have been opened he gets in and drives away. A quarter or fifty cents goes to the first grader when the car is stripped and the parts are sold." Just as modern street gangs recruit "pee-wees" to carry out a range of petty offenses, the "42" Gang understood that should police apprehend these underage youngsters, there was only so much the criminal justice system could do. "The policeman cannot without public censure shoot at youths fifteen or sixteen. Suppose we catch the little fellow, what can be done about him?" Parodl wondered. "He goes to the Juvenile Court and is reprimanded and sent home. The first thing he learns is to keep his mouth shut and hate the police. They never tell us a thing from the time they first open a car door until they are shot and killed and sent to the penitentiary."

In this closed, insulated old-world ghetto, Italian immigrant fathers worked both night and day at low-paying, menial, unskilled jobs to put food on the table. The mother could not control the socially unacceptable actions of their sons who began their journey through the underworld filching clothing items from the clotheslines of their neighbors, stealing pennies from their mother's purse, harassing streetcar peddlers along Maxwell Street, or selling stolen copper wire and iron products for resale.

Sexual experimentation, according to author William Brashler in his book *The Don*, began early. "By the time a boy was seventeen in the Patch, he had not only lost his virginity but he probably had been arrested at least once for rape, a charge that meant only that he was guilty of having had sex with a girl under eighteen. More than likely he had also taken part in innumerable gang rapes, called by the boys 'gang shags.' It happened so often in a garage near the corner of Paulina and Flournoy that the intersection was known as Gang Shag corner."[23]

As Italians displaced the Jews who had supplanted the Irish and Bohemians on the West Side during this remarkable cycle of continuous ethnic resettlement that defined the cyclical nature of Chicago neighborhoods, the "42s" followed an evolutionary process similar to the Market Street Gang, but were less political and more violence driven. Armed robbery, auto theft, mugging, burglary, rape, and occasional contract killing on behalf of the Capones drew their criminal operation into sharper focus in the early 1930s. Although the ranks of the teenage gang were mostly Italian, membership was by no means exclusive. Irish, German, Polish, and Bohemian youths often turned up in the "show-up" (police lineup) following a dragnet. The "42s" were hardcore gun-wielding criminals before they were old enough to vote. They gathered in Bonfiglio's Poolroom at Elburn and Loomis Streets to plan their jobs, and by the end of the 1920s they had become the envy of the neighborhood boys who observed their smart clothes, fast cars, and cocksure swagger.

Law enforcement fingered Sam "Teetz" Battaglia—held over to the grand jury on a $40,000 bond on March 12, 1931, for wounding two police officers in a New Year's Day café robbery on the North Side—as the leader of the "42s."

Battaglia had succeeded twenty-three-year-old Joseph Colaro (nicknamed "Babe Ruth"), the "42" Gang founder, as gang chieftain after Colaro was shot through the back by a police officer while in the process of stripping a stolen car on November 13, 1927. Colaro, like so many other gang leaders, possessed the charisma and natural leadership skills necessary to recruit compliant members and earn their respect. He was aided and abetted by his chum Vito Pelletieri, "Sharkey" Icola, the four Pargoni brothers, Sam Giancana, Battaglia, and others.

By the 1960s Sam Battaglia would control gambling operations on the West and North Sides and serve as overlord of narcotics trafficking for the Chicago mob. On November 24, 1927, following all-night deliberations, a criminal court jury convicted Samuel DeStefano and another youth, Ralph Orlando, of sexually assaulting a seventeen-year-old girl who was walking home with her date. They grabbed the girl, threw her into their automobile, and drove her to a garage where she was gang raped by seven members of the "42s." DeStefano, just eighteen at the time, was sentenced to three years in prison. In time, the certifiably demented DeStefano earned the sobriquet "Mad Sam" for his outrageous courtroom demeanor. An unstable psychopath, murderer, bank robber, extortionist, and torturer, DeStefano served the mob as their most effective executioner and loan shark. He met his demise on April 14, 1973, inside his West Side garage, presumably at the hands of the shotgun-wielding Tony Spilotro.

Chicago's most prominent organized-crime figures of the 1960s and 1970s began their criminal careers as "42" members, including "Milwaukee Phil" Alderisio, Albert "Obie" Frabotta, Willie "Potatoes" Daddano, Vincent Inserro, Marshall Caifano, Charles Nicoletti, Frank Caruso, Fiore "FiFi" Buccieri, Rocco "the Parrot" Potenza, and 1960s syndicate boss Sam "Momo" Giancana, celebrity gangster and occasional associate of Frank Sinatra and boyfriend of singer Phyllis McGuire.

The police and the judiciary could not have possibly foreseen the powerful legacy of this Taylor Street Gang in 1930, but the well-intentioned Judge Francis Borelli of the Des Plaines Street Police Court recognized the inherent danger posed to the community and tried to do something about it. Donning shabby, worn-out clothes, Borelli went undercover into the lair of the "42" Gang to investigate the extent of their criminal operation, their known associates, victims, and focus of activity. Borelli's crusade spurred the police to action. Chief of Detectives William Schoemaker and Deputy Detective Chief Walter Storms sent ten bureau squads into eight geographic sectors of the Taylor Street / Valley District in early December 1931. "You men are to go into their territory," Schoemaker told the detail. "Arrest every man who cannot give a good account of himself. But be sure and get members of the "42" or any other gang. Bring them in and we'll take them before Judge Borelli."

The police cast a wide dragnet from Madison Street south to Twenty-Second Street and west from the Chicago River to Ashland Avenue. The drive against the "42" Gang netted ninety-seven police captives. One by one the parade of young hoodlums appeared before Borelli, who admonished them for the shame they had brought upon the Italian community.

"If I never do another thing in my life, I'm going to break up the '42' Gang," he vowed. "Most of you are of my race and a disgrace to the Italian people. I went into your neighborhood and learned everything said about you is true. You're a gang of thieves, and I'm going to clean up your district. Conditions are horrible with people being terrorized daily." Borelli's warning fell on deaf ears, however, and the "cleanup" ended as quickly as it had begun. Unfazed by police attention, emboldened gang members turned to home invasion. In November 1931, "42" member Frank Tufano and a fellow gunman robbed wealthy socialite William Mitchell and his wife inside their Lake Forest mansion, coming away with $150,000 in jewels. Ten "42s" were rounded up—the youngest was sixteen—in the usual police sweep that followed. Police warned wealthy society people about the perils of displaying expensive jewels at club functions and dinners in the suburb.

The "42s" continued their marauding ways, and always it seemed, the DeStefano brothers, Sam, Mario, and Michael, were in the thick of it. Safely incarcerated in a Wisconsin prison in July 1933 on a charge of bank robbery, "Mad Sam" DeStefano remained active in gang affairs, directing his brother to gather defense funds from Capone gangster "Dago" Lawrence Mangano. After Mangano rebuffed the demand, Mike DeStefano and fellow "42" William Madden spotted Mangano's chauffeur, Frank Laino, loitering in front of a business establishment at 1139 West Taylor. The "42" killers opened up on Laino, but only wounded him. However, a spray of 125 slugs killed bystander Emil Onesta instantly. Although fifty spectators witnessed the crime, only one person stepped forward to testify. Madden was sentenced to life. Michael DeStefano evaded police capture and went on the run. Taylor Street, a mélange of pleasing ethnic Italian restaurants, grocery stores, and vintage upscale housing in the modern day, struggles mightily to escape from its blood-soaked reputation as a place of assassination, sluggings, stabbings, and robberies, much of it the handiwork of the "42" Gang. "They are the terrors of this part of the city," sighed Captain Parodl. "I doubt if any other body of criminals in the country have learned better how to beat the law."

ROGER TOUHY GANG

Roger "the Terrible" Touhy, son of James Touhy, a Chicago police officer born in County Sligo, Ireland, grew up at Polk Street and Damen Avenue in the shadow of "Paddy the Bear's" saloon at Fourteenth and Halsted in the Valley District. Touhy was one of six brothers—four of them turned bad and three were killed in the Prohibition wars, but the boy at least showed some early promise.[24] He was valedictorian of his grammar school class. Formal schooling for Touhy ended there. In his country's service during World War I, Touhy taught Morse code to Navy officers at Harvard University. After he was mustered out of the service, Touhy bought and sold oil leases in Oklahoma for a few years before returning to Chicago in 1922 with a large sum of money in hand. Touhy had no interest in running houses of ill fame, gambling dens, or extortion rackets, but like other young men of the Valley, he got caught up in bootlegging. Touhy and his partner, Matt Kolb, produced a top grade of beer and everyone knew it. "I didn't have to push my beer," he once remarked. "It sold itself. I had a good brewmaster. All the politicians bought from me."[25]

They paid ten cents more for a bushel of hops and malt than his competitors, but not wanting to cross Capone in the old and familiar West Side and South Side battlegrounds, they left the South Side to Frank "Porky" Dillon, armed robber and labor union racketeer previously linked to Joe Saltis while they established a profitable, income-producing beer-running operation in the distant north and northwest suburban "road house" districts of Morton Grove, Des Plaines, and Niles Center (now Skokie) all the way north to the Lake County–Cook County border. Police presence was minimal. Unfortunately for Touhy, the Capone gangsters were everywhere in those days and they wanted to take over "his action." Matt Kolb, affiliated with Joe Aiello and his mob in the early 1920s, emerged as a suburban kingpin of gambling and booze with political influence and protection supplied by his pal and former boss in the ice-distribution business, Cook County sheriff Charles Graydon. Touhy, his brother Tommy, and Kolb undercut the Capone syndicate by selling their superior grade of beer at twenty-five to thirty-five dollars a barrel compared to the exorbitant price of Capone's "downtown" beer, typically fifty-five dollars a gallon. Kolb's assassination inside the Club Morton roadhouse and gambling den at Dempster and Ferris Street, on October 17, 1931, witnessed by Kolb's sister and a roomful of merrymakers, continued the intense feud with Capone that escalated after Prohibition repeal, when Touhy branched out into labor union activity. Two years after the Kolb murder, the Capone mob (minus Capone who by now was serving his sentence for income-tax evasion), staged the phony abduction of Jake "the Barber" Factor, heir to the Factor cosmetics fortune, and an international swindler with extensive underworld ties. Factor aced extradition back to England on tax evasion. He was complicit in a plot to frame Touhy for a crime that never occurred in order to free up Touhy's suburban domain for a quick and painless takeover by Capone. Factor vanished for twelve days in July 1933. The syndicate leaked just enough information to Thomas Courtney, the shady Cook County state's attorney, looking to move up in city politics with an aim to become mayor. The hapless Touhy was among a dozen men arrested and charged with kidnapping. Factor testified that a dozen men had forced his car off of the road and abducted him outside the Dells gambling resort in Morton Grove early in the morning of June 30, 1933. Taken to a "safe house" in Glenview, Factor told of torture and brutality until an alleged $70,000-dollar ransom could be paid by Dr. Herman Soloway. Defense attorney William Scott Stewart outlined the truth of the case in his candid opening statement to the jury. "The syndicate tried every method in the world to force Touhy out of his territory. When that was unsuccessful they began to accuse the Touhys of everything criminal that happened. The syndicate had made inroads also into the government offices, the police department, and the prosecutor's office." The jury deliberated Touhy's fate for thirty-six hours but deadlocked, resulting in a mistrial. Courtney was unfazed by the outcome and pressed on. In the second trial, Isaac Costner, a former member of the Touhy Gang, "confessed" to being one of the kidnappers. Costner had made a secret deal with Courtney to perjure himself in exchange for leniency on a mail-robbery charge. In 1948 Costner admitted he was forced to make a false statement by Courtney, but the lie was enough to put Roger away for ninety-nine years at the Stateville prison in Joliet, Illinois. Touhy caused no problem. He pushed a broom most days, and was a model prisoner, although embittered and increasingly desperate. On October 9, 1942, Roger and six other convicts escaped over the wall of Stateville and raced back to Chicago. He enjoyed two brief months of freedom as a fugitive on the run before the FBI (with a well-guarded J. Edgar Hoover present to slap on the cuffs), surrounded an apartment building in the Uptown community where he was hiding out. Returned to the state penitentiary with another 199 years tacked on to his sentence by Judge Roscoe C. South in Will County, Touhy languished in a cell for another sixteen years for a crime he did not commit. Finally in early 1958, Judge John P. Barnes of the U.S. district court termed the Factor kidnapping a giant hoax, and set in motion the means by which the prisoner could gain his parole. Roger Touhy walked out of Stateville a free man believing that old injustices had finally been set right. However, just twenty-three days after smelling the fresh air of freedom, unknown mob assassins shot down the most cruelly victimized former inmate of the Illinois Department of Corrections on the front porch of his sister's home in the Austin community on the West Side on December 16, 1959. Drawing his last breath, Touhy stammered: "The bastards never forget!" With the slightest exaggeration, the press said that Touhy had never been convicted of anything more serious that a parking ticket.[26]

The *Tribune* commented: "In a world where there are few roses, Roger Touhy did not pretend to be one, but his finish emphasizes that even a man who was not so good may be the victim of men who are worse."[27] Thomas Courtney, the only man to serve twelve years as Cook County state's attorney, never had to answer for the miscarriage of justice he perpetrated against Touhy. Failing in his bid to wrest the mayoralty away from Ed Kelly in 1939, Courtney pushed on. He enjoyed the full backing of the all-powerful Democratic machine and advanced his career. Elevated to the bench, Courtney completed twenty-two years as a judge on the municipal court. He died peacefully on December 3, 1971, his conscience untroubled.

CHICAGO HEIGHTS GANG

Crime fighter Eliot Ness, whose Hollywood-inspired portrayal in motion pictures and television belied his rather meager accomplishments battling Al Capone during the end years of his reign, received his appointment as a Treasury Department Prohibition agent in 1929 through family connections with brother-in-law Alexander Jamie, a federal officer who had married Ness's sister Clara.

Twenty-six-year-old Eliot Ness, a product of Chicago's Roseland community, was fresh out of the University of Chicago and short on experience when he was ordered into the village of Chicago Heights, thirty miles south of Chicago at the southern tip of Cook County, to clean up a rat's nest of vice, bootlegging, gambling, and rampant municipal corruption. Chicago Heights, called the most corrupt town in the Midwest, and its neighboring communities of Burnham and West Hammond (renamed Calumet City), were satellite territories of the Capone mob, first cultivated by James Colosimo and Johnny Torrio at a defining moment early in the century when paved roads made it possible for the crime syndicates to offer its services to a mobile population of gin-sipping thrill seekers. Anthony San Filipo, a local druggist and a man of some breeding and refinement, was the man to see in Chicago Heights in 1920, when their village slowly acquired its steamy reputation. Educated in Italy, San Filipo allocated management of liquor distribution to henchman Philip Piazza, a cabaret owner, and James Lamberta, a jeweler. San Filipo's monopoly ended ingloriously on April 24, 1924, after he had picked up his killers—likely Piazza and Lamberta—near the railroad tracks on the east side of the Heights. From the rear seat of the car, the assassins fired six bullets into his brain. The cops found the murder car the next day smashed into a tree. These two gangland amateurs took over San Filipo's racket and established a headquarters inside Piazza's Milano Café. Believing they were invulnerable to attack, the two men acted like a pair of "junior Al Capones," flaunting their windfall of wealth and making the rounds of the nightspots in this corrupt haven of gangsters and politicians. Their short, violent reign ended June 2, 1926. Lamberta, in the company of Crystal Barrier, a married woman, was shotgunned to death after stepping out of the Derby, a local roadhouse. Drive-by assassins mowed down Piazza two weeks later. By December

1926 the Chicago Heights alcohol wars had claimed fourteen victims. Six months later the death toll had risen to twenty. The vicious nature of these killings gave law enforcement pause. Housewife Katherine Jones, the adulterous paramour of bootlegger Frank Pissani, fully cooperated with police but ended up dead with twelve shotgun pellets in her back while seated at her kitchen table. Gangsters killed police chief Lester Gilbert in similar fashion in December 1928. Chief Gilbert, the father of five, worked closely with assistant U.S. attorney Daniel Anderson in the investigation of the local alcohol ring and the protection afforded by the obliging and corrupt village president, F. W. Hartman.

Cook County coroner Herman Bundesen, a cog in Mayor Thompson's machine, called Hartman "unfit to hold office." It was quite a revelation coming from a member of the Thompson inner circle, but it spoke volumes about conditions in the Heights where Capone gunmen were active on election days by "helping the voters" with their ballots on election. Gilbert was dining with his wife inside his home when he was shot at close range through a window in his living room. "Gilbert told me his predecessor was in league with the Chicago Heights gang and was protected by Hartman," Anderson testified at the inquest. "He furnished me with the names of three of the gang and I know they are a tough gang, an outfit of killers. They set the house of one trustee on fire because he opposed the retention of [former] Chief Erickson." Ness, working under the direction of Alexander Jamie, chief of the federal Prohibition enforcement detail, went after the illegal breweries operated by Lorenzo Juliano, Capone's hand-picked heir and successor to San Filipo, Lamberta, and Piazza. Jamie successfully linked the hitherto unsolved "Diamond Joe" Esposito assassination plus a string of seven other mob murders and the unsolved syndicate bombings at the homes of Senator Charles S. Deneen and state's attorney John A. Swanson in March 1928 at the doorstep of Juliano, a corpulent, mustachioed bootlegger and operator of a South Side poolroom, who began his career as a grocer on the far South Side. Law enforcement revealed that the Esposito hit was a revenge killing engineered by Juliano. Acting under orders, Juliano collected a large campaign-contribution war chest and delivered it to "Diamond Joe" as he had been instructed. But then George Golding, Jamie, the kid Ness and his team of eight marauding Prohibition agents soon to be dubbed "The Untouchables," raided and destroyed hundreds of illegal stills in Blue Island and Chicago Heights before State's Attorney Swanson arrested the Sicilian crime boss running the entire show. Juliano crossed a dangerous line with the bombing of the home of a U.S. senator and the murder of his trusted political ally, Joe Esposito. Now he too had become suddenly expendable. After clocking a bet on the last race at Washington Park Race Track on June 19, 1930, Juliano motored home in a borrowed automobile. Police found the driver and the car mired in a clay ditch on 123rd Street in Blue Island. Juliano's feet protruded out the window and the killer had wrapped the head of the dead man in a towel the cops traced back to the Oak Forest Infirmary. Juliano's head had been crushed and all his ribs were broken. The savagery of the murder made it clear to investigators that someone had a personal score to settle. With Juliano out of the way, the Capones anointed Oliver J. Ellis, beefy kingpin of the slot-machine racket in the far south suburbs and his right-hand man, Howard Caldwell, as the new payoff men overseeing Chicago Heights. State's Attorney Swanson, incensed over the attempt made upon his life, took personal charge of the drive against the Chicago Heights operation. Jamie and his dry agents led a massive raid resulting in the takeover of the Heights on January 3, 1929, impounding 423 slot machines, fifty gallons of alcohol, fifteen cases of whiskey, forty-nine sacks of Canadian beer, and $400,000 worth of cancelled checks found in a garage adjoining Ellis's large country home. At year's end, the government indicted "Boss" Ellis on four counts of income-tax evasion. As fate would have it, the Ellis case was assigned to the courtroom of federal judge James Wilkerson—the jurist that would send Al Capone to the penitentiary eighteen months later.

"We had to weigh our problems and find a vulnerable point," Ness told the *New York Times* years later. "We decided on the breweries because their product is bulky and because they have the toughest transport problem. We knew that regularity was necessary in their operation and it wasn't long before we learned of the special hauls on Friday in preparation for Saturday speakeasy business."[28]

In the closing months of Al Capone's successful conquest of Chicago and its outlying territories, the government transferred Ness, a nervous and obsessively polite man dependent on alcohol and overly fond of women (other than his wife) in his later years, back into the city once the

Heights ring had been smashed. In his short term of active engagement in Chicago, Ness led one noteworthy raid, on June 15, 1930, against a syndicate brewery on South Wabash Avenue that supplied illegal intoxicants to Colosimo's Restaurant.

So much of the meaningful work completed by the Untouchables that helped the government "get" Capone resulted from the spadework of the older men in the unit, supported by fifteen uncredited researchers and investigators going into the neighborhoods and talking to the tavern owners and speakeasy managers. Mostly it was a paper chase through reams of tax records and government filings. Historians and scholars concur that the celluloid crime fighter was largely a 1950s press invention and a footnote character to the larger real-life drama. Asked his opinion about Eliot Ness after his trial on income-tax evasion had run its course, Al Capone merely shrugged his shoulders and asked, "Who is Eliot Ness?"[29]

THE NORTH SIDE GANG | SAMUEL "NAILS" MORTON, DION O'BANION, EARL "HYMIE" WEISS, GEORGE "BUGS" MORAN

The treacherous and increasingly irksome cast of criminal characters defending Little Hell, the Gold Coast, and the other neighborhoods lying due north and northwest of the Chicago River stood in the way of a complete citywide takeover by the Capone mob in the 1920s. While the other gangs south of Madison Street had either made a separate peace with Al Capone, fled the city, or ended up in a grave, the North Side O'Banion Gang violated all agreements set in place during "peace conferences" and escalated gang warfare in the mistaken belief that they alone had the armaments and resources necessary to make "Old Scarface" heel.

The North Side Gang, an outgrowth of "Paddy the Bear" Ryan's outfit over on the West Side regrouped under the direction of war hero and acquitted cop killer "Nails" Morton, who steered the criminal operation into rum-running after the successful hijack of a large inventory of whiskey inside the Flexner Warehouse on Austin Avenue in May 1922. Morton drew in "Dapper" Dan McCarthy, murderer, bootlegger, and the elected leader of the Chicago Journeyman Plumber's Union; the gimpy Dean Charles "Dion" O'Banion, a safe-blower and murderer referred to as "Chicago's arch criminal" by police superintendent Morgan Collins in 1924; Maxie Eisen, the "Simon Legree of the pushcart peddlers"; telephone coin-box thief Vincent "Schemer" Drucci, the token Italian in the bunch; "Two Gun" Louis Alterie, a former Western cowpoke and labor union thug whose real name was Leland Verain; Albert Weinshank, nightclub owner and one of the gang's designates in the Cleaner & Dyer's business; James Clark (née Albert Kachellek), gunman, Teamsters Union local official, and a brother-in-law of George "Bugs" Moran; Willie Marks, the second-in-command to Moran during his period of rule; Earl "Hymie" Weiss, the only gangster known to have performed in a stag film; Ted Newberry, who switched allegiance to the Capones in the aftermath of the St. Valentine's Day Massacre; "Bugs" Moran, a shrewd and vicious criminal better known among his peers as "the Devil" than for his many eccentricities that earned him his famous boyhood nickname; train station mail robbers Peter and Frank "Hock" Gusenberg; Jack Zuta, pimp and vice monger; Leo Mongoven, chauffeur to Moran; and an accompanying cast of killers, hijackers, political fixers, and petty hoodlums. Together, they were a kind of "United Nations" of crime, coming from divergent ethnic backgrounds.

After making his first big score in the booze racket, "Nails" Morton moved into the Congress Hotel on Michigan Avenue, casting aside the squalor and hustle of the West Side "Valley" for a residence befitting his status as a millionaire bootlegger. He bought a stable of horses at the Lincoln Riding Academy on Clark Street, as any well-heeled dude might be known to do. But for all of his notoriety and fame, there was no controlling the skittish steed he mounted for a Sunday morning canter around Lincoln Park on May 13, 1923. In his company that morning were "Dean" O'Banion, who had recently made Morton a business partner in Schofield's Flower Shop, his treasured florist business and gang headquarters at 738 North State Street, opposite Holy Name Cathedral; O'Banion's wife, Viola; and produce commission man Peter Mundane.[30] As the riding party set off from the stable and turned on to Wellington Street near Clark, Morton's horse clamped the bit between his teeth and reared up. "Nails" Morton struggled to bring the animal under control, but a stirrup broke and the rider was thrown to the ground.

Morton might have managed to escape harm, but the outward kick of one of the horse's hooves shattered his skull. "Nails" Morton was dead at age twenty-nine. According to popular legend, the horse was captured, steadied, and returned to the stable, but the vengeful "Two Gun Alterie" saddled up and rode the steed out to the Lincoln Park bridle path the next day and allegedly pumped a bullet into the animal's head. He called the stable and allegedly informed the owner that "we taught that son-of-a-bitch horse of yours a lesson. If you want the saddle go and get it!" The story could well be another press invention dreamed up by a tabloid, scandal-mongering reporter in the crazy 1920s.

The sprightly O'Banion, employed as a singing waiter by John and William McGovern in their Liberty Inn at Clark and Erie, ran with the "Little Hellions" as a boy. The Hellions were too young to make much of an impression on the wizened old Market Street Gang with their skill of jack-rolling drunks in North Side alleys, because the Market Streeters were breaking up around the time O'Banion learned his ABCs at the Holy Name Cathedral School for Boys. James O'Donnell Bennett remembered O'Banion's sunny, optimistic disposition and his familiar mantra "swell fellow!" "He would bestow it upon you at the same time his address was in your death book," Bennett wrote. Superintendent Morgan Collins believed O'Banion responsible for twenty-five murders but he was never arrested and brought to trial for any of them. His criminal record included a meager four arrests for burglary with no convictions.

The North Side Gang chieftain was a brash instigator and something of an enigma to law enforcement. He never touched a drop of alcohol, but rode to fame as the leading purveyor of booze on the North Side. A deeply religious lad, he had served as an acolyte at Holy Name Cathedral for Father Francis O'Brien, but as an adult crime boss he had no qualms about ordering the murder of a rival. In his custom-made, tailored suits he concealed three handguns in separate pockets. The ambidextrous killer with a round face and soft features specialized in pistols and posies and courting North Side politicians and cops with aplomb. During a heated political campaign on November 4, 1924, O'Banion was feted at a fund-raising dinner at the posh Webster Hotel on Lincoln Park West. Present that evening to toast Dean and his hand-picked slate of candidates were chief of detectives Michael Hughes, Colonel Albert

A. Sprague, commissioner of public works under reform Mayor Dever, county clerk Robert M. Sweitzer and several judges of the municipal court, all seated elbow-to-elbow with the Gusenberg brothers, Alterie, and lesser lights of the North Side underworld. Dever demanded an explanation from Hughes, but the detective chief mumbled a feeble excuse that he had been framed. "This banquet was like almost all others. The hoodlums were there," he admitted. "They all go to such affairs. I left soon after I saw who was there. But there were many judges who stayed. I'm being made the goat!"[31] In the Forty-Second Ward, comprising the Gold Coast and Little Hell, the commonly asked question on Election Day, "Who'll carry the Forty-Second and Forty-Third?" had an obvious answer: "O'Banion in his pistol pockets!" Turning to his sidekick, "Hymie" Weiss, one day, he boasted, "We're big business without high hats!"[32]

As Prohibition unfolded, O'Banion made an informal peace agreement promising to respect territorial rights with John Torrio, now in charge of the South Side Levee Gang following "Big Jim" Colosimo's murder in May 1920. Their alliance was shaky and only temporary. The period of quiet quickly ended with the incursion of the Genna brothers into the North Side. O'Banion resented their ambition, but at the same time he looked to diversify and expand his operations south and west. His injudicious remark, "To hell with those Sicilians!" helped seal his own death warrant after he crossed the line with Torrio, Capone, and the Gennas one too many times. At the same time Dean O'Banion the crime boss went about murdering "Sicilians" (lumping gangsters of northern Italian descent together with the Gennas into his favorite pet phrase), Dean O'Banion the business man prepared their lavish floral arrangements for the gangster funerals.

O'Banion's slate of candidates swept the November 4, 1924, city election despite the press uproar over the Webster Hotel testimonial dinner, and the peculiar array of invited guests enjoying O'Banion hospitality. The feast turned out to be more of a "last supper" than the feast of Belshazzar. Exactly six days later, as O'Banion applied the finishing touches to a floral display for the "Sicilians" to honor the memory of cancer victim Mike Merlo, the peace-seeking head of the Unione Siciliana who brokered a shaky truce between the Gennas and O'Banion, the end came for Dean.

Carmen Vacco, city sealer, and James Genna had placed the original order for the flowers and a life-size wax sculpture of their dear old pal Mike Merlo. No expense was spared. The final bill exceeded $10,000. Shortly before ten-thirty on the morning of November 10, 1924, O'Banion received a telephone call advising him that someone would be arriving in five minutes to pick up the order. O'Banion and his porter, William Crutchfield, were the only persons in the store when three swarthy-looking men alighted from a blue Jewett sedan and stepped inside. Extending his right hand in friendship, with his shears in his left hand, O'Banion asked, "Hello boys, you from Mike Merlo's?" One of the Sicilians jerked O'Banion forward and six shots were fired in rapid succession. O'Banion, usually very cautious and alert to danger, recognized the men and did not appear threatened according to Crutchfield's statement. Torrio, the Gennas, and Capone were all questioned but no one talked. In his final report, the Cook County Coroner wrote: "Slayers not apprehended. John Scalise, Alberto Anselmi and Frank Uale suspected but never brought to trial." Among knowledgeable insiders there seemed little doubt that Angelo, Tony, and Mike Genna plotted the assassination, and Scalise and Anselmi, the infamous Mafia killers available for the highest price, were two of the three triggermen.

The O'Banion hit touched off the final, climactic phase of the Prohibition bootleg wars. The Torrio-Capone syndicate had already vanquished or consolidated seven other competitors, leaving only the North Siders standing alone in their of defiance of Torrio-Capone rule. They did not go quietly. "Dapper" Dan McCarthy and "Hymie" Weiss, successor to O'Banion, fixated on Angelo Genna and tracked him down. The bigger target in the revenge scheme hatched by Weiss was Johnny Torrio, at age forty-three, the elder statesman of Chicago gangland. Two lethal killers, Peter Gusenberg and "Bugs" Moran, waited in ambush outside Torrio's apartment building at 7011 Clyde Avenue in South Shore on January 24, 1925. As Torrio and his wife, Anna, alighted from their chauffeur-driven limousine, Moran and Gusenberg raced out of the shadows and pumped four shots into the South Side gang boss who held a bag of groceries in each arm. Despite being shot to pieces Torrio managed to survive. During his recuperation at the Jackson Park Hospital, Torrio told police he knew the identity of the shooters, but would not reveal their names. At his bedside, providing twenty-four-hour security, stood the ever-vigilant former county commissioner Frank Ragen, who's Colts nominally aligned with Torrio-Capone. After a long period of convalescence, Torrio announced that he was through with Chicago, handing over the keys to the criminal operation to Al Capone before departing to New York where he would agree to act as consigliore to the reorganization of the "Five Families" into a national "commission." And so it was all left to Capone, who began his abbreviated but spectacular six-year reign in Chicago to eventually become history's most famous gangster.

The blood on the Torrio sidewalk was barely dry when Genna gang members went looking for "Hymie" Weiss. They drove through Lincoln Park keeping a watchful eye on the Belden Hotel where Weiss resided. The Genna touring car was conspicuous in the neighborhood and Weiss was nobody's fool. He placed a telephone call to Peter Genna, and warned, "If you don't keep these guys away from the Belden Hotel I'll come over and blow your head off!"

Weiss, said to be the only gangland figure Al Capone truly feared, was a cold, impersonal gangster. There could be no peace in Chicago, he said in response to a ceasefire overture from the South Side, until Capone handed over Scalise and Anselmi, O'Banion's presumed assassins. "I wouldn't do that to a yellow dog!" Capone exclaimed.[33] Then Weiss unleashed his gunmen against the South Siders in two separate attacks in September 1926, targeting Capone in his own backyard. In the first assault, Moran led a charge into the South Side badlands, intending to ambush Capone outside of the Four Deuces. Guns blazed, but Capone, seated in his automobile, escaped. His driver, Tony Ross, died behind the wheel. On September 20, 1926, a caravan of motor cars, each of them carrying three machine gunners, drove slowly past the Hawthorne Smoke Shop, Capone's Cicero domain. Capone and his bodyguard, Frank Rio, were seated inside the coffee shop when a fusillade of bullets fired from the slow-moving gangster cars shattered the glass and tore apart the interior. Capone, shielded by Rio, emerged unscathed and covered the cost of the damage. Fearless, but stupid, Weiss pressed on, undoubtedly aware that the Cicero outrage had moved his name to the top of Capone's death list.

The swift and violent end came on October 11, 1926, as Weiss and his entourage crossed State Street on their way to Schofield's Flower Shop after attending the trial of Joe Saltis and Frank "Lefty" Koncil, both under indictment for the murder of John "Mitters" Foley. The Saltis Gang and Weiss had a mutual interest in eliminating Capone, and of late had been working together in a spirit of common purpose. Weiss raised a $75,000 "defense fund" for Saltis—a necessary "business investment." All eyes were on the trial, and not on the movements of gangsters along North State Street. From a sniper's post in a rented room at 740 North State Street, four machine gunners the cops believed to be Frank Nitti, Frank Diamond, and Scalise and Anselmi, fired down on the street. The harsh and deadly crackle of the machine guns sent pedestrians running for cover and chipped the cornerstone of Holy Name Cathedral. Patrick "Paddy" Murray, a minor bootlegger, fell dead in the attack.

Weiss took ten bullets and was pronounced dead at Henrotin Hospital. From his pocket, police pulled out $5,200 in cash and a list of the names of jurors deciding the fate of Saltis. Police did not bother to harass Capone. "It's a waste of time to arrest him," explained Chief Collins. "He's been in before on other murder charges. He has his alibi. He was in Cicero when the shooting occurred."

The resilient North Siders refused to lay down their machine guns and succumb, not with so much profit and political influence at stake. Four days after the Weiss murder, detective chief John Stege announced that street intelligence revealed "Bugs" Moran as the anointed one up on the North Side. Moran's lengthy rap sheet included arrests dating back to 1910 for burglary when he was only eighteen. At various times he occupied penitentiary cells, in 1913 to 1917; 1918 to 1921; and for one day, February 1, 1923. St. Paul, Minnesota, native "Bugs" Moran's final visit to Stateville lasted twenty-four hours because money and political influence helped unlock the cell door. Released back into society, he joined the O'Banion mob, and anointed himself vice president of the Central Cleaner and Dyer's Company, owning one-third of the $300,000 capital investment.

Moran, befitting his rising status, dressed like every other successful, conservative middle-age businessman in his custom-made suit, Hamburg hat, and a long brown woolen trench coat. This was the description of the man Al Capone's team of hired lookouts were ordered to be on the lookout for from their "spotter's post" in the upper floors of two brownstone rooming houses across the street from the Moran liquor depot at 2122 North Clark Street in the heart of the Gold Coast.[34]

The stage was set for the climactic moment of Prohibition-era Chicago and a crime that would shake the sensibilities of the nation and implant in the minds of good people everywhere the notion that Chicago was lawless, dangerous, immoral, and controlled by racketeers. Although mostly true, the city fought hard against negative perceptions but it could never succeed in living down the infamy of the St. Valentine's Day Massacre, occurring at precisely 10:30 on a frozen, snowy morning on February 14, 1929.

The massacre story is familiar and has been retold in numerous Hollywood motion pictures, books, and television documentaries. Seven members of the Moran Gang, their pockets bulging with cash in anticipation of receiving a truckload of recently hijacked booze—Old Log Cabin—gathered inside the grimy S.M.C. Cartage Company garage rented by Adam Heyer under the alias "Snyder." Heyer owned the cartage company.[35] "Bugs" Moran and his lieutenants, Ted Newberry and Willie Marks, were delayed, just five minutes away from participating in their own funeral. For the bosses of the North Side Gang it was the luckiest day of their entire lives.[36]

The rooming-house spotters may have mistakenly identified Dr. Reinhardt Schwimmer, a failed dentist who enjoyed the thrill of keeping company with gangsters, for Moran. With seven men already occupying the one-story building, a discreet phone call was placed to the Circus Café to put the plan in motion. On Wood Street, a vehicle made up to look like a Chicago Police Department cruiser lay in wait to transport four assassins (two dressed as police officers) to 2122 North Clark Street. Arriving at the garage, the four men entered through the front door declaring a police raid, and directed all seven of the Moran men, including car mechanic John May and Dr. Schwimmer, to face the north wall, hands pressed up against the brickwork. The blast of machine guns spraying the backs of the seven men in a sweeping motion, right to left, could be heard above the din of the busy Clark Street traffic outside. Moments later the police cruiser, with the killers safely inside, sped south down Clark Street.

The repercussions of the crime were far-ranging. Capone, wintering in Florida at the time, jokingly told the press, "They don't call that guy Bugs for nothing!" but adamantly denied any personal involvement. In Chicago, the shaken Moran, overwhelmed and hospitalized supposedly with a respiratory infection, had his own message for reporters. "Only Al Capone kills like that."

The massacre was much more than a tabloid crime of passing interest. To many observers of the scene, it was a once-in-a-lifetime occurrence, an "event" of magnitude that awakened the general public and President Herbert Hoover to the undeniable conclusion that there was something terribly wrong in Chicago, the "city of big shoulder holsters," one reporter quipped in a rare moment of jest.

"Who is this Capone?" the president famously asked Colonel McCormick. The "Colonel of Chicago" curtly informed Hoover that Prohibition enforcement was a colossal failure. Too many small-fry drinkers were sent off to jail while the big-shot bootleggers had bribed their way to immunity. The president listened and soon the federal government took a renewed interest in the comings and goings of Al Capone and his flock.

"Never in all history of feuds of gangland has Chicago or the Nation seen anything like today's wholesale slaughter," commented Patrick Roche, an agent of the special intelligence unit of the Internal Revenue Service. Five years earlier Roche gathered the necessary evidence that sent "Dapper Dan" McCarthy and "Hymie" Weiss to jail for one of their many booze hijackings.

Police detectives Thomas Loftus, Joseph Connelley, John Devane, and Captain Thomas Condon of the Thirty-Sixth District sifted through a mountain of clues and transcripts of testimony. Under pressure the detectives conducted a creditable, if not diligent, investigation. "Screwy" Moore (Claude Maddox), armaments supplier, and Vincenzo Gebardi (aka "Machine Gun" Jack McGurn), Capone triggerman in charge of logistics and planning, were hauled in by police with dozens of other gangsters linked to Capone and questioned. Through Moore and his extensive connections, they had a pretty good idea that at least two of the killers had been imported from St. Louis. They also knew that Fred "Killer' Burke, one of the St. Louis gunmen brought in to do the job, wielded a machine gun inside the garage. Major Calvin Goddard, one of the nation's early forensics experts and the founder of the first scientific crime-detection laboratory, installed at Northwestern University, proved that the spent shell casings found inside the garage matched those found at Burke's Michigan farm. The menacing Burke never stood trial for complicity in the massacre, nor did anyone else for that matter. It was not so surprising. Over 1,100 unsolved murders attributed to organized crime gangs in Chicago, dating back to 1919, remain in the books as officially unsolved.

From inside the prison walls in St. Paul, Minnesota, on January 10, 1935, Byron Bolton, a former Egan's Rat and a member of the Fred Barker–Alvin Karpis holdup gang, served as one of the lookouts with Harry and Phil Keywell of the Detroit Purple Gang.[37] He claimed that he had rented one of the surveillance rooms on Clark Street.

Bolton revealed the names of the shooters and planners to disbelieving federal law enforcement. In his confession he told of entering the garage that morning. Fred "Killer" Burke and ex-army pilot, robber, kidnapper, and child rapist Fred Goetz (aka "Shotgun" George Ziegler), were the gunmen disguised in police uniforms. Also named were John Moore (aka Claude Maddox) and Murray "the Camel" Humphries, a "newbie" in 1929 who became a powerful and influential mob figure in the 1950s and 1960s for his ability to suborn political leaders and police. Gus Winkler, the other prominent suspect fingered by Bolton, was slain outside of Cook County commissioner Charley Weber's beer distribution warehouse on October 9, 1933. The inclusion of Winkler is curious, but not entirely improbable. At the time of his death, it was believed that he had taken control of the remnants of Moran's gang, and had become a secret government informant. To this list of suspects, Chicago police added the names of the revenge-seeking Joseph Lolordo, brother of the fallen "Patsy" Lolordo, and James Ray, a St. Louis gangster.

Everyone agreed on Burke as the main suspect, but the feds and the Chicago police were not buying Bolton's story. FBI director J. Edgar Hoover refused to acknowledge the existence of organized crime syndicates until after 1957. Hoover had little interest in the massacre gunmen. He said he would not waste his resources conducting an investigation into Bolton's allegations, claiming that it was a local matter best left to the Chicago Police Department. The slaughter of the seven Moran men remains officially unsolved.

THE AFTERMATH AND AN END TO AN ERA

With a force of seven hundred men (give or take) on his payroll, Capone, by the end of 1929, had mostly eliminated or consolidated all opposing forces despite a $50,000 bounty placed on his head by rival gang chieftains. The holdouts, like Roger Touhy plus a handful of independents that refused to bend, were dealt with severely. "Bugs" Moran attempted to reconstruct his gang and bravely fought on through 1930 and 1931, expanding the business into Lake County, but in the end, he lost the gang, his wealth, and prominence, and reverted back to the aimless life of bank robber, counterfeiter, and itinerant thief and robber. He would spend a number of years locked up. Moran was serving a five-year sentence for a bank robbery he committed in Ansonia, Ohio, back in 1945 when he died of lung cancer behind the walls of Leavenworth on February 25, 1957, at age sixty-four.

President Herbert Hoover's promise to Colonel McCormick to "look into the Capone matter" led to the formation in May 1929 of the National Commission on Law Enforcement and Observance, an investigatory panel of educators, jurists, and attorneys.[38]

"Common sense compels us to realize that grave abuses have occurred which must be remedied," Hoover declared on January 17, 1929, just before taking office. "An organized searching investigation of fact and cause alone can determine the wise method of correcting them. Crime and disobedience of the law cannot be permitted to break down the laws of the Constitution and laws of the United States."

Chaired by former U.S. attorney general George Woodward Wickersham, who served in the administration of President William Howard Taft, this august body, popularly known as the "Wickersham Commission," toured Chicago, New York, New Jersey, Louisiana, and Colorado to study Prohibition enforcement.[39] In fifteen separate published reports the commission, tasked with reassessing the failures and societal benefits of the Noble Experiment, took a long look at lawlessness in America, police corruption, the probation and parole system, and the impact of the Volstead Act upon the nation's youth.

The committee concluded that Prohibition enforcement had done a pretty good job of turning underage juveniles into future criminals. Of the 2,243 young men and women under the age of eighteen who were federal prisoners in 1930, 990 of them—a full 42 percent—had been indicted and convicted on violations of the Volstead Act. Eighteen inmates were less than fourteen years old and 250 were less than sixteen years of age.

Incarceration was formidable and often harsh for these youngsters. "Punishment in the dark cells is given for trivial as well as serious offenses," the report went on to say, "not standing at count, speaking in the dining room, laughing in the cell block, making loud popping noises with the mouth were listed on some of the discipline slips of the federal cases studied. It was related to our field workers that a prisoner was found dead in one of these cells. Those placed in the drill crew are required to keep moving constantly in the yard. They are fed in the dining room twice a day, a slice of bread, a table spoon of potatoes and water."[40]

Although the Wickersham Commission reported these ills, its conservative Republican members officially opposed repeal as a possible remedy to a decade's worth of trouble. There were many dissenting opinions among the members, however, who conceded that the Eighteenth Amendment had simply not worked.

Investigator Guy Nichols closed the final report with the tepid recommendation that "Education and persuasion, it will be found is the only real and lasting way to affect temperance in Illinois," and, "The menacing and very serious problem confronting Chicago is that of clearing the city of graft, political intrigue, bootlegging, and last but not least, by any means, racketeering."[41]

The muddled conclusions nevertheless illuminated a path that would lead to the eventual passage of an amendment repealing Prohibition on March 22, 1933, and it set in motion the long overdue prosecution of Al Capone on income-tax-evasion charges that would ultimately convict him on five of twenty-two counts in Judge Wilkerson's courtroom on October 17, 1931. Wilkerson sentenced Capone to eleven years in federal prison and ordered him to make restitution of $50,000. He entered the federal penitentiary in Atlanta on May 4, 1932.

U.S. attorney George E. Q. Johnson, collaborating with Internal Revenue Service investigator Elmer Irey and Treasury agent Frank J. Wilson were the everyday heroes of the pretrial and trial process. They spent months diving into Capone's tax records and expenditures with critical intelligence supplied by Alexander Jamie, Ness, and the "Secret Six," an undercover unit empowered by the Chicago Association of Commerce and the Chicago Crime Commission.[42]

During the investigation Edward O'Hare, father of World War II Medal of Honor recipient "Butch" O'Hare, tipped off the feds that Wilson and Johnson were marked for death. The desperate Capone had reached out to Torrio and others in New York for five contract killers to travel to the Windy City, do the killing, and make a fast exit. Law enforcement foiled the plot.

Federal informant O'Hare, who managed Capone's dog-racing track and Sportsman's Park in Cicero, paid with his life. On November 8, 1939, at the end of a normal business day, O'Hare motored south down Ogden Avenue from Sportsman's Park when his vehicle was overtaken by Capone gunmen. O'Hare was killed in the ambush. It was later revealed that he had agreed to inform on the Capone mob, knowing full well of the dangers because he needed a governmental recommendation that would allow his son to attend the Naval Academy at Annapolis, Maryland. That was the price of heroism.

Eight days after "E. J." O'Hare's murder, the government paroled Capone. Wracked by syphilis and his mind wavering between long periods of lucidity and utter madness, never again would Alphonse Capone terrorize the City of Chicago. The nation's most famous racketeer died on January 25, 1947. He was only forty-eight years old. New mob bosses rose to power to advance the agenda of this monolithic South Side crime group with roots dating back to the Gay Nineties. The tough youngbloods of the old "42" Gang who made their bones pilfering automobiles, committing rape, jack-rolling drunks, and laughing at the tough admonishments of Judge Borelli in 1930, moved up quickly and soon controlled the destiny of Chicago organized crime into the jet age.

By the 1950s the former Colosimo-Torrio-Capone aggregate had firmly implanted itself as the "Outfit," the Chicago chapter, one of twenty-six identifiable national organized groups knitted together in an embryonic network of formerly independent gangs in the United States—the result of Prohibition. Hyman Roth, the fictional character in Mario Puzo's landmark novel *The Godfather*, summed up the status of organized crime thirty years after Prohibition ended when he confided to young Michael Corleone, "Michael, we are bigger than U.S. Steel."

The end of Prohibition spelled doom for the Cook County Republican Party and the rusting Thompson machine, voted out of office in a 1931 landslide loss to Anton Cermak, the cagey West Side Bohemian boss who forever altered the political landscape of Chicago by reinventing the Democratic machine. He chopped off the dead Republican branches of the municipal tree: the Ellers, Fred Lundin, Robert Crowe; one by one, they all fell.

Cermak ordered John Stege, the old "cleanup man," into the Wabash Avenue station "to make Democrats out of the Negroes of the 2nd and 3rd Wards of the South Side." Cermak handed Stege a sharp directive to be carried out to the letter: Close down every illegal gambling "policy racket" he found for six months and make the "policy kings squirm, and then bleed 'em dry until they have convinced black Chicago to vote in a solid Democratic block behind Cermak and his new patronage chief in city hall, Patrick Nash." Stege did his job too well. He raised hell among the powerful African American gambling bosses overseeing hundreds of neighborhood lotteries, "dream books," and policy wheels until they pleaded with Cermak for relief. "Please remove that 'wild man" from office," they cried. "Vote Democratic next time and the rest will take care of itself," the party hacks replied.[43] From that moment forward the African American community of Chicago turned its back on the Republican Party.

On his last day in office Thompson exited with characteristic huff-and-puff bluster. "I'm tired of working for 3,500,000 people! Now I'll work for myself for a while."

Octogenarian Frank Loesch, the public face of the Chicago Crime Commission for over a decade and a member of the Wickersham Commission, declared final victory over the gangs of Chicago in a fanciful public statement made on February 4, 1934. "Chicago has a bright future" he beamed. "She is known today for her courageous overthrow of a gun government which had left the gangster wealthy; free with the protection his wealth provided, and impudent upon the street. Chicago is now an example for the rest of the nation. Her example is being followed."

Ben Hecht offered a much more sobering, countervailing assessment. "The Prohibition Era helped vitally populate the U.S. with the largest cast of real murderers, thieves, swindlers, muggers, rapists and crooked politicians ever assembled in one land. Our criminals out-number the combined felons of all Western civilization."

The bootlegging wars of the "dry and lawless years" mirror the carnage in the streets of Chicago in our new millennium: gangs of youth fighting for control of the drug traffic, block by block, neighborhood by neighborhood, exacting a frightful toll in lives lost; innocent children walking to school, youngsters on the playground, and others simply caught up in the cross fire. In a very real sense, nothing has changed.

7

SCHOOLS FOR CRIME

With Al Capone languishing in prison and Prohibition having run its course, the City of Chicago looked to a brighter future free of the surge of violent 1920s-style crime. The coming of the World's Fair in 1933 brought joyful anticipation despite the lingering hardships of the Great Depression. "Chicago will no longer know gangs in the form we have known them for the last ten years," predicted U.S. attorney George E. Q. Johnson in his first public pronouncements following the Capone trial. "I do not look for any more spectacular leadership for gangsters and their leaders will know that such leadership will make them shining targets for prosecution."[1]

Optimistic hopes for a crime-free World's Fair city soon faded as the Depression worsened. The example of bootlegging gangs showed inner-city youth how to garner sensational publicity of their serious criminal offenses in a half-dozen daily newspapers and provided for them glamorized depictions of gang life in motion pictures, radio programming, and magazines.

The exploits of George "Machine Gun" Kelly, John Dillinger, "Pretty Boy" Floyd, the Barker Gang, and other Depression-era desperadoes inspired many youthful imitators from across the nation. "Such persistent featuring of crime news and playing it up has much the same effect in inducing imitative conduct as is produced by the constant advertising of commercial products," wrote Frederic Thrasher. "It seems to fire the imaginative activities of the adolescent and stimulate him to follow the pattern this presented, enshrined as it often is in the glamorous setting of adventure and romance."[2]

Hollywood stirred the imagination of youth with the allure of gangland life in the 1930s through such controversial pre-code offerings as *Little Caesar* (1931), *Public Enemy* (1931), and *Scarface* (1932), the latter based on the life of Al Capone. To the consternation of the clergy, educators, and conservative censors, the motion-picture industry released seventy-eight gangster-themed movies between1930 and1933, manipulating public emotion. The *Kansas City Times* assailed these films as vile corrupters of youth, guilty of "misleading, contaminating, and demoralizing children." However, Paul Muni's characterizations of Capone in *Scarface* drew audience applause in theaters across the country but shock and condemnation from the moralists fearing a complete societal breakdown.

Bowing to pressure from religious conservatives, Jack L. Warner of Warner Brothers Studios ceased making these types of films. Hollywood adapted a production code establishing moral guidelines, under the aegis of former postmaster general Will Hays, the appointed censorship czar of the Motion Picture Association of America. The Hays Code came down hard on scriptwriters and producers defying the rigorous standards, but this did not deter the popularity of the genre.

"The box office receipts were staggering for such movies and no one at the Warner Brothers studio lot bothered to consider that their controversial films were influencing a new generation of impoverished youth to become criminals," Daniel Kelley, a film scholar and Chicago educator explained: "These rough and tumble films started during the silent era and continued into the early years of the talkies. Some claim that D. W. Griffith's *The Musketeers of Pig Alley*, made in 1913, was the first gang-themed movie. Unquestionably films like *Underworld*, *The Racket*, and the stage play *Dead End* had an impact. It is interesting to note that it launched the careers of Leo Gorcey and Huntz Hall. The future 'Bowery Boys' were gangbangers at this stage of their careers."[3]

Although the crime thrillers of the 1930s laid out the serious consequences for young men who venture outside the law, the message misfired in the bleak realities of slum living during the Great Depression. Regardless of unhappy endings, the easy attainment of social status, wealth, and power depicted in the rise of the gangster suggested that gang life and a career in crime had its own inherent reward, if only for a short period of time.

In the 1940s Warner Brothers, RKO, Allied Artists, PRC, Republic Pictures, and other studios filled the popular-culture pipeline with a series of low-budget B-grade "gang and gun" dramas starring many back-of-the-lot contract players. These cheaply produced offerings usually preceded the big budget A-list Hollywood motion picture in double-feature movie houses. The morally ambiguous B-film crime dramas of the postwar era were presented in stark visualization, a world of light and shadow.

By no means could these films be considered "high art" by critics until the French coined the term film noir (black film) in 1946 and elevated the status of the forgotten shockers to cinematic masterpieces in the late 1960s. Sociologists, police, and settlement-house workers decried the moral turpitude of the storylines, and believed these films to be a contributing factor to the astonishing rise of boy gangs after the Capone period. "Indecent movies shown regardless of censorship regulations, dance contests for little children in theaters are among the causes for the fast increasing delinquency cases," declared Louise DeKoven Bowen at a luncheon of the Women's City Club.[4]

The abundance of tabloid journalism sensationalizing every aspect of crime and the proliferation of movies, magazines, and radio programming during the era stirred more angry debate. Did these movies in fact contribute to a societal breakdown in the 1920s and 1930s? "The gangster films [of the pre-code period] never intended to puzzle their audiences, narrative or even moral ambiguity was not part of their repertoire since the film makers claimed they were fashioning simple, powerful statements to promote the idea that crime does not pay," wrote Foster Hirsch in his notable film noir study, *The Dark Side of the Screen*.[5]

> The gangster film was really comforting to audiences of the time in a way that *noir* certainly was not. On the one hand audiences in the thirties could revel vicariously in the gangsters' exploits, enjoying the spectacle of the gangster challenging and for a time beating the system; and on the

> other hand the audience could be assured with the gangster's inevitable demise in the final reel, that his illegal and violent methods really did not—and could not work. *Noir* offers no such comfort. It is impossible to derive from its dark stories either a sense of momentary uplift or the moralistic conclusions provided by the gangster picture.[6]

In May 1938 *Tribune* editorialists cautioned "that criminals from fourteen to twenty-three have displaced the Prohibition gangsters and parolees as the leaders in Cook County crime." Chief Justice Cornelius Harrington of the criminal court presented eye-opening data showing that of the 1,070 defendants arraigned before him from September 1937 through March 1938, 790 of them were below the age of twenty-three.

Captain Frank Demski of the Brighton Park Police District pointed to "the lure of easy money spent on candy, food, drink, movies, and similar entertainment" as the motivation for a series of fifteen burglaries that netted a gang of boys from Kelly High School $4,000 in stolen jewelry and other valuables.[7]

The remedies Harrington urged included the creation of an intermediate detention center for troubled youth in order to fill a widening gulf between incarceration among hard-core felons at the Pontiac, Illinois, correctional facility, formerly an institution for felons under the age of twenty-one, or its less harsh counterweight, the St. Charles Training School for Boys.

"The only immediate measures available are a judicial use of the severest penalties where deserved and combined with careful employment of the lighter penalties, such as probation where they may work," added first assistant state's attorney Wilbert F. Crowley. Stern punishment, not reform, codified the treatment of wayward boys at the Illinois State Training School for Boys at St. Charles in Kane County, and a separate affiliated sixty-cell detention center opened June 26, 1942, at Sheridan, Illinois.

Before an underage offender charged with committing a major offense could appear before a sentencing judge, the first stop for the delinquent child was the Audy Home—the juvenile detention center at 2240 Roosevelt Road in the West Side Valley.[8] Opened in 1923 and financed by county and city funds, the three-story, 181,000-square-foot detention center employed a staff of 250 workers to oversee an inmate population of 450—maximum capacity for juveniles under the age of eighteen. In theory, the focus of the mission was to provide group care, but in practice there was little improvement over the failed John Worthy School. Law enforcement and private agencies dumped children as young as three and others suffering developmental disabilities, various physical handicaps, or those abandoned by their parents on the doorstep of the squat, ugly building that was the Audy Home.

The delinquents were mostly short-timers; their average stay was only two to three weeks before the courts determined punishment and correctional placement. The younger children, who were there simply because negligent parents and society did not want them, would remain from six months to three years waiting for placement in another institution.

In this institutional atmosphere of crime and violence, children guilty of nothing worse than pilfering a bicycle or running away from home were intimidated by older gang members. By the 1960s most inmates belonged to street gangs, nominally or in actuality. Cruel and often inhuman treatment of children was reported, ranging from "walking the stairs" (walking up and down four flights for up to an hour and a half) or the "silent treatment," in which children were denied access to books, television, or even conversation with other inmates. Defiance shown a guard resulted in a trip to the Blackstone, the name given to the solitary confinement cells. The girls' cells utilized for the same purpose were called Bluestone. "We use it when we have to," commented Superintendent James Jordan, who ran the institution from 1945 through the 1970s. "Violence, assault, things like that. Don't forget most detention homes in other cities are nothing but a series of individual security cells. Everybody gets one."[9]

A new $32 million Audy Home (officially renamed the Cook County Temporary Juvenile Detention Center) opened at Roosevelt Road and Leavitt Streets in 1973 under the Juvenile Court Act. It was the largest juvenile detention center in the nation but serious problems have lingered. The institution labored under the control of political patronage workers for decades.

Cook County judges were tasked with moving offenders through the system quickly and expeditiously. With limited discretion, they committed juvenile offenders between the ages of ten and seventeen for indefinite periods. The law made no distinction between delinquent boys and hard-core felons, leaving jurists only two choices, Pontiac or St. Charles, neither of them entirely satisfactory for borderline offenders. Without sentencing discretion, judges dumped some of the worst offenders in St. Charles, where they would remain until attaining their age of majority. The boys could be released sooner if they fulfilled special educational and vocational programs and were no longer deemed a threat to society. The boys lived in twelve-bed cottages that were freezing cold in winter and sweltering in the summer months.

Frequent inmate escapes, poor management, overcrowding, correctional jobs doled out to friends of the administration as political plums, hunger strikes, and a litany of social ills plagued the institution almost from the time of its founding in 1903. Social reformers called St. Charles a snake pit and a breeding ground for criminal gangs. Citizens of the Fox Valley region feared the dangers posed by incorrigible boys making a break for freedom. Stern and unforgiving law-and-order advocates criticized the institution as a "soft snap," run by "sob sisters" unwilling to enforce necessary harsh discipline against the more defiant boys, preferring the "faddist notions" of social workers for rehabilitation.

"The tough boys can get away with anything at the school," complained Robert Woods, a discharged civil service employee in an April 1939 press interview. "The stiffest punishment is ten to fifteen days in the Pierce cottage, where they have to shovel coal six hours a day and are deprived of movies. Previous superintendents kept order by limiting the diet of the bad actors and by keeping them in the guardhouse. Now there is no guardhouse. Practically all the boys at St. Charles are tough, but the social workers keep so much pressure for gentleness on [Superintendent William T.] Harmon that there is no punishment."[10]

The St. Charles institution was founded with the best of intentions by a most unlikely pairing, the Gilded Age millionaire Chicago railroad industrialist John W. "Bet a Million" Gates and Judge Richard Tuthill, called the "father of the Chicago Municipal Court." Gates, an ardent race enthusiast who collected $600,000 betting $70,000 on an English thoroughbred in 1900, made the bulk of his fortune promoting barbed wire. His money funded much of the project with contributions from the Commercial Club of Chicago and through private subscription. He pledged $20,000 to fund construction of the compound, contingent upon the state's willingness to locate the training school at Wilson's Farm, a nine-hundred-acre spread two miles northwest of St. Charles in a walnut-tree grove not far from the Chicago & Northwestern Railroad. Near the farm the flamboyant Gates had whiled away his blissful and happy boyhood years. Why shouldn't poor Chicago boys be given the same opportunity?

"It is going to be the greatest school not only in the country but in the world," beamed Gates on August 22, 1902. "The institution will open free of cost to boys of good character between the ages of ten and fourteen."[11]

At the time, it was deemed wise and prudent for the city to remove vulnerable boys from their former evil surroundings far from the corrupting influences of the big-city gangs. Gates and Tuthill agreed that the fresh, wholesome air and the rolling farmlands in the Kane County countryside could rescue boys in danger of becoming delinquent through bad associations and patterns of bad behavior. Speaking to members of the Chicago Federation of Labor on March 15, 1902, in an effort to gain a resolution of support for a proposed $500,000 state appropriation to help fund the project, Judge Tuthill reminded his listeners of the justice system's failure to give boys "good employment in life."

"What has our State been doing?" asked the socially conscious Tuthill. "It has sent out its policemen, club in hand, to take the boys and hurry them to stations, to the justice courts, and then to the Bridewell. What do statistics show? Out of every 100 we find that ninety of these boys have become criminals. We don't want the boys to go to Pontiac, but we want them to be sent where they can be given all the benefits of home. Pontiac is merely a boy's penitentiary. We want these boys sent where they can go to school; be out in the fields, learn to live right and be right."[12]

The promotional materials given to legislators by Gates, Tuthill, Senator Albert J. Hopkins, and other enthusiastic backers touted the many wonderful benefits of the training school. "Close to the cottages to be erected for the boys as planned will be built the shops that will teach the younger generation the trades both in wood, and from working. Everything needful to the line of equipment will be given the boys that find their way to the home. A swimming pool and gymnasium will be provided."[13]

The cottages were constructed of sturdy Georgia pine and red oak. Two large dormitories were fitted with iron bedsteads, with forty boys assigned to each dormitory. Adjacent to the dormitories, guards watched over the locker room where the boys surrendered their clothes each evening before retiring to bed. Given only a nightshirt to wear, the boys were unable to retrieve their day clothes stored in the lockers until dawn in order to deter escape attempts.

Philanthropist and Progressive Era education activist Lucy Louisa Flower had a vested, inbred interest in the welfare of the young. A staunch defender of the implicit need for St. Charles as a countervailing force for good and not a prison, Flower expressed the hope that "one to two years should be and [would be] the average time of detention." The school, Flower added, should never assume responsibility for the permanent care and education of the children. That task, she believed, was best left to the parents in their own homes or the children should be put at Feehanville and Glenwood.[14]

Dependant, uncared for, and neglected children fell within the purview of two institutions. The Feehanville School, founded by Archbishop Patrick Feehan for Chicago fire orphans near the Des Plaines River in the city's northwest suburbs and the Illinois Agricultural and Manual Training School, its nonsectarian counterpart, opened in Norwood Park in 1887 and later moved to Glenwood. At both institutions, administrators made concerted efforts to put up the boys for adoption or indenture in private homes once administrators were able to determine if the youth was qualified to leave the school. Financial support for Feehanville came from the archdiocese, and for Glenwood from the state and the Chicago Commercial Club, inspired by their sense of noblesse oblige.

Although nearly every residential institution shared common stated objectives of achieving juvenile reform through career training and rural segregation, the mission statement of the St. Charles school contained no provision for the care of dependents and long-term residency. John W. Gates did not subscribe to an orphanage approach or a "spare the rod and spoil the child" philosophy to discipline. He never imagined that the school would evolve into a "grade school of crime," as Judge Harlington Wood of Sangamon County described conditions on February 2, 1939.

Politicians of the 1920s engaged social workers to work with school staff, and the decision to import into the institution what the conservative press derided as a pack of "sob sisters" contributed to a laxity in discipline and scandals. "Sentimentalists and sob sisters have been permitted almost continuously to interfere with the operation and policies of the school," the *Tribune* thundered. "They have changed the school from one of strict discipline to one described by one old-time employee as a cream puff or slap on the wrist."

However, the board of trustees had to surrender control of the school after the passage of various acts of legislation that allowed politicians to gain power. The institution became a source of patronage jobs for precinct workers from Chicago and other connected people in towns and cities around the state, and serious problems began to surface.

Media and law enforcement questioned the policy of the administration to award early parole to the toughest boys. They were transferred to local Kane County area farms to work in the fields under a policy of foster-home placing. Critics charged that early release was due to the inability of the school to effectively discipline the most dangerous of the inmate population. Under the law, the parolees were required to be supervised by St. Charles officials upon their release, but so often the scheduled visits rarely occurred. Parole supervision, such as it was, became a farce.

In 1919 the criminal courts were empowered to send more serious offenders between the ages of fourteen and seventeen with police records to St. Charles, but the arrival of the older boys with criminal records caused many problems for the younger, more easily exploited inmates. As early as October 1915, writer Henry M. Hyde pronounced the St. Charles school a failure. "Conditions at St. Charles are rapidly becoming intolerable. The school started to run downhill with great rapidity when Colonel C. B. Adams was practically forced to resign to make room for some political favorite of the State administration. Colonel Adams had given the school a high standing. Under his management the discipline was good and the runaways comparatively few."

In 1913 Governor Edward Dunne replaced the nationally known penologist Colonel Adams, after many years of service, with a political favorite, G. Charles Griffiths. As degreed penologists infused with liberal theories of promoting reform over punishment sparred with law-and-order authoritarians, conditions deteriorated. Inmate escapes, for years a chronic problem at the training school, only worsened. On average in the period 1945 to 1949, the school reported 145 escapes per year. The matter came to a head as the expanding population of Chicago transformed former country towns like St. Charles into city suburbs. Local residents feared home invasions and automobile theft by fleeing inmates. Another worry was diminishing property values in the real estate market. Farmers and homeowners sharing common concerns demanded action from the state to "clamp down" on runaways.

The state searched public agencies for capable administrators to strike a proper balance between respect for inmate civil liberties and excessive discipline, but so often their choices failed. A military man, Major William Butler, took charge of the school and its eight hundred residents in 1927. Butler took a militant stand against the insubordination and defiance by inculcating the military way into disciplinary policy.

"The St. Charles boys have been sent here because neither their parents, nor their school teachers, Sunday school teachers, communities or authorities could make them obey," Butler explained to state officials, after coming under fire in 1928. "We are the last resort and we have found that military training and corporal punishment produce the desired results among these heretofore incorrigible boys."

To Butler's way of thinking, corporal punishment meant the liberal application of the whip upon bare backs. "I have brought the institution from a condition of chaos, wherein corporal punishment was applied surreptitiously and the inmates were coddled, chucked under the chin, patted on the back by every variety of social service worker." Butler claimed his harsh measures yielded positive results in his efforts to tame "42" Gang members, but his assertion is dubious. The "42" Gang threatened reprisals. An anonymous phone call to Butler raised the alarm. "This is the '42' Gang," the caller stated. "Unless you let our pals go, we'll come down there and kill everybody we see. We've got plenty of men and some machine guns." A car was stopped near the gates of the school several nights later.[15] At the wheel was "Crazy Patsy" Steffanelli of Taylor Street, a former "Charley Town" inmate, but neither he nor his compatriots could get any further. Butler complained to the Cook County judiciary that St. Charles was never intended to be a dumping ground for unrepentant criminals. The judges answered that it was often impossible for them to distinguish between the true criminals and errant boys, and therein lies the problem.

The severity of punishment turned troubled boys into hardened criminals.

Refusing to uphold the state's demand that he introduce ensemble singing to the curriculum, and recognize the efficacy of providing regular counseling sessions for the boys with licensed psychiatrists, Butler was summarily removed by the director of the state department of public welfare. Conversely, in equal measure, reformers often came under fire for their policy of "coddling" the boys. No clear-cut strategy seemed to work. The problems were magnified and seemingly insolvable as long as Cook County judges packed the institution with young criminals. Inside the cottages, sexual assaults among the inmates were common. "The school was supposed to be a home for wayward and dependent boys not a jail for hardened thugs," said St. Charles city attorney Drew Green.

In a state-commissioned study published in January 1932, the Department of Public Welfare concluded that in 1925, 72 per cent of six hundred paroled inmates returned to a life of crime once they were back on the streets. "It leads me to express grave doubt of the wisdom of continuing the present policy of treating juvenile offenders against the law in correctional institutions or training schools," said the director, Rodney H. Brandon.

The controversies surrounding the administrative offices of St. Charles dragged on for decades to come. In an October 20, 1948, editorial the *Tribune* warned that "hardened young criminals are not fit subjects for social worker experiments," adding, "To operate St. Charles as a correctional institution may be unfair to the boys who stand in need of guidance, but to operate it as a sociological workshop, releasing young criminals to prey on the surrounding communities is unfair to the public."

Acknowledging that the current problems and past failures at St. Charles could not be satisfactorily resolved through administrative changes alone, Governor Adlai Stevenson bowed to pressure from the press and corrections experts and signed into law a controversial measure to convert the Sheridan facility in LaSalle County into a "halfway" reformatory for boys who were deemed unmanageable in other institutions but yet ready for penitentiary confinement. The measure sailed through the general assembly on July 30, 1949. The *Tribune* applauded the change in the penal system but cautioned the public to be wary of more "sob sister" meddling.

"It is likely that the new correctional institution will be under fire, from time to time from those sentimentalists who believe that all young criminals can be cured by good advice and psychiatric attention. The reformatory will be disliked also by the young toughs who are sent there," editorialists noted. "We hope it is disliked so much that there will be a sharp drop in the membership of teen aged crime gangs."[16]

Residents of "Charley Town," the nickname boys had given St. Charles, feared imminent transfer to Sheridan for the slightest infraction of the house rules. Through the 1960s the school was shaken by reports of brutality, corruption, and widespread inefficiency. Employment in the penal system was a rich patronage trough for politicians to dispense to friends of city and state officeholders. By April 1953, just four years after its reorganization, demands for the immediate closing of Sheridan percolated through Springfield. Human-rights abuses were widespread. Guards payed only lip service to rehabilitation and training in their techniques of behavior suppression. Unruly inmates placed in solitary confinement slept on bare floors wearing only their shorts.

Dismissal proceedings were filed against six correctional officers in March 1961 after seventeen-year-old inmate Thomas Bell accused a guard, Sergeant James O'Grady, of ordering him to beat another boy to a pulp. According to Bell, O'Grady said he should "kill" the youth. Bell beat the lad unconscious. The Illinois Youth Commission examined the reports of brutality and ordered a six-month investigation.

The 1973 death of inmate Anthony Jones from Thorzine-induced respiratory inertia finally compelled the state to close the facility. Locked up in a solitary-confinement cell, correctional officers injected the psychotropic drug Thorzine into Jones to quell his berserk behavior, the result of long hours of solitude. The young man died of strangulation. The inevitable lawsuits were filed in the Circuit Court of Cook County and a ruling unfavorable to the state closed Sheridan for underage offenders.[17]

The matter went before Judge Joseph Schneider, who ruled that indiscriminate application of drugs for the purpose of maintaining institutional control of a child could no longer be permitted. Schneider questioned why poor children were herded into inferior facilities while the more affluent and well-to-do were placed into private schools. "Far too many suffer more in the care of the State," said Schneider who was appointed to spearhead the Governor's Commission to Reform the Mental Health Code in the mid-1970s.[18]

In time the communities of Illinois would pay a deeper price for the failed juvenile-reform campaigns in St. Charles and Sheridan. The decades-old failure to enact a successful program of prevention over punishment came at a tragic human cost measured in lives lost, drug dependence, and an unrelenting cycle of poverty and crime afflicting the poor South and West Sides of the city. By the 1950s ever-increasing numbers of African American youth from the city's widening "black belt" arrived at the doorstep of St. Charles. The institution became an incubator for modern street gangs that would inflict carnage upon their neighborhoods.

The Chicago Crime Commission jumped into the fray by declaring its intent to "attack crime by means of a battle against juvenile delinquency" with the Chicago Area Project. At a meeting of the Mid-Day Club on February 24, 1938, Bertram J. Cahn, chairman of a clothing firm and the new director of the commission, expressed the hope that their shared resources would encourage participation in organized sports and part-time jobs for boys whose parents were most in need. "We have organized crime conquered now and the problem we must face is that of juvenile crime," Cahn remarked.[19] "In the county jail nearly all the prisoners are between the ages of sixteen and twenty-three, girls as well as boys. After one is incarcerated it is hard to save him. Our new objective is to save him before he is jailed."

To no one's great surprise, Department of Public Welfare officials reported that 70 percent of all juvenile delinquents lived in the three blighted inner-city areas of the city surrounding the Loop (downtown Chicago) and in large outlying industrial districts, including the Stockyards and the South Chicago steel mills. Thrasher characterized these areas as the "West Side Wilderness," the "North Side Jungles," and the "South Side Badlands."

"The slums," as poet Carl Sandburg ruefully noted, "seek their own revenge."

The only variant to the demographic profile of juvenile crime was the changing ethnic and racial profile of criminal perpetrators within Thrasher's three inner-city districts. A 1938 study conducted by

Professor Clifford R. Shaw, a member of the Institute for Juvenile Research and the head of the Department of Research Sociology of the National Commission on Law Observance and Enforcement, contrasted data points spanning the period from 1900 through 1930 by nationality and race.

Demographic Profile of Juvenile Crime

Ethnicity/Race	*1900* Cases Classified	*1910* Cases Classified	*1920* Cases Classified	*1930* Cases Classified
	1,035	1,133	1,829	2,307
	Percentage	*Percentage*	*Percentage*	*Percentage*
Caucasian	16.9	16.5	23.0	19.5
African American	4.7	5.5	9.9	21.7
German	20.4	15.5	6.3	1.9
Irish	18.7	12.3	6.1	1.3
Italian	5.1	7.9	12.7	11.7
Polish	15.1	18.6	24.5	21.6
English-Scotch	3.4	2.5	.8	.6
Scandinavian	8.8	2.9	2.3	.8
Czech-Bohemian	4.6	5.5	3.2	4.2
All Others	8.0	11.8	9.1	11.8

Historically Chicago has always remained one of the nation's most volatile, and segregated, cities. Until the African American Great Migration (spanning the years 1910 to 1940), urban neighborhoods were first categorized and identifiable by the ethnic tribes of northern, eastern, and southern Europe and not by race. To understand Chicago is to understand a separate and divided collection of neighborhoods that must be thought of in terms of the "halfway house" analogy: a temporary refuge for a newly arrived group of people as they find their bearings, prosper, and move on to greater opportunity outside the city.

As the table data suggests, over time, improved economic conditions and upward mobility diminished crime rates among nationalities. During this thirty-year cycle of city settlement, Chicago's fast-growing population of African Americans displaced the white ethnics but were made to endure the same paroxysms of violent crime and gang activity as the earlier groups.

"In the 1880s the area bordering the Loop was occupied largely by German, Irish and English immigrants," explained Dr. Shaw. "As later immigrants came in they settled in the same areas and displaced the former occupants. Along Milwaukee Avenue just northwest of the Loop the Scandinavians followed the German and English settlers and displaced them to some extent. In a short time however, all former immigrants in this area gave way to the influx of Polish and Italian immigrants. These in turn are retreating before the Negro settlers. Within the Negro area the same general process takes place. The newest immigrants settle in the areas of greatest deterioration and push the earlier Negro inhabitants out into areas of less deterioration."[20]

Amid profound population shifts and escalating citywide racial segregation, Chicago realtor Carroll Hopkins Sudler Jr., the naive but well-intentioned head of the Chicago Area Project, believed that the work of his group had conquered poverty and improved public and parental attitudes toward child-rearing through a coordinated effort linking worthy public agencies, clubs, and membership groups to the campaign. The Boy Scouts of America doubled their recruitment drive in city neighborhoods. The Chicago Boys Club budgeted for an expansion plan calling for twenty-five new clubhouses accommodating up to seventy-five thousand boys, and the beat cops were encouraged to promote greater cordiality with youth, a strategy presaging the 1990s community policing initiatives put in place in Chicago.

"Experiments begun in 1932 have proved that the fault lies with the communities," Sudler advised. "And by correcting the attitudes of the people in communities toward crime and juvenile delinquency, startling results have been achieved."[21] Holding up police data culled from the Near South Side, Sudler traced a steady drop in the number of juvenile arrests each year from 1931 to 1937. The statistical sample was small, and the reduction in arrests offered only temporary relief. Social and environmental factors, family breakup, the allure of gang life, media influence, and the quest for riches in a time of want ratcheted these numbers sharply upward over the next three decades.

Depression-era juvenile-gang crime percolated through the neighborhoods and into the grammar schools and high schools. Street-corner hustlers interested in material gain without having to work and sacrifice for it organized their friends to "boost" automobiles, perfect the techniques of burglary and armed robbery, employing violence if necessary. Chicago detectives from across the city smashed four boy-bandit gangs in a coordinated effort with the Chicago Park District Police in a

December 1938 coordinated neighborhood sweep that closed out 150 unsolved burglaries, robberies, and automobile thefts.

The West Side Ferraro Gang, captained by a seventeen-year-old genius named Ignatius "Nash" Ferraro, confessed to committing forty robberies and twenty car thefts, mostly in the affluent Sheffield Police District north of the city's Gold Coast. "I wanted to be a big shot," Ferraro bragged to Sergeant William Higgins. "I needed plenty of dough for my wife. I got her a Caracul coat."[22] Three weeks before his arrest, Ferraro and his fifteen-year-old girlfriend, Mary Otey, fled to Crown Point, Indiana, which for years was a no-questions-asked haven for "quickie marriages." She wanted some of life's finer things, and her teenaged husband, with gun in hand, obliged.

The Skylight Gang pulled off fifty successful South Side burglaries over a six-month period in 1938. They too wanted to sample life's finer things. But unlike the gun-wielding teenage thugs copycatting John Dillinger, their sixteen-year-old leader, James Morton "Mutt" Haas, perfected the technique of pirouetting down through retail-store skylights with a clothesline. Grand Crossing District police seized two unloaded revolvers, two screwdrivers, and a pile of money from the gang.

The quest for riches without having to find a job compelled the North Side Ernest Mondt Gang to pull off fifty burglaries including six liquor stores. Frank Pape, the garrulous tough-guy major-crimes investigator who shot and killed nine criminals in his checkered forty-year career in the Chicago PD, pulled down the gang based on a physical description of Mondt, the "burly leader of the smash and grab gang with a big nose who liked fast cars."

Over one hundred robberies, burglaries, and automobile thefts committed by three city gangs were cleared by Chicago detectives in early March 1938 after twenty-two boys, ranging in age from twelve to nineteen, were arrested by police. The gangs worked separately on the North, Northwest, and South Sides, and had never used guns in the commission of crimes. The Northwest Side youths told police that they planned their burglaries after school and had conducted surveillance of the targeted homes for escape outlets before breaking and entering. The oldest boy was just sixteen.

In the North Side Summerdale District, police cleared seven automobile thefts with the arrest of five boys ranging in age from twelve to sixteen. They told detectives that they took the car for joyrides. During regular church services, they took the car keys from the coat pockets of parishioners during prayer services.

All six gangs were white. None engaged in drug trafficking or had the stomach for murder, although guns had been taken from each of them. They were motivated by materialistic gain, big spending on the girls, and enjoyment of nightclub life, with the tacit admission that media portrayals of gangsters inspired them to become lawbreakers.

In the fall of 1941, two months ahead of America's entry into World War II, Captain John T. O'Malley of the Sheffield District broke up two youthful gangs of burglars targeting five elementary schools and scores of groceries, radio stores, and other businesses in a cluster of retail shops up on the North Side. The roundup netted thirteen boys ranging in age from thirteen to twenty-one. With the proceeds of the robberies, the boys squandered the money in ice cream parlors and downtown movies. Chicago police reported that the young thieves entered the school buildings through coal chutes and windows. Items were stolen from teachers' desks, books and pencils thrown about the rooms, and taunting language scrawled on the blackboards.

The privations of the Great Depression left many unemployed parents in the working-class neighborhoods destitute and neglectful of the welfare of their children. Rejection by parents and by society rendered boys without jobs or a sense of purpose exposed and vulnerable to bad influence.

Deprived of the advantages lost when a family's livelihood was taken away, boys turned to street life, said Walter Head, national president of the Boy Scouts of America, in a 1930 speech. "The streets are the logical avenue of escape for boys in the homes [of parents] that are lacking their financial independence, and on the streets there is rapidly growing a spirit of lawlessness or desperation in the pursuit of any kind of pleasure or recreation which circumstances or opportunity might afford."[23]

Petty thieving and pickpocketing were commonplace in Depression Chicago's worst neighborhoods. Gangs formed without supervision or gainful purpose, and mirrored the larger ills of the city's rising levels of poverty and homelessness.

To address the larger social ills of society, the Boy Scouts and the Chicago Boys Clubs initiated remedial measures to curb juvenile delinquency. The Chicago Boys Club opened a $100,000 recreational center in the heart of the Maxwell-Halsted Streets ghetto to provide sixty-nine hundred boys between the ages of ten and nineteen with a recreational and educational center. Facilities for manual training, the arts, sports, and an orchestra were available to boys for a fee of two to five cents per week. "The lack of any recreational or leadership facilities in the neighborhood is largely responsible for delinquency," commented Louis Lincoln Valentine, a retired furniture manufacturer who dedicated the bulk of his fortune to building twenty-five separate facilities for the Chicago Boys Clubs in 1929.[24]

Tireless crusader Frank J. Loesch, whose project work with the Chicago Crime Commission dovetailed with the Chicago Historical Society where he served as a vice president, launched the Pioneer Citizens clubs to inculcate the idea of good citizenship in the minds of seventh- and eighth-grade schoolchildren selected by their principals. "You boys and girls know what a bad condition Chicago is in because there are so many criminals here," Loesch cautioned the children on the occasion of George Washington's birthday in 1930. "You know what a bad reputation Chicago has all over the world for crime. We expect you to be intelligent voters when you grow up. We expect you to free Chicago from gangsters and murderers. One hundred years ago Chicago pioneers were clearing the land to build houses. Your job as pioneers is in another field. You can pioneer here in obeying the law and seeing that others obey the law."[25]

Efforts to reign in juvenile crime through well-meaning community outreach and membership organizations like these achieved only modest results amid contentious unresolved debate between the "punishers" and the "reformers."

In other cities, the crusade to curb delinquency and gangs mostly ran along parallel tracks with the Chicago reform movement. With former Prohibition "Untouchable" Eliot Ness in charge of the city's Public Safety Division, Cleveland sent its police officers into blighted neighborhoods "to make friends" with youthful gang leaders. Ness personally invited forty-five of them over to dinner one night in 1939 to hear their grievances and concerns.

"They told us that they wanted adequate places to spend their spare time in playing, such as swimming pools, baseball diamonds, tennis courts, and gymnasiums; a little spending money and some adventure. We told them we would do all we could do to help them."[26]

Ness gave them abandoned police stations to serve as clubhouses and promoted the formation of clubs over gangs, governed by officers in a parliamentary fashion. The boys formed the Cleveland South Side Improvement Club, and opened a savings account so they would not be tempted to rob and steal during times of unemployment. The City of Cleveland claimed that juvenile delinquency rates dropped by 60 percent by directing the activities of city youth in an organized, structured fashion.

Similarly in New York City, millions of dollars were being spent each year by public, semipublic, and private organizations on special youth programs. Following two serious gang battles in Brooklyn in 1950, the city sent in "detached" social workers from the New York City Youth Board (established 1947) who worked with the police youth patrol to make friends with gang members and guide them toward more socially acceptable activity. Hearing news of an impending "rumble," (otherwise known in gang circles as "bopping or jamming," this violent clash between two rival gangs involved weapons of choice, e.g., tire chains, zip guns, car radio antennas, and switchblades), Youth Board volunteers attempted to broker a negotiated peace as an independent third party.[27, 28]

Encouraged by initial efforts, the "make friends with a gang member" approach fizzled after one of the Brooklyn gangs they had worked closely with killed one of its members. Then more violence erupted in East Harlem. The pattern of gang activity changed markedly in New York beginning in the late 1940s and into the 1950s with large numbers of Puerto Ricans pouring into Spanish East Harlem.

The New York City Youth Board, created for the prevention and control of juvenile delinquency in high-hazard neighborhoods, could not claim any semblance of victory over youth crime in the two decades following World War II. Positive results were only temporary. Rumbles pitting Puerto Ricans against both white and black gangs and each other could not be contained. In 1958 the New York City Police Department estimated that between two hundred and four hundred different gangs terrorized city neighborhoods, the streets, and the subway system. Membership in these gangs varied depending on the neighborhood and ethnic origin. Juvenile delinquency rates in New York doubled over a five-year period, from 1955 to 1960.

As Virgil W. Peterson, executive director of the Chicago Crime Commission, asserted in a 1953 essay, "Long range planning becomes rather difficult however as long as there are such divergent views as to principal causes of delinquent behavior among the experts themselves."[29]

Sociologists generally agreed on the root causes and predictable effect stimulating gang membership: parental hostility, slum conditions, societal rejection, a dearth of recreational facilities, divorce, family breakup, and economic hardship contributed to the boy's lack of self-worth and his need for acceptance, conformity, and identity through a support system, but there were no easy answers or quick fixes.

These common denominators could not be easily applied to members of Chicago's teenage Green Car Gang, a cast of armed and dangerous high school desperadoes growing up in the modestly upscale bedroom communities located on the city's far Northwest Side, miles from the squalor and grind of Thrasher's "wilderness" neighborhoods.

First- and second-generation ethnic Europeans climbing out of poverty staked their claim in the dream of home ownership by moving to secure and isolated Northwest Side bungalow neighborhoods. They never imagined that city problems would follow them into their ideal "suburb within the city" setting. Approaching O'Hare Airport from downtown, Northwest Side residential streets were mostly quiet. Gangs of aimless boys, knowing they would be chased away by vigilant police officers (required by city statute to reside within the city limits), rarely congregated under street lamps illuminating the corners of the dark and dangerous "city" or created undue anxiety in the community. The wail of police sirens, bringing back painful memories of the South and West Sides, were thankfully absent late at night out this way. For a long time people did not even bother to lock their doors at night.

By the late 1940s and into the "baby boom" years of the 1950s and 1960s, once tranquil neighborhood settings in Albany Park, Portage Park, Bowmanville, Hollywood Park, Avondale, Jefferson Park, Montclair, and Galewood noted with alarm a disconcerting rise in juvenile crime.[30]

The Green Car Gang, a moniker given by robbery squad detectives to the Northwest Side teens, came from good homes and caring parents—churchgoing, decent people in total self-denial concerning what their kids were up to. Louis Schultz, father of one of the Green Car Gang ringleaders, Richard Schultz, was a hard-working machinist.

Violence in the family, divorce, alcoholism—all of the usual predictors of future deviant behavior—were strangely absent in this young boy's household environment.

Speaking of her sixteen-year-old son, Richard, a sophomore at Steinmetz High School (the same school that graduated *Playboy* magazine founder Hugh Hefner two years earlier), Bertha Schultz told detectives that he grew up like any other average boy, but "this is the Richard we do not know," she said. "He had everything a normal boy should have. He was a hero to his younger brothers, and even to his cocker spaniel Teddy."[31]

Young Schultz, a former Boy Scout, had no prior run-ins with the law when he ran away from home on July 27, 1946, to begin a wild crime spree with fellow Steinmetz classmate Anthony Kapsis. Bertha Schultz, as many parents of children caught up in the justice system so often do, made excuses and transferred the blame for her son's criminal behavior to "bad associates." Kapsis, police learned, was a "bright boy with above average intelligence." He was a year older than Schultz, attended Sunday school, and enjoyed planting flowers in his backyard. His only altercation involved a stolen car, and a sentence of court supervision.[32]

Together, and in the company of fellow gang members Edgar Keck, a parolee from the St. Charles Training School for Boys, John Follman, Edward Prosek, Fred Getz, William Schwider, and Charles "Tex" Whalen, the acknowledged leader and "brains behind the operation," Schultz and Kapsis went on a rampage and committed eighteen robberies and twenty-eight car thefts over a dizzying six-week period in the summer of 1946.

At gunpoint the emboldened teens robbed Northwest Side fruit stands, a salesman at a used-car lot, innocent pedestrians walking the street, and in their most brazen action, Kapsis and Schultz shot and wounded a waitress and the owner, Robert Miller, of the Country Fair roadhouse in affluent Glencoe. Miller sustained a bullet to the stomach. Battered and bloody, he identified Kapsis as his former employee after narrowly escaping with his life following a fierce struggle that ended with the psychopathic Schultz ("the good boy") firing six errant shots. Kapsis had worked as a dishwasher at Country Fair and decided the tavern was a "good score."

Schultz and Kaspsis fled in a stolen Dodge coupe. An all-points bulletin went out and the newspapers pronounced this a "heater case," with the cops and the public on high alert. Police spotted the fugitives on Northwest Highway and chased them through the streets of Edison Park, but lost them. By now the Green Car Gang had attained the kind of dubious fame and notoriety they imagined when they decided to become "junior John Dillingers" at Steinmetz High.

Their heads bowed in shame, Louis and Bertha Schultz made a direct appeal to their son, over the airwaves of WGN Radio, to surrender before an inevitable clash with heavily armed police could occur. "Son," begged Louis Schultz, "come back home before it is too late. We promise that you shall have every opportunity to redeem yourself."[33]

With strange irony it was a real Boy Scout that helped the cops to bring down the Green Car Gang. Orville Fangrow, walking along the lakeshore to a Scout encampment six miles northeast of Elgin, Illinois, spotted Schultz and Kapsis sleeping inside the red coupe and alerted police. Roads were blockaded and the Illinois State Police moved in. As the cops approached, the fugitives spotted them and raced away on foot through a field of tall corn and dense underbrush.

They made it safely back to downtown Elgin, where they checked into a hotel, tired and spent, hoping to recuperate before their bus ride back to Chicago. A suspicious hotel employee immediately called police chief Joseph Huber who sent three detectives to the scene. Minutes later Kapsis and Schultz left the hotel and went on a shopping spree with their loot money, first to clothing stores for new trousers and shirts and then to a shoe emporium. As they exited the shoe store, Elgin detectives accosted them and clamped on the handcuffs with no resistance offered. Tough guy Schultz, who less than four weeks earlier was an ordinary schoolboy, told the detectives how lucky they were to still be alive. "You were so close," he said to one of the policeman from the night before, "that if I had a gun I would have bumped you off like a pigeon!"

Indictments were hastily filed in Kane and Cook Counties against Schultz and Kapsis. Chief Justice Harold G. Ward of the Cook County Criminal Court meted out tough justice; ten to fourteen years each for assault with intent to kill and one year to life for robbery. One by one the remaining members were rounded up and put away, although Fred

Getz, one of the youngest members, reorganized the Green Car Gang with new members after being prematurely released by the Chicago Parental School.[34] The North Side school for truants was a day school, and Getz was left free to commit larceny, robbery, and purse snatchings at night. In sentencing Getz to what amounted to a slap-on-the-wrist punishment, Judge Frank Bicek said the boy had a "fairly clean record, good intelligence and came from a good home." Harry Ash of the crime prevention board called the boy a "rotten apple" who corrupted other boys at the Chicago Parental School.

The incarceration of ex-Boy Scout Schultz did not mean the end of Schultz the armed bank robber as far as law enforcement was concerned. He emerged from prison a mean, embittered criminal and committed another series of robberies. In an eerie replay of his 1946 capture, police, aided by bloodhounds and helicopters, seized Schultz on August 16, 1961, as he hid himself in a Belvidere, Illinois, cornfield after obtaining $2,413 in the holdup of the First National Bank of Malta.

As Schultz turned toward the door to make a fast getaway from the Malta Bank in Winnebago County, he turned to the teller and said, "This is a hell of a way to make a living!"[35] His pathetic words suggest that if he had even bothered to attempt to find a legitimate job after his release from Pontiac, he was likely thwarted by his criminal record. Few companies are willing to take a chance hiring a violent ex-con.

The era of the political gangs and social-athletic clubs hired by local ward bosses to commit Election Day harassment faded by the 1930s. The Capone gang operated citywide through its own subalterns to attend to voter intimidation and other political work. They operated a criminal monopoly through complicit criminal politicians, who from time to time either engaged street gangs for minor tasks or protected them from police and judicial prosecution to placate loyal ward voters.

The abduction and presumed murder of West Side Valley politician Celinus "Clem" Graver intersected with the doings of one of the most sadistic and troublesome youth gangs to emerge in the city after World War II—the Vito Gang.

The close relationship between Frank Vito Sr., for twenty-five years a down-on-his-luck fruit and vegetable truck driver, with Graver, a product of the old Morris Eller Republican machine and the brother-in-law of Eller gangster Harry Hochstein, is illustrative of parasitical local ward politics. Frank Vito Sr., believing in the Roman Catholic tenet that the faithful "should have as many children as God sends you," fathered eight children with a paycheck that could barely satisfy his own needs.

Papa Vito also understood how the game was played in the corrupt West Side "River Wards." In return for favors, their vote was expected. Constantly in debt, Vito beat a well-worn path to the residence of Republican state legislator Clem Graver at 976 West Eighteenth Place in Pilsen seeking advice, influence, but mostly money. "We would have starved to death if Clem Graver hadn't helped us," Frank Vito told Maxwell Street police. "He was our good friend for twenty years."[36]

Like clockwork, Twenty-First Ward committeeman Graver delivered his two precincts to the Republicans with large pluralities in a district that normally went ten-to-one for the Democratic machine. He was old, reliable, and greatly venerated by the downstate GOP bosses. Bighearted and generous, as were so many of the "ward heelers" who were schooled in old-fashioned nineteenth-century methods of making friends in order to win elections, Graver used his political muscle to keep Frank "Pete" Vito Jr. out of jail.

Vito Jr. was a bad seed, described as "an unmanageable boy just old enough to remember some of the exploits of syndicate gunmen and other heroes of ward children" by reporter George Bliss. At age eighteen he had been sent to the juvenile home after beating and robbing a night watchman. Inside the reformatory, the black-haired son of the Italian peddler organized the Vito Gang. It was 1944 and the eighteen-year-old youth, hell-bent on mimicking his gangster heroes, recruited neighborhood boys Daniel E. Ryan, Lawrence Trumbley, Alex Lipinski, and Willie Sheehan, a youth known to play with explosives, to form the nucleus of his terrorist mob.

Beginning as burglars busting into industrial *warehouses*, the Vito Gang eclipsed the "42" Gang's fearsome reputation as one of the most gun-crazy criminal mobs in city history. Several of its members took jobs as tractor-trailer drivers. With a cargo manifest of booze and cigarettes, the Vito toughs would drive into a garage where the goods would be unloaded and sold in the neighborhood. "We was hijacked!" the Vito drivers sheepishly informed their employers.

They raided warehouses, hijacked trucks, pilfered from the shelves, and beat night watchmen senseless. Each took pride in being slightly "crazy." During a visit to a free medical clinic on November 6, 1951, Frank Vito Jr., according to eyewitnesses, went completely berserk. He tore phones off the walls, beat a physician senseless, and ripped patient medical records to shreds. The Vito Gang, or "mob," as Frank Jr. wanted it to be called, shook down local shop keepers on West Eighteenth Street for protection money. "Pay us now, so we can protect you from robbers and vandals!" they might have said. It was all for profit and for "kicks"—slang that came into vogue in the late 1940s, similar to "bopping," another term meaning fighting likely borrowed from jazz musicians describing the seeking of thrills. The Vito Gang engaged in games of target practice with one another in the alleys, streets, empty lots, and warehouses of Pilsen. In this game of "cops and robbers," the gang members fired rounds of live ammunition. In a June 1950 altercation, Trumbley sustained a gunshot wound that he said happened quite by accident. He shot at a snake in the Cook County Forest Preserve and accidentally wounded himself. When accidents like this happened and a member got nicked in the affray, it was off to the doctor's office to get patched up—the physician asked no questions. He dared not. Ordinary folk understood that to avoid problems, it was important to make way and allow the Vito Gang a wide berth.

In times of trouble, or when one of them had to answer to criminal charges, the parents knew where they could turn. "Graver knew the group and frequently fronted for them when they were involved in comparatively minor crimes," reported George Bliss.[37] Graver, a licensed bondsman in the Maxwell Street Police District, felt duty bound to "help out" his constituents, including greasing the wheels of the state parole board, although Norman Graver later testified that his brother Clem never accepted a dime for his services.

Representative Graver was careful not to get himself mixed up with stickup men and other bad characters, yet accepted $2,500 to help turn the keys of a prison cell at the Joliet Penitentiary where Vito Jr. had been sent after a 1950 armed robbery conviction. However, Graver waffled and did nothing. He later returned the money to the gang after Vito received parole, but he had already made a dangerous enemy in the neighborhood. Graver had good reason to be anxious. Vito and his mob had already murdered one of their own, Frank Ryan, on the suspicion that he had "squealed" to police.

Frank Vito denounced Graver, calling the ward boss "no good" and warning that he had better watch out. Meanwhile Vito, twenty-six years of age in 1952, linked up with Fred W. Bowerman, a professional bank robber out of Niles, Michigan, who coaxed the gang into sticking up the branch office of the National Bank and Trust Company of South Bend, Indiana. The September 19, 1952, holdup of the South Bend bank netted the gang $55,000, although Lawrence Trumbley was seized after he returned to the crime scene trying to retrieve the gang's abandoned getaway car. Over $30,000 of the stolen loot remained missing. Suspicions later arose that the cash had been placed in a strongbox and entrusted to Graver.

"Pete" Vito and his gang planned their jobs inside Tugman's Tavern on Racine Avenue. Glen Chernick, a college football star at Marquette, worked as a bartender one night a week. He made the acquaintance of Vito and earned his trust. Vito told him about a "soft touch" and recruited Chernick for the bank holdup job in St. Louis that he had in mind. William Fred Scholl, twenty-eight, another hanger-on, wanted in. "Vito told me I had a name as a good scrapper and an all around rugged guy. I said okay."

Two weeks later, the gang feasted on roasted duck dinner in a Bohemian restaurant on Twenty-Second Street, before driving to Mound City in an Oldsmobile and a Ford. An informant, unknown to Pete Vito and the gang, supplied law enforcement with the details of the coming robbery attempt before they left Chicago. In St. Louis, Vito and Bowerman spent four days driving up and down the streets, studying the layout of the bank and possible escape routes before making their move.

They entered the bank on April 24, 1953, unaware that one hundred police officers had encircled the bank. As the gang stuffed thick wads of cash into canvas bags, the cops closed in, guns blazing with teargas canisters flying. Bowerman, a sixty-year-old nearing retirement age, was fatally shot. Scholl was wounded in the cross fire. "Pete" Vito fired a bullet into his head rather than surrender. Scholl surrendered and Chernick was apprehended in Chicago. Scholl was sentenced to twenty-five years. Football hero Chernick received twenty years. The cold swagger and gangland terror inflicted by the Vito mob was nearly over, but the missing cash from the earlier Indiana job puzzled the cops.

The mystery deepened following the brazen abduction of Clem Graver a half block from his home on June 11, 1953. Graver had left for the Republican Party headquarters ward meeting at 805 West Eighteenth Street at six o'clock that evening to meet and greet residents and favor seekers and to debrief his staff about his recent adventures in Springfield, the Illinois state capital.

Graver's reputation preceded him. He was known in Twenty-First Ward circles as "an easy man with a buck," always lending a hand when needed. He fixed traffic tickets, provided seven-pound hams to the destitute at Christmas time, and paid midnight calls to hospital administrators if a sickly constituent needed help. Friendly and outgoing, his pleasing demeanor masked a more sinister side. Everyone in the Twenty-First Ward knew and feared his brother-in-law Harry Hochstein, who had gone to work for Al Capone as a chauffeur, personal cook, and confidant after the fall of the Eller empire.[38] Hochstein's influence in the corrupt "River Wards" allowed Graver carte blanche to conduct his secretive business affairs without much oversight or scrutiny from the dwindling number of Cook County Republican bosses.

Graver had rented a garage down the street from his residence. As he opened the door after returning from the ward office, he pulled his late-model Chrysler inside the garage. A black 1950 Ford sedan raced up from behind and slammed on the breaks. Three men pushed their way inside the garage and seized the politician by the arms and dragged him kicking and screaming into the Ford. Clem's wife, Amelia, and their neighbor Walter Pikelis waited on the porch of the house on Eighteenth Place a half block away. They were close enough to witness the kidnapping but were powerless to do anything about it. The car sped away, and that was the last anyone ever saw of Graver.

Police grilled hundreds of suspects, chased down rumors, and searched the city and suburbs for the corpse. A new underground parking garage under construction in Grant Park held one possible clue. Did the assassins bury Graver under fresh concrete? Nothing was found.

No ransom demands were received. The cops had their own pet theories, but without a body case number MPV91903 quickly went cold. The dearth of physical evidence or a confession stymied police. There was very little the department's sharpest detectives could do except ponder the possibilities. Graver had reportedly broken ranks with members of the West Side Bloc.

Case detectives probed the linkage between Graver and the Vito mob. Although the vicious gunman "Pete" Vito had ended his life, elements of the gang remained active in the Twenty-First Ward. Police pressured Milton Putnam, owner of the Snake Pit tavern, another Valley saloon dive popular with neighborhood toughs, to speak up. They had learned from a jailhouse snitch that Putnam's automobile had been used by Graver's abductors. The information was passed along, but no meaningful follow-up measures were taken. Putnam, the father of five, refused to cooperate, and a title search of the vehicle revealed that the title of his 1941 Mercury had been transferred. The kidnappers were known to have driven a Ford. Although the Vito Gang had motive and opportunity, Chicago police abandoned the line of inquiry.

By the close of the 1940s, Chicago youth gangs had increased in size, mobility, and ethnic diversity. Chicago's African American population nearly doubled in the period 1940 to 1950, from 278,000 to nearly a half million. At the same time, the Mexican migration into Chicago accelerated. By decade's end, fifty-six thousand Mexican immigrants settled into the city looking for work and the chance to start anew. Mexican barrios formed in the toughest and most volatile gangland strongholds formerly settled by white ethnics, in the Valley, Lawndale, and Pilsen, where the Vito Gang had spread its pestilence for so long. Partly in response to formidable social problems, issues of race, color, and ethnicity, a new generation of gangs formed to battle one another. They fought protracted wars over matters of turf control, and for or against the preservation/dispersal of the old tribal neighborhood identities, in the backdrop of the struggle for racial desegregation.

The postwar baby boom, increasing affluence of the white middle class, and the dawning of the youth counterculture reflected in popular music, movies, and changing social mores in the 1950s contributed to a separate and distinct gang problem in Chicago's so-called better neighborhoods extending out into the suburbs.

The decade of the 1950s, nostalgically remembered as the last "good decade" by many elderly Americans was neither tranquil nor as warmly assuring as it might have seemed in the large urban centers of the country.

8

GANGS BECOMING NATIONS, 1950–1989

A generation of young men returning from the battlefields of Europe and Asia in 1945–1946 confronted a changing postwar world. Boys who had been drafted into service in 1941–1942 came back to the United States as combat-hardened, cynical men. Postwar restlessness, minimal opportunities for gainful employment among a segment of the population, and the painful readjustment to civilian life contributed to escalating crime waves in large metropolitan areas. Lacking stability and routine, many former servicemen took to the road, forming the first motorcycle gangs, which only added to the stress put upon law enforcement. A generation of children born after World War II suffered from poorer family formation rates as the divorce rate in America soared as the table on the following page illustrates.

In the 1950s increasing numbers of children were growing up in single-parent households with little or no supervision of their after-school activities. The U.S. Department of Justice National Report for 2006 concluded that only 5 percent of youth living with both biological parents reported gang involvement, compared with 12 percent of youth living with one parent or in other alternative arrangements. According to Wade C. Mackey and Ronald S. Immerman in their scholarly study "The Presence of the Social Father in Inhibiting Young

U.S. Marriage and Divorce Rates, 1900–1980

Year	*Marriage Number*	*Marriage Rate*	*Divorce Number*	*Divorce Rate*
1900	709,000	9.3	55,751	0.7
1910	948,166	10.3	83,045	0.9
1920	1,274,476	12.0	170,505	1.6
1930	1,126,856	9.2	195,961	1.6
1940	1,595,679	12.1	264,000	2.0
1950	1,667,231	11.1	385,144	2.6
1960	1,523,000	8.5	393.000	2.2
1970	2,158,802	10.6	708,000	3.5
1975	2,152,662	10.1	1,036,000	4.9
1980	2,406,708	10.6	1,182,000	5.2

Source: U.S. Department of Health and Human Services. Table does not include data from California, Georgia, Hawaii, Indiana, Louisiana, and Minnesota.

Men's Violence," "That data analyzed across the U.S. indicate that father absence, rather than poverty, is the stronger predictor of young men's violent behavior."[1]

M. Anne Hill and June O'Neill concluded that "the likelihood that the young man will engage in criminal activity doubles if he is raised without a father and triples if he lives in a neighborhood with a high concentration of single parent families."[2]

From the poverty-row districts of Chicago's inner city to the affluence of the suburban backyards of the gin-sipping white-collar cocktail generation, the decade of the 1950s spawned an estimated two hundred street gangs and Chicago's highest youth-crime rate in decades. The Chicago Police Department juvenile section pegged the number of gangs to be around four hundred. Lieutenant Michael Delaney, appointed to serve as head of the juvenile section, on December 19, 1954, conceded that many of these gangs were at worst "mischief makers," but added: "There are as many breeds of teen-age gangs as there are neighborhoods. You can't group them according to nationality, creed, or color. They range all the way from gangs that are more noisy than dangerous to those that are downright vicious criminals."[3]

Police and social workers traced the blame to a number of factors, including a dramatic rise in liquor consumption following World War II and a surge in what police termed teenage "wolf pack" gangs in the suburbs. In the city's quieter residential neighborhoods, sociologists pointed to indifferent parenting, increasing numbers of divorced households, and overindulgent parents showering their children with automobiles, fine clothes, and other material trappings instead of giving them needed affection, guidance, discipline, and understanding. "You can't blame the kids," a youth officer confided to reporter Norma Lee Browning in a March 1957 interview. "The only trouble with these kids is their parents. The parents get rich overnight and they don't care what happens to their kids."[4]

The postwar baby boom drove a profound age restructure of the U.S. population.[5] By the end of the 1940s, thirty-two million babies had been born in a ten-year period, compared to just twenty-four million during the Depression. Between 1954 and 1965 the national birthrate continued to rise. The baby-boom generation (and the generation of kids born between 1935 and 1945) ignited in the 1950s a rebellious, inwardly directed youth counterculture revolt against parental control, school authority, conservative social and sexual mores, and the police that would later morph into a broader societal protest to eradicate war, military conscription, racism, sexism, environmental pollution, and corporate elitism during the mid-to-late 1960s.

In the matter of dress and popular taste, 1950s working-class youth abandoned the buttoned-down look of 1930s and 1940s adolescents. Police lineup photos from the 1930s and 1940s of youthful gang members often showed detainees attired in white shirts and ties, fedora hats, and sports jackets. By the 1950s, the "look" had strayed far afield from the suit-and-tie conformity of previous decades. In their search for identity, male adolescents donned chinos, Italian knit shirts and black leather jackets, and greased their hair back with Brylcreem or pomade in the style of Elvis Presley. The jacket (similar to World War II bombardier pilot's garb), the hair, and the scornful, alienated, and sneering attitudes of so many of the boys who adapted this image gave rise to a new term in American slang, "greaser."[6]

Of course not all white adolescents who belonged to gangs were necessarily greasers nor were all greasers members of a street gang. However, the appearance of leather-jacketed young toughs frightened adults, terrorized vulnerable kids, and scared the wits out of school administrators. The leather jacket equated to a predictable pattern of defiant, antisocial classroom behavior. But no one could deny that the movement symbolized a sweeping, open revolt in dress, mannerisms, and music preference mimicking a new and startling antihero popular culture.

Marlon Brando's portrayal of outlaw biker Johnny Strabler in the 1953 motion picture *The Wild One* romanticized defiance against established societal order and encouraged kids to break through conservative social boundaries, to act out and live for the moment. In his abbreviated film career, actor James Dean evoked similar attitudes. Evan Hunter's novel *Blackboard Jungle*, and its 1955 cinematic release, featuring Bill Haley's rock-and-roll anthem *Rock around the Clock* in the opening credits, was a watershed event in the transformation of American *popular* culture into American *youth* culture.

Rock and roll, a fusion of urban blues, country and western, pop ballads, and jazz compositions, was as much an anarchistic statement as 1920s jazz rhythms and 1940s bebop. It thumbed its nose at convention and the rigid, moralistic religious codes of the older generations in frank, revelatory words and lyrics. Billy Ward and the Dominos' "Sixty Minute Man," released in 1951, emphasized guilt-free sexual seduction without consequence in suggestive lyrics. In a similar vein, Hank Ballard and the Midnighters' 1954 rhythm and blues offering "Annie Had a Baby" and an unmarried teenage father's plight: "that's what happens when the goin' gets good!"

This subversive new sound pandered to youth and, in some recordings, to gang life itself. Guitarist Fred Lincoln "Link" Wray's 1958 instrumental hit "Rumble" soared to the top of the musical charts, its title borrowed from the bloody street-gang fights in Chicago, New York, and Los Angeles of that era. Many city gang fighters adapted "Rumble" as their anthem. Fellow guitarist Jimmy Page later said of Wray that he had "a real rebel attitude."

The moral authorities of the 1950s narrowly condemned rock and roll on religious and ethical terms as a dangerous new social current, but they were ridiculed and made to look foolish for their pallid attempts to impose censorship upon the music. Samuel Cardinal Stritch, leading the Chicago archdiocese at the time, banned impressionable young Catholic girls from attending Elvis Presley's concert in the spring of 1957. "When our schools and centers stoop to such things as rock and roll tribal rhythms" he declared, "they are failing seriously in their duty. God grant that this word will have the effect of banning such things in Catholic recreation."[7] The condemnations leveled against Presley and his legion of imitators by the clergy and the PTA seem laughable by today's standards, but the new music was as alarming to that generation of law-abiding middle-class family heads as "gangsta rap," with its promulgation of violence against women and its demeaning antifeminist lyrics, and glorification of gang life is to social critics today.

Setting aside the religious piety of 1950s midwestern Bible thumpers for the moment, can we now take a more sobering view and reasonably deduce that in equal measure, the new-music art forms separated by five decades contributed to increasing lawlessness by encouraging young people to act out in socially irresponsible ways? The popular culture and rock-and-roll music were infused in the greaser subculture. Rising delinquency seemed to be its natural extension.

The spike in youth crime was neither an isolated phenomenon nor a random occurrence. With a $44,000 budget, Senator Robert C. Hendrickson, a New Jersey Republican, chaired a U.S. Senate subcommittee appointed in September 1953 to investigate the juvenile gang problem, delinquency, increased use of narcotics, burglary and strong-arm robbery in twenty American cities including Chicago. Inquiry into crime conditions nationwide revealed a 30 percent increase in juvenile delinquency in a five-year span, from 1948–1953.

The hearings convened in April and continued through November 1954. Chicago officials were summoned by Senator William Langer, a Republican from North Dakota. to the federal courthouse in Chicago to report on existing conditions and offer an assessment of prevailing conditions. "Too many parents take the attitude that it is the duty of the government to raise their children," said Cook County state's attorney John Gutknecht "That is not true. It is the duty of the government to punish parents who neglect their children. I intend to take action against parents who allow their children to stay out until the early morning hours and get into trouble."[8]

In New York, Senate panelists mostly concerned themselves with "licentious and immoral themes" of crime and horror propagated by American comic book publishers. As was the case with the "penny dreadfuls," dime novels and pulp fiction of earlier times, officials attached blame to troubling aspects of the popular culture as a root cause of youth crime.

In their interm report published in 1955, the committee expressed the concern that comic books were instruction tools in the ways and means of comitting crime among impressionable youngsters.

> Another aspect of the contribution of comic books to juvenile delinquency, in the opinion of a number of experts, was the indication that more serious forms of delinquency incorporate knowledge of specific techniques which many comic books provide. This was considered to be another valid criticism of comic books, i.e., they offer juveniles a comprehensive written and pictorial presentation of both methods and techniques of criminal activities.[9]

Writer James F. Short in his scholarly "Study of Delinquency," an essay published in the *International Encyclopedia of the Social Sciences*, noted that:

> In the decade of the 1950s . . . attention was drawn to organized-gang activities more insistently than in the past. Partly this was because of an apparent increase in the amount of violence and crime engaged in by such groups, and partly because it seemed to reflect the nearly universal importance of the gang in industrialized countries. In any event, there were enough differences between the formally organized gangs studied and reported on during the 1950s and the somewhat looser aggregates usually referred to in the earlier studies to generate a new series of theoretical efforts focused on the organized street gang. The central concept that emerged to encompass the phenomenon of the gangs was that of the *delinquent subculture*. The concept "culture" refers to the set of values and norms that guide the behavior of group members; the prefix "sub" indicates that these cultures often emerge in the midst of a more inclusive system. Delinquent subculture refers, then, to a system of values and beliefs encouraging the commission of delinquencies, awarding status on the basis of such acts, and specifying typical relationships to persons who fall outside the delinquents' social world.[10]

To address the growing street-gang threat in 1955, the Chicago Police Department bolstered its juvenile section resources to 141 men. The plan called for the permanent assignment of a juvenile officer in every police district between 8:00 a.m. and midnight. Lieutenant Delaney, an able and hardworking man appointed to his post by Commissioner Timothy O'Connor, launched the department's first database, on index cards, of known street gangs, their leadership and reputed members and hangouts.

Policing, like everything else in American society, changed as modern society evolved. In an earlier era, patrol officers walking the beat kept close tabs on street activity and knew the malefactors in each district. In the modern, mechanized era of policing, the patrol car removed the officers from traditional foot patrol, and the intelligence gained through personal contact evaporated. Patrol officers in squad cars did not see juvenile work as a key part of their responsibilities. The preventative, community-oriented policing championed by Delaney and social outreach agencies was left to the undermanned juvenile division, whose members were dismissed as unimportant and often ridiculed as "diaper dicks" by their peers.[11]

District commanders complained that juvenile-division officers seemed unwilling to share information with frontline patrolmen. However, resources were stretched thin. In some instances a juvenile officer was assigned responsibility in three or four districts. There was little time for any of them to integrate into the community, speak with at-risk youth, and channel their energies in more worthwhile pursuits. Despite setbacks and manpower shortages, the detail succeeded in circumventing flare-ups of violence across the city.

Delaney and his unit were effective at breaking up rumored gang wars, or rumbles. In 1956 the team received word that the Blackhawks, a gang of toughs from Diversey and Leavitt on the North Side, had armed themselves with guns, knives, clubs, and were preparing to go to "war" with the Headhunters and the Lancers from Belmont Avenue and Wolcott Street in a turf battle. With meager street intelligence in hand, juvenile-squad members called upon the Headhunters and Lancers at their homes and known hangouts and spoke with each of them, diffusing a potentially lethal situation.

"It's the best weapon police have had in combating these gangs in years," stated Ben Novoselsky of the Cook County State's Attorney's Office in the Family Court.[12] Before the card database became operational, it was impossible to assess the threat level posed by an embryonic criminal groups like the Frank Vito Gang in the West Side Valley until they had committed a major crime and came to the attention of law enforcement.

Gangs proliferated across the city. Delaney's expanding index-card file kept tabs on nearly all of them. "The Bronkies," a Delaney notation recorded, "these boys, ten and all, are known to carry guns and commit assaults. Ages from sixteen to nineteen and can be found in the area 31st to 33rd Streets and South Parkway to Prairie Avenue."[13]

Delaney's street "intel" revealed that gang leaders were recruited from well outside their neighborhood haunts. The South Side Desert Hawks invaded the North Side Hudson Avenue District, made famous by the St. Valentine's Day Massacre, Chicago's "signature crime," and drew members to local meetings miles away.

Another alarming and growing trend in Chicago youth crime during the 1950s was the sudden rise of girl gangs. Family court statistics tracked an 89 percent increase in the number of girls involved in gang life between 1951 and 1957. To a lesser extent, familiar patterns of violence, extending from the reform school to the streets, presented a vexing set of new problems. In 1957 a thirteen-year-old girl was strangled to death by a fifteen-year-old inside the walls of the Illinois Training School for Girls, the female equivalent of the St. Charles Training School for Boys—"Charleytown"—in Geneva, Illinois.

Girl gangs often formed as adjuncts or auxiliaries to the established male street gangs, who used them to carry guns, drugs, alcohol, and other contraband. Youth officers traced the rise of numerous girls clubs, including the Nobles and Noblettes, the Rex and the Rexettes, the Devils and Devilettes, the Busy Bees, the Hell's Angels, and the Pink Ladies of Taft High School, a late 1950s greaser club later depicted in the Broadway stage play and 1978 Hollywood musical *Grease*, written by Jim Jacobs, Warren Casey, and starring Olivia Newton-John.

Teenage street gangs tread upon the familiar blood-soaked battlegrounds of the 1890s and opening decades of the twentieth century. Crime-scarred areas of the city once terrorized by the Mortell-McGraths, the Feinbergs, and the Valley Gang witnessed fresh outbreaks of gang violence with a new cast of characters in the 1950s. The Sons of Satan, a gang of youths aged twelve to fifteen but answering to older, case-hardened "sponsors," committed acts of vandalism and violence against senior citizens living in the predominantly Jewish Douglas Park. The history of this gang had a familiar but painful echo to youth corrections officials. Its leaders were recent parolees from "Charleytown."

Elderly women were beaten and battered and their purses snatched—each new member had to grab a woman's purse to join the gang. Older members tutored young boys on the ways and means of distracting witnesses to the crime and "swarming" the victim if the person under attack put up resistance. Purse snatchings, automobile theft, and receiving stolen goods were part of their standard modus operandi. Judge Thomas Kluczynski called this gang "the worst of many neighborhood and school gangs" appearing before him in his juvenile (family) court chambers.[14]

If the Sons of Satan represented a failure of the system, social workers were encouraged by the positive results achieved by the Jane Addams Boys Club at 1246 West Taylor Street in neutralizing the threat to the West Side Valley posed by the Dukes, a gang of twenty-five Irish, Italian, and Mexican youths at war with the black gangs slowly overtaking the vicinity of Taylor Street and Western Avenue. To prevent outside interlopers from laying claim to their territory, the Dukes painted their name in large white letters on a fifty-foot stretch of brick wall in the 1300 block of Taylor Street. Any youth who was not a recognized member of the gang had to cross the street rather than walk directly in front of the wall. "That's Duke Heaven, a place none of us wants to visit," said an Egyptian Cobra.[15] The Dukes maintained a twenty-four-hour vigil from rooftops and apartments, on the lookout for trespassers they could beat up.

The Dukes repeatedly sparred with the Cobras—an African American gang from the West Side Fillmore Police District whose membership would eventually swell from fifty-four to six hundred—over racially motivated turf issues.

A Lane Technical High School student belonging to the Dukes had been savagely beaten by African American gang boys and ended up in the hospital with a broken jaw one night in March 1958. The Dukes retaliated by smashing windshields of parked cars near the residences of those they believed responsible. Later that year, Joseph Caliguri, director of the Jane Addams Boys Club, cautiously approached the Dukes individually in an attempt to penetrate the common protective layers of suspicion and mistrust gang members held for "do-gooders" and agents of social reform.

Borrowing a page from the New York City Youth Board playbook, Caliguri and his team struck up conversations with the Dukes over cups of coffee. Members were invited to play billiards and games of table tennis at the club, and were assured that there would always be a youth worker around to talk to as issues arose. Gradually, social barriers were broken down and the Dukes adapted the Boys Club as their "clubhouse." Parties and dances were scheduled, and those resisting this change were asked to leave. A "teen council" was established. The summer of 1958 was the quietest in years in the old Taylor Street District, according to Caliguri. "These changes take time and effort—most of it on the part of the boys," Caliguri said. "After they found that people aren't always waiting to kick them in the pants, things began looking up."[16]

In a similar vein, social worker George Dryden extended the olive branch of friendship to the Egyptian Cobras, offering them recreational opportunities at Stanford Park at Fourteenth Street and Union, where members were invited to play games of softball. Dryden achieved modest results, albeit temporary. A juvenile officer noted that serious gang fights in the district had dropped by 50 percent since Dryden stepped in during the summer of 1959. All bets were off however, after fifteen Cobras beat to death a member of their own gang, nineteen-year-old Jake Jones, on August 14, 1960.

Skeptical cops in the Fillmore District could only shrug their shoulders and say, "I told you so," and declared the Cobras to be devoid of compassion; a gang that acted entirely on compulsion. The point was borne out in February 1962 when Henry "Johnny Ringo" Ponder, gang president, and two other Cobras were indicted for the fatal beating of seventy-two-year-old Lester Wolf, during a robbery of his tailor shop at 1174 East Fifty-Third Street in the South Side Woodlawn community where the Blackstone Rangers ruled the area. In the 1960s, the Cobras and the Rangers, in the tradition of modern corporations, merged to form one "super gang" that succeeded in tearing apart the social fabric of Woodlawn. So much for trying to make friends with a street gang.

Little Hell, never completely free from the pox of gang violence in its bruising hundred-plus-year history of mayhem, became the home turf of the Sharks, a mostly Italian gang from Chicago Avenue and Mohawk Street that formed up in the late 1940s. Their "mission" was linked to "defending" white residents of the Cabrini-Green housing project from the incursion of southern blacks who were tilting the racial scales of the Chicago Housing Authority (CHA) buildings to nearly 100 percent African American by the 1960s. The Italians of Little Hell had a long history of resisting African American settlement of their community. Father Luigi Giambastiani of the St. Philip Benizi Church called upon local realtors and the community to support forced evictions of blacks in 1935 because, as he said, "The Italians resented the invasion of their neighborhood by the colored people, since their neighborhoods had always belonged to them."[17]

Racial mistrust and resentment spilled over from one generation to the next. The bigotry of the community and its leaders pandered to the racist feeling of white youth gangs like the Sharks.

The Sharks were one of the early Chicago gangs to display their "colors" and logo on items of clothing. Members sauntered through the neighborhood in sweaters emblazoned with the gang emblem: an upright shark with a cigarette dangling from its mouth.

Such frills cost money, but to attain this coveted custom-made symbol of gang life, many would steal or sell drugs. The senior Egyptian Cobras designed a snake emblem they stitched to their sweaters. Murders were committed over the theft of an emblem sweater.

In a farcical attempt to break into the ranks of the "big-time" holdup gangs, four members of the Sharks stuffed a cantaloupe in a paper bag then approached the cashier's cage of the Montgomery Ward store at 621 Chicago Avenue on the afternoon of June 11, 1952. "This is a holdup! Don't scream or I'll kill you! I have a bomb in the bag!" Unfazed, cashier Lillian Zannis calmly reached for the telephone to call police. The four Sharks fled, and were arrested minutes later and bound over to the juvenile detail.

According to author Michael Scott in a web posting, the original Sharks were forced out of the neighborhood after the last of the white residents had vacated the Cabrini buildings, but "the cousins and nephews of the original Sharks started their own gangs: Mohawks, Hudson, and the Cleveland Jammers."

"White boys feel they have to keep their area free of Negroes, a common fight they feel they can rally around," said Richard Boone of the YMCA in a 1959 discussion.[18] "This drive is tremendously reinforced by their parents either directly or indirectly through snide remarks." Prejudicial attitudes were imparted to children in such a way that people of color were demonized and racial integration was seen as a calamity and not as the natural process of societal evolution.

The gangs of Chicago claimed primacy in the city parks, as dangerous a place for anyone to be in 1957 as it was back in the racially charged summer months of 1919 when Ragen's Colts and other South Side social-athletic clubs assaulted African Americans venturing into these same "whites only" recreational areas. McKinley Park, adjacent to Brighton Park and Back of the Yards, required extra police attention after well-publicized assaults by aimless youth "hanging out" and looking for trouble. "Ten guys get beat up in that park every week," a crime investigator commented in March 1957. "It's worth your life to walk by there at night. Why do you think we've had to cut out so much of the shrubbery and bushes in Chicago parks? So innocent citizens won't be dragged into them."

Chicago Crime Commission chief investigator Walter Devereaux declared that the "roving gangs of young toughs" had turned the city into a "jungle." Across the nation the problem seemed to have intensified to epidemic proportions. In Washington, D.C., FBI director J. Edgar Hoover described the appalling nationwide juvenile problem as "the crux of our crime problem."

"Wolf pack" gangs, as the Chicago cops labeled them, preyed upon the weakest and most vulnerable members of society: elderly people waiting for the bus on street corners, store owners, and young children (for their lunch money). At Marshall High School on the West Side, armed thugs ambushed young boys from the nearby grammar school to extort their lunch money, threatening physical violence and brandishing switchblades and shards of broken glass. Chicago mayor Richard J. Daley ordered school superintendent Benjamin Willis to assign investigators to the schools after hostile newspaper publicity over these matters took the city's ruling Democratic regime to task.

As the decade wore on, incidences of petty extortion, vandalism of school properties, and random violence escalated and, in some cases, ratcheted up to murder. The 1950s killings, however miniscule in proportion to the numbing rate of gang homicides recorded in the new millennium, signaled the arrival of a transitional period when disorganized gangs evolved into larger, highly structured criminal organizations tied to the procurement, sale, and distribution of illegal narcotics.

The rise of the drug trade in the mid-1960s changed the paradigm of gang life, as police and social workers knew it to be in the 1950s. "It was a remarkable thing," commented Martha Valley, commissioner of New York's youth service agency in a 1970 interview. "The use of drugs while not absolutely forbidden was not condoned. A street gang, with its cadre of paramilitary organizations, would not tolerate the use of drugs within its ranks. A street gang meant teamwork one for all and all for one, but a drug user is all for himself, and therefore could not contribute to the purpose and work of the gang." Although gang drug trafficking in the 1950s lurked in the shadows and could not be linked to youth gangs in a significant way, the cycle of violence marked the rise of the "new" organized crime.[19] The rash of juvenile homicides in the mid-to-late 1950s offered an ugly prelude to worse things yet to come.

Charges of murder, manslaughter, and conspiracy were filed against seven gang youths on October 18, 1956, following a rumble in Cornell Square Park, Fifty-First and Wood Streets, that left Warren White, a senior at St. Joseph's High School, dead. White, like so many other innocent victims caught in the cross fire of warring gangs, had been walking through the park when Frederick Kruse, armed with a .32 caliber pistol fired some "practice shots" at Fifty-Fifth and Karlov prior to the gang fight in the park between the Rebels, a Cornell Square Park gang from Fifty-First and Wolcott, and three other gangs, the Cavaliers, Sons of Italy, and the Sons of Chinatown, from Seventy-First Street and Western.

The motives were traced back to jealous rage. The group of boys from Seventy-First Street aroused the ire of the Rebels because they had had been "picking up" the girlfriends of the Cornell Square Park gang. Kruse turned himself in to police and confessed to the deed.

As absurd as it must have seemed to investigators, such provocations were becoming all too common in teenage gangland. A student at Gage Park High School had apparently "generated steam" (egged on other gang members) by saying, "Come to the candy store tonight. We're ready to swing or jam!" Fourteen youths were held for questioning, but at the inquest many of the parents were notable by their absence. Meanwhile, Frank and Sylvia White, parents of the slain boy, went to church, and in their own words, said they would "pray for our Warren and for the boy who killed him."[20]

The Rebels, a gang from Davis Square seemingly without conscience, had killed before. In March 1957 fifteen teenagers belonging to the Rebels attacked and murdered seventeen-year-old Farragut High

School student Alvin Palmer, a marine reservist, with a mechanic's ball-peen hammer as he waited at a bus stop at Fifty-Ninth and Kedzie Avenue. The motive was racial. Palmer was African American.

Farragut principal William McBride declared, "We hope his death will put a stop to this terrible thing. It is not a race problem. It is not a religious problem. It is a problem for all of us, this terrible thing known as juvenile delinquency."[21] McBride's well-meaning pronouncements counted for little. The Palmer murder reflected the widening chasm in city race relations. The presence of African Americans in Southwest Side neighborhoods, where a pattern of "white flight" was just beginning to unravel the old ethnic-European residential strongholds, underscored how little attitudes had changed since the July 1919 rioting.

City of Chicago health, fire, and building officials responded to the tragedy by closing the candy store at 1855 West Fifty-First Street, where the alley-wise Rebels congregated. In court eighteen-year-old Joseph Schwartz confessed that the idea to kill Palmer was strictly his own. Schwartz, riding in one of two gang cars, said they were just "looking for somebody to roll." Chief Justice Wilbert Crowley sentenced the youth to fifty years in the penitentiary. Five others received lengthy prison sentences. Two more were granted new trials.

Then surprisingly, almost overnight, the gang leadership transformed its image later that year. Members of the Rebels worked with the Boys Clubs to open a clubhouse at 1742 West Forty-Eighth Street in the Back of the Yards to get troubled kids off of the street. Pat Salmon, aka "Fish," one of the founders of Rebels, explained: "They say the Rebels are the toughest gang in the city. And they figure, 'If I'm a Rebel I'm with them and no-one will bother me.' Then they act tough because they think it will impress the Rebels. You get a bunch of boys acting tough to impress each other and what do you have—a gang of punks. Treat the boys like punks and they'll be punks. Help them, guide them and praise them and treat them like decent human beings and that's what they'll be."[22]

A clubhouse to "hang out" in and socialize among peers, Salmon added, is what the Rebels wanted all along. "People see a large group of boys and get scared. They call the police. The police break up the open group and chase them under cover. Then the boys go to parks or alleys where no one can see them. When they're in alleys they act like alley cats. Do people really expect anything else?"[23]

Community intervention by religious groups and social service agencies were ongoing through the 1950s and 1960s. In June 1962 Reverend Billy Graham took time out from his evangelical rally at McCormick Place to meet with the leaders of eighteen rival gangs in a shabby room inside a South Side Christian Center at 3523 South State Street. Members of the white Rebels gang joined with 140 mostly African American representatives of South and West Side gangs, including the Cobras and Abattoirs.

Reverend Graham spoke of Jesus Christ as "a tough guy . . . who could have licked any of you with one hand tied behind him." Several of the boys later said they were "inspired" by the preaching of the charismatic Graham, but a half hour later Chicago police were summoned to break up a gang fight just two blocks from the center.[24]

In Bridgeport, home to five Chicago mayors, the old Hamburg SAC, and an insular community where traditions of family, parish, and politics are lovingly handed down from one generation to the next like cherished heirlooms, the slaying of seventeen-year-old De LaSalle High School student Kenneth Sleboda in July 1955 jarred neighborhood complacency and aroused citywide outrage. A raw, brutal, and senseless shooting, the offender in this case showed little remorse, assuming a cold and defiant "screw the world" attitude that horrified the sensibilities of churchgoing folk desperately trying to rear their children in safe, worry-free surroundings, respectful of God, their parents, and the civil authorities.

Sleboda had just bought his cousin Barbara a Coke at a neighborhood drugstore near Thirty-Second Street and Morgan when a shotgun blast fired from an automobile tore through his chest as he chatted with a group of friends outside a restaurant. Thirteen gang boys riding in a three-car caravan had mistaken Sleboda and his chums for a rival gang. They had sought revenge for a series of alleged beatings and intimidation they had endured and were thirsting for revenge. From inside a stolen Lincoln automobile, fourteen-year-old Clement "Cookie" Macis fired his father's shotgun at Sleboda.

Macis, a freshman at Tilden Technical High School who held down a part-time job as a dockhand at a freight depot, had used tinfoil jumpers to steal the car, and had purchased a box of shotgun shells from a hardware store. The gang of thirteen boys rendezvoused at Boyce Park, at Forty-Second and Lowe Avenue, to plan the attack. The pulled up in front of the restaurant. One youth leapt out of the car and shouted, "We're ready for you!" Macis, a broad-shouldered six-footer that reporter Norma Lee Browning likened to Hollywood heartthrob Tab Hunter in looks, discharged his weapon at that moment.[25] He later told police that he only intended to "fire up in the air."

The father of the dead boy, Bruno Sleboda, who wrapped buns at a commercial bakery for a living, said his son had never been in trouble with the law. "Oh God, whatever happened to him. What are we going to do? Why did they have to murder a kid like that?"[26] The funeral mass at St. Mary of Perpetual Help, located a block from the crime scene, was a solemn affair attended by a large number of grieving Bridgeport residents.

To escape a harsh prison sentence, five members of the gang turned state's evidence against Macis. Anna Macis, the sobbing mother of Clement, said she "did not know" how her husband, Stanley, and she had gone wrong in the upbringing of their son. Parental bewilderment over the actions of these delinquent boys was a common thread in nearly all criminal trials of juvenile offenders.

In the courtroom of Judge Thomas Kluczynski, young Macis appeared calm, detached, and very sure of himself on the witness stand. He maintained all along that the discharge of the weapon was an accident resulting from a sudden lurch of the car. "I didn't know why it happened, but it did," Macis smirked. "I guess I'm too young to get the electric chair, so I guess it doesn't matter."[27]

Kluczynski, disgusted by what he perceived to be the boy's unfeeling, arrogant manner, delivered a harsh, lengthy, sermon before sentencing Macis to a sixteen-year term in the Pontiac prison. "There was nothing wrong with that boy's mind that some good strict discipline at home couldn't have cured," Kluczynski later remarked. "He was belligerent and cocky. He took the attitude that a lot of these young criminals take—'You can't pick on me, I'm a juvenile!'"

The next few years were hellish for "Cookie" Macis. After his first year in Pontiac, the teen was transferred to the correctional facility in Menard, Illinois, to receive psychiatric treatment after being diagnosed with dementia praecox. As Norma Browning bluntly put it, Macis had "cracked up" in confinement. At Menard, he underwent shock treatments and hydrotherapy with injections of Thorzine to bring him out of his debilitation. In September 1956 Macis took a swing at a correctional officer and was placed in a straitjacket. He spent the long, dreary hours of confinement reading movie magazines and crime-adventure stories, forsaking religious services in the prison chapel. In a prison interview, Browning asked Macis what advice he would give to other teens in trouble. "Let 'em figger out their own problems!" he snarled.[28]

Teenage-gang involvement was strongly suspected in two of the decade's most sensational murders, the triple slaying of Northwest Side schoolboys John and Anton Schuessler and their friend Robert Peterson in October 1955, and the December 1956 disappearance of Barbara and Patricia Grimes after they had attended an Elvis Presley movie at the Brighton Park Theater on the South Side. The bodies of all five victims were dumped in heavily forested areas outside the city limits. All five had gone to the movies, and were thought to have been picked up by someone they might have known who lured them into a car and drove them to their place of death—near a stream of water. Days before the murders, Patricia Grimes had told her mother that an older gang boy had accosted her in McKinley Park, a few blocks away from the family home at 3634 South Damen Avenue.

The Grimes case stands as one of Chicago's most chilling cold-case murders. The movements of the teenage sisters after leaving the Brighton Park Theater strongly suggest that they were picked up by a person or persons known to them and taken on a one-way joyride to a hidden rendezvous and then to death in a wooded, unincorporated area of the county, where their bodies were dumped. Nearly forty years after the bodies of Schuessler and Peterson were found, indictments were brought against suburban horse-stable owner Kenneth Hansen. Although Hansen was twice convicted and died in prison, lingering doubts about additional suspects persist. Marauding teenage gangs in the Jefferson Park District, where the three boys lived, had been preying upon young girls and had bullied a number of boys in the schoolyards. The forest preserves, lacking sufficient policing resources, were magnets for rape, robbery, and physical intimidation.

Contrasting the homicide rate of domestic ("acquaintance") murders and street-gang killings, historically the percentage of gang slayings was very small. Chicago Police Department statistics reveal that in 1965, only eleven gang-related murders occurred, representing just 2.8 percent of all homicides. Just five years later the number soared to seventy, the result of a surge in gang warfare involving the Black Gangster Disciple Nation, a South Side African American gang that had grown to the size of an army regiment by the end of the 1960s. The gang murder rate would fluctuate from year to year. This was due primarily to the result of sudden outbreaks of turf wars "defense" of a city block or neighborhood against interlopers, or as a result of the escalating drug trade (after 1965), that spiraled upward from 1955 on.

The juvenile squad identified the Prairie Avenue Police District, a wide swath of the South Side east of Bridgeport between Fourteenth and Sixty-First Streets (encompassing the southern edge of Maxwell and south through the old "Black Belt"), as having the largest concentration of street gangs, both black and white, in the city during the mid-to-late 1950s. Major gangs included the Dukes, the Clockers, the Braves, the Devil's Disciples, the Desert Hawks, the Esquires, the Cottage Grove Gang, and the Thirty-First Street Gang, as well as emerging African American gangs. These various groups held sway in the school playgrounds and parks, but in particular within the vicinity of the Doolittle School at 525 East Thirty-Fifth Street. On the night of June 27, 1955, the school was set ablaze after rampaging youngsters tore through the halls and classrooms breaking glass, overturning furniture and causing major damage pegged at $30,000.

Questioned by police, the neighbors refused to point the finger at any one individual or gang, but admitted that nearly every block had its own gang—and names of the Desert Hawks and Dukes were well-known to nearly all—but the public was afraid to say anything lest they suffer reprisals. "It was none of my business and they weren't damaging my property," said one frazzled restaurant owner. "I don't want to get involved in anything with those kids!"[29]

By the mid-to-late 1960s, attrition significantly reduced the size and activities of Chicago's entrenched white teenage greaser gangs of the 1950s. Membership in such gangs peaked at age twenty. Upon reaching their age of majority, gang boys abandoned street life for marriage, fatherhood, and gainful employment—or in some cases, prison. Loitering on street corners, looking cool and acting tough, painting graffiti on walls of buildings, shaking down weaker boys for lunch money, and defending turf lost much of its appeal as the weighty responsibilities of adulthood rearranged priorities. Although the numbers grew appreciably smaller, there were some notable exceptions—the "legacy gangs" that continued in street life, keeping things going and handing down responsibilities of leadership to succeeding generations, each one becoming more aggressive than the last.

The Gaylords, a white Italian gang from Grand Avenue and Noble Street in the former stronghold of the Black Hand, started innocently enough in the late 1940s as the Junior Postals softball team, playing other social clubs in the public parks. For mysterious reasons, the Postals adapted the name Gaylords in the early 1950s. In various white paper reports on street-gang activity in recent years, the Chicago Crime Commission asserts that "Gaylords" is an acronym for "Great Americans Youth Love Our Race Destroy Spics [sic]." As a white street gang, they congregated in the vicinity of Huron and Throop Streets to take up a "defensive posture" against the influx of Puerto Rican residents pouring into the Humboldt Park neighborhood.

The same deep and pervasive racial and ethnic hatred that characterized so much of the history of these feuding gangs contributed to a series of protracted wars between the Gaylords and the Latin Kings, the oldest and largest Hispanic gang.[30] Year after year, wars were fought block by block as the Gaylords tried to forestall the inevitable transformation of the neighborhood from a dwindling number of whites to black and Hispanic.

In the nightly gunfights, streetlights were knocked out to provide cover as feuding members darted from gangway to alley and across side streets. "It's not hard to start a fight," a Gaylord leader named Streb told *Tribune* reporter Robert Reiss in a 1974 interview. "You take some guy's sweater in another club, or sometimes you just look at someone the wrong way. A fight starts when you represent."[31] Residents of Palmer Street, one of the disputed turf strongholds controlled by the Gaylords, complained that the police showed up late, usually a half hour after gunshots were reported. A pandemic of illegal guns, ranging from .22 caliber pistols to shotguns and semiautomatics, fell into the hands of the street gangs by the early 1970s.

A member of the Latin Kings confided to reporter Reiss that he "remembered when there weren't any guns in gang fighting. We used fists, chains and knives, but not guns until the Vice Lords started fighting. They had zip guns, so we made zip guns. Now we buy guns from people who come from out of state, sometimes boxes of guns. You see when a kid first joins a gang, he sees a big guy do something and he says, 'I can do that better than him,' so instead of a zip gun, the kid gets a .22 and it goes on and on."[32]

In Humboldt Park, not far away, twenty-year-old Richard Medina, leader of the Spanish Cobras, was shot down at Maplewood Avenue and Division—the "gang corner"—one night in 1979 by a member of the Insane Unknowns. The murder ignited a "retaliation war" of killings that dragged on for the next two years.

The sale of illegal, unregistered guns to gangbangers who in turn often resold their surplus weaponry to others on the street evolved into a lucrative cottage industry during this same time period. In December 1974 Chicago police raided several gun suppliers selling pistols by the case or renting then out for two weeks at fifty dollars per weapon. Seized in the bust was the forty-seven-year-old store manager of the Sears Roebuck flagship store in downtown Chicago who had been moonlighting in the gun trade. Hot-dog stands, strictly a cash business, were another good source of cover for guns and drugs. A West Side gun ring transacted business through Pop's Corner, an innocent-looking Vienna hotdog stand at 2214 West Eighteenth Street in Pilsen. The owner boasted to the cops that it was "the best front I've ever had for selling guns."[33] After 1980 the Gaylords eased off of their ethnic and racial philosophy by joining the "People Alliance."[34]

The history of Chicago gangs, as we have noted from its earliest days of conflict in Little Hell, Bridgeport, and Maxwell Streets, runs parallel to the strained patterns of ethnic and racial settlement of the "wilderness" neighborhoods of the city. After World War II, Chicago was crippled by a severe housing shortage as returning GIs, African Americans moving northward from the Mississippi Delta, and Mexicans and Puerto Ricans vied for living space in low- to middle-income neighborhoods on the South and West Sides. The black population increased by 43,549 in the Douglas, Washington Park, and Grand Boulevard communities between 1940 and 1950. Overall the African American population in Chicago rose 214,534, or 77 percent, during this corresponding period, and with it threats of a renewed race war.

From May 1944 to July 1946, forty-six South Side black homes were attacked, twenty-nine of them firebombed. The first black family that attempted to move into the town of Cicero, Al Capone's old bailiwick, on July 11–12, 1951, was driven out by a mob of four thousand harassing whites. Similar to 1919, Chicago was a seething cauldron of racial resentment. For white South Siders in changing neighborhoods hatred was born and nurtured out of fear of plummeting property values, economic loss, and fear of black on white crime. During unsettled times, such as these, white gangs were often encouraged to be on the "look out" for strangers or people of color drifting into the neighborhood, and to deal with them accordingly. Writer Bill Granger remembered that Visitation Parish, the largest Catholic parish in Chicago amd the center of Irish-Catholic life on the South Side for many decades "would stay white because the parish society bought up empty apartments and re-rented them to whites only."[35]

The racial and ethnic conversion of the troubled neighborhoods of the South, North, and West Sides that Frederic Thrasher labeled as the "wilderness" sparked many of the lethal turf battles of the 1950s. However, as the white gangs, outnumbered and overwhelmed by the powerful social currents of urbanization, began to drop away, super gangs emerged, reflecting the changing face of the "new organized crime" in the city.

The Deacons of the Ida B. Wells housing project, a collection of midrise apartments and row houses constructed on the South Side in 1939–1941, was among the first black gang of consequence to emerge in the post-1919 riot era. They ran their operation out of Madden Park, with the girl-gang adjunct, the Deaconettes, and the Little Deacons (age twelve to fifteen). Their principal rivals in the battle for control of the neighborhood were the Destroyers and the 13 Cats. The Clovers were active on the West Side in the late 1950s, battling the Egyptian Cobras for supremacy.

In his book, poet, playwright, and social practitioner Useni Eugene Perkins noted a marked difference between benign gang activity in the 1940s and 1950s and the chronic black-on-black violence characterizing the despair of slum living in the 1960s. "Despite the increase in criminal activities during the fifties, black street gangs as a rule, still maintained some respect for the black community. Nevertheless it was becoming apparent that this respect was eroding and being replaced by behavior that diametrically opposed community norms and sanctions. Indeed, the fifties had spawned a generation of black youth who seemed to thrive on callous behavior, disrespect for adults and senseless violence."[36]

As crime escalated in African American communities, mostly-white social workers attempting intervention and utilizing the same tactics that yielded positive results in the reformation of the Rebels and the Dukes were seen as too "paternalistic," if not patronizing. On the other hand, police were accused of being overly punitive in their dealings. The overall mission of the combined social agencies seemed to be geared to pacifying black street gangs—not rehabilitation. There were associated political overtones to the strategy. The dreaded "long hot summers" of 1960s racial unrest carried with them the constant threat of urban rioting in black neighborhoods. Neutralizing the dangers of gang participation in the fomenting of street disturbances preyed on the mind of Mayor Richard J. Daley and business leaders as the decade wore on.

The early years of the 1960s bore witness to horrific gang violence in impoverished African American communities on the West Side. Lawndale, by now almost entirely black in its racial composition, was the staging ground for violent clashes between the Egyptian Cobras and the Vice Lords, a gang formed in 1958 inside the St. Charles Training School for Boys.

Their leader, Edward Perry, and his associates supplied the name "Vice Lords" after figuring out among themselves that the meaning of the word "vise" meant "strong grip." Returned to the neighborhood from Charleytown, the Vice Lords operated as a quasi-social club sponsoring neighborhood parties as they bolstered their ranks with former members of the Imperial Chaplains, Apaches, El Commandoes, Golden Hawks, and Thunderbirds, and commenced warfare on other youth gangs that had formed in the streets and in the high schools. Over time numerous factions of Vice Lords claimed territorial rights to neighborhood intersections and parks throughout the West Side, particulary in Lawndale.[37]

Social worker Doris Smith of the Chicago Youth Center described in a January 1960 interview that being in a neighborhood like Lawndale "is like visiting another world. As many as fifteen families live in apartment houses constructed for four. Broken windows are never replaced. There are no lights in the hallways. There are no buildings where teenagers can go for recreation in the winter months. It's a strange neighborhood too, because there are few old persons and almost no dogs nor cats. Some youngsters have lived in it all their lives without making a trip downtown or seeing Lake Michigan."[38]

Judge Saul Epton sentenced nineteen-year-old Perry to a year in prison after the youth slashed a member of the rival Imperials gang at a dance held at the Sears Roebuck YMCA in Lawndale in July 1960. The incoming reform-minded Chicago police superintendent, Orlando W. Wilson, ordered an immediate crackdown on teenage hoodlum gangs to erase what he called a "serious blot" on the city's reputation.[39]

Wilson was, in many respects, the most scholarly, forthright, and competent police head in Chicago history, but like others in the Chicago power establishment, he was at a loss as to what to do to curb gang recruitment and put a stop to the outcropping of violence in African American communities, which only grew worse over time. He never fully comprehended the urgent sense of identity and social appeal gang membership held for disenfranchised youth living in tenement districts devoid of recreational outlets and jobs for the young and unskilled. Woodlawn had changed from white to black in a six-year period, 1958 to 1964. The housing stock, meant to comfortably accommodate forty thousand, housed eighty thousand people as the African American population exploded. The overcrowded neighborhood was emotionally charged and tense as the battle for turf control became an obsession of the gangs. Superintendent Wilson and his advisors did not fully comprehend the issue of substandard housing.

Six years after unveiling his highly publicized crackdown, Wilson announced on July 21, 1966, that he had brokered a truce between two of the city's largest and most lethal street gangs, the Blackstone Rangers of the South Side Woodlawn community and the East Side Disciples of Englewood, who would later change their name to the Black Disciples.[40]

Just as the jubilant British prime minister Neville Chamberlain told his subjects that he had secured "peace in our lifetime" after appeasing Adolf Hitler in 1938 at Munich by allowing the annexation of Czechoslovakia, Wilson proclaimed peace in the city streets. However, by agreeing to meet with representatives of both gangs he had in effect granted them de facto recognition of their right to exist.

It was a situation not unlike the attempt of Frank Loesch of the Chicago Crime Commission to request a meeting with Al Capone's cadre to ensure a peaceful mayoral election in 1927. Of course South Side ministers had already reached out to gang leaders in order to redirect their focus to following a more useful path in life, and to build support for the crusade of Reverend Dr. Martin Luther King Jr. Chicago Freedom Movement.

Members of the Blackstone Rangers showed up at Dr. King's July 1966 rally in Soldier Field carrying banners proclaiming "Freedom Now," along with pictures of submachine guns. They accompanied Dr. King into Cicero during his opening-housing march into the segregated hate-mongering white suburb, but were ordered by him to back down from any armed confrontations.

Like Chamberlain's handwritten note from Hitler, Wilson's armistice wasn't worth the paper it was printed on. Just nine days after the signing of the peace agreement, two youths were killed and a dozen more wounded on the South Side. Recognizing the gravity of the problem, Wilson appointed a ten-man Gang Intelligence Unit in 1967 to take the battle to the streets and break up the growing power of the Rangers and their rivals.

By the time of the 1966 "peace conference," the Blackstone Rangers had became the most iconic and feared street gang of the 1960s. At the height of their power the Rangers were the darlings of affluent, but sadly misinformed, white liberals, members of the show-business community, including Sammy Davis Jr., and even within the Richard Nixon White House. In what ranks as a truly astonishing moment, Senator Charles Percy of Illinois invited Ranger founder Jeff Fort and Henry "Mickey" Cogwell to attend the 1969 inauguration of President Richard Nixon.[41] Percy was impressed with Fort's leadership acumen and encouraged his political involvement. However, Fort declined to attend, and sent Cogwell in his place.

The story of the Rangers spins around Jeff Fort, a quiet, unassuming young man from Aberdeen, Mississippi, who moved north with his family during the tail end of the Great Migration era. Born in 1947, Fort ended his schooling in the fourth grade, unable to read or write. Four separate tests revealed that Fort's intelligence quotient (IQ) ranged from forty-eight to fifty-eight.

Caught up in the criminal justice system at an early age, Fort, like other youths before him, wound up in Charleytown, where he befriended Eugene "Bull" Hairston. As young boys in detention c.1959–1960, they founded the Blackstone Rangers, named after a section of Blackstone Avenue, Fort's home ground, between Sixty-Third and Sixty-Seventh Streets, west of Stony Island Avenue in Woodlawn. In the early years the Rangers wore red berets, distinguishing themselves from the general public.

It is believed that Fort and Hairston borrowed the nickname "Rangers" from the crack U.S. Army Ranger unit—among the most highly motivated and precision-trained military fighters in the world. Fort was paroled from the St. Charles Training School in 1962. He gained notoriety with the police in October 1967 after being charged with the murder of a thirteen-year-old boy, but the case was eventually dismissed for lack of evidence. Jeff Fort would amass a criminal rap sheet four-and-a-half pages long before it was all over.

In the early days of the gang's formation, Hairston, larger and more physical than Fort, was considered to be the leader calling the shots. Then, after a period of years, came an inevitable falling out, Fort, the brainier of the two, emerged as the undisputed gang boss. Hairston, sentenced to five to fifteen years in prison in 1968 for solicitation to commit murder after paying six teenagers a dollar a piece to shoot three rivals, survived for two more decades and a failed assassination attempt before being killed execution style on September 22, 1988, near his apartment in the Ida B. Wells housing project. The motive was unclear, but detectives from the Wentworth Area Violent Crime Unit believed it had something to do with the split between Hairston and Fort.

Intuitive and possessing great leadership ability, Jeff Fort had a way of drawing kids into his circle. He was good at bringing opposing gangs together and brokering peace among combatants. For his great skill at diplomacy and negotiation, he earned the nickname "Angel" as the gang evolved into a Mob-like organization that might have rivaled Al Capone's, if not for one important difference. The Rangers and other South and West Sides criminal street gangs never really succeeded in infiltrating mainstream political networks, although in the 1970s, the Vice Lords established the "United Concerned Voter's League," named after the Unknown Conservative Vice Lords faction, while the South

Side Gangster Disciples formed the "Young Voters of Illinois" with little success. In the 1990s they tried a new tack, adapting the slogan "Growth & Development"— believed to be a disguise for the initials of the gang's name, GD.

The alleged political arm of the Gangster Disciples penetrated the Oval Office of the White House in January 1994, when one of its leaders, representing "Better Growth and Development," met with President Bill Clinton. According to George W. Knox, director of the National Gang Crime Research Center, this individual ". . . was out on bond for a charge of criminal trespass to a stolen vehicle and was not supposed to leave the jurisdiction," at the time he conferred with the president.[42]

Gangster political fronts cooked up by Fort and his rivals failed because they lacked friends in high places in city hall and had few or no sympathetic allies in the Cook County offices and within law-enforcement agencies.

By the mid-1960s, Fort had built a monolithic coalition of twenty-one independent gangs, including the Cobras. He organized his coalition of five thousand members under a governing body called the Main 21— twenty-one separate gang leaders designated in military fashion as "generals." They adapted the pyramid symbol composed of twenty-one separate Stones, each representing a Main 21 gang. By the end of 1968, when gang intimidation and killing was at its most rampant point, Fort rebranded his super gang the Almighty Black P. Stone Nation—the letter "P" signified "peace, prosperity, people, and power."

From their humble beginnings, the loose street confederation became highly politicized and now called itself a nation. Their archrival, Black Gangster Disciples, followed suit, so within the span of a decade two South Side street gangs became two separate nations within the City of Chicago.

No one is exactly sure of just how many died during the long and drawn out gang war pitting the Black P. Stone Nation against the Gangster Disciples in the years 1968 to 1970. Estimates range from 150 to 200, easily surpassing the violent Prohibition wars of 1925–1926. In the newsrooms of the major metropolitan papers, city-desk editors, who were numbed to the violence, classified the reports of the daily shootings as "ghetto crime" unworthy of publication except for the high-profile cases involving the "generals" and others high up in the chain of command. Their overt indifference to the plight of families and residents unaffiliated with gang life but trapped in the combat zones was perceived as racist by community leaders, and members of local clergy.

The Black P. Stone Nation enjoyed the support of at least one very influential church advocate in the person of the Reverend John R. Fry, minister of the First Presbyterian Church at 6400 Kimbark Avenue in Lawndale. Fry, a white, middle-age ecumenical leader, seemed oddly out of place and way out of his element. "Offering a creative and courageous approach to extremely difficult urban problems and that he is performing these services in the name of Jesus Christ," so stated the Chicago presbytery in his defense during the summer of 1968, when he was under fire from the City of Chicago and the U.S. government.

With Fry's assistance, Fort secured and completed the necessary forms that would allow them to become a political organization, the first step toward achieving legitimacy and recognition from the white-power establishment. Fort named his fledgling political group the Grassroots Independent Voters of Illinois and set out to broaden his influence. In 1983 Fort's gang worked on Mayor Jane Byrne's unsuccessful reelection campaign and pocketed large sums of money from Democratic Party coffers—although members switched their allegiance to Harold Washington, a former congressman, who went on to become the city's first African American mayor.

Grant money from the city's most influential charitable foundations, including the Community Renewal Society, the W. Clement Stone Foundation, and the Kettering Foundation, poured in, with the naïve hope that the funding would be utilized for the betterment of the community, and the eradication of street violence through job training and job creation. More than anything, Chicago's blighted inner-city communities and its crime-infested housing projects needed some level of economic empowerment.

In Woodlawn, Fort's gang, estimated to have between two thousand and eight thousand members at the peak of its power, threatened and terrorized scores of mostly white, elderly Jewish businessmen who owned small shops serving the community, while at the same time receiving credit for keeping the neighborhood free from arson and looting during the April 1968 riots accompanying the assassination of Dr. Martin Luther King, Jr.

Targeting small businesses, extortion demands were delivered carrying with them the implied threat of violence and destruction to property unless monies were paid. Store owners eventually gave up and moved out of the neighborhood. Essential services were lost, and minus its retail base due to gang extortion of owners of store-front businesses. South Side communities devolved into fractured wastelands of empty weed lots, and boarded up, derelict buildings. Stores that remained in business took precautions. Metal pull-down grates protected commercial facades during off hours and late into the evening. The earmarks of poverty and blight were everywhere, and those suffering the consequences the most were of course the residents wanting nothing more than to live peaceful, ordinary lives.

Meanwhile, Fort's uncanny knack for attaining publicity by courting prominent white liberals and show-business personalities drew him into the national spotlight. Entertainer Sammy Davis Jr. had to seek out police protection after Fort demanded $150,000 from him to finance the purchase of three clothing stores.

We remember those times as the era of "radical chic," when it was popular for jet-setting, fun-loving wealthy socialites attired in Nehru jackets and miniskirts to salve their liberal guilt by inviting gangbangers and persons from the streets to attend Lake Shore Drive cocktail parties.

Law enforcement at the federal and local level was largely unimpressed by the outpouring of support, the mink coats, and the new Cadillacs that Fort drove around in to impress young boys looking to emulate his lifestyle.

In Washington FBI director J. Edgar Hoover authorized the sending of fraudulent and threatening letters from the Black Panther Party to Fort in an attempt to foment trouble between the black nationalist group and the Chicago gang leader.

The government targeted Reverend Fry for perpetuating criminal activity by opening up the church to the Black P. Stone Nation as its headquarters. Lieutenant William Griffin, commander of the Third Police District, told a U.S. Senate permanent investigation subcommittee chaired by Senator John McClellan (Democrat-Arkansas) that Fort held "clandestine meetings to threaten and intimidate members and outline strategy for confrontation with the Disciples" inside the church.[43] Drugs and weapons were reportedly stashed in closets.

Appearing before the subcommittee in Washington, D.C. in June 1967, Reverend Fry urged the government to continue its "manpower and training program" for the Rangers and the Devil's Disciples under the terms of the federal office of the $927,000 grant from the Economic Opportunity to the Woodlawn Organization. Fry listened to testimony alleging that he sanctioned pot parties and sex parties inside the church and personally transmitted an order for a gangland hit from one leader to another and put forth a suggestion that the gangs attack police cars with Molotov cocktails and stage a riot in downtown Chicago. In a published manifesto appearing in the April 15, 1968, edition of *Christianity and Crisis*, titled "Mayor Daley and Chicago Blacks," Fry called upon the African-American community to disrupt the 1968 Democratic National Convention in Chicago as a way of "wrecking Daley's national prestige." Undoubtedly enflamed rhetoric of this kind contributed to the extraordinary security precautions taken by the city to quell demonstrators descending upon Chicago in August 1968.

The accusations piling up against Fry were damning, but the reverend made no apologies and insisted that he was the victim of racism and the target of a larger conspiracy hatched by Mayor Daley and the Chicago Police Department.

With a $927,000 federal grant awarded to the leadership of the Woodlawn Organization in June 1967, four training centers opened, including one in the church to support a federally funded job-training program earmarked for eight hundred young adults in Woodlawn, through the Office of Economic Opportunity.

The Black P. Stone Nation took control of two of the centers and assigned gang members to serve as "classroom instructors" who were paid $5,200 per annum to teach in the facilities. However, "One ten-year-old said the only things he had learned in the center was to steal, cheat and be slick," Griffin testified. "It was not uncommon to hear remarks from participants that they were learning nothing in the centers and enrolled only to receive the $45 in weekly payments." A *Chicago Tribune* probe discovered that kids from the street spent most of their time reading comic books, sleeping on their desks, or playing dice games—except when Office of Economic Opportunity officials dropped in for a visit.

As "center chief" Fort commanded a salary of $6,000 a year in his new role. Hairston was paid $6,500 as an assistant project director. He appointed twenty-one top leaders of the Rangers to serve as "community workers," "teaching faculty," or as "administrators" attending to the record-keeping system, and the purchase of supplies. Paychecks were signed and approved for other gang members to receive forty-five dollars a week. High school dropouts from the area were encouraged to join the program so that they too could collect a stipend. Worse, gang members paraded through the centers armed with shotguns, handguns, and rifles.

For all his good intentions, Reverend Fry never fully comprehended that he was being played. As serious charges swirled around him, aduring the federal hearings looking into the embezzlement of the grant money, he became even more radicalized, hostile, and defensive about his perceived mission. Charging the government with a pattern of institutional racism and the hearings "a function of right wingers," he declared: "My association with the gangs was maliciously misunderstood. "We tried to work for law and order and for peace and against violence."[44]

As might be expected, religious leaders, Hyde Park academicians, and liberal Democrats circled the wagons around Fry and rallied to his cause. "The John Fry I know is a man of honesty, integrity and Christian dedication," commented Martin Marty, associate editor of the *Christian Century* and a divinity professor at the University of Chicago.[45]

The governing body of the Presbyterian Church agreed and cleared Reverend Fry of any wrongdoing, but the controversies continued to swirl until April 1971 when the embattled minister resigned his pastorate and moved to San Francisco to accept a position as visiting professor of social ethics at the San Francisco Theological Seminary. In his final remarks to his congregation he accused the Chicago Police Department of institutional racism and the City of Chicago of "harassing" the Black P. Stone Nation. The police, and not the gangs, he said, were responsible for any criminality that might have occurred.

Jeff Fort refused to tell a U.S. Senate subcommittee how the money was spent, and was held in contempt. The government charged that the funds were used to purchase guns and drugs. They conducted a thorough investigation of the entire setup, and on April 7, 1971, returned a fifty-one page, 132-count indictment against twenty-three members of the Black P. Stone Nation on charges of defrauding $927,000 from the antipoverty program. Although convicted, Mickey Cogwell was granted probation. After stints in the Cook County Jail and the Stateville penitentiary on unrelated charges, Jeff Fort entered the Leavenworth penitentiary on May 23, 1972. He was assigned to work the telephone switchboard and used this opportunity to run his lucrative Chicago drug trade and marshal his troops from inside the walls of the prison. During their confinement in Illinois prisons in Menard, Joliet, and Pontiac, the major gang leaders used their time to recruit members, pass along instructions to members on the outside, and establish the underpinnings of the deadly prison culture we are so familiar with today. Fort never passed up a chance to exploit a situation to his advantage. He would serve four years and six months of a five-year sentence inside Leavenworth.

Released from parole in 1976, he enrolled in a community education program at the University of Wisconsin-Milwaukee and joined the Moorish Science Temple.[46] He reorganized the entire gang operation, replacing his twenty-one generals with just five street bosses. Fort renamed his gang the El Rukn Tribe of the Moorish Science Temple after undergoing a religious conversion while on prison.[47]

In a rare published interview following his parole, Fort told F. Richard Ciccone of the *Tribune*, "We are not related to any one group. Don't confuse us with anyone. Our nationalism is Moor. We are Moors and we are directly tied to Morocco."[48]

Fort, now wishing to be called "Prince Malik," moved into the real estate business as a means to launder money. He acquired the Oakland Theater at 3947 South Drexel Avenue and three storefronts on the ground floor for a $10,000 cash payment—all in singles and five-dollar bills.

Renaming the vermin-infested, run-down, former movie palace "The Fort," the gang leader paid for the restoration, and converted the building, in the poorest, most economically deprived neighborhood of Chicago, into a mosque.

The boss of "The Fort" unveiled the building to the media as the "El Rukn Grand Major Temple." Skeptical gang investigators dismissed the religious significance as a front for a big-time drug-trafficking operation. The mosque was subjected to various police raids over the next few years, although the El Rukns claimed their status as a religious organization with the mosque as their shrine, and therefore exempt from police interference.

In the early 1980s, investigators effectively cultivated key informants from within the gang and the community to build a solid case against the El Rukns. Thomas Hampson, attached to the Illinois Legislative Investigative Commission at the time, developed former member Kenny Morrow to work with the agency in 1981. "I learned that Kenny had been with the Blackstone Rangers since the early days and was a loyal member," Hampson recalled in an interview. "He dropped out of the gang when Mickey Cogwell was murdered. Kenny's brother, a bodyguard for Cogwell, was killed in that ambush. He (Morrow) believed that Fort was responsible for his brothers' murder so he drifted away from the gang but did not burn any bridges. [Kenny's parents] . . . were upset about the path that Kenny and his brother had taken. I interviewed the mother and told her I wanted Kenny's help in building a case against Fort. A few weeks later Kenny called and set up a meeting with me. I talked and gave him my pitch. He listened and several months later he got back to me and said he wanted to do it. And off we went."

Jeff Fort, aka "Prince Malik," returned to prison in December 1983 after being convicted on drug-trafficking charges. The government incarcerated Fort in the Federal Correctional Institution at Bastrop, Texas. He continued to run his gang operation by calling his lieutenants in Chicago using the prison pay phone. The serious breach in prison security allowed Fort to concoct a brazen and bizarre criminal scheme which, had it been successful, might have put at risk the lives of thousands of American citizens.

Fort was tried and convicted in 1987 of ordering his members to meet with Colonel Muammar Gaddafi and the government of Libya to carry out acts of domestic terrorism on U.S. shores for a $2.5 million reward. The fantastic plot was unraveled by the FBI through its Counter Intelligence Program, aimed at disrupting activities of domestic organizations deemed a threat to U.S. interests. The feds listened in on thousands of collect calls from Fort, under the alias "Mr. Wood," using the prison pay phone to talk to El Rukn soldiers in code. Over a five-year period, the government taped thirty-five hundred hours of calls. During this time federal agents overheard the details of the bizarre Gaddafi plot. But in order to build a convincing case, they needed more substantive evidence to bring to court.

A government sting brought the whole thing to light and provided the government with the proof they needed. An El Rukn member attempted to purchase a ground-to-air rocket launcher from an undercover agent. Then another El Rukn member turned state's evidence in exchange for a $10,000 payout to his family. Indictments against Fort and five other El Rukns followed. The El Rukn trial ended after two months of testimony and deliberation. Jeff Fort and the other defendants were all found guilty, and in December 1987 Fort received an eighty-year sentence. He was the first man in the United States to be convicted of terrorism.

In 2006 the feds transferred Fort to the ADX Florence super-max prison in Florence, Colorado. He remains incarcerated in that institution under an order that precludes him from having any human contact.

The final chapter of the El Rukn saga ended ingloriously on October 29, 1989, when Chicago police and federal marshals swooped down on the Grand Major Temple with the force of a tornado, following the indictment of sixty-five gang members and associates on a multitude of charges. Agents sealed the building entrances with steel plates and doors, and bricked up the windows. A "no trespassing" sign was planted in front of the old movie house, which had not shown a movie since the 1960s.

The city declared final victory on June 6, 1990. There were happy smiles and handshakes all around as Mayor Richard M. Daley joined with U.S. attorney General Richard Thornburgh, police superintendent LeRoy Martin, various community and law-enforcement officials, and a crowd of three hundred onlookers to witness the first pass of a six-thousand-pound wrecker's ball. The terra-cotta facade of the blighted theater building crumbled and collapsed. A Chicago police officer volunteered to take pictures and mail them to Fort.

"This building has never been good for anything," commented detective Richard Peck who had arrested Fort and traveled to Mississippi to testify against him in the drug trial. "There was nothing here but narcotics, extortion and recruitment."[49]

It was a strong and resonant message delivered from the City of Chicago and the U.S. government: The El Rukns had been put out of business—gone for good.

Neighbors in the nearby Ida B. Wells project seemed mostly indifferent to the whole thing. "I know that things were being directed from there, but in many ways they made the area safer. Just the name had the people fearful. They had so many lookouts that kids from the other gangs would not dare come by and try to break into your car."[50]

Jeff Fort had succeeded in socially engineering disparate groups of disenfranchised youth trapped in an urban jungle into "nations." Several branches of the old Black P. Stone Nation continue on today as Jet Black Stones, the Corner Stones, and Cobra Stones (later the Mickey Cobras, named after the slain Mickey Cogwell).

Just as modern nations go to war with one another, the gangs of Chicago reorganized, and by the new millennium the number of yearly gang-related homicides had soared. Today Chicago is a city under siege. It is reliably reported by the National Drug Intelligence Center and the Department of Justice that the combined gang membership exceeds 125,000. No city neighborhood is immune. Every suburban community has detected a gang presence.

Jeff Fort left behind a powerful legacy. His lifestyle, attainments, and social prominence, however fleeting, inspired a new generation of African American youth to engage in the gangster life. The story goes that an awe-inspired younger man, standing inside a church where Jeff Fort had spoken, observed the throng of listeners politely step aside to allow Fort to pass. Unknown at the time, he said, "Someday I'm going to get me a mob like that!" The young man's name was Larry Hoover, and he would merge his Supreme Gangsters with the Black Disciples, an Englewood gang commanded by David Barksdale, to form the Black Gangster Disciple Nation, or GDs.[51]

The final demise of the El Rukns in 1989 did not mark the end to a violent era with the restoration of peace and calm. It signaled a dangerous new beginning.

NOTES

CHAPTER 1. OUTLAWRY AND THE RISE OF A CRIMINAL CLASS IN THE EMERGING CITY

1. Hamilton, Henry Raymond, *The Epic of Chicago*. Chicago: Willett, Clark, 1932, p. 73.
2. Lewis, Lloyd, and Smith, Henry Justin, *Chicago: The History of Its Reputation*. New York: Harcourt Brace, 1929, p. 34.
3. Hamilton, *Epic of Chicago*, p. 173.
4. *Chicago Democrat*, November 2, 1835.
5. Kelley, Katherine, "Coming of Beau Brummel Stirs Early Settlers: Gay Tavern Life of 100 Years Ago Told," *Chicago Tribune*, November 14, 1930. See also, Gale, Edwin O. *Reminiscences of Early Chicago*. Chicago: Fleming & Revell, 1902. See pp. 135–136.
6. Beaubien sold the Sauganash to John Murphy in 1834. Murphy eventually changed the name of the business to the United States Hotel. The famous Chicago landmark stood until 1851 when it was destroyed by fire. Nine years later on the same site, developers erected the "Wigwam," a public hall where Abraham Lincoln was nominated to run for president on the Republican ticket. The Wigwam, intended to serve as a temporary structure, was consumed in the Great Chicago Fire.
7. Quoted in Knox, George W., *An Introduction to Gangs*. Bristol, IN: Wyndham Hall Press, 1994, p. 200.

8. Quoted in Karamanski, Theodore J., "The Marseilles of Lake Michigan," *Chicago History Magazine*, Spring 2000, p. 42.

9. Ibid., p. 49.

10. The Bridewell, another name for a nineteenth-century city prison or lockup, was adapted from a hospital built in 1853 in St. Bride's or Bridget's well in London. Chicago's Bridewell opened in December 1851.

11. Hayes, Dorsha, *Chicago: Crossroads of American Enterprise*. New York: Julian Messner, 1944, p. 136.

12. See "A Notorious Character Gone," *Chicago Tribune*, September 17, 1870.

13. Ibid.

14. Constable Quinn remained a forgotten figure of city history until 2002 when amateur historian Rick Barrett, of the U.S. Drug Enforcement resurrected the story while conducting family research. Quinn's name was added to the Honored Star Case, a memorial to slain Chicago police officers.

15. John Sherman opened Chicago's Union Stockyards on Christmas Day, 1865. The yards operated continuously until July 1971.

16. Millionaire financier John Worthy (1841–1894) made his fortune in stone cutting and masonry. He was the president of the Metropolitan Elevated Road and was one of three directors of the Bridewell board and later served as board chairman.

17. Judge Richard Tuthill (1841–1920) served thirty-five years on the bench and was the last Civil War veteran to serve as a jurist in the municipal court. A Republican, Tuthill served as U.S. attorney from 1879 to1884 and was elected to the circuit court bench in 1887. He organized and systemized the juvenile court, the first of its kind in the United States, following passage of the enabling legislation in July 1899. The model he established was copied by Denver, Milwaukee, Baltimore, St. Louis, and Cleveland as those cities established their own courts to try cases involving underage offenders. He replaced Julian Mack as presiding judge of the juvenile court in September 1907.

18. In 1932 inmates at the Riverside institution were transferred to the St. Charles Training School for Boys, discussed in chapter 7.

CHAPTER 2. DOWNTOWN AND NEAR SOUTH: VICTORIAN VICE, GAMBLERS, CARD CHEATS, CHINESE TONGS AND THE RISE OF CHICAGO'S ORGANIZED CRIME GANGS, 1870–1920

1. "Levee" became a generic nineteenth- and twentieth-century designation for big-city vice districts segregated from residential and commercial neighbor-

hoods. The term dates back to the paddle-wheel steamboat era of the 1840s and 1850s when luxury passenger crafts traversed the Ohio and Mississippi Rivers. The presence of gamblers plying their trade onboard the riverboat and the many saloons, bordellos, and gambling establishments lining the wharf (or levee) area of the river town where these boats temporarily moored during layovers became an adaptable term for red-light districts in America. Beginning in the era of the westward expansion, when steamboats traversed the wide expanse of the Mississippi and Ohio Rivers, districts of segregated commercial vice sprouted in the large urban centers of America. Such dangerous and disreputable areas often hugged the waterfront wharves and piers where the paddle-wheel steamers came to port. Gambling, prostitution, and saloons flourished in these "levees," and soon a generic term for vice district crept into the American lexicon. The pragmatic belief among big-city politicians—notably nineteenth- and early twentieth-century Democratic bosses of the large urban machines—was that the traditional vice activities could never be eradicated, so containment in a segregated district near warehouses, train stations, or peripheral neighborhoods, away from residential areas, was the only solution to what nineteenth-century reformers and ecumenical leaders called the "social evil."

2. Author Wallace Rice recalled the era of vice segregation in "When Whoopie Was a War Cry," a series of articles appearing weekly in *The Chicagoan* in July and August 1931.

3. "The Wickedest Block in Chicago Is the West Side of State between Van Buren and Congress," *Chicago American*, March 12, 1901.

4. "Vice on Display at Andy Craig's," *Chicago Tribune*, January 19, 1908.

5. "Craig's Saloon Home of Crime; He the Master," *Chicago Tribune*, December 11, 1903.

6. Ibid.

7. Wooldridge, Clifton Rodman, *Hands Up in the World of Crime: Twelve Years a Detective on the Chicago Police Force*. Chicago: Stanton & VanVliet, 1901, p. 92.

8. The quote is also attributed to Louise "Texas" Guinan, 1920s New York cabaret queen, and Phineas T. Barnum, showman of antebellum America. There is no way to verify the origin of the quote, but McDonald has been cited in numerous books and articles as the originator.

9. John Peter Altgeld, a one-term Democratic governor (1893–1897), is remembered today for issuing pardons to three of the men convicted of complicity in the Haymarket Riot bombing that claimed the lives of seven police officers on May 4, 1886. In truth, Altgeld was a creature of Chicago Democratic machine politics, and his job performance rated subpar. Between 1893 and 1895 he pardoned eighty-one hardened criminals, including nineteen murderers. On his last day in office, January 2, 1897, he freed seven more killers.

10. William Stead (1849–1812) edited the *Pall Mall Gazette* and pioneered the "new journalism"—a blend of tabloid-style reporting and social activism. In 1893/1894 he traveled to Chicago to report on crime, prostitution, corrupt politicians, and the rancid conditions of the "protected" vice districts. He introduced his vividly written and shocking exposé to an audience of prominent businessmen and socialites at Central Music Hall. His book *If Christ Came to Chicago* resulted in a firestorm of municipal outrage and a persistent call for sweeping reform, but the entrenched gangs and vice mongers remained largely unaffected. Stead died on the *Titanic* in 1912.

11. Stead, William T., *If Christ Came to Chicago: A Plea for the Union of All Who Love in the Service of All Who Suffer*. Chicago: Chicago Historical Bookworks, 1990, reprint edition, pp. 243–244.

12. Robert Bruce died of acute alcoholism on January 3, 1895. In his office at Randolph and LaSalle Streets, he tacked up a sign that read: "Death to all thieves."

13. The district was originally known as "Little Cheyenne" before its borders melded into the larger Custom House Place Levee. Biler Avenue, its main artery, extended from Harrison to Polk Streets. Despite bitter complaints emanating from the rabbis of a Jewish synagogue on Pacific Avenue, "Irish Moll," Lillie Shafer, Ruby Bell, and other women in Dan Webster's house solicited men in the streets. The outraged residents of Cheyenne, Wyoming, retaliated by calling their hell's half acre "Little Chicago." Unamused, the Chicago City Council authorized a name change on June 12, 1901. Pacific Avenue officially became LaSalle Street in the belief that to improve the character of the street, it was necessary to change the name. The expanding presence of banking and financial institutions along old Pacific Avenue factored in the council decision.

14. "The Scarlet Sisters Everleigh," *Chicago Tribune*, January 19, 1936.

15. *Chicago Tribune*, June 26, 1905. "Kenna," Huret wrote, "is a little man, slender and blonde wearing doubtful linen . . . a drooping mustache and perhaps forty years old."

16. Doherty, James, "The Story of Bathhouse John: Chicago's Fabulous First Ward Alderman," *Chicago Tribune*, May 24, 1953. Also Kogan, Herman, and Wendt, Lloyd, *Lords of the Levee: The Story of Bathhouse John and Hinky Dink*. New York: Bobbs-Merrill, 1943, pp. 13–22.

17. Ike Bloom operated Freiberg's Dance Hall for twenty-two years. He weathered many police raids, vice crackdowns, and violations of the midnight closing laws. In May 1924 he sold the famous old dive to Jackey Adler, vice monger and "sportsman," and retreated to a property he owned in French Lick, Indiana, to recover his health. Adler renamed the dance hall the Midnight Frolic and capitalized on Prohibition opportunities. Comedian Joe E.

Lewis launched his career in the Frolic, and Al Capone, the gangster overlord responsible for ordering a criminal assault against Lewis in 1927 after the comic broke a contractual agreement to perform at the Green Mill, was a frequent patron. After the old Levee vice rings dispersed from Twenty-Second Street and spread southward into the suburbs straddling the Indiana state line, Bloom recouped and opened the Arrowhead Inn in Burnham, a roadhouse and bordello under the thumb of the Torrio-Capone mob. During Prohibition, Bloom opened the Deauville (named for the famous Parisian nightclub), a downtown Chicago cabaret at 72 West Randolph Street, but the place was constantly raided by dry agents, and even by three armed robbers who stormed into the place on January 20, 1926, and held Ike and his three brothers at gunpoint while they carted away $3,200. Bloom died of an undetermined illness in his North Side residence, 3520 North Sheridan Road, on December 14, 1930. The press reported that he had endured several painful amputations to keep him alive during the last two years of his life.

18. Collins, Charles, "Who Killed Big Jim Colosimo?" *Chicago Tribune*, February 7, 1954. For additional background, see also Sinnick, William, "Still Unsolved—Colosimo Murder," *Chicago Tribune*, June 19, 1938.

19. *Chicago Tribune*, November 13, 1960; and Schoenberg, Robert J., *Mr. Capone: The Real and Complete Story of Al Capone*. New York: William Morrow, 1992, pp. 23–24.

20. Harland, Robert O., *The Vice Bondage of a Great City, or, The Wickedest City in the World*. Chicago: Young People's Civic League, 1911, p. 103.

21. Ibid., p. 130.

22. "White Slave Inquiry On," *Chicago Tribune*, June 19, 1907.

23. The *Tribune* and other Chicago newspapers covered the anti-vice uproar day in and day out in September and October 1912. See, for example, "Wayman Clamps Lid on the Levee," *Chicago Tribune*, October 6, 1912; and Bilek, Arthur J., The *First Vice Lord: Big Jim Colosimo and the Ladies of the Levee*. Nashville, TN: Cumberland House, 2008, pp. 103–112.

24. See the *Chicago Tribune*, October 14, 1909, and the *Chicago American*, October 9–10, 1909.

25. In the frenzy following a July 26, 1914, Morals Squad raid on the "Turf," a Twenty-Second Street bagnio, detectives Fred Amart and Joseph Merrill mistook Birns for part of an advancing throng of menacing Levee hangers-on, and an errant shot killed the officer. Public outrage and negative press publicity is believed to be the final chapter. Press reports tell us that by 1919 the streets resembled a ghost town. However, the final date of the district's shutdown cannot be accurately determined. There were published reports of Levee resorts operating well into the 1920s.

26. John Patton served as Burnham village president continuously from 1907 until his retirement in 1949, at age sixty-six. Testifying before the U.S. Senate-Kefauver Rackets investigation in 1951, Patton freely admitted to being a pal of Al Capone and running illegal racetracks with the rackets boss. Patton died on December 23, 1956, ending a riotous, unprincipled life at age seventy-three.

27. In just one resort, Torrio employed ninety women working three shifts a day, earning the gang $9,000 a month.

28. "Wide Open Aboveboard Town? That's Burnham Says Mayor," *Chicago Tribune*, May 4, 1916.

29. Kelley, John, "Last of Chicago's Chinatown Treks to New Location," *Chicago Tribune*, February 6, 1927.

30. *Chicago Inter-Ocean*, May 26, 1908.

31. In 1910 there were only sixty-five women counted among the Chinese settlement in Chicago. Prostitution *and* the smuggling of Asian women into the country through illegal means was a consequence of the restrictive racial covenants set forth by the government at that time.

32. *Chicago Tribune*, March 2, 1977. Chicago police responded to the dramatic rise of Asian street gangs by forming the Asian Task Force in October 1989, but later disbanded the unit. The International Enterprise Crime Task Force, a larger task force under the direction of the FBI and the Illinois State Police, broadened the scope of the investigatory work and took over primary jurisdiction.

CHAPTER 3. GANGS OF THE SOUTH SIDE: POLITICS, PATRONAGE, AND BARE-KNUCKLE BOYOS, 1860–1930

1. "Chicago in 1840: Interesting Extracts from an Old Letter," *Chicago Tribune*, April 29, 1882. Loco Foco was a nickname applied to a member of the working men's faction of the Democratic Party opposed to state banking interests and monopolies, during the 1830s and 1840s. The term is said to have derived from a meeting in Tammany Hall, New York, October 29, 1835, when after a heated inter-party skirmish the chairman left his seat and the lights in the room were extinguished. Members in favor of extreme measures produced *loco-foco* matches, rekindled the lights, continued the meeting, and accomplished their aims.

2. Steffens, Lincoln, "Half Free and Fighting On," *McClure's Magazine*, October 1903. Reprinted in *The Shame of the Cities*, New York: McClure, Phillips, 1904.

3. Transcript of interview reported in "Murder at Bridgeport," *Chicago Tribune*, December 18, 1871.

4. Hagedorn, John M., *A World of Gangs: Armed Young Man and Gangsta Culture*. Minneapolis: University of Minnesota Press, 2008, p. 66.

5. The modern City of Chicago is comprised of fifty wards, each with one elected alderman. Bridgeport's Fourth and Fifth Wards later merged to become the city's Eleventh Ward, for decades the powerbase of Chicago's Democratic machine.

6. Laid out by General W. B. Archer, a member of the Illinois & Michigan Canal Commission, Archer Avenue followed an old Indian trail. Dubbed the "Archey Road," it was immortalized in the homespun humor of author Finley Peter Dunne through his fictional barkeep "Martin Dooley." Finley Dunne based the character of Dooley upon his personal dealings with downtown saloon keeper James "Red Jim" McGarry and the colorful and outspoken Bridgeport character John J. "Jawn" McKenna, who settled in the neighborhood in 1857 and lived there until his death in 1941. Dunne invented the Martin Dooley character during the World's Fair of 1893 and wrote a number of volumes reviving the whimsical Irish saloon keeper, including *Mr. Dooley in the Hearts of His Countrymen*.

7. McKenna served at various times as mayor of the town of Cicero, and Twenty-Eighth Ward committeeman in Chicago before retiring in 1900.

8. See "Mr Dooley's Pal Recalls Gay Ol McGarry Nights," *Chicago Tribune*, August 21, 1932.

9. A term loosely applied to a cabal of corrupt aldermen from the 1890s that profited from graft schemes, bribe taking, and the wholesale selling off of city utilities (e.g., gas and power, elevated railway rights) to private parties.

10. *Chicago Defender*, July 12, 1919.

11. "Hayne Blames Riot on Political Graft with Police," *Chicago Tribune*, July 29, 1919.

12. Bridgeport resident William Lynch was an important cog in the Daley machine. From the state senate, he leapfrogged to a judgeship in the Federal District Court of Chicago.

13. "Alderman Joseph McDonough Tells How He Was Shot at on South Side Visit—Says Enough Ammunition in Section to Last for Years of Guerilla Warfare," *Chicago Daily News*, July 30, 1919.

14. Edward J. Brundage was the uncle of Avery Brundage (1887–1976), who attained worldwide prominence as the fifth president of the International Olympic Committee, 1952–1972.

15. "Clubs Accused in Riot Arson Plots," *Chicago Daily News*, August 14, 1919.

16. Ibid.

17. From Prohibition through the 1940s, gambler, bootlegger, and labor racketeer Danny Stanton was one of Chicago's most notorious hoodlums. In the early 1940s, his name was added to a growing list of "Public Enemies" by the FBI and local law enforcement. For many years he ruled the South Side territory at Seventy-Seventh and Halsted Streets. On May 5, 1943, Stanton and a petty crook named Louis Dorman were executed by shotgun-wielding assassins inside the 6500 Club at 6500 South May Street. He was arrested numerous times for crimes ranging from bootlegging to bombings and murder, including the sensational slaying of gangster Jack Zuta in 1930. Ballistics showed that Stanton's gun had been used to kill Zuta. However, the Illinois Supreme Court voided his extradition order that would have brought him back from Wisconsin to Illinois after the shooting. A political power in his own right, this former Ragen Colt seized control of the Union of Bartenders, Waiters, and Food Handlers with Louis Romano, a reputed agent of Frank "the Enforcer" Nitti, successor to Al Capone after Capone went to prison in 1931. See Schoenberg, Robert, *Mr. Capone: The Real and Complete Story of Al Capone*. New York: William Morrow, 1992, p. 83.

18. "Policeman Curbs Raging of Ragen," *Chicago Tribune*, December 21, 1913.

19. "Ragen for McCormick's Job," *Chicago Tribune*, April 18, 1914.

20. Thrasher, Frederic Milton. *The Gang: A Study of 1,313 Gangs in Chicago*. Chicago: University of Chicago Press, 1927 (2000 edition published by New Chicago School Press), pp. 82–83; 158.

21. "Clubwomen See Fighting Girls End Wild Dance," *Chicago Tribune*, March 22, 1915, and "New Year Ball of Ragen's Colts Branded as Orgy," *Chicago Tribune*, January 3, 1918.

22. Joseph and Robert Brooks's father, Michael T. Brooks, founded the electrical worker's union 282 in the Stockyards District in the 1890s.

23. "Bad Boy Plague Causes Calling of Big Meeting," *Chicago Tribune*, June 24, 1923.

24. Ibid.

25. "Murder at Club of Ragen's Colts Arouses Dever," *Chicago Tribune*, March 9, 1926.

26. "Ragen Declares Regan Colts Record Good," *Chicago Tribune*, August 6, 1927. Hugo Bezdek (1884–1952) was an outstanding football star playing for Coach Amos Alonzo Stagg at the University of Chicago in 1906 but achieved greater fame as head football coach at Penn State, Arkansas, and Oregon.

27. "Ragen's Colts Deny Riot Responsibility," *Chicago Daily News*, August 2, 1919. "The members are drawn from the territory adjacent to the Stock-

yards and range in age from eighteen years or up to thirty or more. All day, scores hang around the clubhouse, while in the evenings several hundred gather there."

28. Tim Murphy was assassinated in front of his home at 2525 Morse Avenue in the Rogers Park section of Chicago on June 25, 1928. The eternally ambitious Murphy attempted a takeover of the ten-thousand-member Master Cleaning and Dyers Association, a union under the thumb of Al Capone. For this, he paid a high price as .45 caliber slugs, fired from pistol-wielding assassins in a passing car, killed him before he hit the ground.

29. Michael Boyle (1881–1958) allegedly acquired his colorful nickname as businessmen and politicians courting his favor stuffed envelopes of bribe money into the folds of his famous umbrella which he left propped up against the wall of his office.

30. See "Ragen's Union Plans Big Fight on Electric Company," *Chicago Tribune*, March 3, 1920.

31. "Guzik Hearing Explodes after Quiet Start," *Chicago Tribune*, May 14, 1946.

32. The case remained unsolved until the 1990s when a renewed investigation into a bevy of unsolved mob murders established that Lenny Patrick and Dave Yaras of the so-called Jewish Faction of the Chicago syndicate carried out the crime on the orders of mob honchos Guzik and Murray "the Camel" Humphries.

33. "All-American Gang Sought to End Teen Wars," *Chicago Tribune*, August 9, 1950.

34. Dan Ryan Jr. served as Cook County board president from 1954 to 1961. An important cog in the Democratic machine and a powerful ally of Mayor Richard J. Daley, Ryan succeeded his father on the board in 1923 and held his seat continuously until his own death in 1961. He is credited with advancing the plan to build the region's first "superhighway," the Northwest Expressway, later named the John F. Kennedy Expressway.

35. Hagedorn, *A World of Gangs*, p. 73.

CHAPTER 4. MAXWELL STREET, THE WEST SIDE TERROR DISTRICT, 1860–1930

1. "Firemen of '71 Tells Delay in Calling Pumper," *Chicago Tribune*, October 8, 1934.

2. "Centennial Eve Reveals Truth of Great Fire," *Chicago Tribune*, September 26, 1904.

3. "Moral Support," *Chicago Tribune*, October 11, 1872. See also Bales, Richard, *Great Chicago Fire and the Myth of Mrs. O'Leary's Cow*. Jefferson, NC: McFarland, 2005, pp. 90–95. Scouring through property index records from October 1871, Mr. Bales's meticulous research concludes that Daniel "Peg Leg" Sullivan, a local ne'er-do-well, was the likely culprit responsible for the fire's origin. Sullivan, who was identified in a much earlier history titled *The Great Chicago Fire*, authored by Chicago book critic Robert Cromie, is portrayed as something of a hero in the personal recollections of Mary Callahan. Mr. Bales believes it is improbable that Callahan and her friends would have returned to the party inside the McLaughlin barn in a calm, composed manner, pretending nothing had happened. However, this was the account Callahan provided to the press decades later. The debate over who was responsible for the fire that destroyed "The Garden City" remains a contentious one among historians, although Mr. Bales's hypothesis trumps most other theories, including the far-fetched notion that a comet struck Chicago that night.

4. *Chicago Globe*, January 21, 1889. The City Council Ordinance of 1902 defined a tenement house as "any house or building or portion thereof which is intended to or designed to be occupied or leased for occupation or actually occupied as a home or residence for three or more families living in separate apartments, each family doing cooking upon the premises."

5. For a good discussion of squalid tenement housing in Chicago, see Abbott, Edith, *The Tenements of Chicago: 1908–1935*. New York: Arno Press, 1970, pp. 28–31; 198–200.

6. "City Builder, 85, Tells Origins of Blighted Areas," *Chicago Tribune*, March 8, 1951. Born in Bavaria, Schmidt remembered witnessing the Chicago Fire as a small boy.

7. Maxwell Street was named after Dr. Philip Maxwell, the military surgeon at old Fort Dearborn. The famous open-air market was as much a state of mind as it was a melting pot of ethnic tribes; races and religions comingled with gang crime and political intrigue. For a good overview of Maxwell Street through the years, see Berkow, Ira, *Maxwell Street: Survival in a Bazaar*. Garden City, NY: Doubleday, 1977, pp. 5–11.

8. "Valley's Past Shines through Cloud of Today," *Chicago Tribune*, July 22, 1928.

9. "The Wickedest Spot in Chicago," *Chicago Tribune*, December 5, 1897.

10. Reprinted from the November 14, 1892, central station police blotter in the *Chicago Tribune*, November 13, 1892.

11. "Dr. John A Benson on Murder: He Analyzes the Crime and Disposition Thereto, Applying His Argument to Merry's Case," *Chicago Tribune*, December 20, 1897.

12. Henry Street was the original name of Fourteenth Place. Trucking warehouses and industrial buildings in-fill this former ghetto neighborhood in the modern day. It is hard to imagine that this area was once a densely crowded, dangerous slum.

13. "How Gangs of Boy Bandits Terrorize and Murder 100 People a Year," *Chicago Tribune*, January 28, 1906.

14. Ibid.

15. Moses Goodman was the first Jewish resident in the Maxwell Street District. He settled there in 1858.

16. "Mother Jails Boy Cop," *Chicago Tribune*, February 9, 1905.

17. "Ghetto in Terror over Bomb Tales," *Chicago Tribune*, May 26, 1908.

18. See "School Race War Costs Boy's Life," *Chicago Tribune*, March 11, 1906; and "Breaking Up Boy's Gangs," *Chicago Tribune*, March 13, 1906.

19. Founded by society matron Louise DeKoven Bowen, the JPA was not intended to serve as a charitable association or relief society, but rather to minimize delinquency among children, monitor social conditions, and guard against the "pitfalls" of neighborhood life leading to arrest. The association supported a detention home and paid the salary of Chicago's first probation officers, whom it selected and supervised. In later years, the association evolved into a watchdog agency concerned with community conditions and city and state legislation impacting youth.

20. The City of Chicago later changed the name of Johnson Street to Peoria Street, which it is today.

21. "Goggin Let's Go a Book," *Chicago Tribune*, August 29, 1896. Pugnacious, irrepressible Judge Goggin was a staunch Democrat who kept a safe distance from both reformers and the "bummer" element of his party controlled by Mike McDonald's ring of gamblers and saloon politicians. He never finished the book that he promised would blow the lid off of police corruption in the city, nor did he leave the City of Chicago. Goggin passed away from liver disease on March 29, 1898.

22. This is the same Charles Walgreen who founded Walgreens, the prominent national drugstore chain of the modern day.

23. "Dying Bandit Dictates Farewell to Wife," *Chicago American*, January 1, 1905; "Harry Feinberg Cheats Gallows: Dies in Hospital," *Chicago American*, January 5, 1905. The *American* reported that Feinberg and Gagen were close friends of the North Side "Car Barn Bandits" ring, discussed in chapter 5.

24. Founded in 1882 by Chicago's first archbishop, Patrick Feehan, as an orphan asylum, the school evolved into a manual training school. Cook County judges were granted the power to send dependent boys found on the streets to this institution.

25. For accounts of "Scully de Robber" and his progression from street urchin thievery to a career in crime, see the *Chicago Tribune*, June 22, 1884; August 27, 1890; August 29, 1896; and June 6, 1909.

26. *Chicago Tribune*, December 12, 1900.

27. Moe Annenberg, a product of the West Side ghetto, operated the National Racing Wire and established a publishing empire after buying the *Inquirer* in 1936. Annenberg was the father of Walter Annenberg, philanthropist and U.S. ambassador to the United Kingdom, 1969–1974, appointed by President Richard Nixon.

28. Political boss Manny Abrahams (1866–1913) brokered free peddler permits, bridewell pardons, and jobs. His aldermanic victory over Dennis Egan was tainted by allegations of election fraud in the spring of 1913, but he enjoyed the strong support of Mayor Carter Harrison II and the *Chicago Herald-Examiner*, the Democratic newspaper published by William Randolph Hearst. A product of the ghetto, Abrahams operated a saloon at 921 West Twelfth Street and Sangamon, which was twice bombed during his 1913 aldermanic run. He received his first political appointment in 1898 as bailiff of the Maxwell Street Police Court from Harrison. After delivering a long oration in city council chambers on July 1, 1913, Abrahams collapsed in his chair, the victim of a fatal heart attack.

29. Goldstein said that he was empowered to collect these fees by the corporation counsel's office. The Jefferson Street businessmen's plea that their street remain unchanged was ignored (*Chicago Tribune*, June 10, 1913).

30. "Dictator of Fish Market Charged with Conspiracy," *Chicago Tribune*, July 20, 1928.

31. Eller's son Emmanuel served as a municipal court judge. With his father, he was indicted in 1929 and later acquitted of election-fraud charges. Fifteen other Eller henchmen went to jail however.

32. "Morton, Miller Tell How They Killed Police," *Chicago Tribune*, January 7, 1922.

33. Ibid.

34. Lyle, John A., *The Dry and Lawless Years: The Crusade against Public Enemies and Corrupt Officials in Chicago*. New York: Prentice Hall, 1960, pp. 137–138; *Chicago Herald & Examiner*, January 8, 1922.

35. "Bomb, Bullets for Hershie," *Chicago Tribune*, March 14, 1924. The shaky business partnership between the Miller brothers and North Side bootlegger Dion O'Banion, and the bad blood that followed, is told in Keefe, Rose, *Guns and Roses: The Untold Story of Dion O'Banion, Chicago's Big Shot before Al Capone*. Nashville, TN: Cumberland House, 2003, pp. 155–158.

CHAPTER 5. THE GOLD COAST AND THE GANGS: NORTH SIDE AFFLUENCE, LITTLE HELL, AND GANG CRIME, 1860–1930

1. Goose Island is situated in the North Branch of the Chicago River and is utilized primarily for industrial output. For more on the Kilgubbin settlement in this location, see Robinson, J. Nicole, "The Irish of Kilgubbin," *Chicago History Magazine*, Fall 2014, vol. 39, no. 3.

2. *Chicago Tribune*, August 30, 1868.

3. "Market Street Gang: Chicago's Noted Criminal Band," *Chicago Sunday Herald*, January 6, 1895.

4. Educator and philanthropist Eli Bates (1805–1881) established the first Unitarian church in Chicago. Changing neighborhood demographics and the improved recreational facilities closed the Bates House in 1938. In March of that year it was formally dissolved by order of Judge Cornelius Harrington of the circuit court. The Chicago Community Trust acquired the assets of the charity.

5. "Prosperity and Poverty, Fashion and Crime Are Near Neighbors on the North Side," *Chicago Tribune*, March 18, 1906.

6. "Politics Were Colorful in the Days of John F. O'Malley," *Chicago Tribune*, September 13, 1953.

7. It was common in nineteenth-century Chicago for opportunistic and unsavory gambler-saloon politicians to jump parties in order to win an aldermanic or legislative seat as the most expedient way to safeguard their business interests. John Rogers, another aspiring politico mired in the illegal gambling rackets in the West Side Eighteenth Ward, claimed an aldermanic seat on the Republican ticket after being rejected by the Democrats.

8. Dr. Patrick Henry Cronin was a prominent Chicago physician and a member of Clan Na Gael, known to its members as the United Brotherhood, an American political organization for promoting Irish independence. It was formed to replace the Fenian Brotherhood, which was discredited in America after its ill-conceived attempt to invade Canada in 1866. Cronin's murder was the result of a conspiracy motivated by personal ambivalence and political reasons. Dan Coughlin, iceman Patrick O'Sullivan, and Martin Burke were convicted of murder and sent to prison for life. John Beggs was acquitted while John Kunze was convicted of manslaughter and sent to prison for three years. It was revealed that a significant contingent of cops secretly belonged to Clan Na Gael, and devoted much of their working time serving the society rather than carrying out their law-enforcement duties.

Dickie Dean passed away February 7, 1919. The well-traveled Market Street conman had been removed from his constable's post and lived out his life as a conman.

9. "O'Malley at Home Again: Cheers Follow Him from the Criminal Court," *Chicago Tribune*, February 14, 1897.

10. "Mayor Takes the Stump," *Chicago Tribune*, March 31, 1900. Also, "Sampson Wins the Day," *Chicago Tribune*, March 13, 1900.

11. "Stormy Life Nearing End," *Chicago Tribune*, November 17, 1904.

12. "Constables Held to Grand Jury," *Chicago Tribune*, September 6, 1901.

13. "McCabe, Wright and Phalen Held," *Chicago Tribune*, July 8, 1891, and "Epidemic of Shooting," *Chicago Tribune*, July 8, 1891.

14. Thrasher, Frederic Milton, *The Gang: A Study of 1,313 Gangs in Chicago*. Chicago: University of Chicago Press, 1927, p. 20.

15. "Tell of Murder Record: Scrapbook of Doings of Automatic Trio Was Kept," *Chicago Tribune*, July 26, 1904.

16. Asbury, Herbert, *Chicago: Gem of the Prairie*. New York: Alfred Knopf, 1940, p. 225. The *Chicago Tribune* published an interesting retrospective on the case, February 5, 1939: "Chicago's Car Barn Bandits: Relentless Killers, They Met Relentless Law."

17. Asbury, *Chicago: Gem of the Prairie*, pp. 224–225.

18. William Blaul rose to the rank of deputy chief of detectives in 1932. He was a part of that old-line cadre of Chicago police officers who saw nothing wrong with imposing on uncooperative suspects whatever physical punishment deemed necessary. The "third degree sweat," the infamous practice of extracting a confession from a criminal suspect, came frequently under fire from civil libertarians throughout departmental history. Blaul was cited for heroism many times and won the Carter H. Harrison Medal for bravery in the take-down of the Car Barn Bandits. He died on June 25, 1939, at age seventy-two.

19. "Tells How Marx Slew Policeman," *Chicago Tribune*, February 12, 1904.

20. "Car Barn Bandits Tired of Murder Taken in Battle," *Chicago Tribune*, November 28, 1903.

21. "Roeski's Life One of Fear," *Chicago Tribune*, November 28, 1903.

22. "Bandit Jury in Weary Deadlock," *Chicago Tribune*, March 12, 1904. See also *Chicago Inter-Ocean*, January 6, 1904. Selection of twelve venire men lacking prejudice against the defendants in this case was particularly challenging for the four attorneys handling the defense.

23. "Begs for Van Dine's Life in Last Plea for Bandit," *Chicago Tribune*, March 4, 1904.

24. Ibid.

25. "Bandit Jury in Weary Deadlock," *Chicago Tribune*, March 12, 1904.

26. "Car Barn Bandits Die on Gallows," *Chicago Inter-Ocean*, April 22, 1904.

27. "Henning Recalls Gun and Murder Spree of the Car Barn Gang," *Chicago Tribune*, January 5, 1954. For chilling accounts of the execution of the Car Barn Bandits in front of two hundred witnesses in the Cook County Jail, see the *Chicago Inter-Ocean* and the *Chicago Daily Journal*, April 22, 1904.

28. "Six Murders Are Charged to Band Led by Wheed," *Chicago Tribune*, September 5, 1917.

29. The Eddie Wheed crime spree spurred indignant civic elites into action on many fronts. The formation of the venerable Chicago Crime Commission, one of the nation's oldest civilian watchdog agencies, followed. Virgil W. Peterson, the commission's high-profile and long-serving executive director, discussed the Wheed case as a catalyst for the birth of the organization in "How Ammunition Eddie Wheed Triggered City's War on Crime," an article he published in the *Tribune*, February 19, 1961.

30. "Gemmill Toots Fiery Blast at Crime Shouters," *Chicago Tribune*, May 15, 1920.

31. Ibid.

32. "Coroner Traeger, in Annual Report, Says Carrying of Concealed Weapons Is One Great Cause of Homicides—Official Statement Has Supporting Facts," *Chicago Inter-Ocean*, December 3, 1903. The handgun crisis in Chicago is nearly as old as the city itself, and just as unstoppable. Traeger reported that out of 118 homicides in 1903, only eleven were found to be "justified." Seventy-eight deaths were caused by shooting. Ninety-one were held to the grand jury on charges of murder, and twelve as accessories. Concealed handguns were at the root of the problem. Purchasers of guns were not required to register their names, addresses, or provide identification at this time.

33. Ibid. Others echoed this sentiment. One Frank Johnson, in the same article, added: "The saloon dives and the extensive advertising of criminals by the yellow press encourage a great deal of crime. The yellow journals make the criminals appear like heroes. By closing the saloons where criminals hide, the hold-up men would be without refuge."

34. Morici was eventually convicted of murder—the first successful Black Hand conviction in Chicago.

35. Lombardo, Robert M., *The Black Hand: Terror by Letter in Chicago*. Chicago: University of Illinois Press, 2009, pp. 17–18.

36. Between June 1914 and June 1915, Chicago police recorded 300 shootings in the North Side Italian colony. Most, it appears, were Black Hand-related. Catalanetto, a self-described olive oil vendor, inspired fear and loathing among the residents of Little Italy. Alternately known as "Silver

King" and "Don Pietro, King of the Black Hand," he was felled by Michael Locascio. One of his extortion victims put an end to the demands for money by shooting Catalanetto on the North Side. A predictable act of vengeance followed. A Black Hand assassin had pumped six bullets into Locascio's fifty-one-year-old mother, Angelina. Then John Locascio extracted a final revenge by gunning down John Catalanetto. And so went the primitive, old-world barbarity year after year.

37. "Black Hand Warns Sleuth to Drop Kidnapping Inquiry," *Chicago Tribune*, August 28, 1911. For more on Black Hand mail extortion, see "Black Hand Art Seen in Letters," *Chicago Tribune*, May 8, 1914.

38. Lombardo, *The Black Hand*, pp. 89–90. Also "Kidnappers Free, Victims Suffer," *Chicago Tribune*, May 4, 1914; *Chicago Daily Journal*, May 4, 1914.

39. "Launch Battle on Delinquency in Little Hell," *Chicago Tribune*, July 21, 1934.

40. Perkins, Useni Eugene, *Explosion of Chicago's Black Street Gangs: 1900 to the Present*. Chicago: Third World Press, 1987, pp. 19–20.

41. Jacobs, Jane, *The Death and Life of Great American Cities*. New York: Random House, 1961, pp. 170–171.

42. See "Byrne Moves into Cabrini; Gang Raided," *Chicago Tribune*, April 1, 1981; "Byrne Leaves Cabrini for Now," *Chicago Tribune*, April 22, 1981.

43. See Wellman, James K., *The Gold Coast Church and the Ghetto: Christ & Culture in Mainline Protestantism*. Champaign, IL: University of Illinois Press, 1999, pp. 171–175.

44. In 2002 Currie won a $3 million dollar judgment from the CHA after filing a lawsuit alleging that the CHA and the security guards they employed had failed to protect her. The convicted assailant responsible for this horrific crime had procured the roach poison from an adjoining apartment.

45. Gallun, Alby, "Around Cabrini-Green, the Future Looks Bright," *Crain's Chicago Business*, July 19, 2014.

CHAPTER 6. THE GANGS OF PROHIBITION-ERA CHICAGO

1. "On Temperance Day," *Chicago Tribune*, October 7, 1894.
2. "The Temperance Temple," *Chicago Tribune*, May 3, 1890.
3. "United Societies Flay Blue Laws," *Chicago Tribune*, February 10, 1909.
4. "Wets Turn Guns on Saloon Foes," *Chicago Tribune*, May 30, 1910.
5. "Prohibition—Still Rankling after 25 Years," *Chicago Tribune*, November 30, 1958.

6. Quoted in Gottfried, Alex, *Boss Cermak of Chicago*. Chicago: University of Chicago Press, 1962, p. 118.

7. Hecht, Ben, "The Noble Experiment," *Playboy*, December 1963, pp. 174–175; 222–230; 233.

8. "Memoirs, Thompson, Part IV," *Chicago Tribune*, August 1, 1954. Although they were of the same party in their political loyalties, *Tribune* publisher Colonel Robert R. McCormick remained a bitter and strident foe of Mayor Thompson. At one point in the 1920s Thompson sued the *Tribune* for libel, but the mayor came up a loser in the civil litigation.

9. Fred Lundin, a born showman with a passion for politics and self-promotion, arrived in Chicago a penniless twelve-year-old Swedish immigrant barely able to speak ten words of English. Throughout his career in public life, he prided himself on his humble roots, adapting the nickname "The Poor Swede." Like many nineteenth-century street urchins, he got his start bootblacking and peddling newspapers on the street. He made the rounds of the political saloons and became a favorite of the roistering lads of Quincy No. 9, a popular hangout for reporters and politicians. Donning a long-tailed frock coat, a string tie, slouch hat, and amber-colored eyeglasses, Lundin went around downtown and the outlying districts in what might reasonably be called a "circus cart," promoting and selling a home-brewed temperance beverage he called "Juniper Ade." His two helpers sang and strummed banjos to draw in customers who listened to Lundin's blathering. His peculiarities and undeniable crowd appeal drew the attention of Henry L. Hertz, a West Side Republican political boss. Lundin, sensing a greater political harvest with U.S. senator William Lorimer, helped Lorimer claim Hertz's territory and was rewarded with the party's support in the 1894 election. Voters sent Lundin to the Illinois House for one term, and later to Washington as a congressman from the Seventh District. After Congress impeached Lorimer and removed him from the U.S. Senate in 1901 for malfeasance, Lundin returned to Chicago and built a strong North Side political organization and cast his lot with Thompson, who rewarded him with the job of patronage boss. By 1921 he controlled the destiny of forty thousand city, county, and state workers. Not long after, he and twenty-three other political types were indicted on a charge of defrauding the Chicago Public Schools out of $1 million. Lundin avoided a conviction and jail time through the brilliant courtroom defense put up by Clarence Darrow. Thompson and Lundin parted company and became bitter enemies. Prohibition sealed the doom of the Republican Party in Cook County, and the "Poor Swede" exited the political picture by 1938. He died in Beverly Hills, California, in 1947.

10. "Big Bill Sets His Big Rats on Old Pals," *Chicago Tribune*, April 7, 1926; and *Chicago Herald & Examiner*, April 7, 1926.

11. "Swedish Club Raps Thompson for Rat Exhibit," *Chicago Tribune*, December 18, 1926.

12. It is believed that Capone and his top advisors, including Pacelli and several other political types, secretly met here in October 1928 to formulate secret plans to eliminate the North Side Gang controlled by George "Bugs" Moran once and for all. Capone and his brothers had owned the heavily fortified compound, including a bunkhouse and caretaker's cottage, beginning in 1925. Guarded by a stone gun tower and a guesthouse with eighteen-inch-thick walls, the property sits on 407 acres and overlooks Blueberry Lake. A handcut stone fireplace and custom-made spiral staircases imported from Chicago reflect the extravagance of Capone, a chronic spendthrift. Years later the new owners opened the building as a restaurant and tourist destination called "Capone's Hideaway," but the venture failed, forcing a public auction conducted by Sawyer County, Wisconsin, in 2009. The Chippewa Valley Bank paid $2.6 million to acquire the entire property. They were the only bidders.

13. See "Serritella and Capone Deliver for Thompson," *Chicago Tribune*, February 20, 1931. Serritella's influence reached deep into the Chicago police cadre. Crime Commission investigator Shirley Kub testified that he controlled "the action" in the First District, and regulated policing of the cabarets and after-hours haunts. "Spy Tells Jury Serritella Is Loop Dictator," *Chicago Tribune*, March 27, 1931.

14. "I Remember Prohibition, Part Six—Portrait of a Gangster," *Chicago Tribune*, March 11, 1951.

15. Thrasher, Frederic Milton, *The Gang: A Study of 1,313 Gangs in Chicago*. Chicago: University of Chicago Press, 1927, pp. 6–7.

16. "Take Gunmen or Kill Them," *Chicago Tribune*, October 26, 1925.

17. Schoenberg, Robert, *Mr. Capone: The Real and Complete Story of Al Capone*. New York: William Morrow, 1992, p. 59.

18. "Frankie Lake Goes to Dance: Lands in Jail," *Chicago Tribune*, January 28, 1930.

19. "Mustache Pete" was a street term applied to older, out-of-step with the times, pre-Prohibition crime bosses from Sicily or the Italian mainland by younger American-born hoodlums looking to move up in the criminal world. "Big Jim" Colosimo, slain on May 11, 1920, in the vestibule of his restaurant by killers unknown, and "Diamond Joe" Esposito fall into this class.

20. Cavallero was later identified as Tony Spano, a former henchman imported from Italy to provide "street muscle," who became a bitter foe of the Gennas. Police suspected Spano was responsible for more than just the one Genna murder. Retaliation came in August 1926, when Spano was gunned

down outside of a barber shop on West Division Street. A twelve-year-old boy named Tony Aiello was named as the shooter.

21. In April 1929 Detective Chief John Stege put out a nationwide bulletin for the arrest of Frank Marco, a New York and Chicago gunman linked to Aiello as Lombardo's shooter.

22. See Bergreen, Laurence, *Capone: The Man and the Era*. New York: Touchstone, 1996, pp. 314–315.

23. Brashler, William, *The Don: The Life and Death of Sam Giancana*. New York: Harper & Row, 1975, pp. 22–23.

24. James Touhy Jr. was killed by a police officer during a 1917 robbery attempt. John Touhy was accidentally shot to death by one of his own men inside the Lone Tree Inn, straddling the Niles-Chicago boundary line, on December 28, 1927, while trying to strong-arm the owner into buying his beer. Brother Joe Touhy was killed in an exchange of gunfire with Victor Willert, owner of the Windmill Tavern in Schiller Park, on October 11, 1929, after he had failed to get Willert to agree to buy his beer.

25. "The Roger Touhy Story: The Syndicate Wanted His Territory," *Chicago Tribune*, March 9, 1958. See also the full-length autobiography written with Ray Brennan, *The Stolen Years*. Cleveland, OH: Pennington Press, 1959.

26. In truth, Roger Touhy's record showed two arrests for disorderly conduct in 1921 and a charge of carrying a concealed weapon in 1933. He never served time for these offenses.

27. "The Murder of Roger Touhy," *Chicago Tribune*, December 18, 1959.

28. Lindberg, Richard, *To Serve and Collect: Chicago Politics and Police Corruption from the Lager Beer Riot to the Summerdale Scandal, 1855–1960*. Westport, CT: Praeger, 1991, quoted on p. 204.

29. Following the repeal of Prohibition, Eliot Ness (1903–1957) was transferred to the mid-South / border states region as a tax agent to arrest hillbilly moonshiners in Ohio, Kentucky, and Tennessee refusing to register and pay taxes to the government. In 1934 he was sent to Cleveland to serve as the Director of Public Safety with authority over all policing agencies, but he achieved negligible results. Ness was unsuccessful in identifying the mysterious "Torso Killer," otherwise known as the "Mad Butcher of Kingsbury Run," that had terrorized the city 1935–1938. At least twelve and possibly many more victims were attributed to this unknown killer. Failing in his bid to win the Cleveland mayoralty, he moved to Washington, D.C., and eventually retired in obscurity. After several disastrous marriages, and Ness's death on May 16, 1957, author Oscar Fraley published a flattering but wildly exaggerated biography of the forgotten Chicago crime fighter that was picked up by DesiLu Productions in Hollywood and turned into a

television anthology series, *The Untouchables*, starring tough guy Robert Stack in the lead role. The show ran from 1959 to 1963. Stack's deadpan, prickly persona in no way reflected the real-life Eliot Ness.

30. Schofield's Flower Shop, a relic of Chicago's gang wars, fell to the wrecker's ball on August 13, 1960. Ironically the former home of a band of killers had been utilized by the Young People's Club of Holy Name Cathedral in its final years. Today the site is a parking lot.

31. As a direct consequence, Morgan Collins demoted and transferred Hughes to the Irving Park Station on November 19, 1924, as punishment for his collegiality with known gangsters in the Forty-Second Ward. He refused the demotion and quit, but returned to the department after William Hale Thompson won the mayoralty in 1927. With a good-natured slap on the back, Thompson welcomed Hughes and said, "Go get 'em Mike!" Hughes completed a thirty-nine-year police career in 1935.

32. Pasley, Fred D., *Al Capone: The Biography of a Self-Made Man*. New York: Ives Washington, 1930, p. 43.

33. Schoenberg, *Mr. Capone*, p. 161.

34. The SMC Cartage building, a squat, innocuous low-slung two-story structure, was a transshipment point for liquor distribution.

35. Ownership of the Moran-Heyer garage at 2122 North Clark Street changed hands after the massacre. Charles Werner and his wife, Alma, purchased the building and operated it as an antiques warehouse and storage company from 1949 up through July 1967 when the city's Department of Urban Renewal demolished it. The Werners were frustrated by the endless procession of tourists and curiosity seekers coming in off the street asking to view the wall. Many of them would not take no for an answer. The demolition of the dubious old landmark ironically coincided with the release of the motion picture *The St. Valentine's Day Massacre*, starring Jason Robards and George Segal. After the Werners exited the business, and the building was reduced to rubble, nightclub owner George Patey, in Vancouver, Canada, purchased 417 chipped, bullet-scarred bricks and built them into the interior wall of the men's room of the Banjo Palace in back of the urinals. Later, after the nightclub closed, the bricks were reportedly auctioned off, and many of them are in the hands of private collectors. The massacre site is today an empty lot adjacent to a senior citizen's home that went up in 1967. Because of its dubious notoriety, the City of Chicago refuses to place a commemorative plaque or historical marker on the site, although the deeply held fascination with the crime and with the era has never waned.

36. Keefe, Rose, *Guns and Roses: The Untold Story of Dion O'Banion, Chicago's Big Shot before Al Capone*. Nashville, TN: Cumberland House,

2003. Rose Keefe postulates that Moran and Ted Newberry arrived outside the garage seconds after the killers alighted from the phony police cruiser and entered the building. Thinking that it was a legitimate raid, they retreated to a coffee shop to wait it out.

37. Harry Keywell served thirty-four years of a life sentence for murdering three Chicago gangsters trying to infiltrate the Detroit underworld in 1931. This famous Michigan crime was also termed a "massacre"—the Collingwood Manor Apartment Massacre.

38. See "Wickersham Heads Hoover Crime Board," *Chicago Tribune*, May 21, 1929.

39. Historians are unanimous in the opinion that the Wickersham Report misfired in its simplistic conclusions, sticking the taxpayers with an immense bill for research documents that, according to author Bill Helmer, "joined other mammoth and costly government studies quickly entombed in the bowels of libraries that hold Congressional records." The Wickersham Committee assigned agent Guy L. Nichols to Chicago to drive about the city snapping photographs of known gangster haunts. Nichols visited downstate towns and villages concluding that Springfield, the capital city, Danville, Quincy, Rockford, East St. Louis, Peoria, Bloomington, and Joliet were all "equally bad." The serious committee work relied heavily on the scholarship of John Landesco, an important and respected sociologist from the University of Chicago and the author of *The Illinois Crime Survey*. Landesco rightfully traced the blame for lawlessness in Chicago to a larger issue. Rampant crime was not merely due to an influx of criminals into the system and a faulty justice and penal system allowing them free reign, but systemic patterns of corruption, collusion, and parasitic cooperation between the underworld and politicians that had flourished and grown stronger for decades prior to the passage of the Volstead Act. See Helmer, William J., with Mattix, Rick, *Public Enemies: America's Criminal Past 1919–1940*. New York: Checkmark Books, 1998, pp. 61–66.

40. "Another Wickersham Report," *Chicago Tribune*, July 10, 1931. The dead inmate was incarcerated at the Washington State Reformatory.

41. "Rakes Chicago as Wide Open: Ruled by Gangs," *Chicago Tribune*, March 4, 1931; and "Chicago's Gang Life Described by U.S. Report," *Chicago Tribune*, March 5, 1931.

42. Although their methods were often questionable, the Secret Six helped put an end to the worst of the bootlegging wars through their campaign to rid the city of Capone. The "Six" included Frank Loesch; Colonel Robert Isham Randolph, president of the Chicago Association of Commerce; banker and socialite J. Russell Forgan; and philanthropist Julius Rosenwald. Day-to-day investigative work, surveillance, and infiltration duties were assigned

to: Alexander Jamie; Chicago police detectives Michael Ahern (chief of the Traffic Division); Captain Roy Steffans; Lieutenant Charles Tousinski; Jamie's assistant, Edgar Dudley; and Shirley Kub, police stool pigeon and the duplicitous ex-girlfriend of gangster Jack Zuta and a double agent serving both the gangsters and the Six. Colonel Randolph fired Mrs. Kub on January 18, 1933. Because of Kub's embarrassing antics and pending lawsuits, the Secret Six disbanded under pressure on April 19, 1933. For further insight into the Chicago Crime Commission and the Secret Six, see Helmer and Mattix, *Public Enemies*, pp. 291–292.

43. See "John Stege: Fighting Cop," *Chicago Tribune*, May 25, 1952, for a good career retrospective of this tough but honest police official by James Doherty.

CHAPTER 7. SCHOOLS FOR CRIME

1. "Gangs Seen Broken," *Chicago Tribune*, May 5, 1932.
2. Thrasher, Frederic Milton, *The Gang: A Study of 1,313 Gangs in Chicago*. Chicago: University of Chicago Press, 1927, pp. 112–113.
3. Author interview with Daniel Kelley, January 16, 2015.
4. "Officials and Parents Share Crime Blame," *Chicago Tribune*, December 15, 1926.
5. Hirsch, Foster, *The Dark Side of the Screen*. New York: Da Capo Press, 1981, p. 72.
6. Ibid.
7. "Youths Replace Gangs in Crime, Courts Disclose," *Chicago Tribune*, March 16, 1938.
8. At the behest of the Cook County Board, the name of the Juvenile Detention Center was officially changed to the Audy Home in June 1950 after Arthur J. Audy, the thirty-eight-year-old superintendent, who died of a heart attack on March 2, 1950. Audy ran the institution for ten years, from 1940 to 1950.
9. Galamoy, Terry, "Audy: Way Station for Kids Nobody Wants," *Chicago Tribune Magazine*, March 9, 1969.
10. "Bare Coddling of Tough Boys at St. Charles," *Chicago Tribune*, April 12, 1939.
11. See "Gates Aids with $10,000," *Chicago Tribune*, May 1, 1902. Gates's rainmaking ability brought in $22,000 from New York financiers.
12. "Votes for St. Charles Home," *Chicago Tribune*, March 16, 1903.
13. Ibid.

14. "Plan of St. Charles Home," *Chicago Tribune*, September 24, 1902. The Illinois School of Agriculture and Manual Training for Boys, at Glenwood, opened in 1888. The school was placed under the inspectional control of the State Commissioner of Public Charities. In its first eleven years, Glenwood received 2,333 boys. In its promotional literature, the institution closely followed the "ordinary grammar schools, pupils being trained in eight grades substantially along the lines established in the public schools." See related article by Hash, Phillip M., "The Glenwood Manual Training School Band," *Journal of Band Research*, Spring 2012.

15. Brashler, William, *The Don: The Life and Death of Sam Giancana*. New York: Harper & Row, 1977, pp. 45–46.

16. "A Reformatory at Last," *Chicago Tribune*, July 31, 1949.

17. Wooden, Kenneth, *Weeping in the Playtime of Others: America's Incarcerated Children*. 2nd ed. Columbus, OH: Ohio State University Press, 2000, p. 144. The state converted the 270-acre, six-hundred-thousand-square-foot Sheridan Correctional Center into an adult prison on August 13, 1973.

18. "A Judge Fights for Society's Castoffs," *Chicago Tribune*, October 15, 1974.

19. "War on Juvenile Crime Declared by Commission," *Chicago Tribune*, February 25, 1928.

20. "Juvenile Crime a Weed in City's Social Garden," *Chicago Tribune*, March 22, 1938.

21. "War on Juvenile Crime Declared by Commission," *Chicago Tribune*, February 25, 1938.

22. "Smash Four Boy Bandit Gangs," *Chicago Tribune*, December 7, 1938.

23. "Gangs of Boys Part of City's Poverty Growth," *Chicago Tribune*, December 11, 1931.

24. "New Club Aims to Keep Boys Out of Gangs," *Chicago Tribune*, February 8, 1931. Louis Valentine (1866–1940), president of the Valentine-Seaver Furniture Company, was a major benefactor and national director of the Chicago Boys Clubs. He donated nearly $600,000 of his fortune to promote the work of the organization. "Because we have no children of our own, we want to help the sons of others," he announced on May 31, 1929. "Mrs. Valentine and I, after discussing the matter, decided that since we made our wealth in Chicago we should give back to the city. There is no better way than to build manhood." He funded construction of the Valentine Boys Club at Thirty-Fourth and Emerald in Bridgeport, erected as a memorial to his wife in 1939.

25. "Calls on Pupils to Help Banish Gangs," *Chicago Tribune*, February 23, 1930.

26. "Cleveland Woos Its Young Gangs into Clubhouses," *Chicago Tribune*, July 21, 1939.

27. Street gangs of the late 1940s and 1950s adapted "bopping" and "jamming," the common "jive" argot of younger-generation jazz musicians stylizing a free-form fast tempo minus the orchestration of traditional 1930s swing music. The chaotic rhythms symbolized a broader rejection of societal standards and altered popular music tastes in profound ways by fomenting a subversive lifestyle attractive to youth. The drug-addled lives of many of the bebop jazz men presaged the counterculture by two decades, but in many ways inadvertently inspired a rising tide of juvenile delinquency and violent street gangs in the 1950s.

28. Similar efforts were later inaugurated in Boston and around the country. Boston's "Operation Cease Fire," launched in 1996, sought to implement a method of problem-oriented policing to curb youth violence. The program was aimed at a core group of youths responsible for much of the city's escalating homicide problem. The impact was immediate. In the first two years the number of youth homicides fell to ten. However, priorities shifted and the program was curtailed, and not surprisingly the youth homicide rate escalated.

29. Peterson, Virgil W., "The Problem of Teen-Age Gangs," *Chicago Tribune*, October 4, 1953.

30. The City of Chicago in the modern day is divided into seventy-seven distinct geographic neighborhoods, each given a place name.

31. "Elgin Police Seize Two Green Car Bandits," *Chicago Tribune*, August 23, 1946.

32. "Bad boy" Tony Kapsis served eight years in the Pontiac Correctional Center for his involvement in the Green Car robberies. Through the intervention of Monsignor James Whalen, the Catholic priest assigned to the prison, Kapsis turned his life around. He learned the barber's trade, moved to Hartford, Connecticut, and earned a college degree.

33. "Parents Urge Killer Suspect to Surrender," *Chicago Tribune*, August 11, 1946.

34. The Chicago Parental School, which opened on July 4, 1902, spread across a forty-acre tract of North Side land, was built for truants and wayward boys showing antisocial classroom behavior. The Board of Education, urged on by the Chicago Women's Club and a successful lobbying effort in Springfield, were satisfied that they had succeeded in providing "parental care, discipline, and instruction" to miscreant boys in a rural "cottage setting" minus forced confinement in dormitories that were akin to prison cells. For nearly six decades the Parental School operated as a *real* school, in its strictest sense, with a mission to disavow the harsh penal aspects common in institutions charged with

reforming young men in trouble with the law. Administrators boasted that this was neither a reform school nor a detention center but instead, in the learned view of contemporary educators, a progressive educational movement to obviate the many abuses, brutalities, and scandals of the past. By the late 1950s the Parental School (renamed in its final years the Chicago Residential School) began to empty. The school's long, slow period of decline continued up until 1974 when changing public attitudes concerning the forced confinement of truants finally softened. The inability to secure state funding signaled the end of the line for the seventy-two-year-old institution that same year.

35. "Nab Illinois Bandit in Corn Field," *Chicago Tribune*, August 17, 1961.

36. "Why Did Vito Gang Hate Graver?" *Chicago Tribune*, May 14, 1954.

37. "Clem Graver's Kidnapping Tied to Vicious Gang by Two Bits of Evidence," *Chicago Tribune*, May 16, 1954.

38. In 1947 Chicago ward boundaries were remapped and the famous "Bloody Twentieth Ward" of yesteryear, encompassing the Valley District and Maxwell Street, became the Twenty-First Ward.

CHAPTER 8. GANGS BECOMING NATIONS, 1950–1989

1. Mackey, Wade C., and Immerman, Ronald S., "The Presence of the Social Father in Inhibiting Young Men's Violence," *Mankind Quarterly*, vol. 44, Spring 2004. See pp. 339–366.

2. Quoted in Hirschmann, Nancy J., and Liebert, Ulrike, eds., *Women and Welfare: Theory and Practice in the United States and Europe.* Piscataway, NJ: Rutgers University Press, 2001. See Kittay, Eva Feder, "From Welfare to Public Ethic Care," p. 41.

3. "Parents Held to Blame for Young Gangs," *Chicago Tribune*, March 18, 1957.

4. Ibid.

5. Sociologists and demographers identify those born between 1946 and 1964 as the "baby boom generation."

6. In Great Britain the greaser style was adapted by the so-called Teddy Boys.

7. "Stritch Urges Catholics: Ban Rock and Roll," *Chicago Tribune*, March 1, 1957.

8. "Laws to Punish Parents Urged by Gutknecht," *Chicago Tribune*, October 28, 1954.

9. Hearings before the Subcommittee to Investigate Juvenile Delinquency (Comic Books) of the Committeee of the Judiiciary,U.S. Senate, 83rd Congress, 1954. Comic books and Juvenile Delinquency, 84th Congress, First Session,

Report no. 62, "Crime and Horror Comics as a Contributing Factor in Juvenile Delingquency," section iv. Washington, D.C.: Committee on the Judiciary, 1955.

10. Short, James F., Jr., "The Study of Delinquency." In Sills, David L., and Merton, Robert K., eds., *The International Encyclopedia of the Social Sciences*. Vol. 4. New York: Macmillan, 1968.

11. In April 1993, Superintendent Matt Rodriguez inaugurated the Chicago Alternative Police Strategy (CAPS), a modern community policing initiative that borrowed heavily from the "constable on patrol" beat watch of yesteryear. CAPS encouraged dialogue between community members and district officers through ongoing beat meetings coordinated by district advisory committees. Predictably, attendance at beat meetings was highest in poorer inner-city neighborhoods with soaring crime rates, bad schools, and gang presence. Between 1991 and 2002, violent crime decreased by 49 percent and property crime by 36 percent, according to the 2004 Chicago Community Policing Evaluation Consortium. However gang-related and drug-related homicides proved more difficult to counter. In general, the attending drop in crime paralleled other large cities during this ten-year period.

12. "File on Teen-Age Gangs Averts Bloody War," *Chicago Tribune*, November 13, 1956. Delaney was firm but fair in his dealings with troubled youth. Promoted to captain, Michael Delaney oversaw the Crime Prevention Bureau (Youth Division) from 1955 to 1968. During that time he expanded its resources from a staff of twenty-nine to over four hundred.

13. *Chicago Tribune*, March 18, 1957.

14. "Young Toughs Organize Crime Combine and Share Loot," *Chicago Tribune*, May 26, 1954. Judge Thomas E. Kluczynski (1904–1994) served as chief justice of the Cook County Criminal Court in 1951 and head of the Juvenile (Family) Court in 1952–1953. He was elected to the Illinois State Supreme Court in 1966, serving until 1976, and again from 1978 to 1980. The Kluczynski Federal Building in downtown Chicago is named after his late brother, John, a former U.S. congressman.

15. "'Y' Aid Fights Gang by Winning Trust," *Chicago Tribune*, May 8, 1960.

16. "Dukes No Longer Have Their Dukes Up, Here's Why," *Chicago Tribune*, October 5, 1958.

17. See Lombardo, Calogero, "A Brief History of Chicago's Little Sicily Neighborhood and the Saint Philip Benizi Parish," Chicago Catholic Immigrant's Conference, posted at http://blogs.lib.luc.edu/ccic/little-sicily-st-philip-benizi-parish-fr-luigi-giambastiani/ November 2, 2013. The author of this article asserts that the father had renounced any racist views by 1956, although he remained in opposition to the CHA. Through Father Giambastiani's advocacy, the Cabrini-Green housing development was named after Mother Frances X.

Cabrini. Also Lombardo, Robert, *The Black Hand: Terror by Letter in Chicago*. Chicago: University of Illinois Press, 2009, p. 203.

18. "Probe Gangs to See What Ticks," *Chicago Tribune*, November 15, 1959.

19. Federal and local law enforcement classifies the Mafia and the twenty-six national crime families that came to power during and after Prohibition as "traditional organized crime." The "new organized crime," a designation that came into vogue during the 1990s, refers to national, drug-dealing street "gangster nations," e.g., the Gangster Disciples in Chicago, the Crips and Bloods in Los Angeles, etc.

20. "Police Probe Two Teen Gangs in Gun Killing," *Chicago Tribune*, October 19, 1956.

21. "Pastor Cites Civic Crises at Palmer Rites," *Chicago Tribune*, March 20, 1957.

22. "Rebel Founder Tells Whys of Gang Trouble," *Chicago Tribune*, April 2, 1957. Also "Founder of Gang Sees Solution in Sports Program," *Chicago Tribune*, April 1, 1957.

23. Ibid.

24. "Teen Gang Leaders Hear Billy Graham," *Chicago Tribune*, June 10, 1962.

25. See Norma Browning's prison interview with Macis in "Cookie Macis Slayer at 14 Learns Hard Way," *Chicago Tribune*, March 31, 1957.

26. "Teen-Mob Slaying Inquest Launched," *Chicago Tribune*, July 6, 1955; also the *Chicago Sun-Times*, July 6, 1955.

27. "Prison for Nine Teen Killers," *Chicago Tribune*, February 17, 1956.

28. "Cookie Macis Slayer at 14 Learns Hard Way," *Chicago Tribune*, March 31, 1957.

29. "Fear of Reprisal Big Weapon of Gangs Harassing Citizens," *Chicago Tribune*, July 16, 1955.

30. The Latin Kings were organized in Humboldt Park in the early 1960s to fight both black and white street gangs. The Chicago Crime Commission estimates that the two factions of Latin Kings, Mexican and Puerto Rican, have ten thousand members and ninety factions inclusive of whites, African Americans, and Middle Easterners. They are active in every Hispanic neighborhood of the city and across thirty-three states in the United States. Their motto is "once a King, always a King."

31. "Neighborhood Protection," *Chicago Tribune*, April 4, 1974.

32. "North Side Story: Gangs Are Holding on to Their Turf," *Chicago Tribune*, April 4, 1974.

33. "Ten Seized as Arms Suppliers to Gangs," *Chicago Tribune*, December 2, 1974.

34. In the mid-1970s Chicago street gangs, formerly divided by race, identity, and mostly obsessed with the protection of neighborhood boundaries, coalesced into two separate alliances, "People" and "Folks," because the focus of gang life shifted to attainment of profitability through criminal activity, e.g. drug trafficking.

35. "A Youth's View of a Changing Neighborhood: Fear, Sadness," *Chicago Tribune*, March 22, 1983.

36. Perkins, Useni Eugene, *Explosion of Chicago's Black Street Gangs: 1900 to the Present*. Chicago: Third World Press, 1987, p. 29.

37. See Keiser, R. Lincoln, *Vice Lords: Case Studies in Cultural Anthropology*. New York: Holt, Rinehart & Winston, 1979, pp. 1–4.

38. "Fight to Save City's Youth Never Ends: Worker," *Chicago Tribune*, January 13, 1963.

39. O. W. Wilson (1900–1972), an esteemed professor of criminology at the University of California at Berkeley, and a recognized authority on police administration, stepped in as Chicago police superintendent in the aftermath of the city's worst police corruption scandal, involving eight uniformed officers who had randomly looted North Side retail stores with the connivance of a cat burglar named Richard Morrison. The reforms Wilson put in place in the aftermath of the embarrassing 1960 "Summerdale Scandal" to a great extent modernized the department, provided opportunity for younger, college-educated men to step over the entrenched "old guard" patronage system that rewarded incompetence and scorned new ideas. Wilson was given carte blanche by Mayor Daley to do what was necessary because Summerdale had left Daley exposed and vulnerable to political attack from the remnants of the Cook County Republican Party. Wilson stepped down in 1967. Daley, done with costly expenditures of Wilson's reform movement by this time, restored the cadre of "*ancien regime*" hierarchy to power. Daley's former driver, James Conlisk, was named superintendent of police.

40. The Disciples first turned up in the police rap sheets during the 1950s when they were known as the "Gents." In 1967 it became a coalition gang known as the "Disciple Nation."

41. James Cogwell founded the Egyptian Cobras in 1954 near Maxwell and Roosevelt Roads. By 1960 the Cobras shifted their home base to Woodlawn, where they formed an alliance with the Rangers. Henry "Mickey" Cogwell, called the "Al Capone of the black community," became the new leader and changed the name of the gang to the Cobra Stones in 1966. He merged the former Cobra gang into Jeff Fort's organization to become part of the Main 21 confederation. Cogwell, who took control of Fort's gang while Fort was incarcerated in Leavenworth, was assassinated on February 25, 1977, at 3:45 in

the morning as he walked to his home in the 7800 block of Seeley Avenue. His murder occurred just months after Fort's parole. Unknown shooters pumped three shots into his back.

42. Knox, George W., *An Introduction to Gangs*. 2nd ed. Bristol, IN: Wyndham Hall Press, 1994, p. 138.

43. "Rev. Fry Gave Rangers Status Senate Probers Told," *Chicago Tribune*, July 2, 1968.

44. "Rev. Fry Tells Plans after Resignation," *Chicago Tribune*, April 19, 1971.

45. "Many Civic Leaders in Rev. Fry's Corner," *Chicago Tribune*, June 28, 1968.

46. Founded in 1913 by Timothy Drew (Prophet Noble Drew Ali), the Moorish Science Temple of America based its mission on the belief that African Americans were descended from the Moors and their chosen faith was Islam.

47. El Rukn is Arabic for "pillar."

48. "Jeff Fort's Nation Gets a Chief Priest," *Chicago Tribune*, April 11, 1976.

49. "El Rukn Razing Doesn't End Gangs," *Chicago Tribune*, June 7, 1990.

50. "Seizure of Rukn Headquarters Stirs Change," *Chicago Tribune*, October 30, 1989.

51. By 1974 Hoover's GDs had taken control of much of the South Side narcotics trafficking. By the 1990s gang membership surpassed ten thousand. While in prison, Hoover helped organize the "Folks" alliance of gangs. Weary and resigned, law enforcement had seen it all before. Disciples leader David Barksdale, a proficient boxer who claimed allegiance to the Black Panther Party, became a moving target of the Black P. Stone Nation. In May 1968 Barksdale's car was shot up in a failed assassination attempt. After leaving a South Side bar on June 7, 1970, he was shot in the abdomen. He died of kidney-related complications four years later.

BIBLIOGRAPHY

BOOKS

Abbott, Edith. *The Tenements of Chicago: 1908–1935*. New York: Arno Press, 1970.

Adler, Jeffrey S. *First in Violence Deepest in Dirt: Homicide in Chicago*. Cambridge, MA: Harvard University Press, 2006.

Asbury, Herbert. *Chicago: Gem of the Prairie*. New York: Alfred Knopf, 1940.

———. *The Gangs of New York*. New York: Alfred Knopf, 1928.

Bales, Richard. *Great Chicago Fire and the Myth of Mrs. O'Leary's Cow*. Jefferson, NC: McFarland, 2005.

Bergreen, Laurence. *Capone: The Man and the Era*. New York: Touchstone, 1996.

Berkow, Ira. *Maxwell Street: Survival in a Bazaar*. Garden City, NY: Doubleday, 1977.

Bilek, Arthur. *The First Vice Lord: Big Jim Colosimo and the Ladies of the Levee*. Nashville, TN: Cumberland House, 2008.

Brashler, William. *The Don: The Life and Death of Sam Giancana*. New York: Harper & Row, 1977.

Cohen, Adam, and Taylor, Elizabeth. *American Pharaoh: Mayor Richard J. Daley: His Battle for Chicago and the Nation*. New York: Little, Brown, 2000.

Danckers, Ullrich, and Meredith, Jane. *Early Chicago to 1835, the Year the Indians Left*. River Forest, IL: Early Chicago Incorporated, 2000.

Fry, Rev. John R. *Locked Out Americans: A Memoir*. New York: Harper & Row, 1973.

Gale, Edwin O. *Reminiscences of Early Chicago and Vicinity*. Chicago: Fleming H. Revell, 1902.

Glaab, Charles N., and Brown, A. Theodore. *A History of Urban America*. New York: Macmillan, 1976.

Grant, Bruce. *Fight for a City: The Story of the Union League Club and Its Times, 1880–1955*. Chicago: Rand McNally, 1955.

Grimshaw, William J. *Bitter Fruit: Black Politics and the Chicago Machine*. Chicago: University of Chicago Press, 1992.

Hagedorn, John. *A World of Gangs: Armed Young Men and Gangsta Culture* (Globalization and Community). Minneapolis: University of Minnesota Press, 2008.

Halper, Albert, ed. *The Chicago Crime Book*. New York: World Publishing Group, 1967.

Hamilton, Henry Raymond. *The Epic of Chicago*. Chicago: Willett, Clark, 1932.

Harland, Robert O. *The Vice Bondage of a Great City, or, The Wickedest City in the World*. Chicago: Young People's Civic League, 1911.

Hayes, Dorsha B. *Chicago: Crossroads of American Enterprise*. New York: Julian Messner, 1944.

Helmer, William J., with Mattix, Rick. *Public Enemies: America's Criminal Past, 1919–1940*. New York: Checkmark Books, 1998.

Hirsch, Foster. *The Dark Side of the Screen*. New York: Da Capo Press, 1981.

Hirschmann, Nancy J., and Liebert, Ulrike, eds. *Women and Welfare: Theory and Practice in the United States and Europe*. Piscataway, NJ: Rutgers University Press, 2001.

Jacobs, Jane. *The Death and Life of Great American Cities*. New York: Random House, 1961.

Keefe, Rose. *Guns and Roses: The Untold Story of Dion O'Banion: Chicago's Big Shot before Al Capone*. Nashville, TN: Cumberland House, 2003.

Kennedy, Eugene. *Himself: The Life and Times of Mayor Richard J. Daley*. New York: Viking, 1978.

Knox, George. *An Introduction to Gangs*. 2nd edition. Bristol, IN: Wyndham Hall Press, 1994.

Lewis, Lloyd. *Chicago: The History of Its Reputation*. New York: Harcourt Brace, 1929.

Lindberg, Richard C. *To Serve and Collect: Chicago Politics and Police Corruption from the Lager Beer Riot to the Summerdale Scandal*, 1855–1960. Westport, CT: Praeger, 1991.

———. *The Gambler King of Clark Street: Michael C. McDonald and the Rise of Chicago's Democratic Machine*. Carbondale: Southern Illinois University Press, 2009.

Lombardo, Robert M. *The Black Hand: Terror by Letter in Chicago*. Chicago: University of Illinois Press, 2009.

Lyle, John A. *The Dry and Lawless Years: The Crusade against Public Enemies and Corrupt Officials in Chicago*. New York: Prentice Hall, 1960.

Pacyga, Dominic A. *Chicago: A Biography*. Chicago: University of Chicago Press, 2009.

Pasley, Fred D. *Al Capone: The Biography of a Self-Made Man*. New York: Ives Washburn, 1930.

Perkins, Useni Eugene. *Explosion of Chicago's Black Street Gangs: 1900 to the Present*. Chicago: Third World Press, 1987.

Robinson, J. Nicole. "The Irish of Kilgubbin." *Chicago History Magazine*, vol. 39, no. 3, Fall 2014.

Royko, Mike. *Boss: Richard J. Daley of Chicago*. New York: Penguin, 1972.

Schoenberg, Robert. *Mr. Capone: The Real and Complete Story of Al Capone*. New York: William Morrow, 1992.

Sills, David L., and Merton, Robert K., eds. *The International Encyclopedia of the Social Sciences*. Vol. 4. New York: Macmillan, 1968.

Stead, William T. *If Christ Came to Chicago: A Plea for the Union of All Who Love in the Service of All Who Suffer*. Chicago: Chicago Historical Bookworks, 1990. Reprint edition.

Suttles, Gerald D. *The Social Order of the Slum*. Chicago: University of Chicago Press, 1968.

Thrasher, Frederic Milton. *The Gang: A Study of 1,313 Gangs in Chicago*. Chicago: University of Chicago Press, 1927.

Tuttle, William M., Jr. *Race Riot: Chicago in the Red Summer of 1919*. New York: Atheneum, 1970.

Wellman, James K., *The Gold Coast Church and the Ghetto: Christ & Culture in Mainline Protestantism*. Champaign: University of Illinois Press, 1999.

Wooden, Kenneth. *Weeping in the Playtime of Others: America's Incarcerated Children*. 2nd edition. Columbus, OH: Ohio State University Press, 2000.

Wooldridge, Clifton Rodman. *Hands Up in the World of Crime: Twelve Years a Detective on the Chicago Police Force*. Chicago: Stanton & VanVliet, 1901.

Zorbaugh, Harvey Warren. *The Gold Coast and the Slum: A Sociological Study of Chicago's North Side*. Chicago: University of Chicago Press, 1929.

ARTICLES AND REPORTS

Block, Richard, and Block, Carolyn Rebecca. *Street Gang Crime in Chicago*. Research in Brief. Washington, DC: U.S. Department of Justice, Office of Justice Programs, National Institute of Justice, December 1993.

Chicago Crime Commission Gang Book. Chicago: Chicago Crime Commission, 1997, 2006, 2012.

Deeney, Jeff. "How to Discipline Students without Turning School into a Prison," *The Atlantic*, January 9, 2014.

Hearings before the Subcommittee to Investigate Juvenile Delinquency (Comic Books) of the Committee of the Judiciary, U.S. Senate, 83rd Congress, 1954. Comic Books and Juvenile Delinquency, 84th Congress, First Session, Report no. 62, "Crime and Horror Comics as a Contributing Factor in Juvenile Delinquency," section IV, Committee on the Judiciary, Washington, D.C., 1955.

Hecht, Ben. "The Noble Experiment." *Playboy Magazine*, December 1963.

Karamanski, Theodore J. "The Marseilles of Lake Michigan." *Chicago History Magazine*, Spring 2000.

Mackey, Wade C., and Immerman, Ronald S., "The Presence of the Social Father in Inhibiting Young Men's Violence." *Mankind Quarterly*, vol. 44, Spring 2004.

Skogan, Wesley G., and Steiner, Lynn. *CAPS at Ten, Community Policing in Chicago: An Evaluation of Chicago's Alternative Policing Strategy*. Chicago: Chicago Community Policing Evaluation Consortium, January 2004.

Vale, Lawrence J. "Up from Little Hell." *Chicago History Magazine*, Fall 2014.

Wardle, Lynn D. "The Fall of Marital Family Stability and the Rise of Juvenile Delinquency." *Journal of Law and Family Studies*, vol. 10, no. 1, pp. 84–86.

NEWSPAPERS

Chicago American
Chicago Daily News
Chicago Defender
Chicago Globe
Chicago Herald & Examiner
Chicago Inter-Ocean
Chicago Journal
Chicago Sun-Times
Chicago Times
Chicago Tribune
Crain's Chicago Business
New York Times

INDEX

Pages references for photos are italicized.

ABOUT THE AUTHOR

Richard C. Lindberg is an award-winning author and Chicago historian, who has authored sixteen previous books. His recent titles include: *Whiskey Breakfast: My Swedish Family, My American Life*, winner of the Chicago Writers Association's Best Nonfiction Award for 2011; *Heartland Serial Killers: Belle Gunness, Johann Hoch and Murder for Profit in Gaslight Era Chicago* (2011); *The Gambler King of Clark Street: Michael C. McDonald and the Rise of Chicago's Democratic Machine*, winner of the 2009 Best Biography Award presented by the Society of Midland Authors; *Chicago Yesterday and Today* (2009); *Shattered Sense of Innocence: The Chicago Child Murders of 1955* (2006); *Total White Sox* (2006); *Return Again to the Scene of the Crime: A Guide to Even More Infamous Places in Chicago* (2001); *Return to the Scene of the Crime: A Guide to Infamous Places in Chicago* (1995), and others.

Mr. Lindberg is a past president of the Illinois Academy of Criminology, and as a member of the Chicago Crime Commission in 1995, he helped draft "Street Gangs, Public Enemy Number One."

Over the years, Mr. Lindberg has provided commentary for numerous television documentaries and radio talk-show programs of local, national, and international origin, including material for A&E, Investigation Discovery, the History Channel, CBS News Overnight, and the Travel Channel.